Incompleteness: Donald Trump, Populism and Citizenship

by
Francis B. Nyamnjoh

Langaa Research & Publishing CIG
Mankon, Bamenda

Publisher:
Langaa RPCIG
Langaa Research & Publishing Common Initiative Group
P.O. Box 902 Mankon
Bamenda
North West Region
Cameroon
Langaagrp@gmail.com
www.langaa-rpcig.net

Distributed in and outside N. America by African Books Collective
orders@africanbookscollective.com
www.africanbookscollective.com

ISBN-10: 9956-552-87-9

ISBN-13: 978-9956-552-87-0

Acknowledgements

The acknowledgements page is a necessary reminder that writing is and should be seen as a collaborative endeavour. Not only does one write in conversation with the written words of others, one benefits in the writing process from the goodwill and generosity of others – among whom perfect strangers and fleeting acquaintances – in a myriad of ways. This makes every piece of writing a collective project, even when authorship is assigned to or claimed by one person.

This book epitomises writing as a process of debt and indebtedness that I could never acknowledge enough. As I wrote this book, I set off like a day-old bird learning to fly but with little to show for feathers. Through my interactions with others, their ideas, their time, their intellect, their attention and their words, I have accumulated feathers that have charged, propelled and propped me up in this challenging flight of incompleteness, even as I have mostly been immobilised from January 2020 to October 2021, a period that included a nine-month study and research leave for which I am sincerely grateful to the University of Cape Town. As some semblance of normalcy returns, and as we regain hope in our struggle against Covid-19, it would be a mistake, to continue with our bird metaphor, for me to fly off solo into the fantasy world of credentialism, however intoxicated I am with my delusions of autonomy and contrivance of authorship.

Thus, it is worth stressing, ad nauseam. This book, incomplete as it is, could not have been possible without the Ubuntu of others. Here, I would like to acknowledge some of them whose names readily come to mind, without in any way suggesting that I have exhausted the list of possible contributors – an impossible task in a world of incompleteness.

The idea to study Donald Trump, populism and citizenship came to me in late 2016, following a residency at the Rockefeller Bellagio Center in Italy, from 25 August–22 September, where I worked on "Amos Tutuola and the Elusiveness of Completeness". Several high profile American scholars and public figures were my cohort of residents with whom I shared memorable and productive conversations on the unfolding presidential campaign that eventually led to Trump's election. I had predicted that Trump would win, without quite knowing why at the time, and much to the bemusement of some of my fellow residents who knew the American political scene well. We have remained in contact, using a mailing list that we unanimously agreed to name "Il Convivio", partly in recognition of Dante, but mostly because the word "conviviality" proliferated itself in our conversations. I want to thank my fellow residents for their encouraging comments and insights on my research around the idea of "incompleteness" and "conviviality". I thank them especially for the conversations that kindled my interest in Donald Trump, populism and citizenship as intriguing phenomena.

In the course of writing a book, one becomes like Chinua Achebe's dancing masquerade, with a nimble-footedness that leads to many enriching encounters, not all of which I can recall, but all of which I would like to acknowledge. Thank you all for making this book possible, even when you were unaware that you were contributing to an unfolding conversation.

Over and above a general vote of thanks, I would like to single out a few names for their contributions. First, to Henrietta: Without the flourishing love, patience, family and intellectual climate you have actively enabled and generously sustained over the years, I would not be able to do what I do. I owe you and our children an infinite debt of gratitude.

For reading, commenting and providing suggestions on the entire manuscript or sections thereof, my sincere gratitude goes to the following in no particular order: Piet Konings, Bernard Lategan, Milton Krieger, Jimu Malizani, Anye Nkwenti Nyamnjoh, Leah Junck, Joel Carpenter, Kristin Kobes DuMez, Kathryn Toure, Winston Mano, Hassan M. Yosimbom, Edmond Agyeman, Aalyia Sadruddin, Petr Skalnik, Artwell Nhemachena, Thelma Nyarhi, Ochega Ataguba, Petr Skalnik, Divine Fuh, Lauren Paremoer, Mufor Atanga, Charles Prempeh and Sophie Oldfield.

I have been fortunate to know Muhammed Umar over the years and to have benefitted from his energic resourcefulness in ferreting for and sharing relevant online newspaper stories. My gratitude to him is profound. For assisting with relevant research and sourcing newspaper articles and online publications, I am grateful to Miriam Aurora Hammeren Pedersen and Inge-Amè Botes. For his indefatigable and enthusiastic search, downloading and sharing relevant literature on populism, especially on the USA and as pertains to Trump, Tekletsadik Belachew deserves immeasurable thanks. I would also like to acknowledge the research assistance of the algorithms of Google and Amazon for feeding me more of the same once they figured they understood what my searches and clicks were about in the course of researching this book.

Fuhlem Emile Fuh, the 3-year-old who visited (along with his elder sister Sirri Inès Fuh), and played with me during the writing of this book, enhanced, unknowingly, my understanding of Daniel W. Drezner's book –*The Toddler in Chief: What Donald Trump Teaches Us About the Modern Presidency* – and related psychoanalytical literature. I thank him sincerely for this.

Special thanks go to Nic Cheeseman and Milton Krieger, who generously agreed to write the forewords, and Bernard Lategan, for so kindly writing an afterword.

Last but not least, I acknowledge with profound gratitude the editorial contributions of Kathryn Toure, Lucien Mufor Atanga and Rae Dalton.

Table of Contents

Populism: Myths, Metaphors and Metamorphosis

Populism is one of the most important political phenomena of our time, but is also one of the least understood. This is partly because it is one of the most ambiguous and nebulous terms in our lexicon. Especially if one moves away from academic texts to media reports and everyday conversations, the concept of populism can appear to be as vague as it is ubiquitous due to the promiscuous way in which it is used. Over the last decade, a remarkably diverse set of figures – known for espousing radically different ideologies – have been labelled as populist. This includes Donald Trump, former President of the United States, one of his main critics, US Senator Bernie Saunders, the current Ugandan President Yoweri Museveni and his youthful rival Bobbi Wine, and British Prime Minister Boris Johnson and former Labour leader – and hence Johnson rival – Jeremy Corbyn. A similarly elastic deployment of the populist label has also taken place with regards to social movements, newspapers and even movies. In some cases, the term has been used as a signifier of little more specific than that a leader has aspirations to be wildly popular – and which presidential candidate doesn't? It is almost as if the concept is following the example of some of the leaders who deploy it, seeking to be all things to all people – and in the process, losing much of its analytical value.

Yet despite the conceptual stretching that has plagued the term, it remains indispensable. Neither political scientists and anthropologists nor journalists and commentators have been able to come up with anything that has greater resonance or analytical precision thus far. To paraphrase a contributor to a recent conference in South Africa, in this respect populism is not unlike pornography because, in the oft-quoted words of Justice Potter Steward, while we struggle to define it, we are fairly sure that we "know it when we see it". But what is it that we see? What lies at the heart of the populist project and is so instantly recognisable – at least in theory – to observers of contemporary politics? Is it perhaps the performative nature of populists; the way in which they act out their promise of rapid change through dynamic performances at rallies, such as when

Zambian opposition leader, Michael Sata, described President Levy Mwanawasa – who had previously suffered a stroke – as a "cabbage", and then proceeded to destroy a cabbage on stage? Or is it the nature of the claims made by populist leaders that distinguishes them – the suggestion that they, and they alone, not only understand the "people" and their needs, but actually represent the physical embodiment of the "common man"? Perhaps the key commonality is less how populists communicate and more how they govern, centralising power in a cult of personality that erodes institutional processes and so undermines checks and balances?

The growing literature on populism has done little to forge a consensus around when the term should be used – and, just as importantly, when it is inappropriate. Given this impasse, we are fortunate that a scholar as insightful and knowledgeable as Francis Nyamnjoh has decided to enter the fray. By drawing on a sophisticated and complex set of experiences, understanding and metaphors, Nyamnjoh shines new light on a familiar debate. His distinctive approach is so creative that it even manages to further illuminate those areas so thoroughly traversed that they already appeared to be well lit. My personal favourite example of Nyamnjoh's ability to draw on different kinds of texts – both non-fiction and fiction – to build his own narrative is the use of the story of the three blind men and the elephant in Part 1. In the classic parable, which originated in the Indian subcontinent, three blind men attempt to identify the essence of the elephant by touching it. But because they each touch a different part of the elephant – in most versions, the trunk, an ear, and a leg – they come away with very different understandings of what the animal must be like, and have no hope of coming to a consensus. This is without doubt the best metaphor I have come across of the tendency for different academic disciplines to approach the topic of populism from different directions and, as a result, to emphasise different characteristics and so talk past one another. The "blind men" discussion is just one example of how Nyamnjoh recasts old problems in new ways – and it is far from the only way that the book breaks new ground.

One reason that *Incompleteness* is able to tell us something new is that Nyamnjoh looks at the rise of Donald Trump and populism in the United States through a distinctive lens that not only offers fresh answers, but also suggests that we may have been asking the wrong questions. In other words, Nyamnjoh doesn't simply hand the reader a powerful torch in order to brighten a couple of dark corners of the topic that have hitherto been underexplored; rather, he asks readers to look at the whole issue afresh from a completely different perspective. The key that unlocks the mystery of populism in this book is not economic decline, or globalisation, or falling class mobility, but rather citizenship and incompleteness. Once one looks through this new lens, it is immediately apparent that the contours of the landscape have been transformed, and that previously obscured points have become legible – as if a pair of infrared binoculars had been lifted up to our eyes.

When we begin to follow the new roadmap that Nyamnjoh sketches it quickly becomes clear that we cannot hope to fully get to grips with contemporary populism unless we first understand the nature of citizenship, and the fact that projects of citizenship – like our own human projects – are inherently incomplete. As he puts it, the business of citizenship is both "unfinished and unfinishable". Yet that is not all: Nyamnjoh argues that we need to recognise that one of the core factors that drives our own actions is a sense of incompleteness, and that this is no bad thing. We should not view incompleteness as a negative phenomenon but instead as "something to embrace and celebrate, as we, in all humility, seek to act and interact with one another, with the things we create to extend ourselves, and with the normal and supersensory worlds relevant to our sense of being and becoming". Incompleteness can be a positive force if we recognise that it is an inherent feature of our existence, and then choose to celebrate it by developing a "disposition that privileges interconnections, interdependences and the reality of debt and indebtedness as essential aspect of being and belonging together". If we do this, our own incompleteness, and that of our society, can become a source of strength – a shared understanding of both our limitations and our possibilities that can bind us closer together. But if we instead idolise and chase after a sense of completeness in the mistaken belief that we and our societies can somehow be perfected and made absolute, we will fall into the trap of seeking to achieve a kind of social and political dominance. Those who do this, Nyamnjoh warns, "believe in their untamed power to define themselves, define others, and define into existence or oblivion in tune with their every whim and caprice". Seen through Nyamnjoh's eyes, populist fascism can thus be understood as an extreme attempt to "complete" human beings and society through the assertion of dominant force. This process not only failed, but was *bound to fail.*

Nyamnjoh's argument about the ubiquity of incompleteness and the importance of how we respond to it is critical not only because it helps to explain why populist appeals have such enduring resonance, but also because it highlights why populism has such divisive potential. It is only when we start by recognising the inherently incomplete nature of citizenship in our countries, and the persistence of disagreements over who is and is not a "true" citizen, that the divisive potential of any leader claiming to represent "the people" comes to the fore. In turn, the centrality of citizenship means that any scholarly attempt to engage with contemporary populism must begin by looking at the composition of society, the main sources of unity and disunity that exist, and the way in which local perceptions of who does and does not belong has evolved over time.

After all, while there is remarkable variation in the language and policies of populists, a common feature – and perhaps the only central element that most researchers would agree on – is that they claim to have a special relationship with the "common man" (and it is worth noticing that this terminology is not accidental – populist mythology is almost always hyper-masculine). In the extreme version of this assertion, they claim not only to have a distinctive understanding of the people but – despite often being wealthier and more fortunate than the average citizen – to actually *be* the common man. In other words, they present themselves to be the personal embodiment of the "folk" and to have a special and unmediated connection to what the folk want and need. As Nyamnjoh recognises, this form of politics, in which "the people" play both a mobilising and legitimising function, means that the question of who does and does not belong is absolutely fundamental to the populist project and the form that it takes.

Citizenship and what Nyamnjoh calls the "prism of incompleteness" are not only relevant for our understanding of North America and Europe – they are equally significant if we turn our attention to other parts of the world. Take my own work on populism in East and Southern Africa with Miles Larmer, for example. Our research concluded that a central challenge facing populist leaders such as Michael Sata, the late president of Zambia, was how to articular populist messages that would both resonate with a cross-ethnic support base in urban areas while appealing to rural voters who had traditionally been targeted with more "ethnic" appeals. The feasibility of uniting these different constituencies, and hence the potential to build a more inclusive form of what we called "ethno-populism", falls when political competition increases the salience of ethnic identities, and rises when processes of urbanisation – and urban–rural migration – have created overlapping beliefs and preferences between urban and rural areas.

Indeed, in making the connection between populism, citizenship and *Incompleteness*, Nyamnjoh demonstrates the value of bringing insights and lessons from sub-Saharan Africa to bear on American – and we could also say British, German, French and Indian – political processes. Thirty years ago, the study of populism was dominated by scholars from the Latin American countries in which it was seen to be most pronounced. More recently, the rise of first the Tea Party and later Donald Trump has triggered an explosion of research by North American scholars. New literature has also emerged in Europe around Brexit and the rise of right-wing populists in a number of countries, such as Hungary – evoking sad and alarming memories of the rise of fascism seventy years previous. The conceptual toolkits of these scholars, as with any researchers, has tended to be shaped by their political and cultural experiences, and the national preoccupations these have given rise to. In particular, the success of populism is often said to be rooted in a specific set of economic conditions, from the way that the Great Depression facilitated the ascent of Hitler and Mussolini through to the link that is often made between globalisation, declining class mobility and the rise of Orbán and Trump over the last two decades.

While he recognises the significance of economic drivers, Nyamnjoh's take is refreshing because it comes at populism from a very different starting point. Having written important books on citizenship and the politics of belonging, he has a deep understanding of how identity politics operate, and how debates about citizenship and identity are manipulated by political leaders. As a Professor of Social Anthropology, Nyamnjoh is also able to conceptualise the public appetite for populism, and for leaders of various different persuasions, on the basis of a more grounded perspective that allows for nuance and recognises the vast array of factors that shape political subjectivities. This is particularly valuable, because it moves us away from the reductive tendency to see the human beings as robotic units that are inevitably more willing to support radical political leaders whenever the economy goes through a bad patch. Indeed, the various scholarly projects that Nyamnjoh has completed in a remarkably productive career provide a range of distinctive perspectives on how attitudes towards citizenship are formed, from the role of the media to the drivers of xenophobia and the politics of belonging, and on to the common human desire for sociality and inclusivity. All of these perspectives are collected here, in chapters that look at the effervescence of populism and the role of digital social media as a "magic multiplier" of narcissism and the quest for completeness.

Seen from this kaleidoscope of perspectives, which provides important insights both from above and below, the questions we need to answer in the populism debate start to shift. The issue is not simply what kinds of economic change catalyse radical politics and how, but rather how incomplete processes of nation and state-building generate opportunities for leaders to make political gains by leveraging populist appeals – and always will do. What is particularly striking about this approach is that it suggests a very different way of responding to the threat of exclusionary populism. The best way to avoid populist excesses is not to try and build the perfect society that would be immune to divisive appeals. To do this, Nyamnjoh argues, is to make the same mistake as the populists themselves, and to imagine that we are societies that can be made complete. A better approach, he suggests, is to start by accepting our incompleteness, and recognising it as the true universal characteristic that connects us to all other humans. Once we have done that, we open the door to recognising not only the value of conviviality and compromise, but also their innate necessity. This, rather than a quest to build the perfectly united society, is the antidote to political polarisation and intolerance.

To find out exactly why and how this strategy can help to protect against the worst demons of our nature, you will of course have to read the pages that follow with great care and attention. This foreword, much like ourselves, must remain forever incomplete.

Nic Cheeseman
Professor of Democracy, University of Birmingham
Lilongwe, 5 October 2021

Foreword 2

The Road from Lakabum to Bellagio and Beyond

Francis Nyamnjoh's writings, now in their fourth decade, consistently open fresh, varied and original lines of scholarship and advocacy. Belying and transcending this book's Trumpian title and content, discoveries and pleasures await below if he's new to you. They could take you to places you haven't read about or been.

That's so even if it means going through the omnipresent (or lurking), ceaselessly headlined Trump, to "get to him", and to where I think Francis also wants to take us here. Along an intricate path, informed by a vast literature current to late 2021, Nyamnjoh plunges into Trump and the vocabulary and experience he generates: populism and citizenship (as the book's title specifies), the Cartesian method and its impact since its time and place of origin, neo-liberal capitalism and globalisation, contemporary media, the emerging contest between democracy and autocracy or tyranny, and more. The path makes particular use of an idiosyncratic but posthumously praised Nigerian author, Amos Tutuola (1920–1997), to identify what Nyamnjoh offers here: an African epistemology to challenge the alarmingly dystopic Trump. Profiles of Nyamnjoh himself and Tutuola open the way below to Francis's reading of Trump World, and how a better one beyond it might be found.

***

Framing the production and circulation of knowledge about and throughout Africa is an ever more indigenous project. Generations of Africans have put their own hands, minds, imaginations and hearts to this work. Nyamnjoh's profile and contribution as he reaches age sixty late in 2021 is among those currently most notable. Fragments of his autobiography reveal his bearings, starting with the youth he described in the last pages of a 2002 publication. It locates his 1961 birth in Lakabum chieftaincy, a remote hamlet in the hills thirty kilometers beyond the village of Fonfuka where he attended primary school, in the Grassfields region of Anglophone Cameroon, the very year its independence, linked with Francophones in a bilingual republic, was achieved. Cameroon's been an ever more tangled and vexing union to this day, and a good apprenticeship for this study of Trump, as some of Nyamnjoh's writings address, but his personal touches are a key to that 2002 text for the purpose here. Its title: "A Child is One Person's Only in the Womb". Its core: his paternity. He recounts, first, a rich but "commoner" cattle-owning biological father, Ndong, he never met until his third year in college. Then came two subsequent fathers, both royals, he acquired through maternal kinship, who housed him and financed his education; the *fon* (king or paramount chief) of Bum in a still rural but highly sophisticated domain, serving for a wider apprenticeship, through Francis's early schooling, then, in his upper school and early university years the *fon* of Mankon in his peri-urban palace on the outskirts of the provincial capital, Bamenda, 140 (then and now) sparsely paved kilometers from Fonfuka.

His sense of the matter as his narrative developed: "I was left with three active fathers, two royal and one commoner, and in my own little way have sought to satisfy their competing demands for attention ever since." Its last sentence quoted at this paragraph's end, summarised his experience to 2002. It looked back on his paternity, more properly paternities, a core part of his life and identity, and found fluidity, with constant negotiation and "palaver" (Ndong tried to assert a naming right, which Francis refused, then did not attend "his son's" wedding). It reads like Francis's manifesto, for himself, and Africans at large: "The way forward lies in recognizing the creative and intersubjective ways in which Africans merge their traditions with exogenous influences to create modernities that are not reducible to either but superior to both."

This microcosmic glimpse into Nyamnjoh's sense of his 2002 self provides a pivot for this foreword and for Nyamnjoh's platform in the macrocosmic study of Trump he's written here. By 2009, from a deeply rural childhood and a more metropolitan young adulthood through first degrees in anthropology within Cameroon, he reached a cosmopolitan adulthood via sociology of communication studies for the Ph.D. at Leicester, university teaching posts in Cameroon and Botswana, and a senior position as communications director at CODESRIA (Council for the Development of Social Science Research in Africa) in Dakar. The next dozen years added a senior academic post at the University of Cape Town, a 2018 award, from the United Kingdom's Africa scholars' association for the best book about Africa, his study of South Africa's "Rhodes Must Fall" movement (a foreshadowing parallel to Robert E. Lee statues' fates more recently in Virginia), and not just an African but also a globally informed and collaborative scholarship. Its capacity and range lead to this book about Trump, which may familiarise him to American readers as never before, and more.

***

That "more" paving the path to Trump requires another pivot along the way, because Nyamnjoh peppers this book with prompts to the above-mentioned Tutuola that could, if ignored here, puzzle readers below. They come from Nyamnjoh's 2017 book about him, with a title evoking palm wine and its equivalents elsewhere in Africa, *Drinking from the Cosmic Gourd: How Amos Tutuola Can Change Our Minds*. Tutuola was among the early African novelists published abroad, with *The Palm-Wine Drinkard* (1952) and *My Life in the Bush of Ghosts* (1954) the hallmarks. He remained relatively marginal during his lifetime compared with the academically and commercially canonical Chinua Achebe, Wole Soyinka and other, mostly younger contemporaries from Nigeria and Africa at large. But Tutuola's early, against the grain abandonment of literary styles and vocabularies brought from elsewhere ("European modernity") into local classrooms and bookstores, instead favoured domestic, indigenous expression framed by street, marketplace and especially traditional story-telling practice. He challenged the plot lines and genres of an imposed grand narrative that crowded out the vernacular experience, using a unique lexicon to frame the disruptive agencies of tapsters, tricksters, diviners, body parts dealers and the like.

This caught Francis's attention. Expressed as what he called Tutuola's "cosmic gourd of incompleteness" (2017:. 217), Nyamnjoh concluded his Tutuola study in a way that foreshadows this book about Trump and Trumpism: "It is a pity that delusions of completeness and linear articulations of being human, being modern and being civilized should stand in the way of recognition of the full magnitude and depth of Tutuola's creative imagination and its importance to meaning and sense making, and to knowledge production and consumption ... Tutuola's epistemological order stresses instead a mix between individual rights and interests on the one hand, and the rights and interests of groups and collectivities on

xvii

the other. There is little room in it for zero-sum games of winner take all. (2017: 272–4.) Tutuola offered an open-textured and, in important anti- and post-colonial ways, prismatic and transgressive African expression and experience.

Soyinka in 2014 had already written the introduction to a reissue of *The Palm-Wine Drinkard* that signified Tutuola's place in a revised African canon. Nyamnjoh's book-length 2017 study further valorised Tutuola's shape-shifting work and affirmed its authenticity. It's worthwhile as we turn to Nyamnjoh in 2022, with his attention to the USA as never before, to note Tutuola's African-American counterparts in materials Zora Neale Hurston and Henry Louis Gates in particular have brought to light.

***

Nyamnjoh here and now makes the USA a major focus of his scholarship for the first time. Trump World is his platform and vehicle. "The Donald", whose single and singular father is famously (not in a good way: no ambiguity here) central to *his* story, dominates a fully "winner take all" world he's shaped and ruthlessly inhabits. Francis covers its opportunism, fault lines and menaces, and its unpredicted successes. Readers may find some detours along the way, but Nyamnjoh's journey here is inclusive; stones are unturned, many illuminate the Trump phenomenon.

Currently prominent social science and policy literature, both American and global, fuel Nyamnjoh's Parts I and II on populism and Trump's emergence. Drawing on his cultural anthropologist's sense of his surroundings, one brief excursion from the book's USA repertoire can stand for many others. As Trump's presidential campaign geared up, Francis spent two months at Ohio University's African Studies programme in late 2015. This placed him near Trump arch-acolyte Congressman Jim Jordan's electoral district, and where J. D. Vance's 2016 book, *Hillbilly Elegy*, disclosed local disorders in economy and society, with their visceral causes and effects the very "winner take all" Trump campaign exploited nationally, drawing heavily on the vocabulary of "elite-popular" and "two coast-heartland" antagonisms. The story keeps building through 2021. Both Tutuola's repertoire – think of an already strained body politic Trump divided into warring body parts – and more conventional academic analysis feature throughout. Nyamnjoh addresses narrow and competing populisms' challenges (a few from the "left" but most from the "right") to an already vulnerable democratic citizenship practice, and widens his lens to Orban, Bolsonaro, Duterte and others (and their challengers) in Trump's global orbit.

Part III draws on Nyamnjoh's communications study and work background, and traces the role of media and digital technologies in populism's rise. Another USA fragment exemplifies the book's sweeping approach and analysis by briefly recounting Freud's nephew, Edward Bernays, a World War I-era trans-Atlantic migrant from Vienna, and relating how this public relations industry pioneer, through much of the century, built the foundations for modern "political messaging". Powered algorithmically since 2000, it's cut a vast commercial and digital swath, capable of major mischief, with Trump an early practitioner and now a prime beneficiary. This is how, to quote Nyamnjoh in Part III's sub-titles in a way that will orient you, the reader, "Magic Multipliers" lead to the "Pandemic of Narcissism" in a "Digitally Mediated Post-Truth U.S.A.", a citizenry's body parts, indeed, exposed to rampant manipulation.

The title of Nyamnjoh's Introduction here, "The Prism of Incompleteness", cues Part IV and the book's "Concluding Thoughts". The latter draws on and applies his reading of Tutuola, whose challenge to the colonially imposed grand narrative, idiosyncratic rather than programmatic, kick starts the three-fathered Nyamnjoh to deploy his muse's aesthetic and cosmology more analytically, to a world made vulnerable by the insistence on certainties. Here's where I think Francis (as above) "also wants to take us". Why not push past Trump, and all his and others' claims that don't bend or yield, in the absence of court jesters speaking truth in the palaces of wealth and power, like Trump's? Why not call out the very idea of completeness with (quoting near this book's end) its "problematic dichotomies and zero-sum games of absolute winners and absolute losers" and seek instead a "democratic pluralism of political checks and balances reinforced by social checks and balances"? Why not look to Tutuola's version of the human experience, which Africans know well, for more nuanced and shared bearings on an ever more precarious human condition?

No firm answers to such (perhaps) Quixotic questions emerge: where is our Star Wars' Princess Leia to dispatch our real-world Jabba the Hutt? But such trajectories and fresh paths have driven Nyamnjoh's advocacy in publications for many years, conveyed in latter parts of this book by his call for "conviviality" as "a practice of humility" that can foster a "common humanity". His generic use of the word "conviviality" for African communality (similar to Archbishop Tutu's use of the Bantu languages' generic "ubuntu") dates back at least a decade. It was sharpened when, a year after meeting Trump World in Ohio, in 2016 at the Rockefeller Center in Bellagio, he learned of Dante's compendium of knowledge *Il Convivio* (The Banquet) written 700 years ago, not in the then dominant Latin but (another Tutuola touch?) an emerging vernacular that would contribute to "Italian". That's where and when he started this book, and also predicted to colleagues that Trump would take the presidency a few weeks later –nothing Quixotic here, just good applied research along the road from Lakabum to Bellagio.

***

It's paved with critical and satirical essays, plays and novels, academic books like this one, articles, a long "contributions to" list and collaborations, principally in The Netherlands and Japan. And there's something else, quite unusual: the publishing house he started in Cameroon, 2004, Langaa RPCIG, putting his communications expertise from Leicester and Dakar to further use. As prolific and genre-varied as Francis himself, it's published over 500 titles by writers from twenty-five continental and off-shore African nations, plus Haiti, including his own British award-winner. Among Africans now articulating Africa in their own kaleidoscopic ways, his role as both writer and interlocutor for his peers stands out. This book and his entire repertoire are worthy of the wider audience, including the USA's, they should now attract.

References
Francis Nyamnjoh, 'A Child is One Person's Only in the Womb', in Richard Werbner (ed.), *Domestication, Agency and Subjectivity in the Cameroonian Grassfields* (Zed Books, 2002), pp. 111–138.
_____, *Drinking from the Cosmic Gourd: How Amos Tutuola Can Change Our Minds* (Langaa RPCIG, 2017).

Milton Krieger, Emeritus Professor
Department of Global Humanities and Religions
Western Washington University

Introduction

The Prism of Incompleteness

As someone interested in Donald John Trump – or what some have simply termed "the Trump Phenomenon" (Kellner 2016; Kivisto 2017) – as an American and a global phenomenon, I have decided to delve into the deep ocean of abundant literature of newspaper articles, opinion pieces and commentary on television and in social media linking Trump with populism. These sources are supplemented with relevant books and journal articles on Trump, populism and democracy. This book explores how and the extent to which the term populism has been employed, especially in journalistic discourse, in relation to Trump, particularly but not exclusively, from when he campaigned for and assumed office as the one-term 45th President of the United States of America (USA). The book canvasses a broad range of opinions, mostly by journalists and political commentators, on the Trump candidacy (2016) and presidency (20 January 2017–20 January 2021) as an entry point to illuminate key contemporary debates about the context, cause, character and significance of contemporary populism in the USA and the West most especially.

Underpinning this exploration of Trump and populism, as represented in the media, are questions about nationality, citizenship and belonging as inclusionary and exclusionary possibilities and permanent works in progress. To what extent could it be argued that populism points a torchlight at the urgency of addressing problematic hierarchies that seep in, highjack, skew and curtail the materialisation of democracy, citizenship, belonging and nationality, even when these are provided for under the law and guaranteed constitutionally? How is the history of mobility mobilised to include and exclude, to lay or deny, contest and reconcile claims of belonging to particular territories in particular configurations and hierarchies? And how should one account for these developments and positions in understanding the role populism plays in a given context?

How one answers the above and related questions depends on one's sense of being and belonging through mobility (bodily, physical, social, economic, cultural, political and otherwise), encounters, relationships with others (fellow humans and non-humans alike), and one's sense of debt and indebtedness in the making and reproduction of the identities one claims as an individual or as a collectivity or as both. The framework I propose is like a road companion in reading this text and seeking to understand the nexus between populism and the unfinished and unfinishable business of citizenship.

The Prism of Incompleteness

To understand populism and its impact on citizenship and belonging, I argue that incompleteness is normal and universal. Incompleteness is not a negative attribute of being but something to embrace and celebrate, as we, in all humility, seek to act and interact with one another, with the things we create to extend ourselves, and with the natural and suprasensory worlds relevant to our sense of being and becoming. To recognise and provide for incompleteness is not to plead guilty, inadequate, inferior or helpless vis-à-vis supposedly complete pacesetting others against whom one is called to measure oneself and one's accomplishments. Instead, incompleteness is a disposition that enables us to act in particular ways to achieve our ends in a world or universe of myriad interconnections of incomplete beings, human and non-human, natural and suprasensory, and amenable and not amenable to perception through our senses.

In a universe of incompleteness, the quest to activate oneself for the potency required to fulfil a desire or a need entails motion that brings one into contact and interaction with equally incomplete mobile others. Some people move around with the idea of getting by in a spirit of mutual respect of the sensitivities and sensibilities of those they encounter. They reach out to others and draw on them in their incompleteness, tapping into attributes they need to enhance themselves. The logic and reality of mutuality and symbiosis may be conscious or unconscious. If it takes eating to survive and subsist, it takes being eaten in turn to ensure survival and subsistence for incomplete others (Nyamnjoh 2018a). Mobility is a universal constant, even as it is differential. Everything and everyone moves, not always in the same ways or with the same potential, and life would not be possible without mobility. We would be incapable of doing much in our incompleteness if we could not move around – physically and otherwise – and encounter and interact with equally incomplete others to mutually activate ourselves to fulfil various ends. Yet, precisely because of the necessity for mobility, incompleteness is never static, so it cannot be outgrown. As new encounters offer solutions to the incompleteness that we are used to and would like to mitigate through interactions with incomplete others, so too do those very encounters and extensions generate new incompleteness. Thus, we are always incomplete even as we appear to accumulate mileage in our quest for attention to the incompleteness of which we are aware.

Throughout history, people have used both their incompleteness and their mobility in different ways. Some think that incompleteness is negative, something to transcend via a linear progression to something one might call completeness, sustained through the eternal production and reproduction of oppression, repression and suppression, aided and abated by contrived and radically exclusionary identities and identity politics of purity and purification. They believe that completeness is possible, that it comes from using one's mobility to reaching out and encounter others in unequal ways, conquering them and imposing one's superiority. They believe that mobility entails survival for the fittest, the fittest being those who are either more naturally endowed or who transgress borders and boundaries with impunity to dispossess, humiliate and humble those they encounter with dehumanising indignities and repressive technologies of control, containment and confinement. They believe in their untamed power to define themselves, define others, and define into existence or oblivion in tune with their every whim and caprice (Nyamnjoh 2016). However, not every mobility has to be animated by such ambitions of conquest, domination or suppression. Just as survival of the fittest is far less about dominance (physical and otherwise) than it is about the ability to reproduce through relationships of inclusivity and conviviality.

Some, on the other hand, move around, informed by the understanding that incompleteness is the norm. Completeness, on the other hand, is a perilous illusion, especially if defined in zero-sum terms as independence or autonomy. Suppose one does not recognise that incompleteness will always be with one even in one's supposed superiority and autonomy. Then one could easily develop arrogance by not recognising one's debts and indebtedness to others. With erasures and disavowals of histories of entanglements and indebtedness one could conveniently forget by claiming exclusive ownership of shared patrimonies and/or of the things and inheritances of others. One could even turn the tables on the reality of unequal encounters and claim that it is actually the victims of one's ambitions of conquest – those one has dispossessed and dehumanised – who are in one's debt. One could, for instance, parade the illusion that the debt of civilisation and modernisation that one has brought others through one's aggressive transgressions of their borders and their humanity is immeasurably greater than the debt of dispossession and dehumanisation that they owe them. Hence, far from claiming restoration and restitution, one's victims should actually demonstrate eternal gratitude and recognise their debt and indebtedness to one. Such warped logic, it could be argued, is commonplace in imperial and colonial encounters, as well as in capitalist relations where nothing seems valuable enough unless as a commodity (Fuchs 2018: 262–263). Incompleteness thus pushes us to problematise and rethink current assumptions of debt and indebtedness informed by the dominant logic that completeness is possible, attainable, desirable, valuable and a superior state of being (Nyamnjoh 2015).

When one provides for incompleteness as a permanent feature and disabuses oneself of ambitions of dominance, one develops a disposition that privileges interconnections, interdependences and the reality of debt and indebtedness as an essential aspect of being and belonging together. One develops as well, a permanent suspicion towards absolutes. It cannot be emphasised enough that a life of incompleteness is ultimately about recognising and providing for debt and indebtedness, of which no one – humans and non-humans alike – is free. Put differently, we are who we are through a process of interdependence and indebtedness that living and letting live entails. Life, ultimately, is all about eating and being eaten. This recognition facilitates the cultivation of a disposition of humility that enables one to see and provide for interconnections that guarantee the flow of life. One is who one is because of others. Even if one does not always service one's debts, let alone repay them, one is conscious that one is not self-made. And not to be self-made is not something one should feel ashamed about. One is not an underachiever by owning up to the fact of not being self-made. Rather, the truth of each and every one is that we are all the product of various networks of interconnections, to the production and reproduction of which one actively contributes. The current debate about populism in the USA, Europe and elsewhere, and how it impinges on citizenship, I posit, could be enriched by the notions of incompleteness and conviviality. Conviviality as a disposition that makes accommodating and being accommodated possible arises from and is constantly enriched by a consciousness and alertness to the reality and universality of incompleteness, and the need for flexible mobilities and encounters and interactions with incomplete others that are generative of mutual activation and potency for efficacious actions and interaction. I develop this further below.

The late Nigerian writer, Amos Tutuola – author of *The Palm-Wine Drinkard* and *My Life in the Bush of Ghosts*, published respectively in 1952 and 1954 in London by Faber and Faber – was a genius at depicting the universes of incompleteness popular across West and Central Africa (Nyamnjoh 2017). One example from *The Palm-Wine Drinkard* illustrates the point of this book superbly. The story revolves around a very dependent, overly materially endowed Drinkard, who believes that he is independent because of the predictable regularity of service and servitude he receives from his faithful, virtually enslaved, caretaker and harvester of palm wine.

Instead of celebrating the fact of belonging with and because of others, the Drinkard dramatises his illusions of propped-up independence, power and privilege. He and his friends enjoy the fruit of the tireless toil of the harvester, while treating him as a lesser human. Far from appreciating their indebtedness to the harvester and his labour, the Drinkard expects gratitude from the harvester for the luck to be chosen to be of service and servitude – something that would resonate with those familiar with the British historical drama television series, *Downton Abbey*. Then, suddenly, the Drinkard is made aware of just how dependent he really is, when the palm wine harvester and provider falls from a tall palm tree and dies. During his quest for his palm wine provider who has suddenly dropped dead – a quest best understood as a masterclass of a guided tour on the infinite possibilities of incompleteness by Tutuola – the Drinkard comes to a town where a beautiful young woman has been lured away

5

by "The Complete Gentleman" into the distant bushes inhabited by curious creatures.

It happens that "The Complete Gentleman" is not that complete. There is a lot less to his glitter and sparkle than meets the eye. His charm and handsomeness are less than skin deep. Indeed, almost everything about him belongs to others. He is in every way a composite or cosmopolitan being – a sort of Ubuntu human. He belongs with a community of curious creatures who are reduced to a bare-bones lifestyle, deep in the bushes – they live their lives as skulls, an almost end of history existence. This curious creature reasons that a young woman in town who turns down every man's hand in marriage must want as husband an otherworldly man. So, he decides to try his luck. He embarks on a self-enhancement journey by borrowing body parts from others along the way to the town of the young woman with high standards. He borrows all the body parts he needs, as well as a lovely outfit and a horse. Thus, equipped with these technologies of self-extension, he sets out to make a compelling case of his self-sufficiency, by bending the will of the young woman to his desires. As a composite being, he feels genuinely handsome in his cosmopolitanism of body parts and outfit. In Tutuola's words, "The Skull" turns human, thanks to his borrowing, and ultimately becomes "The Complete Gentleman". Both the Drinkard and "The Skull" present us with complementary indicators of incompleteness and delusions of completeness. From both, we gather that our sense of completeness (independence, omnipotence, invincibility and superabundance) is not merely derived from our mental, psychological or emotional state of being, but can also be cultivated and internalised from how we perceive and relate to ourselves and to other humans, non-humans and the wider external world.

As soon as the young woman sets eyes on him, she decides to follow him. Unlike the Drinkard who is oblivious of what makes him who he is, "The Skull" activated into a gentleman is as gentlemanly as he appears to be complete. He is conscious of his dependent existence. He does not seek to conceal the reality that he is who he is thanks to the generosity of others. He recognises the fact of his debt and indebtedness to them. He warns the young woman repeatedly that there is a lot less to him than meets the eye. He would not be "The Complete Gentleman" or cosmopolitan being that she was seeing if he had not mobilised others to prop him up with body parts

6

that made him dazzle and pass for a truly impressive fellow. But the young woman insists that she has found what she desires: a handsome gentleman of substance – the realisation of her dreams. Her eyes know what they have seen, and she trusts them.

At the crossroads, the penultimate symbol of his compositeness or cosmopolitanism of being, he warns her for the last time. When she insists, he branches off and takes the path leading back to his community of skulls deep in the bushes. Crossroads in Tutuola's universe are significant. They are places of encounter and creative conversations that challenge regressive logics of nativism or autochthony and exclusionary claims and articulations of identities and achievements that seek to deny the histories and realities of productive mobilities and the inextricable entanglements of multiple incomplete beings enriched by the impurities of limitless encounters. As such, they are creative confluences of tensions and possibilities. Having acquired the wife he had set out to win, and being the gentleman that he indeed is, the man begins the process of self-deactivation, self-decomposition or self-unravelling by returning all the things (material and cultural indicators of privilege, wealth and handsomeness) and body parts that he had borrowed for the occasion and paying the agreed price to the lenders. The bride learns how deceptive appearances sometimes are. She learns that as human beings, the reality of our dependence on forces external to ourselves is not always obvious. If only "The Complete Gentleman" were not so much of a gentleman as to insist on recognising and paying back the debt of things and body parts he owed to others, if only he were more selfish and self-centred as to unfairly, in the manner of a trickster, dispossess others permanently, he just might have continued to live a lie. Put differently, if only he were readier to fight to keep the illusion of completeness, omnipotence or self-sufficiency, he may have opted to default on his gentleman's agreement to return the body parts and outfit that he had borrowed.

The story of "The Skull" – that can activate itself from an end of history existence into a complete gentleman to achieve an end, and then reverse itself to being just a skull once again – provides us with a prism through which to make sense of being, becoming, belonging and citizenship, as a permanent work in progress in an interconnected world of incompleteness. The story suggests that everything in the world and in life is incomplete: nature is incomplete, the suprasensory is incomplete, humans are incomplete, and so are human action and human achievement. Such incompleteness implies that people are not singular and unified in their form and content, even as their appearance might suggest that they are. And so are other creatures and things. As the fruit of our creation as incomplete humans, our societies, cultures and civilisations are no different from us. Fluidity, compositeness of being and the capacity to be omnipresent in whole or in fragments are core characteristics of the reality and ontology of incompleteness, and the ethic of conviviality, Ubuntu and cosmopolitanism that they entail.

It is in recognition of incompleteness that human beings are ever so eager to seek ways of enhancing themselves through relationships with other human beings. In using their creativity and imagination to forge solidarities, they acquire magical qualities and useful objects or technologies that can help improve their relationships with fellow humans. These new acquisitions are either embodied as techniques of being and doing through standardised and routinised collective processes of cultivation or are adopted and adapted as complementary objectives external to one's person. Such qualities, objects and technologies also come in handy in dealing with the whims and caprices of natural and supernatural forces and agents. Thanks to this never-ending exchange, human beings grow constantly even if they can never be complete.

Being incomplete necessitates and explains mobility and action to pursue activation for individual and collective fulfilment. Being and becoming are possible only through endless and flexible mobility in quest for activation, potency and efficacy. Even the predictably constituted can move and reconstitute itself in familiar and unfamiliar ways. Nothing is ever entirely what it seems. There is always a lot more or a lot less to things than meets the eye.

It is thus essential to factor into our perception and analysis the reality of social action informed by the constancy of mobility occasioned by the permanence of incompleteness. Whatever the claims made to the contrary, our perception and analysis of reality are impoverished whenever we lose sight of the fact that everything moves – people, things and ideas – in predictable and unpredictable ways. The circulation of things, ideas and people is not the monopoly of any particular group, social category, community or society.

Mobility and circulation lead to encounters of various forms, encounters that are (re)defining in myriad ways.

If people, their possessions and ideas circulate, it follows that their identities, personal or collective, move as well. And through encounters with others, mobile people constantly have to navigate, negotiate, accommodate or reject difference (in things, ideas, beliefs, practices and relations) in a manner that makes of them a permanent work in progress. Like Tutuola's crossroads encounters, no mobility or interaction with others leaves anyone, anything or any idea indifferent, even if such interactions are not always equal and do not always result in immediate, palpable or tangible change. No encounter results in uncontested domination or total passivity. Even as some may wilt in the face of domination, some resist it fervently. Others can navigate and negotiate the tensions and contradictions brought about by the reality of domination in complex, creative and innovative ways. Sometimes this holds the potential for new and more convivial forms of identity and identification.

Mobility is a permanence because incompleteness is an enduring condition. The quest for extensions to repair one's state of incompleteness only makes one realise one's incompleteness when confronted with all manner of extensions that one has not mastered. Moreover, extensions tend to work only partly, and only some of the time – and some of them do undermine the degree of completion one thought one had achieved. The fact that the pursuit of completeness is elusive and illusory (and can only unleash sterile ambitions of conquest and zero-sum games of superiority) is an invitation to explore, contemplate and provide for a world of infinite rhizomic interconnections, fluidities and conviviality. It is an invitation to a world in which no one (and no social, racial, ethnic, gender, age, class or physical category) has the monopoly of power or powerlessness, in which humans and things complement each other and double as one another.

Power is fluid, and so is weakness; both are constantly changing places in a fashion akin to the American *Tom and Jerry* animated cartoon movie series. We are self-consciously incomplete beings, constantly in need of activation, potency and enhancement through conviviality and Ubuntu relationships with incomplete others. Those who ignore this reality and insist on claiming momentary or short-term victories in zero-sum terms sooner or later run themselves into

9

cul-de-sacs where they are forced to reckon with their debt and indebtedness to others – those they have dispossessed and left behind, the debris or those rather mistakenly seen as "unassimilable excess" (Laclau 2005: xi) of their purported achievements – when these others, through popular uprisings and populist movements, mobilise themselves as debt collectors seeking restitution and restoration.

In light of the ubiquity of incompleteness, Ubuntu as a social organising principle encourages a life of mutuality, obligation and reciprocity. Ubuntu emphasises a continuous act of sharing (giving) to maintain a balance of reciprocity between oneself and others. Only through continuous circulation of relationships and things can one guarantee activation, potency and efficacy for competing and complementing incompleteness that account for our flexible compositeness of being. Ubuntu and conviviality insist on interconnections and interdependencies (Nyamnjoh 2015). They suggest a perception and an approach to life, sociality, encounters and relationships mindful of the importance and centrality of charging, discharging and recharging. One can only stay permanently charged if one is in splendid isolation, disconnected, aloof and inactive. Even then, one's charge risks leaking or wasting away (draining itself out unproductively for lack of interactivity). With that, one's life eventually also drains away with little to bequeath to society and the world, which has given so generously to one.

Being social and in relationship and interaction with others requires and simultaneously makes possible actively charging, discharging and recharging oneself and the others involved. Discharging within relationships is not a wasteful exercise because it entails charging others (energy expended is not necessarily energy depleted). Just as recharging entails drawing from the charge of (or being energised by) others. Symbiotic relationships and sociality are full of charge, discharge and recharge. When one loses one's charge to others in a social relationship, that cannot be considered as sterile leakage or wastefulness, as long as recharge or reactivation is possible. Ultimately, being human is all about debt and indebtedness. It is about the need to recognise and provide for the fact that life is all about the circulation of debt. It is crucial to recognise the reality of one's eternal indebtedness to others – be these fellow human beings, the natural environment and its resources, the supernatural forces and one's ancestors or any other set of relationships, real or imagined, that charge or energise and inspire us in our ambitions to fulfil ourselves in all humility and consideration for one another.

This is the framework I would like you to consider as a road companion as you navigate the discussion of Trump, populism and citizenship in this book. I believe, with incompleteness, mobility and conviviality in mind, we are better able to appreciate when populism is used to articulate inclusionary or exclusionary forms of being, becoming and belonging informed by unequal encounters fuelled by ambitions of superiority and zero-sum games of conquest. The book challenges the reader to reflect on how stifling frameworks of citizenship and belonging predicated upon hierarchies of humanity and mobility and driven by a burning but elusive quest for completeness can be productively transcended by humility and conviviality inspired by taking incompleteness seriously and positively.

Throughout the book, I argue that the logic and practice of incompleteness is a healthy antidote to the cheap and toxic recipe of name-calling and scapegoating of others as undesirable outsiders depending on the brand of populism at play. Besides, incompleteness also helps to question sterile and problematic binaries such as those between elites and the impoverished masses among whom populists go to fish for political visibility, prominence and success. Both the elites and the populists among them need to realise and acknowledge – challenging though this is in reality, especially for one who has not been brought up in a culture of care, unending negotiation and give and take – their indebtedness to those that they are excluding in the world with obvious and subtle technologies of oppression, suppression and repression at their beck and call. The mere appeal either to pluralism or populism does not help to make good one's debts and indebtedness to others, locally or globally or anywhere in between.

Part I

The Global Rise and Effervescence of Populism

Populism: Everything and Nothing

As someone making a foray into the attention-catching world of populism, I am curious about what strikes me as the potency of the ambiguity of populism as a phenomenon, a way of structuring being and relating, and a concept. In the age of relativism and the ephemeral, although extensively defined, the meaning of populism remains elusive. I use the analogy of the three blind men and the elephant to demonstrate the experience of those who seek to provide a sense of what is populism. In the story of the three blind men narrated below, each insists their incomplete experience of the elephant represents the whole animal.

Nevertheless, populism as a phenomenon seems unperturbed by the apparent inability among its observers and depicters to capture the complexities, nuances and dynamism that makes it a permanent work in progress as a phenomenon and in its strategies. Those who embrace populism, not from the vantage point of scholarship, truth-seekers and chroniclers of social action, seem to knowingly galvanise towards the evangelical and salvationist promises and messianic pronouncements of a charismatic leader, who emerges, often from an unconventional political itinerary, claiming an exclusive ability to save "the people" from the grip of a sinful overreaching elite. The idea of "the people" is as ambiguous and vague as the idea of populism, hence the need to see both, as Laclau suggests, more as contingent and particular forms and ways of articulating demands and of constructing or structuring the political than necessarily as delimitable phenomena (Laclau 2005). Hence, the side of the political spectrum this messiah finds themself, will foretell who "the people" are and what constitutes populism. What is seldom ambiguous is the ambition of the populists to turn the tables on "the establishment" and elites by riding the horse of popular outrage that they help whip up.

In the present-day USA, for example, what makes both Trump and Sanders populists, is that they both bash "elites" and "the establishment", and whilst they disagree to a large extent about who this establishment is, they manage to frame "the people" that they appeal to as voters, as victims of this establishment, and utilise their anger fuelled by "popular disdain, disillusionment, and disenchantment" provoked by "dispossession, inequality, and disenfranchisement" under neoliberalism as political propellers in what Maskovsky and Bjork-James have appropriately termed "*angry politics*" (Maskovsky and Bjork-James 2020a: 1–2). The populist with messianic pretensions, when otherwise ticking the boxes of what passes as the elite, tends to downplay their own elitism. As illustrated throughout this book, Trump attempts to downplay the privileges that hoisted him into his position; even as Trump being Trump, he cannot help himself but play them up boastfully ever so often. Unlike Tutuola's "The Complete Gentleman", Trump's agenda does not recognise his incompleteness and the imperative for conviviality. Instead, Trump draws on a narrative that prioritises purity over conviviality and winning as a zero-sum pursuit. Even if illusory, Trump's investment in purity is an irony in the USA viewed through the prism of a nation of generational immigrants and a melting pot of diversities.

As discussed in detail below, populism does work in its ability to recognise those who feel displaced by liberal democracy across political vantage points and global geographies. An answer may be to insist on a middle ground if the fate of populism is not simply to replace disgruntled groups with each other year-in and year-out, or following every election cycle. In this regard, how ready are those seeking redress under the banner of populism, amenable to the populism of conviviality? If one draws on the pendulum swings, the middle seems the most compassionate ground, bringing the left and the right to a productive and inclusive conversation in which there are neither losers nor winners in a zero-sum and permanent fashion. The disgruntled swings of populist pendulums are surely not productive for an inclusive future if they keep on being a rerun of the radical undoing of past winners by the current winners in an unending zero-sum game. The creation of zero sums of haves and have nots by toxic capitalism and its enablers seems a power play unwilling to acknowledge the give and take that will inevitably need to happen if all conviviality is not to collapse in favour of eternal orgies of violence and violations.

First things first. Let's take a closer look at populism and its articulation in the literature.

When something can mean everything and nothing, depending on the vantage point of the perceiver, that thing is a victim of relativism gone berserk. It would appear that this is the fate of populism, if what we read and hear about it is anything to go by. When I embarked on this exercise, based on what I had read and heard linking Donald J. Trump and populism, I thought, initially, that the journey would be a straightforward one. I was wrong to be hopeful. Like with Trump, nothing about populism is straightforward. Both have been the subject of voluminous writing, but the more one reads, the more repetitive the writing is, with less and less confidence to claim any actual knowledge of Trump and populism as phenomena. They are both global phenomena that defy definition with precision. The point that populism suffers from proverbial definitional precariousness (Urbinati 2019) and conceptual fragmentation occasioned by "a dizzying proliferation" of competing definitions that are seldom complementary (Gagnon et al. 2018: v) is just as true of Trump. Although, Singh argues, Trump confirms more about populism and its conceptual elasticity, plasticity, malleability or fluidity than populism reveals about Trump as an improvisational person with a nose for money who defies coherence and principles (Singh 2017). Trump and populism, I have come to think, are like a door that opens in all directions.

But all those writings – by authors most of whom it could be argued are part of the elite class who seem to agree and disagree in the manner of team A and team B of the same football club – are written in earnest. Something must be going on, and if the characteristics are sufficiently distinctive, that something needs to be named or categorised. This is what the writers and commentators have tried to do about populism and about Trump. It is possible that as writers and commentators we may, like the blind men and the elephant, be dealing with a story of incompleteness and incomplete knowledge, a story that invites us to privilege conversation over conversion and to champion inclusivity over exclusivity. It is a story worth revisiting in detail here for new and deeper understanding of linkages between populism and a man like Trump. The story is also worth revisiting for what it tells us about the complementarity between knowledge and ignorance, knowing and not knowing.

Several versions of the story of the blind men and the elephant exist. Some mention three blind men and others six, and still others involve more men. The blind men were curious to encounter an elephant, rather than contenting themselves with stories about this "queer" and "strange" animal, the aspects of the creature varying from one version of the tale to another.

In one version, the three blind men collaborate, holding hands in anticipation. The merchant who offers to take them to an elephant leads the way. They each contemplate and imagine how they will touch the elephant. The merchant coordinates and controls the encounter like a scientist conducting a laboratory experiment. Arriving at the destination where his herd of elephants are, the merchant asks the blind men to sit on the ground and wait. Then he leads them, one by one, to touch the elephant. The first blind man feels the left foreleg and then the right, and in a moment akin to Archimedes' "Eureka!" he exclaims, "So, the queer animal feels like *that*!" Then he slowly returns to the group to announce his findings. It is now the turn of the second blind man. Whether by design or not, the merchant leads him to the rear of the elephant. The blind man touches the tail, which wiggles a few times, and he exclaims with satisfaction, "Ha! Truly a queer animal! Truly odd! I know now. I know." He hurriedly steps aside to make way for the third blind man, who touches the elephant's trunk, which moves back and forth, turning and twisting. He thinks, "That's it! I've learned."

The three blind men thank the merchant and go on their way, bubbling with excitement. Back together, they decide to share and discuss their findings. The second blind man takes the lead in their panel discussion. "This queer animal is like our straw fans swinging back and forth to give us a breeze. However, it's not so big or well made. The main portion is rather wispy," he proclaims. "No, no!" shouts the first blind man in disagreement. "This queer animal resembles two big trees without any branches." "You're both wrong," replies the third blind man. "This queer animal is similar to a snake; it's long and round, and very strong."

They argue, each insisting that he alone is correct. Of course, there is no conclusion for not one has thoroughly examined the whole elephant. Yet how were they to know? They were not able to see the animal. How could they describe it in whole? Sight would have enabled the blind men to see the elephant, and not simply touch it.

But seeing does not necessarily translate into knowledge. Even if they possessed all the physical senses and used them to good effect in bringing the elephant home to their senses, it is still possible to question the extent to which they could claim to know the elephant in full. If, as some would argue, reality is much more than that which we can see, hear, touch, smell and taste, this means there is knowledge over and above what our senses tell us (Rauch 2013[2003], 2021). To know as humans is particularly challenging, given, as Rauch indicates, that we "have no direct access to an objective world independent of our minds and senses, and subjective certainty is no guarantee of truth" (Rauch 2021: 86).

The focus in this story of the elephant is not on physical blindness or sight but on ways of perceiving and knowing. Thus, the same story could be told of three men with full capacities for sight and all their other senses intact. The challenge would still be to represent the elephant, which they had never encountered before. The story is a metaphor for another kind of blindness – that which comes from preconceptions, prejudices and assumptions about what constitutes reality, a blindness which all humans possess and practise.

How does one keep one's preconceptions in check so as to do justice to encounters with difference and diversity? Put differently, is it possible to achieve the level of objectivity needed to perceive and represent the elephant for what it truly is – a complex and nuanced reality that cannot be easily reduced to its constituent parts or limited to sensory perceptions? Does it matter what the elephant has to say (if it could speak) about how it is perceived and represented? Is it adequate to claim validity and veracity by providing for an intersubjective account informed by the observer's and the elephant's representation of *being* an elephant? How does one account for the eventuality that the elephant could be beyond knowing by one individual or even by all blind men together and the elephant combined? We must grant that intimate encounters with the elephant, however deep and convincing, are always approached from particular angles and perspectives – for example maleness – and that such encounters are further compounded by the dimensions of being an elephant that are beyond appearances and beyond representation, as in the encounter described above between the young woman and "The Complete Gentleman".

Even the most industrious and creative of explorers can achieve only a partial account of what the elephant is. And this includes the elephant as self-explorer. Like ethnographers, the blind men are so focused on their areas that they are, consciously or not, oblivious to the existence of other areas – a situation made worse by their reluctance to accept that others could be right about the elephant as well. The fact that the elephant is larger than the individual or even collective experiences of it is lost on each of the men. If they were scientists, they might have understood that science is a collective pursuit and that no one has a monopoly on insights and the truth. Social truth being negotiable by virtue of its public nature, critical public debate and social checking (Rauch 2013[1993]: 165–174), it requires humility and mutual accommodation through open-ended conversations on the part of those who lay claim to it (Rauch 2021: 1–19). As Rauch rightly observes, the open society as a marketplace of ideas "is sometimes a cross we bear, but it is also a sword we wield, and we are defenseless without it" (Rauch 2013[1993]: 180). Hence his call for the passionate pursuit of truth by a reality-based community of socially networked practitioners of liberal science motivated by the relentless quest for objectivity, factuality and rationality, "while remaining coolly mindful" of the "elusiveness" of truth (Rauch 2021: 233). Knowing and knowledge production require the humility of incompleteness and an openness to conviviality. Thus, amply equipped with the stories of "The Skull", "The Complete Gentleman" and the "blind men and the elephant", let us turn our attention to what writers and commentators from different horizons and of multiple ilk are saying about populism and Trump.

The 21st century world is marked by a global rise in populism, an ambiguous word or "chameleon" concept[1] which means different things to different people (Laclau 2005; Gherghina and Soare 2013; Benveniste et al. 2016; Singh 2017; Finchelstein 2017), an outfit that seems to excite and concern reactionary and revolutionary shoppers alike. In their "very short introduction" to populism, Mudde and Kaltwasser suggest that the confusion generated by the concept comes in part from "the fact that populism is a label seldom claimed by people or organizations themselves", but rather "it is ascribed to others, most often with a negative connotation" (Mudde and Kaltwasser 2017: 2). If those so labelled were given more of a say in how they are understood and defined, populism might perhaps be more empirically grounded. Like the elephant in our story above that captured the attention of the blind men seeking to make sense of it, populism has attracted and continues to attract burgeoning though fragmentary literature and the proliferation of scholarship described by the editors of the 2017 *Oxford Handbook of Populism* as "unwieldy", even as these musings provide a very useful overview of the origins, history and state of the art of the concept (Kaltwasser et al. 2017: 1). It could be argued that scholarship has come a long way from 1969 when Ionescu and Gellner described populism as an elusive but important concept: "There can, at present, be no doubt about the *importance* of populism. But no one is quite clear just what it *is*", to draw attention to what exactly it was that made of populism a phenomenon with distinctive characteristics or clear defining features. The questions raised by Ionescu and Gellner about the extent to which "populism is a unitary concept, regardless of the variety of its incarnations" or "simply a word wrongly used in completely heterogenous contexts", and to what extent populism is "primarily an ideology (or ideologies) or a movement (or movements) or both" have certainly received some attention (Ionescu and Gellner 1969: 1–3). However, much work remains to be done on the conceptualisation and theorisation of populism. According to Müller, the fragmentary and often country specific nature of the literature means that, "We simply do not have anything like a *theory* of populism, and we seem to lack coherent criteria for deciding when political actors turn populist in some meaningful sense" (Müller 2016: 2).

To Mouffe – who, inspired by Ernesto Laclau (2005), thinks of populism less as an ideology and more in terms of "a political strategy of constructing a political frontier" in a divided, conflictual and antagonistic partisan context where democracy is less about procedures and institutions for generating consensus than it is about institutions and procedures for the management of conflict – it is unfortunate that populism is widely misused to label and dismiss things we do not like.[2] She shares Laclau's critique of the tendency in some of the literature to approach "populism in terms of abnormality, deviance or manipulation" and to demote and denigrate it, instead of seeing it as "a distinctive and always present possibility of structuration of political life" (Laclau 2005: 13).

Fukuyama laments the fact that the term populism "has been used so broadly" to the point of being rendered "meaningless" in certain ways. "Everything has been called populism".[3] In the course of reading for this book, I have come across a rich menu of qualifiers for populism, amongst which are the following: new, modern, contemporary, economic, political, cultural, identity, religious, ethno, agrarian, poverty, protest, authoritarian, pessimistic, progressive, reactionary, left-wing, right-wing, exclusionary, bad, good, politicians', intellectual, empirical/"actually existing", literary, local, global, neoliberal, transnational, native working-class, antisystem, electoral, media, digital, demagogic, polarising triadic, true, faux, fake, platonic and meta. It is with this in mind that some writers, Traverso for example, find meaning in Isaiah's observation that "many scholars have developed a curious Cinderella Complex: 'there is a shoe—the word "populism"—for which somewhere there must exist a foot'" (Traverso 2019: Chapter 1). Gagnon et al., on the other hand, suggest six broad definitional categories to enable an approach that sees populism as "a shape-shifting phenomenon which moves along multiple, crosscutting cleavages" (Gagnon et al. 2018: v), namely: "(1) *authoritarian and democratic*, (2) *market fundamentalist (libertarian) and redistributive*, (3) *exclusionary and inclusionary (antipluralist and pluralist)*, (4) *xenophobic and cosmopolitan*, (5) *electoral and participatory (thick)* (6) *nostalgic and aspirational*" (Gagnon et al. 2018: vii, italics in original).

Aware of the "tension between different approaches" as well as "the controversies and new directions that characterise activity" by researchers on populism, Heinisch et al. call for "further research" and invite greater transdisciplinary conversations, scholarship and insights "on populism as it relates to political actors, political mobilisation, political institutions, as well as political discourse and style" (Heinisch et al. 2017: 5–7). Gherghina and Soare argue for greater theoretical coherence informed by detailed individual and comparative case studies that are empirically grounded and methodologically rigorous (Gherghina and Soare 2013: 2). Weyland and Madrid offer useful comparative insights drawn from European and Latin American experiences with populism, in their critical interrogation of the challenges posed by Trumpian populism to American democracy (Weyland and Madrid 2019). On his part, Finchelstein draws on the diverse global history of populism to argue for theory building that is grounded on the complex history and protean nature of the concept (Fichelstein 2017).

Kaltwasser et al. regret the fact that "the study of populism has not been recognized even by its own scholars and there has been a marked reluctance to systematically and comprehensively make use of work on populism from other regions or other historical period" (Kaltwasser et al. 2017: 10). This, Chini and Moroni (2018) argue, poses the challenge of how to make an analytical category of populism. This is a challenge Mudde and Kaltwasser believe could be addressed by positioning "populism first and foremost within the context of liberal democracy" and not within democracy more generally, or any other form of government (Mudde and Kaltwasser 2017: 1–2; see also Mudde 2019: Introduction). Populism suggests an unravelling – not unfamiliar to the deactivation of Tutuola's "The Complete Gentleman" discussed above – that is both luring and alienating, depending on who one is and from what vantage point one is following the unfolding. Regardless of the vantage point, Gherghina and Soare point to a unifying attribute of populism as a phenomenon that "emphasises instinct and emotion at the expense of the rational legal spirit", and promotes "a simplified antagonistic vision of society, in which the ruled people are betrayed by a detached ruling class", as well as "the possibility to restore the equilibrium between the ruled majority and the ruling minority by empowering the latter". Hence "the sacralisation of the people" as "an instrument in the fight against the corrupted elites, which increasingly become alienated and alienating". The challenge this poses to the populist leader, however, is how to enable "a relation of proximity that is no longer valued by contemporary society" (Gherghina and Soare 2013: 7–8). Love it or hate it, populism, even as it is fundamentally critical of experts and the excesses of expertise, is an expert at centring issues of mobility, belonging, citizenship and debt and indebtedness. Populism resurfaces these issues that may have seemed to have been settled in the nation-state, purportedly the most effective framework for organising life together in large-scale modern societies. Although difficult to analyse because of what Cooper describes as its "cultural and political ambiguities", the concept of "popular" (populist and populism) suggests that "struggles over the legitimacy of authority and status are very much unresolved" (1987: 100), whatever those who wield political and cultural power might think or say.

Compared to Tutuola's universe of incompleteness, populism would seem to signal that "The Complete Gentleman" has failed to live up to his part of the bargain by defaulting on his debts or failing to recognise the fact of his indebtedness to others. This calls for debt collection (populism) and debt collectors (populists) as a way of deflating "The Complete Gentleman" that has opted to live off the sweat and toil of others, and in callous disregard of their predicaments. He must be stripped of all his pretensions. In this regard, it makes sense to stress, as do Levitsky and Ziblatt, that:

> Populists are antiestablishment politicians—figures who, claiming to represent the voice of "the people," wage war on what they depict as a corrupt and conspiratorial elite. Populists tend to deny the legitimacy of established parties, attacking them as undemocratic and even unpatriotic. They tell voters that the existing system is not really a democracy but instead has been hijacked, corrupted, or rigged by the elite. And they promise to bury that elite and return power to "the people." (Levitsky and Ziblatt 2018: Chapter 1).

Whether or not the actions of populists match their anti-establishmentarianism is an empirical question, according to Makulilo, whose study of populism in Tanzania, South Africa and Zambia leads him to conclude that as "much as populists may claim to be antipolitical, anti-institutions, and anti-elite, they ultimately use these very same institutions to solicit support for power" (Makulilo 2013: 197).

Populism could thus be likened to a form of debt collection and populists to those who opt to serve as debt collectors from those who have insisted on borrowing without acknowledging and on dispossessing with impunity. Whether the debt collectors are genuine or are con-people just keeping up appearances while maintaining ambiguous relationships with the debtors is a central question of this book. It should be acknowledged, however, that populists are not always necessarily anti-democratic just because they are critical of the "establishment" and cultivate a "they" versus "us" narrative. To seek to express the ideas of "the people", however defined or delimited, is not inherently problematic. Trying to express the ideas of "the people" becomes problematic only when it incorporates the moral entitlement of being the only one who can do the speaking on behalf of "the people" and address their needs while simultaneously dehumanising those who are excluded from their definition of "the people". In other words, it is problematic to speak of "the people" in an unsubstantiated manner in contexts characterised by hierarchies and exclusionary practices informed by categories such as race, place, culture, class, gender, sex and age.

To Martinelli, populism, as both a loose or thin ideology and as a strategy of consensus organisation by leaders seeking unmediated non-institutionalised access to supporters, was employed across the world in the 20th and 21st centuries to mount anti-elitist appeals against established interests or mainstream parties of both the political left and right (Martinelli 2016, 2018). He adds:

> Although present in the language of almost all political leaders as a rhetorical style and an attempt to connect empathically with the masses, populism acquires the features of a full-fledged ideology when the political discourse is organised around a few core distinctive features: the two concepts of "people" (as the legitimate source of power) and "community" (as the legitimate criterion for defining the people), the antagonistic relationship between two homogeneous groups, We (the pure, virtuous people) and Them (the corrupt, inefficient, and negligent elite or establishment); the absolute right of the majority against the minority; the denial of pluralism and intermediation (Martinelli 2018: 17).

Seen in such stark dichotomies, populism assumes the character of a zero-sum dualism with clear and irreconcilable battle lines of the irredeemably bad elite and the eternally good people. Kivisto agrees, observing that in populism, "Elites are typically depicted as not only corrupt, but as inept and as failures in terms of meeting the needs of the people, while the people are portrayed as victims of elites" (Kivisto 2017: 30). This could be overly simplistic, as in the case of Trump voters in the 2016 presidential election, who "are not a homogeneous group", yet they share an "embrace — sometimes explicitly, at other times more implicitly; sometimes assertively, sometimes quietly — of the ideology of right-wing populism" (Kivisto 2017: 67). Equally, the closer one looks, the clearer it becomes that even the elites are not as homogenous and unified and predictable as is often assumed by those who categorise them as singular and unified. Many who fly the flag of populism would pass the litmus test of elitism with flying colours.

Harkening to this call to fight for the people against a corrupt elite, Donald Trump, himself an elite – economic, cultural and political – (Kazin 2016), as the elected debt collector for the people of the USA in Tutuola's terms, stressed in his inaugural address on 20 January 2017 that "government is controlled by the people" and "a nation exists to serve its citizens". Trump insisted that power was being transferred "not merely […] from one administration to another" but from Washington DC directly back to the people, who from the day of his inauguration would become "the rulers of this nation again". He promised that, "The forgotten men and women of our country will be forgotten no longer." He would drain the swamp of Washington DC, where "a small group" "flourished but the people did not share in its wealth" and where politicians prospered and "reaped the rewards of government while the people have borne the cost". He blamed "The Establishment" for protecting itself "but not the citizens of our country" and for failing to make its triumphs the triumphs of the struggling families across the country, that have had "little to celebrate" even as the establishment has been celebrating[4] (see also Mudde 2019: Introduction; Nance 2019: Chapter 10).

This book explores the extent to which Trump has lived up to this promise of inclusivity and pluralism of his inaugural speech, especially given Müller's pertinent remark that, "In addition to being antielitist, populists are always *antipluralist*" (Müller 2016: 3).

Hawkins et al. provide a minimal definition of populism – stripped of additional features "such as charismatic, outsider leadership; movement-based organization; short-sighted economic policies; or the presence of certain types of coalitions" – "as a Manichaean discourse that sees politics as a struggle between a reified will of the people and a conspiring elite" (Hawkins et al. 2016: 95), and that as a discourse, populism "stands in opposition to a pluralist one in which political opponents are not demonised, and disagreement and compromise are seen as valued and natural features of democracy" (Hawkins and Hawkins 2018: 48). However, as Benveniste et al. (2016: 5) argue, the fact that "as an ideology, populism does not tell us who the elite and the people are, what they do and what they think" accounts for the proliferation of definitions that are "contingent on the existing relationships between government and society".

The use of the term "the people" in present day populist speak in Europe is ambiguous. It clearly does not coincide in any way with the people of "the nation as bounded by the territory of the nation state" (Benveniste et al. 2016: 8). It undermines the idea of the nation-state as a plural community of unity in diversity. Writing specifically about the USA, Kazin suggests that, "It may be impossible to come up with a credible definition of 'the people' that can mobilize the dizzying plurality of class, gender, and ethnic identities which co-exist, often unhappily, in America today. But ambitious populists will probably not stop trying to concoct one" (Kazin 2017[1995]: xv). In the absence of clear indicators of what constitutes populism and, especially given the fact that the governing elites are almost always targeted by its rhetoric, it is not surprising that "populism has always been used in a negative sense by governing elites to characterise any form of opposition that claims to represent the 'people's voice' without basing its policy declarations on real facts and viable solutions to actual problems" (Benveniste et al. 2016: 5). All caveats aside, common to all forms of populism, it could be argued, is the idea of "protest against the establishment, loudly expressed in a way that encourages large audiences" (Benveniste et al. 2016: 11). For students of populism, Espejo argues, "Making clear what we mean when we say 'the people' is crucial to understanding both populism and democracy", especially given that "democratic legitimacy rests on the idea of a unified people", yet "the people are always indeterminate". Equally of significance for defining and theory building on populism is addressing questions such as: "How does the people emerge as a unified body (if it can ever do so)? How can a people decide? Who gets to speak for the people? How does it legitimize rule?" The idea of "people as process" is a useful prism through which to examine the extent to which populists speaking on behalf of the people live up to or betray the ideals of democracy that they claim to endorse (Espejo 2017: 607–608).

Like Kalwasser et al. (2017), *The Economist* attempts to give a historical overview and explanation of the term "populism". The point of departure is Donald J. Trump, described by Smith and Oltermann of *The Guardian* in December 2016 as "the brash businessman who rose to power on a populist tide"[5] or simply as "the populist American president-elect". But the article in *The Economist* goes on to observe that almost anything or anyone can be considered populist, depending on one's vantage point and who is doing the categorisation. This suggests a flexibility of meaning and/or usage that could have populism serving in political ping-pong and being a hot potato for politicians and others (the professional elite for example) seen to be encouraging or shying away from it. To *The Economist*, "Populists may be militarists, pacifists, admirers of Che Guevara or of Ayn Rand; they may be tree-hugging pipeline opponents or drill-baby-drill climate-change deniers. What makes them all 'populists', and does the word actually mean anything?"[6]

Michael Kazin contends that "the power of populism lies in its adaptable nature" (Kazin 2017[1995]: xi). This accounts for why political commentators:

> [...] seem eager to paste the label on forces and individuals who really have just one big thing in common: they are effective at blasting "elites" or "the establishment" for harming the interests and betraying the ideals of "the people"—proud in their ordinariness—in nations which are committed, at least officially, to democratic principles. Thus, President Donald Trump and Senator Bernie Sanders both get called populist, despite their mutual hostility and starkly different stances on nearly every issue from health care to business regulation to climate change. The term is also routinely affixed to both Jeremy Corbyn and Viktor Orbán, although the right-wing Hungarian prime minister would like to destroy every key element of the social-democratic agenda the current head of the British Labour Party wants to preserve and strengthen. Clearly, there can be no Populist Manifesto worthy of the name (Kazin 2017[1995]: xi).

In its capacity to attract or appeal to all and sundry (Müller 2016), populism resembles Tutuola's "The Complete Gentleman" in its compositeness. Like "The Complete Gentleman" who is a patchwork of borrowed body parts and accoutrements, populism is a catch-all net of interests and meanings. A case could be made that Trump, despite being a teetotaller, has much in common with the Drinkard in terms of a dependent and protected life of power and privilege sustained by inheritance and a very supportive father. Trump has been described by Tim O'Brien, his biographer (O'Brien

2015[2005]), as having "a consuming desire to always be centre stage, yet he never wants to reveal who he really is". He "masks his finances, his taxes, his friendships, his ongoing family conflicts of interest, his ignorance and his inadequacies", and is "constantly making up areas of expertise he doesn't have".[7] As Rohde emphasises, Trump knows that "information is power" and while strictly limiting "the release of information about himself", he does not hesitate to attack "the credibility of information from rivals" (Rohde 2020: Epilogue). As someone who means different things to different people, who reportedly has no strong principles or firm ideological leanings, who has no permanent friends or foes, and on whom everyone seems to have a strong opinion, it could be argued that Trump is also very much like "The Complete Gentleman" and like populism, if not as Siamese twins, then as mirror images of each other. Trump is like "The Complete Gentleman" who doubles as the emperor in his make-believe new clothes. Without principles to hold everybody to the same standards, how can common purpose, accountability and democracy be possible with Trump, or his double, populism?

Populism, like Trump, emphasises the idea of a nation-state that is divided within between us and them, insiders and outsiders, those who belong legitimately, those whose belonging is contested or contestable, or, as Marcia Pally suggests, between the truly deserving sons and daughters of the soil and "bastards" (recent immigrants and other suspect groups) who deserve to be thrown out.[8] In other words, populism, its justifications or legitimacy notwithstanding, is comparable to "The Complete Gentleman" that gives up on its cosmopolitan pretensions to embark on an unravelling journey and free fall into ever compounding nativism and its echo chamber bubbles. In the case of Tutuola's fiction, this is to illustrate a point about the value and humility of incompleteness, a lesson that does not seem apparent in many an investment in populism which, beyond rhetoric, tends to embrace and celebrate exclusionism and the policing of thought and practice. Justified religiously, such disentanglements and autochthony or nativism suggest a radically exclusionary solution inspired by ever diminishing circles of inclusion in which "a troubled world will be set right when evil forces are purged".[9] Nativist unravelling suggests a situation where one's enemies (depending on who one is as well as on one's power and privilege to define and confine and to cancel out dissent) have transgressed one's borders and infiltrated the arteries of one's blood system like a virus. Such nativism is, put differently, raising an identity red flag against obvious strangers or those caught betwixt and between who have dared to imagine that fulfilment and full integration were possible in a determinedly zero-sum game of being and belonging.

The mere act of labelling immigrants or the outsider more generally as criminals serves as a justification to treat them as pollution and hence mobilise the language and acts of law and order, and even war, to fight off invasions and infections, and to police borders and boundaries to safeguard citizens and/or insiders, protect jobs and ensure that scarce resources are expressly directed to bona fide insiders. The reasoning in such logic is that when the body politic is infected, one requires surgical interventions to cure it of the infections and re-establish health and, most importantly, a sanitised and protected purity of being (Ignatieff 1995; Geschiere 2009) comparable to that of the thoroughbred (Isenberg 2016). Populists play with this idea of the importance of purity of blood and the need to protect and defend the biological and cultural essence of the nation or the dominant group. Put differently, they are keen to promote democracy not only as an individual right, but also and often, more importantly, as a group right as well, to be limited to groups whose belonging is rigorously vetted by the populists in question, using nebulous and subjective criteria. Populism thus arises when the nation-state's capacity to outsource its headaches and contradictions to an external enemy, real or imagined, is seriously limited in a world where the sites of contestation are increasingly very local and grounded in everyday existential relationships. Even when not obviously stated, populism materialises as a contestation of the idea that mobility (physical, social, economic, cultural and other) could, in real terms, provide a basis for a much more flexible and open-ended framework and practice of citizenship and belonging to cultural and political communities at local, national and global levels.

In a universe where completeness remains an ambition, a possibility and an investment, populism arises from a number of intersecting perceived grievances, loss, dispossession and anxieties, but most significantly from a feeling of being left out economically, culturally and socially, and not having one's voice heard, politically, through established democratic mechanisms. In other words, populism arises from a feeling of inadequate activation of one's citizenship and a sense that one's rights and entitlements, whether or not provided for in a constitution or in principle, are not effectively enacted in concrete terms or translated in the relationships that one has with others. Populism arises when one feels remote and radically cut off from a world one believes to be one's own and for which one is ready to fight. Thus, as Hawkins et al. argue:

> [...] populism is much more than a claim for material rewards or a privileging of traditional values, and certainly more than an emotional reaction born of low education. It is a claim that citizens are not being given equality before the law – that their fundamental rights as democratic citizens are being violated. Worse, their rights are being violated by a selfish elite that is not just deaf to their concerns, but consciously working against them. Merely redressing material concerns or traditional values will not respond to this deeper claim and, perhaps just as importantly, addressing the deeper claim may make it unnecessary to fully respond to other material or values-based claims. On the contrary, it opens up novel compromises (Hawkins et al. 2016: 105).

When populism arises, it tends to fault the ruling (political and technocratic) and/or economic (national and global) elite which it portrays as enemies of ordinary folks – hapless victims of uncaring policies and practices by the elites. However, in some instances, Chandler argues, using Vladimir Putin and pension reforms in Russia as a case in point, "a strategy to court voters can impel [populist] leaders to postpone or delay important decisions" (Chandler 2020: 148). Known for their big promises, populist leaders, Chandler suggests:

> [...] may be vulnerable to social policy mistakes, because of several political propensities: first, an impulse to launch major policy changes suddenly with little consultation; second, a reluctance to undertake measures that might be unpopular with key constituencies, but which might merely postpone action to address a problem; and third, a tendency to raise expectations of citizens through grand (and ultimately unrealistic) promises (Chandler 2020: 149).

The "populist ethic tends to glorify [...] the *ordinary* individual" and "populism is often a romanticization of the ordinary" (Mazrui and Engholm 1968: 21).

Whatever the vulnerabilities of populist leaders may be, Goodhart credits contemporary populism in Europe and North America for pushing Western politics to make "room for a new set of voices preoccupied with national borders and pace of change, appealing to people who feel displaced by a more open, ethnically fluid, graduate favouring economy and society, designed by and for the new elites" (Goodhart 2017: 2). Populism, in other words, is all about holding democracy, neoliberal globalisation and globalism to account for its debris and the dystopian side effects of their effusive utopian pursuits. Seen through the prism of incompleteness within a framework that provides for completeness as a possibility, the current waves of populism in Europe and North America challenge democracy, neoliberal globalisation and globalism to prioritise those who consider themselves as worthy of the status of primary beneficiaries and as autochthons. The message seems to be one of charity begins at home occupying the topmost rungs of the ladder of success. No culture, civilisation or social order, however tall on its ideals and achievements, can be considered to be truly successful when it fails woefully to ensure inclusivity in how the benefits of success are distributed, embodied and harnessed in change and continuity. Thus, whether driven by cultural resentment, economic marginalisation or both, populism presents itself as a wakeup call for remedial measures to a perceived lack of accountability by the driving forces of particular societal and political projects. , Titlestad stresses the importance to provide for populism as "a way of making sense of an increasingly opaque world", instead of simply dismissing it on the basis of its propensity to reinforce, however paradoxically, injustice, prejudice, brutality, bigotry and exploitation. Populism deserves greater compassion and understanding than it tends to get (Titlestad 2020: 2).

Populism is also a direct consequence of political opportunism by populist leaders seeking office not so much with a carefully considered and inclusive programme of action, but with sweet-sounding, luring slogans and clichés that are seldom anchored institutionally and are overly reliant on the personal charisma, anti-system and anti-establishment rhetoric of the leader in question. As

Müller affirms, "Populists claim that they, and they alone, represent the people" (Müller 2016: 3). The populist leader assumes messianic qualities that are often evangelical in their appeal, charisma and propensity for fearmongering, stoking hatred, and claims of being "the sole voice capable of representing and embodying 'the People'" (Chini and Moroni 2018: 5). Such rhetoric includes but is not limited to: "I alone can fix it" and "I'm the only one that matters" – in the manner of Donald Trump the "very stable genius" (Singh 2017; Finchelstein 2017; Nance 2019; Rucker and Leonnig 2020; Leonnig and Rucker 2021). As Sims echoes, "Trump believes he alone, often through sheer force of will, can solve certain problems", just as he believes "that all of life is a negotiation, and that every negotiation is a zero-sum game". In other words, with Trump, there is "no such thing as a 'win-win'; someone will win and someone will lose" (Sims 2019: Chapter 7). Trump is all about the total annihilation of incompleteness, which he insists on seeing as a weakness, with delusions of supremacy. As Fukuyama recounts:

> When Donald Trump accepted the Republican nomination in 2016, he said something truly remarkable: "I alone understand your problems and I alone can fix them." He has gone on to attack virtually every institution in the American government that he feels has threatened him. He began with the intelligence community because they were saying the Russians helped him win the election. He went on to include the FBI and the Justice Department. In a Stalinist turn of phrase, he and his allies in parts of the media now characterise these institutions as "enemies of the American people".[10]

Countries with names such as People's Republic of China, Polish People's Republic and Korean People's Democratic Republic, and that often tend to have political parties that are similarly named, with an emphasis on "the people", draw attention to some form of populism at work, in principle as least. With perhaps the exception of Japan where, according to Penn, "populism is so unpopular",[11] the entire world seems to be haunted by the spectre of populism, as Ghita Ionescu and Ernest Gellner described it in their introduction to an edited book on the meaning and national characteristics of populism in 1969. Since then, the populism bandwagon has attracted more and more attention. Mishra observes that:

[…] the world at large – from the US to Indonesia – is undergoing a militant tribalisation. The new demagogues combine xenophobia with progressivist rhetoric about decent housing, efficient healthcare systems and better schools. Insisting on linguistic, religious, ethnic, and racial differences, they don't just threaten free trade, or the globalist dream of achieving cosmopolitan unity through intensified commerce and digital communications. They seem to be deforming nothing less than the secular and egalitarian ideals of modernity.[12]

Like messiahs, the new demagogues appeal to the debris and/or those left behind by neoliberalism and its globalisation bandwagon to weaponise their frustrations, anger and hate, and join them in a crusade against the establishment power elite. They are critical of the latter for enjoying power without accountability and responsibility along with frequent flyer, flexible global citizenship with scant regard for their compatriots abandoned to waste their lives away at the margins of their painful economic, social and cultural modernist programmes, experiments or fantasies. They claim to be the voice of the people, asking for power to be returned to the people (Kellner 2016; Coles 2017; Lind 2020; Nichols 2021).

Babones believes that the privileges enjoyed by the cosmopolitan global expert class in the contemporary world are of such magnitude that it is hardly surprising why "populist nativism" is "so abhorrent to them". To Babones, the political liberalism of this global expert class ranges from "the instinctive affinity for personal freedoms and human rights that comes from years of higher education" to the instinct for "self-preservation" through "the natural propensity of experts to embrace a political ideology that looks to them as the authoritative sources of wisdom". Hence, it is no coincidence, Babones argues, that in every field, the world's leading experts "are the greatest beneficiaries of transnational liberal rights" such as "the right to invest across borders, the right to intellectual property protection, the right to have disputes resolved outside of potentially biased national court systems, the right of non-discrimination in employment, and the right to work in the country of one's choice". Thanks to their personal mobility, these professionals are able to "shop for freedoms, and even citizenships, when the governments in their home countries prove unsatisfactory" (Babones 2018: Chapter 3).

Put differently, this class of experts is keener to personalise and privatise the benefits of rights and freedoms applied globally, than to extend these to their compatriots who are more grounded and local, and less exposed to the same opportunities. They want their achievements unencumbered by the responsibility of accountability to anyone but themselves (Judis 2018; Lind 2020). As Goodhart details with reference to Britain and Brexit politics, while these flexibly mobile modern elites can afford a kaleidoscopic view of the world from anywhere, they must not be oblivious to or condescending about the reality and predicament of more rooted people who, most of the time, can only afford to see the world from the somewhere of their more grounded existence (Goodhart 2017). Often, as Kakutani remarks, populist leaders tend to "inflame these feelings of fear and anger and disenfranchisement, offering scapegoats instead of solutions" (Kakutani 2018: 25). They capitalise on the unique ability of feelings and beliefs to trump facts (Ioanide 2015), and of demagoguery and rhetoric to deflate scrutiny for the lack of action and failure to provide solutions (Skinnell 2018a; Steudeman 2018; Young 2018). Such leaders are comforted by the tendency in angry people to suffer a significant reduction in their need for "complete and rational explanations", to be "more indiscriminately punitive, particularly to out-groups" and to "underestimate the risk of negative outcomes" (Wylie 2019: Chapter 7).

Representations that oppose populism to cosmopolitanism impoverish both ideas, according to Ingram. To see populism as inherently and inevitably in contradiction with cosmopolitanism comes from "a hasty, overly cynical interpretation of both ideas, one that narrows populism to communitarian self-interest and self-aggrandizement, and cosmopolitanism to elite self-interest and self-aggrandizement" (Ingram 2017: 644–652). Ingram elaborates:

There have been and continue to be more and less cosmopolitan, universalistic, and inclusive populisms, just as there have been and continue to be more and less popular, common, and inclusive cosmopolitanisms. It is important to recall this not only [...] to avoid a distorted or one-sided view of either object, but also for practical purposes: by predetermining the nature of such multifarious phenomena, we deprive ourselves of tools for making ethical and political judgments (Ingram 2017: 656).

Being cosmopolitan is not confined to passing for a citizen of the world or having loyalties that transcend local belonging and national citizenship. Cosmopolitanism is as much a disposition of open-mindedness and open-heartedness as it is an experience of cultural diversity, transnationalism, in some cases, and continual transformation. It is about being rooted and nimble-footed, grounded and rhizomic.

Many conflate populism with right-wing populism, but as Judis argues with reference to the USA, there is left-wing populism as well. Judis makes a subtle distinction between the two:

> Leftwing populists champion the people against an elite or an establishment. Theirs is a vertical politics of the bottom and middle arrayed against the top. Rightwing populists champion the people against an elite that they accuse of coddling a third group, which can consist, for instance, of immigrants, Islamists, or African American militants. Leftwing populism is dyadic. Rightwing populism is triadic. It looks upward, but also down upon an out group (Judis 2016: 15).

According to Mouffe, the fact that "the social is always discursively constructed" with no "final rational foundations" possible, makes the case for both left-wing and right-wing populism in that "the people can be constructed in different ways".[13] She elaborates as follows:

> "The people" is neither an empirical referent, nor a sociological category, but is always a political construction, and it can be constructed differently, so you can have a people constructed according to right-wing populism and according to left-wing populism. The "people" of left populism consists in the articulation of a multiplicity of democratic demands around issues concerning exploitation, domination of discrimination.[14]

There is an abundance of examples around the world of left-wing populism, and almost every leader and politician, right, left and centre, can be said to have a populist inclination or policy now and again. Examples of left-wing populism include but are not limited to certain movements against the globalisation of neoliberalism as a racialised form of consumer capitalism. Such movements may target certain consumer items, corporations or franchises that are widely perceived as symbols of what is disenfranchising, dispossessing and ultimately dehumanising in the globalisation of capitalism with reckless abandon. In other words, left-wing populism "turns society's attention to unequal social and economic conditions" that in some instances includes "questioning even the dogmas of neoliberal austerity measures and the supposed neutrality of technocratic business-oriented solutions" (Finchelstein 2017: Prologue). Contemplated in an interconnected and globalised world, left-wing populism ought not conflict with calls for "global solidarity and universal human rights" and the privileging of "global solutions" over "narcissistic nationalism and the capitalist death drive" (Samuels 2016: Chapter 5). It is such malleability or catch-all-net character of populism that leads Traverso to argue that populism as a concept "erases the distinction between left and right, thus blurring a useful compass to understand politics" (Traverso 2019: Chapter 1).

Knopff provides much food for thought by drawing our attention to what populism has in common with the judicialised politics of rights, and the impact of both on representative democracy as a system and practice of moderation, compromise and deliberation. He argues that populism and the judicialised politics of rights work in opposite directions. Thus, contrary to populism which "seeks to move power down, away from representatives to the people, the politics of rights moves power up, away from elected representatives to appointed judges". In addition, "populists see the judicialization of politics as handing even more power to elites and 'special interests,' while rights advocates see populism as giving even more scope to the 'tyranny of the majority'". Both "feed off each other, with the very existence of each strengthening the other". What they share is "their common opposition to representative democracy" (Knopff 1998: 683–684), an ambition that is often hidden "behind the banners of both rights and the people". Hence, Knopff calls for the institutionalisation of "both the liberalism and the democracy of liberal democracy [...] through the careful structure and arrangement of representative institutions". This would ensure that "representative democracy" effectively assumes "a middle ground

35

between populism and rights, a way of blending both without giving in to the extremist tendencies of either". It ensures as well that representative democracy is "both responsive to public opinion and sufficiently distant from it to permit and encourage sound deliberation", and that it protects rights, but in a way that resists "the uncompromising tendency of 'rights talk'" (Knopff 1998: 704).

Although this book is not about Africa, it is worth noting in passing that populism may be more present in Africa than it is studied (Saul 1969). According to Mazrui and Engholm, both intellectualised and empirical populism were evident in the political thought and practice of many immediate post-independence African leaders, with the ideas of Jean Jacques Rousseau finding much fertile ground amongst them in the "cults of ordinariness", "the ethos of antipluralism", "the ethic of mass involvement" and the form of egalitarianism his ideas inspired (Mazrui and Engholm 1968: 27–29). As argued by Maghimbi, Mwalimu Julius Kambarage Nyerere emerged as a foremost theorist and rare large-scale practitioner of populism in Africa inspired by Rousseau among others, with his "African socialism" or "*Ujamaa*", which focused on a flexible approach to the peasantry, and emerged as his lasting legacy of theory in action (Maghimbi 2012). This is in tune with the idea of populism as being about worshipping the people, especially "the meek and miserable", of which peasants in the underdeveloped societies are "the most miserable of the lot", and thus the most amenable to being worshipped (Ionescu and Gellner 1969: 4). The importance of taking intellectual populism seriously Mazrui and Engholm argue, lies in the possibility that a leader, African or not, "may propound populist ideas and yet pursue different policies". They stress the need to study populism both at the empirical and the intellectual levels, as it is not unthinkable that "African ideologies can have important populist components even if African policies are not always in accord with them" (Mazrui and Engholm 1968: 20–21).

Banywesize remarks on the paucity of studies on populism in Africa as well as "the ambiguity of the term, the sensibility of the subject itself, and the scarce bibliography" on the phenomenon (Banywesize 2013: 230). That populism in Africa is little studied could also be part of "politics of demobilisation", which, according to Makulilo, is a political strategy employed by most African governments to deter mass political participation (2013). To some scholars, the paucity of studies could also be explained by populism not having found traction on the political landscape of the continent until recently. Writing in 2005, Giovanni Carbone observed that for many post-independence African governments the political strategies for over 30 years "were largely aimed at the political demobilisation of the masses", with the consequence that "African citizens themselves, in turn, often minimised their links with states that proved to be predatory more often than not". The result in some countries was that "the people" were either "formally excluded" or "became de facto marginalised from the political arena". Another consequence of these dominant political strategies is that, with a few exceptions, populist leaders and regimes have not played a central role in post-independence political developments (Carbone 2005: 2).

The exceptions include leaders such as Jerry Rawlings of Ghana and Thomas Sankara of Burkina Faso, who came to power in the 1980s on the back of military coups that they justified "as the only means of ousting corrupt incumbents who had exacerbated macroeconomic mismanagement and undermined citizens' welfare" (Resnick 2017: 102). Others include Yoweri Museveni of Uganda who took power in 1986, and sought to set up and govern through parallel structures to established political institutions (Carbone 2005; Resnick 2017). Laurent Gbagbo in Cote d'Ivoire could be considered as another populist. His embrace of *Ivoireté* appeals to the continued struggle against foreign domination (Bahi 2013), and marketing himself as the only true alternative and promise of a better future qualify him as a populist (Banywesize 2013: 224–225). Banywesize presents Gbagbo, together with Ahmed Sékou Touré of Guinea, Mobutu Sese Seko of Zaire and Idi Amin Dada of Uganda, as excellent illustrations of "identity populism and poverty populism". These are forms of populism which:

> [...] capitalise upon the issue of the people's identity and the idea of national belonging, denouncing the abject poverty in which the vast majority of the population lives and disparaging thereby any foreign elements, the great powers (more precisely, the former colonial powers) and a part of the national elite (Banywesize 2013: 203).

Using as pretext the defence of "the people's interests" at the national, local and/or ethnic level, Banywesize posits, has given rise

37

to "various totalitarian regimes" that have tended to promote or turn a blind eye on "government-sanctioned pillaging, excessive spending, and unjustified resource squandering", in addition to building "a xenophobic universe of discrimination and exclusion" (Banywesize 2013: 230). Using the examples of Raila Odinga of Kenya and Michael Sata of Zambia, Cheeseman and Larmer explore how in some instances opposition leaders have catapulted themselves into prominence by skilfully blending narratives of exclusion and poverty with discourses of marginalisation, victimisation and xenophobia to harness support through "ethnopopulism" – a fusion of populist and ethno-regional constituencies in contexts of myriad resilient rural–urban political, economic and cultural interconnections (Cheeseman and Larmer 2015).

African leaders, whether in pursuit of identity, poverty or protest populism, Resnick argues, were populist in that "they attempted to establish direct ties with their populations through new, local level, avowedly participatory structures"; "grounded their populism in an anti-establishment discourse and, by portraying their usurpation of power as people's revolutions, they implied that they were acting in the interests of the 'general will' and against the 'enemy of the people'". Those considered enemies of the people were "the disappointing independence-era political elite" as well as "former colonial powers that had exploited African economies and undermined their prospects for genuine economic liberation". Populist African leaders "tended to pursue relatively similar economic strategies focused on heavy state intervention, import substitution industrialization (ISI), and rural collectivization schemes" and "were committed to equity and distribution through social welfare spending, subsidized commodities, and attempted land reforms in rural areas". They "aimed for a broader societal transformation predicated on modernization and equality by promoting women's rights and attacking traditional patriarchy, especially chiefly privilege in rural areas" and "their populism was not easily compatible with genuine democracy" (Resnick 2017: 103–104).

While the immediate post-independence leaders were more interested in personal rule through neo-patrimonial networks, the continent has increasingly flirted with populism, especially with the growing economic challenges and the adoption of structural adjustments programmes insisted upon by the International

Monetary Fund and the World Bank, as well as the return or establishment of multi-party democratic systems, and the demise of the one-party era. These developments have given rise to exclusionary populism and disturbing strategies to redefine the parameters of citizenship in often opportunistic, disingenuous, insidious and xenophobic ways (Nyamnjoh 2006, 2016; Geschiere 2009; Resnick 2014, 2015, 2017). New charismatic populist politicians with often unmediated ties to disenchanted urban poor among other resonances, appeared, from Cameroon's John Fru Ndi to Zambia's Michael Chilufya Sata and Frederick Jacob Titus Chiluba, through Kenya's Raila Odinga, Senegal's Abdoulaye Wade, and South Africa's Jacob Gedleyihlekisa Zuma and Julius Sello Malema. More have followed, with recent waves of populism globally and on the continent (Krieger 2008; Cheeseman and Larmer 2015; Resnick 2014, 2017; Banywesize 2013; Makulilo 2013; Kapanga 2020).

In South Africa, it could be argued that a left-wing – which could also be viewed as right-wing from the vantage point of the previously disadvantaged black population seeking land restitution as bona fide sons and daughters of the native soil – populist form of politics has emerged following the end of apartheid in 1994, which populism coalesces around a struggle for "radical economic transformation", against what is commonly referred to as "white monopoly capital", and pursues land restitution with little or no compensation, even as the populists in power are called to answer accusations of "state capture" and widespread corruption amid pandemics of inequality, poverty and violence. This populist platform (championed by Jacob Zuma and Ace Magashule) is situated within a liberation movement turned into political parties including the African National Congress (ANC) led by Cyril Ramaphosa and the Economic Freedom Fighters (EFF) led by Julius Malema, a former leader of the youth wing of the ANC (Hart 2014; Melber 2018). Both parties, according to Melber, use populism as:

> [...] a means to legitimise the continued governance of former liberation movements by appealing to the continued struggle against foreign domination and thereby marketing oneself as the only true alternative and promise of a better future. It is a kind of retrospectively applied populism vis-à-vis a colonial dominance left behind but accused

of seeking to regain power. It is reclaiming ownership over history and society not by seeking but by remaining in power (Melber 2018: 679).

It is worthy of note as well that the ANC leadership, which is predominantly black, in their speeches refer to "our people" in a manner suggestive of inclusivity, but not without equivocation, especially in a post-apartheid context where the racialised categories of White, Indian, Coloured and African are still authoritative and a common currency, and racism is yet to be a thing of the past. Attwell faults what he terms the ingrained "deference to popular mobilization" in South African cultural expression for the failure of "a forthright critique of populism" to materialise in South African literature (Attwell 2020: 127).

As Resnick observes, in Africa, driving the populism of the 1980s and populism since the 2000s is a "disappointment with democratic experiments and the emergence of a corrupt elite that appeared detached from the poor masses" and the anti-elitist discourses that this has generated. While the populism of the 1980s was "generally driven by outsiders, particularly military leaders, who often had the latitude to implement radical plans for restructuring society and who sidelined existing bureaucratic administrative structures in favor of new grassroots structures ostensibly aimed at facilitating popular participation" especially in rural communities, more recent populists have tended to be "highly variegated" in their economic ideologies focusing on young urban poor and courting when and where necessary "traditional authorities" for votes in ethnic and religious communities. Whatever the differences in focus and ideology, Resnick concludes that "populist leaders in Africa have exhibited a certain intolerance for independent institutions, civil liberties, and internal dissent within their parties. Consequently, the lines between the pure people and the corrupt elite inevitably become blurred, confusing whose general will is in fact actually being pursued" (Resnick 2017: 114–117). When politicians (populists and others) and people involved in social movements in Africa and elsewhere scream for a return of "power to the people", who exactly are the people, and how ready are the people to sign a blank cheque for those seeking to speak on their behalf, and with what regrets, if any? To what extent do populists, the elites and leaders of social movements alike, credit the people with a capacity to think and act rationally, and to determine what their interests are individually and collectively? (Torre 2015a). To Torre, "The people is individual and collective, active and passive, whole and part, the despised mob and the redeeming People that on occasion rise up in unison against injustices" (Torre 2015a: 11). Those, like Donald Trump, who urge a return of power to the people have the obligation to demonstrate that the expression has more value than merely as a slogan, a sugar-coated emptiness or an enchanting but dangerous illusion (Brabazon et al. 2019).

In the USA and globally, the Black Lives Matter movement could be seen and appreciated through the prism of left-wing populism that seeks redress for the continued subjugation of black humanity under the global America-championed capitalist, imperialistic, exclusionary, extractive and exploitative democratic order. This system has been experienced by black people globally, mainly in terms of racialised subjugation, repression and suppression. To seek dignity in citizenship nationally and globally as a black person through populism is to make a statement against structures and systems that insist on the impunity of propelling whiteness and white interests forward while blacks and blackness are kept in captivity – shackled: body, mind and soul. Far from questioning the humanity of others, Black Lives Matter are seeking redress for the inhumanity of systems that need to be reformed. In this regard, Black Lives Matter, if populist, is best understood to be inclusive, not regressive, and to be fighting for a common, universal humanism, dignity and equality – unmitigated and undiluted by race and culture. It would be the sort of populism that takes Donald Trump to task for the double standard of urging governors to mobilise the police and the military "to dominate the streets" and "clamp down very, very strong" on Black Lives Matter demonstrators protesting the savage brutality of the police in the killing of George Floyd in Minneapolis[15] (Dean and Altemeyer 2020: Chapter 1; Leonnig and Rucker 2021: Chapter 7) – notwithstanding Trump, reportedly, being initially "visibly disturbed by Floyd's death" and exhibiting "more genuine empathy than his advisers had ever seen in him" (Leonnig and Rucker 2021: Chapter 7) – while, on the other hand, actively encouraging and protecting his steadfast predominantly white supporters who mob-stormed the Capitol in an attempt to stop Congress from certifying an election result that he falsely claimed to have won (Leonnig 2021: Epilogue;

Leonnig and Rucker 2021: Chapter 21; Wolff 2021a: Chapters 2, 3 & 8; Woodward and Costa 2021). While Trump referred to Black Lives Matter protestors as "anarchists, agitators, looters or lowlifes" (9:34 AM 6/19/2020 tweet), he called the white mob who stormed the Capitol "patriots" and told them "we love you, you are special" (Leonnig and Rucker 2021: Chapter 21).

Ultimately, left-wing populism, consensually and inclusively pursued, amounts to radically challenging the dominant elite minority and historic structures of oppression and dehumanisation, manipulating identity and belonging in a racialised and/or ethnicised economically skewed society to its benefit, while paying lip service to the humanity of the (black/coloured and white) majority and the pursuit of market-driven democracy. Both left-wing populism and right-wing populism share the trait of framing themselves as the quest to reclaim human dignity and the possibilities of citizenship for the oppressed and downtrodden – those left behind by the economic, cultural and political elite and their bandwagon of modernism, modernisation and rugged individualism. They are a necessary reminder that the rule of law and protection under the constitution is jeopardised when it fails to materialise systematically and profoundly in the lives of all and sundry who call upon and expect it to regulate everyday life and relationships with self-evident certainty that generates and sustains mass confidence and belief.

When allowed to fester into deep painful wounds and recurrent grievances, such neglect becomes easy prey for prophets of gloom and doom and evangelists of anxiety, fear, hate and conspiracism that assaults reality and insults common sense with unsubstantiated accusations (Muirhead and Rosenblum 2019). It is thus not surprising to argue or observe that left-wing populism and right-wing populism are equally amenable to being endangered or hijacked by hate and fear of a carefully constructed other as an inconvenience, an undesirable, a pollution, a danger, an infection – and as less than human: a thing that does not deserve consideration, and as inferior even to one's pets – that play into the hands of populist prophets of gloom and doom.

Thanks to manipulation of the truth by various populist leaders and engineers of consent-seeking political capital by harnessing peoples' predicaments, those militating under either wing of populism are made to see one another as enemies, while in reality they are united by a common frustration: unfulfilled humanity and citizenship. But, as an African proverb goes, "the truth may become skinny, but will never perish" (Opoku 2012). Elite modernity specialises in the mass production of unattended human debris, regardless of race, ethnicity, geography, gender, sexuality and age category. In this regard, both wings of populism could be said to suffer a double jeopardy: jeopardised by structural inequalities skewed to serve as dispensers of power, privilege and resources for the elite few (taken collectively and without distinction) and subsequently jeopardised by the co-opting politics of opportunism played by the purportedly discerning elite among themselves, where they can afford themselves the luxury of quibbling over who cares the most about the marginalised, dispossessed and vulnerable masses.

How do the survivors of such elitism not see the game for what it is when the politics of opportunism begins to distinguish between "our" downtrodden and "other" downtrodden; "our" debris or human waste and wasted humanities and those of "others"? Is it beyond the possible to care for every victim of modernity? To care about those left behind, regardless of nationality, race, ethnicity, geography, class, gender, sexuality, religion or political party? As Melber suggests in relation to southern Africa, "Populist forms of mobilisation take advantage of the understanding and practice of liberal democracy while being in their core utterly illiberal". He draws attention to the markedly "broad disparity between the propagated and claimed ideal and the reality, or between promises and deliveries", arguing that at a closer look, "populists care about their own interests, not those of the people and wider society" (Melber 2018: 678). Hence, even with populism, the problem of how the dispossessed repossess their very beings and rights and place in society in a manner that does not create new cycles of malcontents persists. If populism is sometimes the answer but populists seldom are, how does one balance the equation of a modernism unduly skewed in favour of the elites?

It is understandable why, regardless of wing (right or left), populism usually always frames "elites" as enemies of the "common people" and as conmen and conwomen or simply as conpeople, even when those doing the framing are by every objective indication possible the most con of them all. As Hofstadter (1963) documents, it is usually insinuated, if not stated outrightly, that, given the opportunity to run their own affairs, the common people, in their omnicompetence, would come through superbly well, beating the elite hands down, and putting many an expert, specialist and intellectual to shame. In the USA for example, Folan claims that populism is fuelled by a populist anger and widespread "dissatisfaction with the way things work in Washington, coupled with a conviction that local governments know best".[16]

Magri asserts in his introduction to *Beyond Trump: Populism on the Rise* that in Europe the ability of national governments to deliver has been constrained in part by a loss of sovereignty to global trends and to a European Union (EU) which has turned out to be unable to fix the problems that national governments have outsourced to it. With such diminishing sovereignty and inability to deliver, Europe has noticed a re-emergence of old cleavages, which have combined with the crisis of representative democracy and of mainstream political parties and the negative effects of the global economic and financial crisis, to kindle a wave of populism (Magri 2016). The rise of populist parties in Europe has been reflected in significant surges in votes at elections, including important wins (Benveniste et al. 2016; Lazaridis et al. 2016; Martinelli 2016, 2018; Judis 2016; Goodhart 2017; Eatwell and Goodwin 2018; Albertazzi and Vampa 2021).

Globally, Bremmer affirms, populism is having the effect of decentralising "power away from central state actors toward local officials, at the expense of international cooperation".[17] Desired as such decentralisation might be, what is lost, Mazarr argues, is "global integration and liberalization" that comes from "encouraging free-trade agreements, developing international law, and fostering global communications networks".[18] If both decentralisation and global integration are needed, then to do both effectively, in a manner that satisfies in equal measure the elites and the disenchanted masses on behalf of whom the populists speak, would require serious conversations in all humility and disabused of the propensity to settle for nothing short of stark dichotomies between winning and losing and among winners and losers.

According to Mounk, populism arises as elites become "insulated from ordinary voters' preferences", which creates a "wide-open space for appeals – often tribal and profoundly chauvinist – to communal unity and popular self-defense". Mounk sees this wide-open space with tribalistic appeals as a potential threat to liberal democracy. Paradoxically framed as liberation, the populists step into the space and promise to restore lost rights, freedoms, material wellbeing, proud cultural traditions and cherished conservative values. Such sweeping promises often meet with the yearning approval of people thirsting to reinvent and reendow themselves with dignity and pride, even if in the end it becomes a case of wildly overpromising and underdelivering. "Alienated from an unresponsive political establishment," Mounk argues, voters flock "to populists who claim to embody the pure voice of the people." Both too much and too little democracy can be interpreted by citizens that their political preferences are not heard. Populist politics has gained in popularity both because of too much democracy (in that voters now have the choice to reject the technocrat leaders and opt for populist leaders) and too little democracy (in that citizens feel they do not have a say in the complicated political processes and thereby opt for populist candidates that offer the bypassing of the given systems and institutional roadblocks – something facilitated by the growth in digital technologies and alternative channels to conventional media such as social media (Facebook, Twitter, WhatsApp, etc.) – which Wu (2016) refers to as "online attention merchants" – and their propensity to pander to tribal cocoons and echo chamber bubbles),[19] driven by such "hubristic allure" as "Facebook's call to 'move fast and break things'" (Wylie 2019: Chapter 1). These insights are further developed in Mounk (2018).

As Manucci aptly affirms, social media have come to "represent a perfect channel for the diffusion of populist messages". Populist actors view the mainstream media to be controlled by the mainstream political elites, and turn to "the new social media as the only neutral and independent arena". With social media, they are able to communicate directly with ordinary people, and are thus able to "reinforce their image of being approachable" by the electorate. Populists are attracted by the more informal nature of social media, which favours "a populist discursive style" with "a type of communication close to colloquial language, based on emotions rather than on reasoning" (Manucci 2017: 475–476).

The potential for these digital technologies to bring about a better and more inclusive world notwithstanding, Martinelli observes that in the hands of populists who despise expertise and enjoy manipulation, social media and its capacity for instant availability and reachability (Mounk 2018: 137–150) has been:

> [...] widely used for blaming and shaming adversaries, seeking scapegoats, expressing personal frustrations and prejudices, rather than for developing practices of deliberative democracy, which are based on respect for different opinions, a willingness to confront and compare and to reach reasonable compromises (Martinelli 2016: 22).

Welfens echoes Martinelli, and criticises "digital populism" for the frequency with which it "pushes news/information which has no basis in reality, but rather reflects and reinforces the prejudices already common amongst part of the less educated strata of society". To Welfens, the practice is to use made-up stories by leading government actors "to undermine the confidence of society and of voters" in "the constitution and the established leading parties and institutions" (Welfens 2019: 26).

Hampton observes that, from espousing the positive relevance of the internet and social media to electoral campaigns, participation and outcomes, scholars seem to have shifted focus to "the deleterious role of social media in influencing" the outcome of elections, especially in contexts of deep inequalities, rising immigration, rising intolerance, rising populism and the growing popularity of populist leaders like Trump (Hampton 2018: 159). Rauch regrets the missed opportunity for digital media to harness its potential to put in place much more "truth-friendly digital architectures". Rather, "digital media have turned out to be better attuned to outrage and disinformation than to conversation and knowledge". Digital media have found themselves battling with "two insurgencies", the one being a predominantly right-wing and populist "troll culture" that "employs chaos and confusion" to "spread viral disinformation and alternative realities", and the other a predominantly left-wing and elitist "cancel culture" that employs "social coercion" to call out political incorrections and enforce "conformity and ideological blacklisting" (Rauch 2021: 17–18), leaving their victims feeling uncomfortably closeted, hemmed in and having "to hide their true selves to please society" (Wylie 2019: Chapter 7). This diminishes instead of enhancing creativity and innovation, as the emphasis, paradoxically, is on the sterile reproduction of ever-diminishing circles of inclusion in a world where the accelerated mobility of people, ideas and things is creating more and more opportunities for cosmopolitanism and conviviality. Both troll and cancel cultures bypass "rational persuasion to seek truth", by manipulating "the social and media environments for political advantage" (Rauch 2021: 17–18), disinterested as they are in fair criticism or persuasion. By opting to reward "instantaneity and impulsivity" in lieu of "slowing down information by reviewing and testing it before passing it along", digital media has accelerated untruths and privileged emotion over dispassion. It has also downplayed accountability in favour of anonymity, and elevated amateurism and celebrity over professionalism (Rauch 2021: 133–134).

A well-known case in point of digital or electronic populism in the USA, notoriously popular in right-wing circles, whose blurring of the lines between news and entertainment earned him a presidential Medal of Freedom from Donald Trump at the 2020 State of the Union address, was the conservative talk radio host Rush Limbaugh[20] (Du Mez 2020: 133–134). According to Reid, "conservative talk radio programs hosted by high-voltage performers like Rush Limbaugh" in a bid to keep their core audience "exercised", shared with Fox News "a determination to find the 'truth' the mainstream media was 'hiding' about the 'dangers' of illegal immigration, 'unpatriotic' kneeling by NFL players, and 'lawless' Black Lives Matter activists who 'hate police'" (Reid 2019: Chapter 8). If the mainstream media were all about ferreting and disseminating what they insisted was the objective truth dutifully harvested in line with the golden rules of factual journalism, right-wing media were all about protecting their viewers from being contaminated by such extravagant liberal claims to a disembedded shared universal truth in which identities, be these cultural or otherwise, did not matter. To Fox News and the right-wing family of media outlets, racialised cultural and group identities mattered beyond what and how individuals thought of and presented themselves in abstract liberal terms (Hassan 2019: Chapter 6).

The blurring between news and entertainment, truth and falsehood brings about what Mounk describes as "illiberal democracy [...] democracy without rights [...] undemocratic liberalism [...] rights without democracy". The outcome of this, according to Mounk, and if one must think in binary terms, is the political equivalent of Sophie's choice: "sacrifice our rights to save our democracy, or abandon democracy to preserve our rights". He warns, however, that the "nasty rhetoric" of the populists "should leave little doubt about what they hope to achieve: a clampdown on individual rights, particularly those of the people [...] whom they scapegoat in their speeches to such great effect".[21] They fight for their rights at the expense of the rights of others (Mounk 2018).

However, as Kaletsky argues, the "opposite of populist nationalism" may not be "globalist elitism" but rather "economic realism". Sooner or later countries that opt for populism "will learn the hard way that reality always eventually wins" and that "scapegoating foreign influences, whether through trade or immigration, will do nothing to lift living standards or address the sources of political discontent".[22] In other words, while the chasms in citizenship between the elite and the masses are real and demand urgent attention, shortcuts and short-term opportunism cannot replace policies and political action articulated around genuine participation and inclusivity and an openness to the dynamism that makes identities and identification, being and becoming, nationalism and citizenship a permanent work in progress. This is an important argument and way forward.

Nothing is to be taken for granted. Nothing lasts forever, and democracy is no exception. All human achievements are reversible. It takes a carefully articulated consensus to keep things the way they are, reproduce them, and creatively, innovatively and meaningfully evolve them over time. A democracy stands a chance only to the extent that it is able to reconcile principles and practice, winners and losers, success and failure, power and responsibility, recognition and redistribution, insiders and outsiders, being and becoming. It is either inclusive in principle and practice, or it is not a democracy. There is no room for equivocation and dissemblance. With democracy, nothing short of the authentic, not even an expert copy, is good enough. This is how different variants of populism, without the distraction of opportunistic populist leaders left, right and centre, ought to be understood. Thus, as Levitsky and Ziblatt argue, we should be worried about the threat of authoritarianism, when a politician "rejects, in words or action, the democratic rules of the game"; "denies the legitimacy of opponents"; "tolerates or encourages violence"; or "indicates a willingness to curtail the civil liberties of opponents, including the media" (Levitsky and Ziblatt 2018: Chapter 1).

The current populism unfolding in the West deserves a closer and critical look. Describing it as "the new class war" around "social power", Lind believes that "Europe and North America are experiencing the greatest revolutionary wave of political protest since the 1960s or perhaps the 1930s", but one that has "remained nonviolent" with the exception of the yellow vest protests in France. The revolutionary waves, regardless of the immediate antecedents in particular contexts, share the same underlying cause: "long-smoldering rage by non-college-educated workers against damage done to their economic bargaining power, political influence, and cultural dignity during the half-century revolution from above of technocratic neoliberalism" (Lind 2020: Chapter 8).

The popular rebellions are contesting "the material interests and intangible values of the college-educated minority of managers and professionals", who have taken over from the "old-fashioned bourgeois capitalists as the dominant elite". They are also making a case for a break with the "technocratic neoliberalism" of "their arrogant and meddlesome overlords" in favour of a return to genuine "democratic pluralism" (Lind 2020: Introduction & Chapter 8). Such legitimate protests have, like carcasses, attracted the vultures of populist demagoguery and charlatanism (Steudeman 2018; Simpson and Fritsch 2019: Chapter 3; Lind 2020: Introduction; Bartlett 2020: Introduction). As Lind explains, populist demagogues "have opportunistically championed legitimate positions" and "concerns about trade and immigration" popular with many voters whose voices have been ignored for decades by the managerial ruling class (Lind 2020: Chapter 5). Legitimate "populist rebellion from below […] has been exploited, often with disastrous results, by demagogues, many of them opportunists from elite backgrounds, like Donald Trump and Boris Johnson" (Lind 2020: Chapter 8).

Hence, Lind's argument that, for the dispossessed and disenfranchised of Europe and North America to secure any lasting victories for democratic pluralism and social power for all and sundry, there is need to challenge both the strategies of co-optation, repression and cosmetic reforms of the managerial elite on the one hand, and the false promises of the populist demagogues on the other. As he puts it:

Achieving a genuine class peace in the democracies of the West will require uniting and empowering both native and immigrant workers while restoring genuine decision-making power to the non-university-educated majority in all three realms of social power—the economy, politics, and culture.

Demagogic populism is a symptom. Technocratic neoliberalism is the disease. Democratic pluralism is the cure (Lind 2020: Introduction).

What exactly does Lind mean by democratic pluralism? With democratic pluralism, he argues, "free and fair elections are a necessary but not sufficient condition for genuine democracy". The emphasis is far less on a narrowly defined political realm of electoral democracy, and much more on ensuring an effective system of "power-sharing arrangements among classes and subcultures in the realms of the economy and the culture". It should insist on "social checks and balances in addition to political checks and balances", and ensure that decisions are "based as much as possible on hard-won and lasting consensus among negotiating parties, classes and creeds, not on fluctuating numerical majorities" (Lind 2020: Chapter 9).

Indeed, Lind cautions those seeking genuine democratic pluralism to be mindful that "technocratic neoliberalism and demagogic populism represent different highways to the hell of autocracy". For, while technocratic neoliberalism champions the idea that "an elite of experts insulated from mass prejudice and ignorance can best promote the public interest", populism invest in the belief that "a single Caesarist or Bonapartist figure with a mystical, personal connection to the masses can represent the people as a whole" (Lind 2020: Chapter 5). Proposing a position that resonates with the framework of incompleteness proposed in this book, Lind maintains that nothing short of "a new democratic pluralism that compels managerial elites to share power with the multiracial, religiously pluralistic working class in the economy, politics, and the culture can end the cycle of oscillation between oppressive technocracy and destructive populism" (Lind 2020: Chapter 6).

Demagogic populism is indeed no less of a problem than the technocratic neoliberalism of which it is highly critical. Both endanger democratic pluralism in which there is more than token participation for otherwise disempowered ordinary working-class citizens (Lind 2020: Chapter 8). By opting for unproblematised regressive rhetoric and policies, populists in Europe and North America have, as Petras rightly observes of Britain and the USA, "opened the door for the rise of the extreme right" even in historically progressive areas.[23]

While the ideology and implementation of meritocracy may have created victims of those it was meant to inspire and reward, a solution to its failure is hardly simply to bounce to the other end of the pendulum. A consensual middle is worth serious consideration, if the populists of the day are not to end up laying the groundwork for the populism of the future by simply seeking to replace one disgruntled group of "the People" with another. The challenge is how to halt the creation and amassing of debris by providing for a radically inclusive and truly participatory democracy. As Luce explains, the US and Britain in particular "suffer from an illusion about the value of qualifications" and are overly dramatic about "their meritocracies".[24] Justifying their power and privilege in terms of merit, the professional, economic and political elites have revolted the working classes that are seen as largely responsible for the rising waves of populism. It is thus obvious that many a populist is making political capital of such over-prioritisation of credentialism to the point of making the overwhelming majority of the citizenry who fall through the cracks feel like wasted humanity.

Humility and realism on the part of the meritocratic elites would help. As Krastev argues, what many populists find duplicitous and hypocritical among elites is the exaggerated claim that all it takes to succeed is hard work and good qualifications. "Europe's meritocratic elites aren't hated simply because of populists' bigoted stupidity or the confusion of ordinary people" Krastev explains. "What makes meritocrats so unbearable to their critics is not so much their success", but rather their insistent claim that "they have succeeded because they worked harder than others, because they happened to be more qualified than others and because they passed the tests that others failed". To Krastev, from the vantage point of "the meritocratic elites, their success outside of their country is a proof of their talents", while from the perspective of "many people, this very mobility is a reason not to trust them".[25]

Thus, while the meritocratic elites have harnessed their credentialism and mobility to propel themselves productively into true globetrotters for whom boundaries and borders are fluid and the prospects of flexible citizenship all too real, their insensitivities to the sensibilities and predicaments of their less mobile and less credentialled compatriots have created chasms and tensions that have hollowed the contents and attractions of citizenship and nationality. Home and away, they are an ephemeral exception to the more grounded existence of the more ordinary folks that they are trying to inspire with their model of meritocracy and globalism.

Like vultures and hyenas who have discovered a carcass abandoned by the kings of the jungle at the Okavango delta, populist leaders can smell an opportunity from miles away. And they have the right rhetoric to sweeten their words for the ears and hearts of the depressed, the repressed, the oppressed and the suppressed. Populist leaders consistently portray themselves as champions for the common people left behind by meritocratic and other types of elites. In the contemporary world, "common people" usually refers to the people who feel left out by the neoliberal economic policies that have characterised globalisation so far. Whether right-wing or left-wing, the populist parties that prey on their disaffection are, as Gros remarks in the case of Europe, "embracing identity politics, playing on popular fears and frustrations – from 'dangerous' immigration to the 'loss of sovereignty' to the European Union – to fuel nationalist sentiment".[26]

Pieraccini writes of the likelihood of future changes in Europe as a result of failed policies and Europe's uncurbed subservience to American interests to the detriment of the interests of European citizens. It is partly for this reason, Pieraccini thinks, that many parties considered populist and nationalist are "turning to the East and pursuing cooperation that for too long has been denied by the stupidity of Western elites".[27] The East, as used here, refers to Putin's Russia, in particular. Many of the new crop of populists in the West, far from being repulsed by Putin, are drawn to his model of propaganda, which according to Kakutani has been labelled as "the firehose of falsehood" because it takes the form of "an unremitting, high-intensity stream of lies, partial truths, and complete fictions spewed forth with tireless aggression to obfuscate the truth and overwhelm and confuse anyone trying to pay attention", with the ultimate objective of exhausting critical thinking and annihilating the truth (Kakutani 2018: 141–144).

The whole purpose of online propaganda, Rauch maintains, is "*to organize or manipulate the social and media environment to demoralize, deplatform, isolate, or intimidate an adversary*", and being effective in this regard entails attacking "not just individual people or facts but the whole information space", even if it means "*flood*[ing] *the zone with shit*" (Rauch 2021: 162–163, italics in original). This willingness by European populists to bring Putin and Russia in from the cold as well as adopt Putin's model of propaganda is significant, especially when buttressed by Donald Trump's perplexingly intimate and protective relationship with Putin, whose propaganda is generally credited with having helped Trump to the presidency in 2016 (Kakutani 2018; Miller 2018; Watts 2018; Bennett 2019; McCallion 2019; Nance 2019; *The Washington Post* 2019; Stengel 2019; Wylie 2019).

It is also possible, as Lind suggests, that "the Russia scare story" is little more than a narrative used by "embattled members of the Western establishment […] to explain the rise of transatlantic populism in a way that demonizes populist voters and politicians". Hence, his point that the greatest threat to liberal democracy "is not its imminent overthrow by meme-manipulating masterminds in Moscow", but rather, "the gradual decay" into something like banana republics "of North America and Europe under well-educated, well-mannered, and well-funded centrist neoliberal politicians" (Lind 2020: Chapter 6). For liberal democracy to meet its national and global ambitions, those promoting it would need to ensure that it is not all about "a lot of liberalism and very little democracy" (Lind 2020: Chapter 9).

The populists of Europe and the USA are keen to substitute the meritocratic elites and whatever professionalism and expertise, knowledge and institutionalised mechanisms of doing, being and belonging they practise and sustain as part of a consensual system of values. In their obsession and compulsion with "I alone can fix it", the populist leader displays a violent rejection or antipathy of anything established, procedures and processes, substituting them with ad hoc and highly personalised alternatives, which may seem justified in the language of democracy but are effectively a style and approach hostile to democracy. Wolff, writing after Trump left office, sums up Trump's disregard of process thus:

If process is the true theater of government—its glue, its logic, its language—then Trump, by his disregard for it, and lack of understanding of it, and yet insistence on his own domination over it, broke the proscenium over and over again (Wolff 2021a: Chapter 12).

Hence, as some have hastened to argue, the only thing that can make a country truly great again, is not a person but principles (Stevens 2020). And principles make sense only to the extent that they are applicable and applied systematically, consistently and without prejudice.

Among other things, populists in Europe and North America are perceived to jeopardise liberal democracy through their overt or muted sympathies with and efforts to normalise racialised extremist far right ideologies, beliefs, hostilities to inclusivity of and violence towards minorities (cultural, religious, sexual, etc.) and immigrants (Mudde 2019). Traverso argues that the dramatic surge in far-right activism and identity politics throughout the European Union has re-actualised in powerful ways the ghosts of the past and raised afresh questions around the extent to which fascism is truly dead and buried in the 21st century (Traverso 2019: Chapter 1). While some argue that Europe and the USA are witnessing a return to fascism in its undiluted prior existence (Finchelstein 2017), Traverso suggests that "the concept of fascism seems both inappropriate and indispensable for grasping this new reality", which he terms "*postfascism*", to imply "both continuity and transformation" (Traverso 2019: Chapter 1). As Lloyd notes with particular reference to the rise of populism in European liberal democracies since the end of the Cold War, there is the increasing lack of political civility, and the increasing use of "hate speech, or grossly exaggerated warnings of fascism" by European leaders. The populists calculate that "the public either does not know, or does not remember" the insults that they have been subjected to before. Eventually, such hate speech and insults become commonplace and erode ideas of civility, honesty, dialogue and the appreciation of diverse opinions in politics and politicians that have long been taken for granted as a core ingredient of citizenship and belonging together under the same legal canopy.[28] Such politics, however compelling in the heat of the moment, cannot be a long-term fix.

There is, admittedly, pressure on democratic rule from all sides of the political spectrum and in many long-standing democratic countries. The rhetoric of populist politics, however grounded in legitimate frustrations, is not anchored on rationality and Enlightenment morality, which, as Lasch argues, "are increasingly seen as a cover for power, and the prospect that the world can be governed by reason seems more remote than at any time since the eighteenth century". Lasch laments the "citizen of the world" that the Enlightenment philosophers have failed to materialise with the globalisation of markets. "Instead of generating a new appreciation of common interests and inclinations—of the essential sameness of human beings everywhere—the global market seems to intensify the awareness of ethnic and national differences. The unification of the market goes hand in hand with the fragmentation of culture" (Lasch 1995: 93).

Political leaders representative of the end of political decency include: Jean-Marie Le Pen and Marine Le Pen (France), who have openly compared Muslim religious freedom in France to Nazism; Nigel Farage and Boris Johnson (UK), perhaps the face of Brexit and who have also compared the EU to a Nazi-like authority; Beppe Grillo (Italy), who has openly shamed and used mocking names to refer to fellow politicians; Donald Trump (USA), known not the least for a suggestion of not allowing any more Muslims into America (Martinelli 2016, 2018; Traverso 2019; Lind 2020: Chapter 5).

These populist politicians quickly attempt to turn the truth to suit their political desire and fulfil a popularity vote in their respective democracies. The danger is that the mockery and lack of decency seem to be attracting millions of supporters and voters, many of whom share similar authoritarian dispositions with the leader, as Dean and Altemeyer (2020) argue of Trump and his supporters in the USA. It remains unclear how these leaders are to govern the diverse and free societies that do not necessarily share their views, were they to purport to be leaders for all their nationals and citizens – for all of "the people" so to speak, given that in a cosmopolitan Europe and USA, not only one sex, race or ethnic group (to name just these three categories) is victimised by an uncaring and corrupt meritocratic elite.[29] If one takes seriously the accusation that the meritocratic elites are to blame for the feeling of alienation in the masses, what is achieved in terms of credibility, if, in lieu of a more inclusive solution, one merely resorts to furthering the very same divisiveness of the elites, by differentiating between "our poor and marginalised" and "other poor and marginalised", even when these are nationals and citizens of the same country? (Espejo 2017).

Hate is a weapon of choice in the armoury of populists who are at heart far more impatient with democracy than they make believe. As Corrales elaborates, hate is a political tactic of choice among populist politicians, regardless of their positions on the political ladder in the societies where they seek political power. Populists would target an authority figure, be this a capitalist or any other elite figure, including "senior politicians, respected journalists, renowned professors, members of the clergy, policy gurus, celebrities, professional athletes and […] mayors", to name a few. Corrales argues that "Some of the world's most famous populists in the last decade have been masters at this game of hate" fuelled by scaremongering, the manipulation of fear and the outsourcing of blame. Recep Tayyip Erdogan in Turkey, Viktor Orbán in Hungary and Hugo Chávez in Venezuela have all used "hatred as a way to polarize and thus survive in office".[30] When Trump ran for president in 2016, one of the reasons he gave for doing so was his desire "'To be the most famous man in the world'" (Wolff 2021b: Introduction). In other words, he craved "'sold-out performances everywhere'" for "'The show [that] is Trump'" (Barrett 2016[1992]: Foreword), hopefully, with the added advantage of an endorsement by White Evangical Christians as "God's Strongman" (Posner 2020: Chapter 2).

However sympathetic one is towards the predicaments of those on behalf of whom populists militate, one cannot be oblivious to the implications for democracy if hate and fearmongering were to be institutionalised and systematically normalised as tools for attaining and maintaining power in a country that purports to be united by a common set of values and aspirations requiring all and sundry to embrace and celebrate unreservedly. Evans laments the growing polarisation and hollowing out of the political centre in many countries, with democratic institutions coming under fire and right-wing populists and demagogues taking the reins of power. With long taken-for-granted liberal values no longer holding sway over the policies of many countries, it is hardly surprising that "Putin has announced that the 'liberal idea' has become 'obsolete' in the world".[31] Putin may have good reason to declare liberalism dead, given how much Russia under his leadership has been associated with sowing disinformation with the run-up to elections in many a Western country and beyond, in addition to mounting "concerted propaganda efforts to discredit and destabilize democracies" (Kakutani 2018: 14; see also Miller 2018; Bennett 2019; McCallion 2019; Nance 2019; *The Washington Post* 2019; Stengel 2019; Wylie 2019), as if to deride as "radically premature" Francis Fukuyama's "optimistic assessment" celebrating the triumph of liberal democracy and "the end of history" (Kakutani 2018: 50).

As provocative as Putin's claim may be, it should not be dismissed in a hurry. The crisis of liberal and Western culture has been a long time coming, according to Lasch, who describes liberalism as both politically and intellectually bankrupt (1991[1979]: xiii). According to Hunter and Owen IV, evidence that liberal democracy is facing a crisis of legitimacy is a continuous and deepening fragmentation characterised by:

> [...] an increasing skew in the distribution of wealth; decay in traditional institutions, from civic associations to labor unions to the family; a loss of trust in authority—political, religious, scientific, journalistic—and among citizens themselves; growing disillusionment with progress in effecting equal justice for all; above all, perhaps, the persistent and widening polarization between those who want increasingly open and experimental societies and those who want to conserve various traditional institutions and practices. (Hunter and Owen IV 2018: ix–x)

In "David Cameron and the great sell-out" in *NewStatesman* in April 2021, John Gray writes that it is a "certainty [...] that a 'rules based' liberal order is history" and that "This is undeniably a period of Western decline" even if "a new order" is yet to emerge.[32]

In *Why Liberalism Failed*, Deneen faults liberalism for its determined and unabashed celebration of individual autonomy, downplaying the importance of the state, and proving helpless in containing the breakdown of family, community and religious norms and institutions (Deneen 2018: xiv). Liberalism's relentless prioritisation of "private over public things, self-interest over civic spirit, and aggregation of individual opinion over common good",

Deneen maintains, has resulted in the "degradation of citizenship" (Deneen 2018: 154–155). He concludes that liberalism is beyond redemption following decades of decline into "authoritarian *illiberalism*". Deneen finds the decline is ironical in that it has been occasioned or exacerbated by the dismantlement of cultural norms and political habits critical of the very same self-governance that liberalism promotes in principle. To Deneen, liberalism is incapable of saving itself. It cannot be patched up or reformed, principally because: "Liberalism created the conditions, and the tools, for the ascent of its own worst nightmare, yet it lacks the self-knowledge to understand its own culpability" (Deneen 2018: xiv).

In seesaw fashion, liberalism is on the decline, and it seems that populism is on the rise. What is needed is a carefully negotiated balance between the two forces. However, as Lind advises, to be successful, populism must be more than merely reactionary. Rather than simply contenting themselves with reacting "against what the dominant overclass establishment does", it is incumbent on populists to develop and implement "a positive and constructive agenda of their own" by moving beyond the status of "a counterculture" to that of "a counterestablishment" (Lind 2020: Chapter 5).

Even with populism, no political community or identity, local, national, regional or global, can or should be taken for granted, because everything is reversable, in the manner of the unravelling of "The Complete Gentleman" in the work of Tutuola. And as the experience of the Drinkard demonstrates, interdependence is much more productive than illusions of independence that simply result in the mass production of dependency. To draw on Lasch (1991[1979]: xiii), it is understandable that people will lose faith in leaders who have used up their "store of constructive ideas" and "lost both the capacity and the will to confront the difficulties that threaten to overwhelm" the society they promised to lead. "What looks to political scientists like voter apathy", Lasch observes, "may represent a healthy skepticism about a political system in which public lying has become endemic and routine". Hence, "A distrust of experts may help to diminish the dependence on experts that has crippled the capacity for self-help" (1991[1979]: xv).

Some questions are worth asking. If populists are not there to put together the attractions of democracy, citizenship and belonging, which various forces – from neoliberalism to global and local elites through the governing professionals or deep state – have put asunder, if they cannot learn and apply lessons from the alleged mistakes of all those they are trigger hungry to criticise and castigate, what is the purpose of claiming to share a common political community – society, country, nation or state? Should populism, whatever the legitimacy of the grievances of those mobilising it for their political battles, be so illiberal that it exudes a dehumanising lack of empathy for (often forced) mobilities? What is productive about power that seeks to excel at little else than a politics of division and misrule? What is to be gained in a citizenship characterised by ever-decreasing circles of inclusion and visibility? What becomes of a nation-state of immigrants that chooses to unravel nonstop in the elusive pursuit of purity in ever-diminishing circles of inclusion? Would such a nation-state be surprised if it ended up like Tutuola's "The Skull" – stripped of all the borrowed body parts that had transformed it into "The Complete Gentleman"? Radically arrested in its nation building and disembodied of its immigrant history, such a nation-state of bare bones would consist purely of first peoples or native sons and daughters that every nimble-footed newcomer from distant lands found in place, and through sustained dehumanisation and subjugation, reduced to, as Desmond Tutu would put it, "picking up crumbs of compassion thrown from the table of someone".[33] That someone, in this case, being settlers in their variations, gradations and configurations, who consider themselves superior to or better than those they found in place.

If regression without end is the game, native populations are right in challenging the politics of division. Why would they let any wayfaring strangers pollute – with the sterile politics of autochthony – the land of legendary generosity? The benefits of unravelling diversity and cosmopolitanism are short lived even for purportedly more entitled native populations. Regression is ultimately endless, because even native populations are not as homogenous and bounded in their indigeneity as is often assumed in a world where the dominant template for relationality is to compare and contrast between a bounded aggressively globalising capitalist West and the rest, who, a priori, are defined as culturally different and homogenous and as operating outside of history prior to encounters with the civilising and modernising West. Such assumptions of homogeneity are expensive fallacies (De la Cadena and Starn 2007) mobilised to justify the cannibalisation with impunity of those encountered by the West in its global adventures of conquest.

Far from being simply indigenous, a notion that is rather limiting, native populations are more appropriately understood as endogenous populations, to evoke the dynamism informed by myriad encounters and interchanges, negotiability, adaptability, and capacity for autonomy and interdependence, creativity, and innovation in the societies so categorised. The term endogenous provides for mobility and histories of making, contesting and remaking of identities. It counters the widespread and stubborn misrepresentation of native populations as static, bounded and primitive in culture, and as needing the infusion of benevolence and enlightenment of colonialism and neoliberal capitalist penetration to jumpstart them into forms of meaningful modern existence (Hountondji 1997). And because endogeneity is not a monopoly of non-Western societies, the West could draw inspiration from such indigeneity in action to understand the current eruptions into populism fuelled by nostalgia for real or imagined autochthony. Replacing indigenous with the concept of endogenous should render more complex and nuanced the blanket claims of Western culture and Western modernity in Europe and North America, as if this were one gigantic timeless glacier or iceberg.

Populism and Nationalism

The rise of populism coincides with a resurgence of nationalism, and in effect, conservatism – this leads many observers to state that liberalism needs to stand up for itself. The call relates to a need for the pendulum of democracy to swing and hopefully spend as much time as possible in the moderate middle. Remembering that populism can exist on all sides of the political spectrum, it is worth noting that populism is always a form of identity politics of accelerated inclusion or exclusion, and/or seeking to regain what has been lost. The geographical expansion of nationalism is part of this identity politics. The supposed West claims an exclusionary purity that disallows participation for those who are not autochthonous (and autochthons forced into silent minorities by more powerful settlers), seemingly forgetting its previous imperialist dreams of having all the world become westernised.

The rise of the current waves of populism seems to have coincided with the resurgence of nationalism (Martinelli 2018; Hawkins and Hawkins 2018; Hazony 2018), which, Lepore claims, "doesn't die" simply because historians have abandoned studying it and scholars have stopped trying to "write a common history for a people". Far from withering away, nationalism instead, as Lepore suggests, "eats liberalism".[34] *The Economist* writes: "Wherever you look, nationalism is rising." If nationalism thrives by making a meal of liberalism, the implications of this for "People who cross borders and cultures easily, and who prosper as they do so" – those symbolised by "The Complete Gentleman", so to speak – is that they "find this new nationalism disturbing. They see it hindering peaceful countries from trading, mingling and co-operating on the world's problems".[35]

This is a fact which perhaps accounts for Hazony's argument, with reference to Britain and America, that the fear for the worst that has gripped many a liberal, from public figures to journalists and academics, and led them to deplore "the return of nationalism to [...] public life in the harshest terms", must not blind one to "the virtue of nationalism". Such virtue lies in a principled commitment to a world that is best governed when nations, without resorting to imperialism or globalism, "are able to chart their own independent course, cultivating their own traditions and pursuing their own interests without interference" but with patriotism (Hazony 2018: Introduction). Hazony sees the virtue of the nation-state in its capacity to drive "war to the borders of a large, politically ordered region, establishing a protected space in which peace and prosperity can take hold", but which, unlike an empire, prioritises an independence that "inculcates an aversion to adventures of conquest in distant lands" (Hazony 2018: Conclusion).

A nationalism that emphasises unravelling cannot be patient with cobbling, cosmopolitanism, compositeness and the humility of incompleteness. Optimistic nimble-footed and concerned cosmopolitans "tend to think that it will pass, like a fever".[36] However, this new wave of nationalism, if a fever, is no ordinary fever. For *The Economist* to portray such nationalism as an expectation that will soon pass seems to underestimate what is happening. Nationalism, to *The Economist*, "is an abiding legacy of the Enlightenment", which "is capable of bringing out the best in people as well as the worst". *The Economist* concludes: "Sadly, the new nationalism plays to the paranoid, intolerant side of this legacy."[37]

Be that as it may, *The Economist* calls for a return to the ideas of the great liberal thinkers, namely: a commitment to good faith and reasoned argument; individual freedom; and a faith in progress. "Today's challenges are real. But far from shrinking from the task, the liberal thinkers of yesteryear would have rolled up their sleeves and got down to making the world a better place".[38] In other words, *The Economist*, like Welfens (2019), is challenging liberalism to stand up for itself, to resist being bullied into fodder by the rising tides of nationalism.

If liberalism cannot survive without the elites that have championed it, the call by *The Economist* for the liberal elites is to close ranks, rally their forces and defend their order or forever perish. Such a defence, it cannot be emphasised enough, would likely fail if it were simply to amount to an exercise at the fetishisation of reason and rationality with scant regard to how being rational is not divorced from the emotional and the affective dimensions of how reason and rationality are shaped by their embodiment and enactment. While not denying the possibility of a unified and universal knowledge, it would be wrong to assume it in a rushed manner or for it to be imposed by the current wielders of political, economic and cultural power. Any such reductionism, totalising pretensions or hyperrationality only alienates and disenchants. A democracy ought to be like a pendulum that never stands still, through its capacity to celebrate diversity and the coexistence of people, things and ideas, and in ways of knowing, doing and being.

Some have argued that liberals are largely to blame for the precarious position of liberalism in the 21st century. Singled out for criticism is the perceived elitism and superiority syndrome of the liberals, who, given their prominence in conventional media institutions and in public debates, as well as their gatekeeper roles in how public opinion is shaped, are effectively players and umpires in the game of ensuring coexistence and mutual accommodation between nationalism and internationalism, localism and globalism, insiders and outsiders, us and them (Babones 2018; Coles 2017; Judis 2018; Zito and Todd 2018).

In this regard, Jacobson is uncomfortable with the rather dismissive and condescending attitude among liberals who, regrettably, "still regard populism as an authoritarian anti-politics and denigrate its supporters as plebeians yet to evolve from animal laborans to zoon politikon". Jacobson cites Jan-Werner Müller for whom populism is a "permanent shadow of modern representative politics" and who considers it "a danger to democracy" to dismiss populism "as a gross manifestation of unreason". Rather, it must be borne in mind that "populism has stood for a range of societal changes that have spurred 'the people' to common purpose".[39]

Put differently, every success story, civilisation or societal project must account for its debris or those perceived and related to as "an unassimilable excess" (Laclau 2005: xi), to avoid the embarrassment of contestation by those who feel left behind by the arrogance of zero-sum games of winner takes all. Indeed, Kagan writes, the "belief among liberal democracies that ideological competition had ended with the fall of communism" was wrong.[40] If the new populism is a timely reminder that ideological competition is far from dead, as predicated by Francis Fukuyama in *The End of History and the Last Man* (Fukuyama 1992), in what form (guise or disguise) is such competition manifesting itself? Fukuyama attempts an answer in a discussion of the rise of identity politics in modern liberal democracies and the challenge this poses to a universal understanding of human dignity in a world of disruptive accelerated mobilities (Fukuyama 2018).

Müller aptly remarks that "populism is always *a form of identity politics* (though not all versions of identity politics are populist)" and "an exclusionary form of identity politics" at that (Müller 2016: 3). In Europe – which is increasingly marked by what Michta describes as "progressive civilizational fracturing and decomposition, fed by the growing disconnect between political and cultural elites and the publics"[41] – Rooduijn claims "Populism is sexy". In other words, decomposition and unravelling are sexy in contemporary Europe. Writing in November 2018, with reference to the sex appeal of populism, Rooduijn notes: "Particularly since 2016 – the year of the Brexit referendum and the election of Donald Trump – it seems as if journalists just cannot get enough of it". The ideological debris in this post-Cold War period is contesting its voicelessness in a manner attractive not only to journalists but also and perhaps, more importantly, to a new breed of political actors with a nose for opportunity and opportunism. "The increasing popularity of the term [populism] is no coincidence," Rooduijn writes. Published in November 2018, Rooduijn's article shares the following statistics: "Populist parties have tripled their vote in Europe over the past 20 years. They are in government in 11 European countries. More than a quarter of Europeans voted populist in their last elections." Rooduijn discusses why this has happened, diving into the causes of the recent rise of populism country by country. [42] According to Traverso, "In 2018, the governments of eight countries of the European Union (Austria, Belgium, Denmark, Finland, Italy, Poland, Hungary, and Slovakia)" were "led by far-right, nationalist, and xenophobic parties" with a surging capacity to polarise political debate and practice as illustrated by the experience of France, Italy and Germany (Traverso 2019: Chapter 1).

For non-Europeans, especially people in former colonies where memories of European plunder are stubbornly fresh and where much unhappiness is blamed on Europe, it boggles the mind that a fantasy space of sumptuous abundance like Europe would be guilty of mass frustration to the point of widespread hatred, fear and anger among ordinary people. A question worth asking – especially by those previously dazzled by Europe and its ambitions of universalising its modernity and civilisation, in light of the growing popularity of populism informed by nativism or autochthony – is quite simply this: whatever happened to Europe and Western Civilisation as the best thing ever? As the very rationale for all sorts of excesses – from the slave trade to neocolonialism through imperialism and colonial conquest – perpetrated all in the name of a purported *mission civilisatrice*? I can understand why non-European observers of populist nationalism in Europe and the rest of the West would be miffed, when Western populists create and perpetuate the narrative that the West is seemingly being conquered by "the Rest". Notions of autochthonous purity insist that only a particular type of native is native enough, and that certain natives are stripped of their title, whereas mobile citizens are made citizens everywhere elite indicators of meritocracy allow. How ironic that European and other Western nationals and citizens are fighting for their right to be token autochthonous natives in the West, when not so long ago, the term was kept exclusively for "other" less developed parts of the world – when native meant subject and governed by the regime of tradition, customs and culture, and citizen meant settler rulers with modern political and legal rights (Mamdani 1996; De la Cadena and Starn 2007). Now citizenship does not equate belonging as categories become outdated in a world where more than just the mobility of colonising and imperial forces is defined as impactful.

How could Europe and the West turn around to embrace the same primitive nativism that they had asked everyone the world over who cared to listen to abandon in a hurry and in the interest of large-scale cosmopolitan nation-states? Additional questions: How could the Western elites have been so greedy and so self-absorbed to keep entirely to themselves all the benefits that have accrued from the systematic and reckless dehumanisation and enslavement of non-Western others, the exploits of conquest and empire, and the windfalls and proceeds of impunities of the colonial treasure-hunting expeditions into the lands of others? How could the elites have been insensitive to the point of not providing for a measure of trickle-down largesse and munificence to placate the masses of the conquering metropolis? Could the elites really have been that insensitive? Or have they simply forgotten, all these decades later, of the looting to bring the world back home to the fatherland? Did they forget to cultivate the masses at home to acquire the habit of appreciating one's privileges, even when these may not be evident to one and thus tend to be taken for granted? A final thought: One wonders how many of the masses or ordinary men and women of Europe and North America, who are currently drawn to populist nationalism, would join ranks with the populations of former colonies and with their very own formally enslaved ethnic minorities to demand restitution and reparations from their unaccountable elites as a symbol of global solidarity of the side-stepped, the dispossessed and the thingified.

The new nationalism and populism defy old categories

Populist nationalism and its politics of unravelling are bankrupting language by purging words of their carefully and generously cultivated repertoire of meaning. With autochthonous purity being priority on the nationalism forefront, terms like "native", "immigrant", "citizen", "democracy", "belonging" and other relevant terms, are no longer representative of the complexities of their current usage and cosmopolitan potentials. As purported native citizens feel left behind and opt for an exclusionary insistence of their inclusion, they mobilise bounded notions of culture which the West used to criticise in those they sought to colonise and dispossess, rather than or over and above the economic and material predicaments which led to their experiences of being left behind by their nimble-footed globalising elites. Trivialised is the need to recognise that those who are currently being mobilised against by various concoctions of nativist populism often did not invite themselves to the West, but rather, were mobilised by the West to do their bidding, even if that bidding ended benefitting mostly the elites. Whilst populism is dangerous in its promotion of nationalism, it is promising in pointing out the failures of a democracy that has caused those on the right and left to feel left behind. Distaste for elitism, although mostly being a conservative phenomenon, has also contributed to the popularity of populism. Populism invites a levelling of the playing field, which, in the case of the West and through the prism of populist nationalism, has been unduly narrowed to reproduce the power and privileges of a globetrotting elite to the detriment of millions who feel entitled to lay claim to being bona fide sons and daughters of the native soil.

According to Brubaker, the new nationalism and populism combine in a manner that defies old categories. Of particular contention is a preoccupation with a heightened need to safeguard the cultural purity of presumed "natives" (nationals and citizens, preferably by blood and birth) from contamination or dilution by the purportedly "dangerous" cultures and/or civilisations of immigrants (who in certain instances are conflated with bona fide nationals and citizens by birth) in the countries doing the policing of identities. On the marked and rising hostility to immigrants in Europe, Brubaker observes that "many anti-immigrant parties [...] have developed a new political discourse", which he terms "civilizationism" and which "posits a pan-European civilizational identity that it asserts is threatened by, and in fundamental conflict with, Islam, understood as a separate and alien civilization". He is of the opinion that, "By proclaiming in ever-harsher terms the incompatibility of Europe and Islam, the new civilizationism cannot help but deepen the alienation of Europe's Muslims and the mistrust between them and the continent's nominally Christian majority."[43]

Driving the cultural backlash at the heart of new nationalism and populism is what Norris and Inglehart term "the authoritarian reflex", by which they mean:

> [...] a defensive reaction strongest among socially conservative groups feeling threatened by the rapid processes of economic, social, and cultural change, rejecting unconventional social mores and moral norms, and finding reassurance from a collective community of like-minded people, where transgressive strongman leaders express socially incorrect views while defending traditional values and beliefs (Norris and Inglehart 2019: 16).

Norris and Inglehart argue that the authoritarian reflex, which arises from "long-term processes of cultural change" is strongest in rural communities and among older citizens, "who feel the most threatened by the spread of multicultural diversity", and not as strong "among the younger generations and university-educated professionals who commonly study, live, and work in metropolitan areas that are typically more socially and ethnically diverse". The authoritarian reflex can easily "be accelerated and deepened by fears of economic insecurity", such as "the loss of secure, well-paid blue-collar jobs" by an individual, and being forced as a collectivity to experience living in "declining communities of the left-behinds". Groups experiencing material hardship are likely to be "more susceptible to the anti-establishment appeals of authoritarian-populist actors, offering simple slogans blaming 'Them' for stripping prosperity, job opportunities, and public services from 'Us'" (Norris and Inglehart 2019: 18).

Material predicaments notwithstanding, the emphasis in the form of nationalism and populism that feeds from and into the authoritarian reflex is on culture and civilisation, and not so much on economic opportunities being taken away by invading immigrants (Goodhart 2017; Eatwell and Goodwin 2018). Although, it must be added, a focus on the imperative to protect cultural and civilisational values does not preclude a preoccupation with endangered lives and livelihoods of those who see themselves as bona fide cultural and civilisational citizens.

As Fukuyama explains, in modern liberal democracies characterised by accelerated immigration and where people who are not willing to play by the rules may be given undue advantages, "Economic distress is often perceived by individuals not as resource deprivation, but as a loss of identity" (Fukuyama 2018: 89). He elaborates:

> The nationalist can translate loss of relative economic position into loss of identity and status: you have always been a core member of our great nation, but foreigners, immigrants, and your own elite compatriots have been conspiring to hold you down; your country is no longer your own, and you are not respected in your own land. Similarly, the religious partisan can say something almost identical: You are a member of a great community of believers who have been traduced by nonbelievers; this betrayal has led not just to your impoverishment, but is a crime against God himself. You may be invisible to your fellow citizens, but you are not invisible to God. (Fukuyama 2018: 89).

While recognising that "economic anxiety cannot explain away our political or cultural divisions", Klein argues that only "a special kind of condescension" can make one believe that "voters suffering economically are so distracted by the identity politics of the Right that they have overlooked the direct solutions to the economic problems offered by the Left" (Klein 2020: 122).

It is thus not a contradiction to seek to reconcile what Gray terms "'left-wing' economics with 'right-wing' cultural values".[44]

For many in the former colonies of Europe, it is more than perplexing that Europeans should engage in a culture war with the rest of the world, when colonialism and its *mission civilisatrice* were all about inviting the colonial subjects to suspend or forget about their cultures and embrace the alternatives that the colonialists dangled before them. The logic was that it was possible to acquire another culture, one that presented itself as more civilised, and that members of the colonising culture were happy to see themselves and their values embodied by the colonial subject. If the colonial subject had proved adept at imbibing the superior culture to the point of migrating to the metropolis, it must really be perplexing for members of that superior culture to, all of a sudden, embrace the language of cultural resistance. Are we, now, to believe that the cultural conversions of the colonial era are no longer a possibility in the 21st century? Is the West tired of others acquiring and excelling at

Western cultural values? Or have they suddenly realised that these cultures and values are so precious that they are better guarded jealously? Or simply that they are much more incomplete than they ever imagined? The cultural mimics of the former colonies must, like Mrs Hyacinth Bucket of *Keeping Up Appearances*, be cursing: "If there's one thing I can't stand, it's snobbery and one-upmanship. People trying to pretend they're superior. Makes it so much harder for those of us who really are".[45]

From Britain to Hungary, through France, the Netherlands and Austria, and indeed, across much of what is generally referred to as the Western world, there has been a noted rise in populist ethnonationalism, and in the unscrupulous politics of opportunism that this has given rise to among certain politicians, argues Applebaum. While previously there was, according to Appelbaum, a consensus in the Western world that "the globe is flattening", this is no longer the case. There is a noted increase in sentiments for far-right politics and "populist ethno-nationalism" coupled with a growing "failure of empathy" and "failure of imagination". An unproductive distinction between the nation-state and the world out there, and between nationals and immigrants, has stifled the need to provide for complexity and nuance, and for the rich histories of mobility in the constitution and reconstitution of nation-states in Europe as well as elsewhere. Appelbaum critiques the stark choice voters are left with which embraces an "all-or-nothing vision of globalisation". She concludes with a wishful thought whether political elites can "display enough empathy to convince the angry" and "enough imagination to offer a positive vision of the future".[46]

Under the new nationalism and populism, scapegoating of real or imagined immigrants using real or imagined cultural differences is the order of the day. The substance and subtleties of difference are also overly simplified to superficial appearances and indicators (such as how one looks, speaks, dresses and/or behaves in public) that are often misleading. Hedges suggests that "Europe, especially EU countries on the fringes of the union, is devolving into proto-fascism", which is characterised by movements that "are rabidly xenophobic, racist, Islamophobic and homophobic" and that "demonize immigrants and brand internal dissent as treason".[47] The riches of globalisation are drained or distilled away, resulting in nostalgia for a golden past of belonging in a culturally congruent polity by those who see themselves as bona fide sons and daughters of the native land (Martinelli 2016, 2018; Goodhart 2017; Eatwell and Goodwin 2018; Traverso 2019). Put differently, when the tables are turned and those who used to be encountered in exotic and remote locations by the nimble-footed treasure-hunting European adventurer become the nimble-footed adventurer, it dawns on Europeans who care to empathise just how magnanimous one must be to open one's doors to a perfect stranger, even under duress.

If one takes a closer look at the coincidence between populism and nationalism in Britain, for example, a country well known for its erstwhile ambitions of global dominance with ideas of liberal parliamentary democracy, one realises an unravelling that speaks to an unmaking of the sort of civilisation that champions the possibility of a shared humanity, shared citizenship and shared belonging at both small- and large-scale levels. Being an outsider or an insider is layered and contextual, and the contestation of citizenship and belonging by purported insiders does not end simply by removing the obvious outsiders of the moment, usually referred to as immigrants or strangers. A logic of unravelling informed by ever-diminishing circles of inclusion would continue and hold its ground even with the last man standing. For, what is there to stop the body parts of the last man standing warring with one another on who is more entitled or more indebted to whom?

Writing on the disturbing rise of a radical English nationalism that threatens British nationalism, *The Economist* describes the present English nationalism as more political than cultural, and as "radical and angry" and characterised by "flags are everywhere". Those drawn to this brand of nationalism:

> [...] describe themselves as "English" first and foremost [and] are more likely to feel "left behind"—either because they live in unfashionable corners of the country, such as seaside towns, or because they are older or less educated. But grievance is animated by a strong set of values: commitment to fair play and parliamentary democracy, and a fierce pride in England's history. The English feel that by pocketing more money than they deserve, the Scots are not playing fair; membership of the EU was wrong because Parliament is the only legitimate source of power; English history has provided "our island

nation" with both a web of ties with the Anglo-sphere and a unique global economic and strategic niche.[48]

The England (and Britain) of old was all about expansionism ad infinitum, while the England of the populist moment (post-Brexit) is all about shrinking or unravelling *à la* Tutuola's "The Skull" and ever diminishing circles of inclusion. It is one in which whiteness, Englishness and the Crown as unifiers are not to be taken for granted, even at the level of mere symbolism. Put differently, the England and Britain of the populist moment is one in which the likes of Cecil John Rhodes and his imperial pretensions and transnational articulations of whiteness – even if pursued under the misguided belief of the supremacy and divinely ordained British and their cultural values – would not recognise himself (Geary et al. 2020).

Bhadrakumar maintains that the EU's "populist approach" to immigration "fundamentally signifies the decline and collapse of the left". He sees democratic elections in Europe as "increasingly turning into referendums on immigration" as right-wing movements skilfully exploit the fears of blue-collar voters, "while social-democratic parties have suffered historic losses" in France, the Netherlands, Germany and Italy, for instance. "This could have far-reaching consequences", Bhadrakumar concludes.[49] Accounting for the rise of populist movements and the growth of nationalism and xenophobia, Das includes the increasing dissatisfaction with the failure of "governments to deliver on promises to restore growth and prosperity in return for sacrifice".[50] When the justifications for the upsurge in populism are not cultural, they are economic or both.

To some, the continued existence of the West as a dominant global force could very well depend on the extent to which Western governments are able to find satisfactory solutions to the present currents of nationalism and populism. The concerns, Batchelor reports, are with the fact that "populist movements are feeding off the vacuum in political leadership with groups swapping tactics and increasingly cooperating across borders to maximise their influence". It is a state of affairs for which "Western countries are themselves partly to blame [...] for carrying out sweeping societal and economic changes too quickly".[51] Whatever happened to Fabianism? The radical changes occasioned by globalisation and globalism have been shocking and unsettling to the native sons and daughters of the West (especially as a white European world). Conversely, the changes have opened up humanity in new ways to other peoples, cultures and philosophies of being, and their respective elites to join the ranks of the liberal Western elites with scant regard to the plight of the masses in the West and the rest of the world. Kaufmann explains the rise of populism as stemming "first and foremost, from ethnocultural anxiety", which is driven by the fear by members of the majority populations of the West, of "an erosion of the connection between their communities of shared ancestry and their perceived homelands".[52]

As Krastev and Holmes put it, the origins of populism lie partly in the "humiliations associated with [becoming] an inferior copy of a superior model".[53] To Kaufmann, the solution to the populist nationalist challenge "is neither to dismiss these concerns as racist— which only increases right-wing populist support—nor to promise, as the populists do, that the clock can be turned back to a time of more homogeneity". Rather, he invites "advocates of immigration" to "focus on telling conservative whites", and the general public by extension, "positive, true stories of intermarriage and voluntary assimilation".[54] The solution, to put it differently, lies in the liberal victors of globalisation cultivating the humility and compassion to disabuse themselves of the zero-sum logic of elitism, through policies and practices that destigmatise those left in the wreckage of their globalism and left behind in the processes of compressing time and space and transgressing physical, cultural and social borders (Babones 2018; Coles 2017). The solution is in learning and embracing the principle of collective success as summed up in two slogans: "a person is a person because of others" and "united we stand, divided we fall".

The Economist sounds a warning alarm with the argument that, even though there is a basis for it to claim a certain degree of truthfulness and plausibility, the "wave of populism that is rapidly destroying the foundations of the post-war international order and producing a far more unstable world" is dangerous in that:

> [...] it is self-reinforcing. It contains just enough truth to be plausible. It may be nonsense that "the people" are infallible repositories of common sense, but there is no doubt that liberal elites have been smug and self-serving. And populism feeds on its own failures. [...] As

economic stagnation breeds populism, so excessive regard for the popular will reinforces stagnation.[55]

The Economist is thus unequivocal about its stance on populism. Understandable though the phenomenon is, it clearly is a dangerous force and all must be done to contain it. As Eatwell and Goodwin (2018) would argue, this position could not have been written by anyone critical of the liberal elite order or the elite class.

As Cox remarks, "even the most cursory glance at the literature (with a few notable exceptions) reveals [...] a distinct liberal bias against populists and populism", with opinions that are often sneering and patronising, as if to delegitimate it and the problems it purports to highlight. Cox rightly argues that as scholars and social critics, we "do not have to like or agree with populists", but we should not allow "our own political or ideological preferences" and "moral outrage" to cloud our need to understand populism as a phenomenon worthy of social scientific curiosity (Cox 2017: 11–12).

Such curiosity, Mazzarella reminds us, would require a critical interrogation of categories (liberal and otherwise) often taken for granted in the social sciences. Just as it would require carefully negotiating a balance of how to hold onto scholarship that is timely and takes time, and that is imaginative and empirical, in a context of emergencies where heightened incendiary political rhetoric makes everything urgent (Mazzarella 2019: 45–46).

One must not lose sight of an equally important emphasis in much of the literature that populism, if dangerous, is just as promising, a point superbly made in *The Promise and Perils of Populism* edited by Carlos de la Torre (De la Torre 2015b). There is little reason to dismiss a priori the potential of populism "for the democratic regeneration of ostracized and exclusionary political systems". Hence the need for patient scholarly documentation – theoretical and empirical in nature – of "the democratizing promises and the authoritarian threats of populism" (De la Torre 2015a: 2).

Addressing questions such as the following would render the concept of populism less elusive, according to Ayyangar:

> How do populists govern? Is there variation in whether and how they centralise decision-making, address their campaign promises, respond to democratic institutions and promote reforms? Further, do

we have enough evidence to understand their legacies once they demit office or lose their salience in the political field? Have they in fact made their democracies more democratic or otherwise? (Ayyangar 2017: 2–3).

Implicit in Ayyangar's questions is an invitation for scholars of populism not to prejudge its outcomes or assign, a priori, a moral judgement before a careful and rigorous investigation of populism in action. Even when a populist admits barely two weeks into his presidency, as did Donald Trump, that "This job is a lot harder than I thought it'd be" (Sims 2019: Chapter 5), it is not evidence enough to conclude that the populist in question finds governing challenging. There is a need to observe populists in the act of actually governing for evidence to support their affirmations.

The concept of populism, to be useful, ought to help highlight "how much of what kind of populism is desirable and how much of what kind undesirable or dangerous, when, where, and why" (Ingram 2017: 657). Like "The Skull", populism, a priori, is neither good nor bad. To automatically and in abstraction assign to it the label of right or false consciousness is to miss the point. How it is activated and the purpose or consciousness with which it is imbued matter. The context as well matters. Infused with zero-sum games of total winners and absolute losers, populism is likely to be just as exclusionary as the establishment elite that have cared little about those left behind by their modernism and ambitions of local and global dominance. Agreeing that populism is what any society and its citizens want to make of it, Norris and Inglehart argue that "populism by itself can be a useful corrective for liberal democracy, if it encourages innovative forms of direct participation, highlights genuine public concerns neglected or quarantined by cosmopolitan liberal elites, and brings the cynical back into politics". In view of liberal democracy's "many flaws", populism may thus render service to liberal democracies (Norris and Inglehart 2019: 22).

Even as anti-populism is growing in support – attracting high profile endorsements such as from Pope Francis, who says "populism is evil and ends badly"[56] – opinion is split on the future of liberalism, in view of its shortcomings and rising criticism, left, right and centre. Some believe that it has reached its sell-by date and should simply be forgotten and replaced. Those who have reached this conclusion challenge one another and the wider society to imagine and propose alternatives. Some of them would agree in part with those who are currently drawn to populism, not necessarily as a viable alternative, but as a wake-up call to the governing, economic and cultural elites to get to work and propose a new order propelled by the imperative to be more inclusive. Others, even as they recognise the many flaws of liberalism, refuse to give up on it entirely. They believe that liberalism can reinvent itself by jolting itself out of its business-as-usual mode. They characterise populism as an easy fix that cannot work, and are keener to single out and criticise the opportunism and manipulativeness of populist leaders who employ luring slogans and make promises that they cannot possibly keep to their helpless supporters and gullible masses. The need to see populism "not only as a symptom of decline of representative institutions but also as an opportunity for rejuvenating democracy" (Urbinati 2019: 112) cannot be overemphasised, and requires "awareness of the historicity and context specificity of [...] liberal democracy" beyond its ideological and normative credentials (Urbinati 2019: 124).

If the idea of incompleteness and the stories of the dependent Drinkard with delusions of independence, and of "The Skull" and "The Complete Gentleman" are anything to go by, a truly inclusive society and future ought to invest not in zero-sum games of recrimination fuelled by violent hatred and fears, but in marshalling and taking each and everyone on board the bandwagon of being and becoming as a permanent work in progress.

Problematic Distinctions between the Elite and the Popular

Beyond its connivance and complicity with nationalism, further inflaming the raging tankers of populism is a tendency among elites to resort to hierarchies of humanity, credibility and entitlement based on nebulous and often unproblematised, from the perspective of the popular classes mainly, indicators of excellence and meritocracy (Hofstadter 1963) and of being civilised (Elias 1994). An excellent illustration of the perceived snobbery or smugness of liberal elites is in the following distinction between elite and popular art forms given by Kirsch and Schillinger:

Populism is easy to understand; it's the force that courts the tastes of the masses. Elitism is trickier. The word is loaded with associations of snobbery and exclusivity. To fully enjoy a populist art form — like an airport novel, a reality show, a rock concert or a cartoon — you need only bring your ears and eyes. To fully enjoy an elite art form — like opera, epic poetry or ballet — audiences need a certain level of education. [...] The populist mind-set keenly resents the presumption that such foreknowledge matters.[57]

The authors proceed to distinguish between a popular and an elite writer as follows:

A popular writer is one at home with the conventions and expectations of his moment, which is why his work is immediately understandable to many readers. But for that very reason, his popularity is likely to be short-lived [...] An 'elitist' writer, on the other hand, is not one who desires only a small audience — few writers have any interest in turning readers away. Rather, she is one whose vision of the world and style of expression are defamiliarizing, who does not reproduce the world in words but transforms it.[58]

In these definitions, the source and content of a text are more important than what the text means to the consumer as a discerning consumer who is free and entitled to an interpretation that may or may not coincide with that of the author and/or the expert reader and critic. Such snobbery or smugness, intended or not, accounts for much of the anti-intellectualism, anti-elite, anti-specialist and anti-expert on which populism thrives (Hofstadter 1963). It accounts for the popular but misguided assumption in populist circles that the more inexpert, ordinary, regular and everyday one is the more likely one is to be right. It accounts as well, for the common but often unsubstantiated claims by populist leaders that their decisions, actions and policies are entirely dictated by the people's will, and that, in reality, they are not leaders but followers and interpreters of the people. Just as a good servant is in effect the master, a good master is a servant. A good leader is one who follows the people and attends to their needs like a servant.

When victims of the snobbery and smugness of the cultural and intellectual elite start keeping up appearances in order to be seen to belong, they are subjected to even more ridicule by those who see themselves to belong in a more authentic manner, and by those who have been schooled to accept their lowly status in the hierarchies. The importance of such differentiation to those who crave it, is demonstrated by Mrs Hyacinth Bucket (pronounced "Bouquet" upon her insistence) of the BBC Sitcom, *Keeping Up Appearances*, originally aired from 1990 to 1995. Mrs Bucket, who insists that one must stick to one's own, identifies with the classy and the nobility who read full size newspapers, will never strike up a conversation with anyone who reads the tabloids that are associated with the working class and the barely educated. *Keeping Up Appearances* revolves around Mrs Bucket's:

> [...] attempts to prove her social superiority, and to gain standing with those she considers upper class. Her attempts are constantly hampered by her lower class extended family, whom she is desperate to hide. Much of the humour comes from the conflict between Hyacinth's vision of herself and the reality of her underclass background. In each episode, she lands in a farcical situation as she battles to protect her social credibility.[59]

In an episode titled "How to go on holiday without really trying", Mrs Bucket says to her husband, Richard, who like everyone else knows that she is all about appearances, "If there's one thing I can't stand, it's snobbery and one-upmanship. People trying to pretend they're superior. Makes it so much harder for those of us who really are".[60]

Brooks echoes the distinction by Kirsch and Schillinger, recalling how, "Most of the 20th-century radicals were wrong to put their faith in a revolutionary vanguard, a small group who could see farther and know better."[61] What seems to have happened instead has been the crystallisation and consolidation of a powerful and privileged elite whom Sheng and Geng believe are more to blame for the rise of populism. In their words, it is wrong to blame, as many do, "today's populist rebellion in the West on the far right, which has won votes by claiming to be responding to working-class grievances, while stoking fear and promoting polarization". Rather, they argue, those who attribute blame to "leaders who have seized on popular anger", "overlook the power of that anger itself, which is aimed at elites whose wealth has skyrocketed in the last 30 years, while that of the middle and working classes has remained stagnant".[62] This argument is shared and further explored by contributors to *Beyond Populism: Angry Politics and the Twilight of Neoliberalism* (Maskovsky and Bjork-James 2020b), through the prism of three kinds of anger, namely: "*neoliberal disenchantment, racialized resentments*, and the *rage of the downtrodden and repressed*" (Maskovsky and Bjork-James 2020a: 8–12, italics in original). If the distinguishing features of elite and popular writing and art by Kirsch and Schillinger are anything to go by, the cultural elite are just as blameworthy as the economic and political elite. Populism is the result of snobbery and smugness gone wild.

Younge makes an important distinction between the position toward elites held by right-wing and left-wing populism. "When left populists rail against elites," writes Younge, "they are generally referring to economic and political power." On the other hand, "when right-wing populists focus on elites they are mostly referring to culture." The right-wing populists "pillory opinion-formers for looking down on 'ordinary people' as being ignorant, bigoted and uncouth. And they are always careful to invent 'ordinary people' in their own image". Younge challenges "The Left" to "do worse than admit that it has given the right considerable material to work with" and discusses ways for the left to invigorate itself.[63]

Putting things in historical perspective, Elliot believes that one would have to go back to the 1930s for "acute fears of a populist backlash against the prevailing orthodoxy" similar to the current. As then, current waves of populism are the result of a prolonged period of poor economic performance has led to a political questioning of the prevalent approach to the economy. Hence his conclusion that, in the mid-2010s, just like in the 1930s, there is growing sense that "the political establishment has lost the confidence of large numbers of voters, who have rejected 'business as usual' and backed politicians they see as challenging the status quo".[64]

According to Buruma, the Anglo-American world has championed and ridden the waves of globalism "as beacons of freedom and heroism", beckoning all and sundry to embrace "Anglophilia and the American Dream as 'shining' examples for the world at large". Now the Anglo-American world is losing considerable "international prestige and gravitas from the rise and grip of right-wing populism". "A terrifying irony of contemporary

Anglo-American populism", according to Buruma, is to be found in phrases "traditionally used by enemies of the English-speaking countries" that have become common currency. He suggests that the very idea of Anglo-American exceptionalism – as self-flattery and a sense of entitlement – may have helped make "populism [...] more potent".[65] To McBain, these developments might actually be good. "America's national identity," she argues, "is built on the dream of individual aspiration and self-improvement, but for a long time this has existed more as a kind of mental state than a real feature of American society."[66]

To Fukuyama, "it should not be surprising that in today's globalized world, many people are upset that vast technological and social forces constantly disrupt established social practices, even if they are better off materially". In order to curb this trend, he calls for "better systems for buffering people against disruption, even as we recognize that disruption is inevitable".[67] Kurbjuweit urges Europe to "resist populism, with a smart mixture of taking fears seriously and confronting the rage, but without curbing freedoms".[68] This is easier said than done if not translated into policy, practice and culture.

As Moak observes, in practice, "democracy remains restricted to the 'privileged few,' those who are well organized and connected or with the resources to influence public policies".[69] Yet, effective democracy ought to explore and enact broad-based participation as well as remedial measures for holding the privileged few accountable. Derviş calls on "the cosmopolitan elites who are making consequential decisions in critical sectors, from business and finance to politics" to "pay more attention to the grievances of the less fortunate, the less educated, and the less connected".[70] It should be added, though, that those seeking a more inclusive democracy should disabuse themselves of the idea that power is located in particular and predictable places, and, in a spirit of incompleteness, embrace the idea of identifying and harnessing power in unsuspecting places. Derviş stresses the need for "redistributive policies" and "inclusive growth", which could well involve submitting "the very rich [...] to a form of regulation and taxation, including international rules, that cost them substantial wealth in the long run"[71] yet lead to better, healthier and more convivial relations between them and society in general. This is a position shared by left-wing populists such as Bernie Sanders, as well as by some materially wealthy people, among whom are some of those Sanders loves to refer to as "the top 1 percent" and/or "the richest 1 percent" (Sanders 2011, 2016, 2018; Tasini 2015; Parmar 2017).[72]

The very future and survival of the West and liberal democracy depend on this dismantling of the concentration of material wealth, in Mason's opinion, with a warning, that: "if xenophobic populism triumphs, there will be no 'West' to aspire to". Europe would have to curb its own populism excesses as no external power is likely to come to its rescue. "Our last great hope will be ourselves. And there are enough of us to stop this second great collapse towards oligarchy and nationalism".[73] To save democracy, Berman argues in a review of Mounk's *The People Vs. Democracy: Why Our Freedom Is in Danger and How to Save It*, that there is "need to unite citizens around a common conception of their nation; to give them real hope for their economic future; and to make them more resistant to the lies and the hate they encounter on social media each and every day"[74] (See also Mounk 2018). Notwithstanding its destructive dimensions, anger or rage could be liberating or empowering, according to Nichols (2021: Chapter 3). Burkeman argues that while anger as a human emotion is not, in principle, a bad thing, "We've built a world that's extremely good at generating causes for anger, but extremely bad at giving us anything constructive to do with it". He illustrates with what he terms: "the twisted genius of social media", which is more adept at generating and spreading anger, despite its capacity, in principle, "to provide something constructive to do, by engaging with posts". With social media, populist leaders have adopted a two-part strategy: "acknowledge the reality of anger" and then "keep it bubbling".[75]

Hoffmann stresses the need to recognise that "polarized, divided societies […] rife with failed integration" are everywhere. With this in mind, she cautions against confronting "criticism and attacks with intellectual and moral arrogance" and seeking to dismiss criticism and attacks "as ignorance from those who have been left behind". It is equally unhelpful for those criticised and attacked to retort with "we are progressive and you are regressive". In her opinion, "Democracy is going to have to engage with its opponents."[76] Münchau agrees that democracy has been unable to cope with the economic shocks accompanying globalisation and this is the cause of voters' frustration. Whilst some countries like Germany attempted reform, their short-term benefits reaped Eurozone chaos. Reforms have not necessarily resulted in better performance to make a difference in the face of populist rhetoric. If moderate politicians do not change their tune, voters will.[77]

Buruma provides important food for thought by reiterating the need to problematise the continued relevance of the right/left distinction. He asserts that "distinctions between left and right have indeed collapsed", and the "old idea of a left representing the downtrodden proletariat against the interests of big business and the bourgeoisie is gone". In France, however, the "left" also encompasses ideas of "citizenship as a legal concept, not one based on blood and soil", and such a "division still holds in the age of Macron and Le Pen". Buruma points to a crisis on both the right (making "chauvinistic, nativist populism" coexist with outward-looking capitalism) and the left (how to forge a new alignment with traditionally marginalised people).[78] Put differently, rising populism is a call to level the playing field between the elite and the popular, the local and the global, nationalism and internationalism, business as usual and business unusual. Populism is also demystifying politics and expertise in a manner that attracts greater credibility and less cynicism from the general, and especially working-class, public (Babones 2018).

In terms of incompleteness, populism is an invitation to giving "The Complete Gentleman" of patchwork of borrowed body parts a chance on condition that he is not carried away by hubris, but cultivates the humility and consciousness that he is who he is thanks to the generosity and credit of others. Hence the imperative to service his debts by ensuring the circulation of success and life chances for all and sundry.

Liberalism-Bashing National Populism in Perspective

This section explores the abounding emergent narratives of the juxtaposition of liberalism and populism. On the one hand, populism is seen as a critique of liberalism and its hierarchies of exclusion, or more crudely, liberalism-bashing. On the other, populism is seen as a threat to political and economic liberalism.

As a critique of liberalism, populism foregrounds a condition of alienation, premised on racial and class fault lines, as characteristic of political life devoid of meaning. Meaning, seen to be continually eroded by concessions to finance capitalism and rootless cosmopolitan consensus. Both seem to be actively promoted by an equally alienated elitist liberal establishment. National populism as a nationalist challenge to mainstream elite politics in liberal democracies of the West thus seeks a prioritisation of the culture and interests of the nation and its purportedly more bona fide citizenships, and the giving of a voice to the neglected and the left behind by the liberal elites and their reckless pursuit of globalism. Such populism amounts to a questioning of elite insulation from ordinary people's concerns, an inquisition of the accommodating nation-state as the undisputed organiser of the political and social lives in Western societies and interrogation of Western societies' incapacity to rapidly manage immigration, growing economic inequality, cosmopolitanism and the West's globalising agendas.

The tendency to assume, almost a priori and without much critical thought, that liberal democracy is the unquestionable perfect alternative to every other form of government imaginable is challenged by national populism. What empirical substantiation is there to argue that a liberal democratic state is better equipped than an authoritarian state to grapple with the inevitable conflicts that arise in diverse societies when both forms of government are at the expense of the masses that the ruling, economic and cultural elites regularly ignore? The following question articulates one aspect of the emergent debate in this regard: If the appropriate response to populism-as-critique is to reinscribe meaning in politics, does this involve the search for or creation of (new) enemies to rally against, or the creation of a positive political project?

Especially noting the parallel narrative that populism is a threat to liberalism, it is worth exploring arguments that posit populism as the illumination of already existing pathologies of liberal democracy. Representatives within liberal democracy, through concessions of neoliberalism, outsource governance to the market and hollow out the very institutions that would ordinarily respond to the grievances of the ordinary people – whose causes populists purport to champion – precisely at those moments that require their robustness. As such, even if we were to say that right-wing populism in the figure of Trump constitutes an assault on institutions, it should not be missed that much softening up occurred before his ascendancy.

Worth bearing in mind even if not explored at length, there are insights to be gained by juxtaposing populism alongside postcolonial and decolonial critiques of liberalism. The liberalism that national populism has been struggling to unseat is the same liberalism that has plundered and cannibalised the rest of the world for the benefit of the West, defining itself, defining and confining others with a touch of totalitarianism, dogmatic prescriptions and self-righteousness. It is interesting to be mindful of this dynamic and contradiction, for it foregrounds whether liberalism is worth saving. This theme is further explored by engaging those who interpret the populism moment as a threat, as necessitating a defence of liberalism.

Populism, as a threat to liberalism, is developed mainly through the figure of Trump. This brief introduction to liberalism-bashing analyses both its mode of governance and Trump as a lens through which to account for the demand of populism.

Let's take a closer look.

"National populism", according to Eatwell and Goodwin "is here to stay". It mobilises a nationalist challenge to mainstream politics in liberal democracies of the West, by prioritising "the culture and interests of the nation" and by promising to "give voice to a people who feel that they have been neglected, even held in contempt, by distant and often corrupt elites". While some national-populist leaders, like Hungary's Viktor Orbán, may be guilty of "creating a new form of 'illiberal democracy'", Eatwell and Goodwin argue that "voters want *more* democracy – *more* referendums and *more* empathetic and listening politicians that give *more* power to the people and less power to established economic and political elites". National populism questions "the way in which elites have become more and more insulated from the lives and concerns of ordinary people". It also calls into question the nation state, which the elites see as "the only construct that has proven capable of organizing [...] political and social lives" in Western societies. National populism questions the incapacity of Western societies to rapidly manage immigration and "hyper ethnic change" to the satisfaction of nationals. It questions the growing economic inequality that leaves behind swathes of people, just as it questions the cosmopolitan and globalising agendas of Western societies. (Eatwell and Goodwin 2018: Introduction). Those who vote national populism are not transactional voters, argue Eatwell and Goodwin:

Rather, they are driven by a deeper desire to bring a broader set of values back onto the agenda and to regain their voice: to reassert the primacy of the nation over distant and unaccountable international organizations; to reassert cherished and rooted national identities over rootless and diffuse transnational ones; to reassert the importance of stability and conformity over the never-ending and disruptive instability that flows from globalization and rapid ethnic change; and to reassert the will of the people over those of elitist liberal democrats who appear increasingly detached from the life experiences and outlooks of the average citizen (Eatwell and Goodwin 2018: Introduction).

Determined in turn to undo national populism, some argue in defence of liberalism (Mounk 2018: 253–266; Welfens 2019; Norris and Inglehart 2019), pointing to "the rise of 'critical citizens,' who endorse democracy as the ideal form of government while distrusting politicians as a class" (Norris and Inglehart 2019: 15). The roots of the rising waves of populism across Europe and in the USA are in fear of cultural and social change, and especially of increasing migration, according to Zakaria, leading to "public anxiety". He calls for governments to actively deal with issues relating to immigration, instead of refusing to fix them because of political sensibilities and sensitivities among other reasons.[79] Social, cultural, political or economic "high inequality", as Wolf puts it, is at the heart of "Populism (of both left and right)", and until such inequality is significantly attended to, populists such as Donald Trump and Bernie Sanders have a happy hunting ground among those afflicted by it.[80] The persistence of inequalities play into the hands of populism, even when it is "dangerous" and "may lead to grossly irresponsible policies" and, at worst, "lead to dictatorship".[81] As Finchelstein argues with inspiration from history, "populism can be a reactionary force leading society into a more authoritarian mode", just as it can, "in its progressive variants", initiate or promote "democratization in a situation of inequality while also undermining the rights or legitimacy of political minorities to its right and to its left" (Finchelstein 2017: Prologue).

Stephen maintains that the risk that populism poses is of such magnitude that it demands the defence of liberalism. To him, words such as "I disagree; I refuse; you're wrong; *etiam si omnes — ego non*", "define our individuality, give us our freedom, enjoin our tolerance, enlarge our perspectives, seize our attention, energize our progress, make our democracies real, and give hope and courage to oppressed people everywhere". Hence, he argues, to yield easily to populist dictatorship is to fail at this task. As he indicates, the inability to listen, question and disagree results in geographic, personal and digital polarisation. Stephen calls for "journalism in defense of liberalism".[82] It is a call echoed by Rauch, who argues for a liberal science at the service of modern liberalism as a marketplace of ideas and an epistemic order that frowns on the policing of thought (Rauch 2013[2003], 2021).

Brooks argues that, for those who subscribe politically and socially to "the idea that the autonomous self-interested individual is the basic unit of society", it is understandable that they "wind up with an individualistic culture that widens the maneuvering room between people but shreds the relationships and community between people". He proposes an alternative, in the case of America, that consists of a "politics of weaving", which "grows out of the acknowledgment that there is no dominant majority in America", just as there "is no moderate center". It is a politics informed by the realisation that one's "group will never pulverize and eliminate" the opposing groups. "There's no choice but to set up better collaborative systems across difference. This is not a problem, it's an adventure".[83] Coming together from different families, different races and different cultures among other differences, to take a road trip together is indeed an adventure that offers those concerned an opportunity to begin the process of weaving a shared belonging through shared experiences, shared stories and shared memories. Van Slyck extends this imagery of weaving together a common belonging through journeying together to the imperative of reimagining and reshaping national and international discourse by emphasising inclusivity rather than exclusivity. She uses her discussion of how the experiences of immigrants by community college students in the US as a template on how to respond in "useful and provocative ways" to xenophobia and anti-immigrant rhetoric in Trump's America, foster global literacy and encourage students "to develop a deeper understanding of others" through participation "in online exchanges across national and cultural borders" (Van Slyck 2020: 104).

Kuran draws on Walter Scheidel in *The Great Leveler* to question the extent to which "gradual, consensual, and peaceful paths to greater equality exist" for redressing inequalities. To Scheidel, the democratic process as currently structured and practised "cannot be counted on to reduce inequality", for, "Even in countries with free and fair elections, the formation of bottom-up coalitions that support redistribution is rare." Also, the world over, in addition to spreading conspiracy theories, "elites have promoted ideologies that focus the poor's attention on noneconomic flash points, such as culture, ethnicity, and religion".[84] Picheta sees the drive towards conspiracy theories as fuelled by the desire to "maintain a positive view of the self and the groups we belong to", as well as by "an underlying need for power and control" aimed at getting "a better handle on life and the universe".[85]

Kelly is less pessimistic about democracy. "Representative democracy", he opines, drawing inspiration from A. C. Grayling's *Democracy and Its Crisis*, "ticks more of the boxes citizens want from their government than any other system we've tried to design". It is when we lose sight of this, Kelly argues, that "rancorous populism and plebiscitary politics take hold, and we need to be given an old-fashioned history lesson to warn of the dangers ahead". While "democracy understood as the rule of the majority, has never been sufficient in itself," Kelly maintains, it most definitely is more productive when practised in combination with other measures such as "enshrining constitutional rules to avoid the arbitrary exercise of power, imposing standards of behavior on elected officials or supporting a healthy ambivalence toward rulers by the ruled."[86]

It must be reiterated, however, as Edsall explains, that although "Liberal democracies are better equipped than authoritarian states to grapple with the inevitable conflicts that arise in diverse societies", liberal democracies "also contain the seeds of their own destruction" in that:

> […] if they fail to deal with these challenges and allow xenophobic populists to hijack the public debate, then the votes of frustrated and disaffected citizens will increasingly go to the anti-immigrant right, societies will become less open, nativist parties will grow more powerful, and racist rhetoric that promotes a narrow and exclusionary sense of national identity will be legitimized.[87]

Sitaraman stresses the need to keep the balance, with reference to present day USA, where, as he argues, growing economic inequalities have tested the Constitution – designed at a period of an "extraordinary degree of economic equality within the political community" as was defined by the founders at the time – because it "was not built for a country with so much wealth concentrated at the very top nor for the threats that invariably accompany it: oligarchs and populist demagogues".[88] By making "full use of the demagogic playbook" – lying repeatedly, spreading falsehoods and attacking the credibility, motives and patriotism of others and especially of witnesses to his misdeeds – to put asunder what the founders had delicately tried to put together, Trump, in Bauer's opinion, became "the Founders' Worst Nightmare".[89]

The liberalism that is x-rayed and criticised in the West is the very same liberalism that has globalised itself with reckless abandon, enslaved non-Western people with impunity and benefitted enormously from dispossessing them and from their service and servitude as labour. It is the same liberalism that promotes policies and practices of selective migration and widespread monitoring and control of those from the non-Western world who dare to move on their own terms and for their own reasons. Put differently, it is a liberalism that has plundered and cannibalised the rest of the world for the benefit of the West, which enjoys a monopoly of defining itself, defining others and ensuring that these definitions stick and that they cancel out every other. In other words, it is a liberalism with a touch of totalitarianism in its rigid dogmatic prescriptions and self-righteousness. It matters little that "Compliance is forced less by the state than by elites who form public opinion, and by private corporations that, thanks to technology, control our lives far more than we would like to admit" (Dreher 2020: Chapter one).

Seen from the perspective of the non-Western victims of such liberalism, it is shocking beyond comprehension to listen to ordinary people in the West – "the people" so to speak – resort to cultural and national populism to make their voices heard on the material and cultural indignities that they have suffered, even though the excuse given all along by their plundering elite was that such plunders, cannibalism, indignities and impunities to which others were subjected were being carried out in the interest of "the people" of the enslaving, colonising and conquering societies of the West. Little wonder, therefore, that populism, be this left-wing or right-wing, is united by a common sense of excruciating injustice, of being taken for granted for far too long by liberal elites, national and global, who seemed too carried away by their ambitions of dominance and narcissism to think seriously of those rejected by or falling out of their bandwagon of modernity and globalisation.

Like Tutuola's Drinkard, the liberal elites, in their ambitions of dominance and narcissism, seem incapable of seeing and living in a world in which they are not at the centre of things. Everything is about them. To feed their illusions of completeness, they must actively consume others and their life chances, in a sterile form of cannibalism. Their very power and privilege depend on them working extra hard to politely but firmly impose their lifestyles, priorities and hierarchies of being and becoming on others by cancelling out alternative sources of self-activation, self-cultivation and self-extension, all in the name of a phoney or contrived meritocracy.

Part II

Trump, the USA and the Populism Bandwagon

The dominant argument here dovetails with the brief discussion of liberalism-bashing above, focusing on Trump, which is mainly perceived as a threat to liberal values and norms like democratic representation and tolerance. What is it in American society that nurtures populisms and populists like Trump? This section takes a cursory look at some of these factors, which include: perceived failures of contemporary neoliberalism; obsessional narcissism of the neoliberal elite; a sense of overarching meaninglessness in political and cultural life; the hollowing of people's life by classical liberalism forcing them to turn to ideology, religion, xenophobia, nationalism, exclusionary politics and anti-immigration; and democracy's abandonment of its public life and public good to unregulated privatisation, militarisation and individualisation. These nurturers, it could be argued, have sustained the USA's long tradition of right-wing populism from the anti-communist movement through McCarthyism and the Tea Party to the coming to power of Trump, whose political populism feeds on the forlorn stagnation of people at the fringes of the American economy (Kalb 2018; Young 2018).

Drawing on numerous sources, I argue that, whether seen as classic populism, thuggish populism, reactionary populism, fake populism or the struggle to create an alternative and more personalised deep-state, Trumpism and Trump's leadership, like many of its type, is a testimony of crude exploitation of the fear of social change and the crisis of identity experienced by many whites. Trump has braggadociously revealed that the democratic system in America is only as good as the person who is entrusted with its preservation. Because there is no one more elite than Trump, one could argue that the elites are the financial and political winners of either neoliberalism or populism. By notably pointing to the significance of the 6 January 2021 insurrection, Trump is argued to have successfully convinced a significant portion of the population to turn against democracy (just as did the liberal elites whom he repeatedly criticised) or, at the very least, be unconcerned with its demise, as long as his strongman ambitions were fulfilled. In this connection, Trump's Chairman of the Joint Chiefs of Staff, General Mark A. Milley, could have a point when he suggests that the 6 January insurrection might well have been a dress rehearsal or "a precursor to something far worse down the road" (Woodward and Cosata 2021: Epilogue). And, if Trump's post-White House rallies are anything to go by, the country may well not have seen the last of him. In a 26 June 2021 rally in Wellington, Ohio, for instance, Trump reportedly declared:

> "We will not bend," […] "We will not break. We will not yield. We will never give in. We will never give up. We will never back down. We will never, ever surrender. My fellow Americans, our movement is far from over. In fact, our fight has only just begun." (Woodward and Cosata 2021: Epilogue).

The liberal establishment against which Trump has turned by embracing populism has not hesitated in fighting back. They have sought to portray Trump and populism as a threat to democracy. How does the figure of Trump show populism as a threat to democracy? The keyword here is authoritarianism. Below, I mobilise a range of arguments that show Trump as authoritarian in person and in his mode of governance and in a comparative perspective to authoritarian politicians globally. In addition, Trump is presented as a vessel for popular authoritarian energies flowing from his supporters, informed by cultural and economic anxieties, that undermine the possibility of pluralism. Trump's visible contempt for democracy illustrates this: the decimation of the institutions and norms of procedural democracy; a willingness to hold democracy to ransom by exploiting fear, hate, polarisation and by threatening instability, and thus undermining the rule of law that he otherwise should champion as president; the cultivation of a thug-like cult of personality through the personalisation of political authority comprising constant and narcissistic demands for deference, respect and loyalty, evident in routine complaints of being victimised by witch-hunts and the disciplining of dissent; and an embrace and endorsement of dictators globally.

Let's take a closer look.

A new wave of populism has been a long time coming across the Western world. This argument is widespread. In the USA for example, Samuels places the rise of Trump squarely at the feet of the failures of contemporary neoliberalism and the obsessional narcissism of the neoliberal elite (Samuels 2016). Rachman observes that the spread of democracy and political freedom "seems to have gone into reverse". This has given way to an "authoritarian wave that began outside the established democracies of the west" to "spread to the US and Europe". He shows that governments with "authoritarian tendencies" have come to power in several countries, and in countries where they are yet to work their way to power, the faith in democratic institutions has declined.[90] There are "perceived failures of democratic representation" (Hawkins et al. 2016: 102), which have led to the rise in authoritarianism, including among others Trump and his committed support base (Dean and Altemeyer 2020). "Authoritarian thinking," Kivisto recalls, "is characterized by being rigid, simplistic, and exclusionary — viewing the world in terms of stark black-and-white polarities that divide social actors into us-them categories" (Kivisto 2017: 53), as abundantly articulated in the literature we have examined so far.

Like Judis (2016, 2018), Martinelli (2016: 25–26) and Maskovsky and Bjork-James (2020a), Barkin discusses how "The global financial crisis of 2008/9" together with the rising concern about an upsurge in migration in 2015/16 "exposed the impotence of politicians, deepening public disillusion and pushing people towards populists who offered simple explanations and solutions".[91] As Mahbubani and Summers argue, at the heart of the surge in what they qualify as "pessimistic populism" is "a widespread loss of confidence in the West about its own systems and future potential".[92] As they put it:

> Sluggish growth across the developed world, stagnant incomes for much of the population, rising economic inequality, political gridlock, and the emergence of populist insurgencies on both sides of the political spectrum have fueled a widespread sense that Western models of governance and economic management are floundering.[93]

This, according to Green, accounts for what Shadi Hamid has termed as "a sense of overarching meaninglessness in political and cultural life in [Western democratic] countries". Hamid explains that although classical liberalism makes sense intellectually, it does not fill the gap in people's lives, and this explains why they turn to "ideology, religion, xenophobia, nationalism, populism, exclusionary politics or anti-immigrant policies." All of these aspects contribute to a sense of something greater. In the same way that Islam is reconciling pre-modern Islamic law with the modern nation state, so Western democracy may also need to reconcile meaning and politics.[94] There is need as well to understand the meaning of representation, particularly in politics.

Whites in Europe and the USA who feel left behind "are economically protectionist and socially conservative" insists Goodwin. They are equally, "deeply anxious about economic disadvantage and threats to their identity, values and ways of life".[95] As Møller argues, those left behind feel like they have "been sacrificed in pursuit of the higher cost-benefit or cost-efficiency—or whatever slogan was used—necessary to justify the privatization" of wealth. They lose the feeling of "living in the same nation with equal access to public services" as the nation becomes more bifurcated. "Any society and any nation depends on trust between its citizens and the authorities," Møller explains. "Trust governs a society when citizens feel a public officer's decision would have been the same if the roles had been reversed." However, as "intransparency and obscurity" in nations grow, the tendency is to abandon the "human factor and person-to-person communication". When this happens, "citizens do not have the faintest clue about who makes decisions on important issues that may be vital for them". Additionally, there is the increasingly likelihood that citizens would "classify politicians and business leaders as 'not like us' and thus take less of an interest in politics".[96] It could be argued, as some have with reference to the USA, that no democracy can survive when its public good and public life are so privatised, militarised and individualised, leaving many to fend unproductively at the forgotten margins where populist opportunists regularly go to shop.

The voters rallying to populist insurgents are, according to Freedland, usually "those who feel failed by conventional politics, left behind either economically or culturally". On their part, the new populists "insist that the entire system is broken" and must be replaced, instead of simply saying that "the ruling party has failed and now the opposition should have a turn". Freedland warns that "if voters increasingly assume democracy to be impotent, they will trust less and less those politicians who so much as attempt to inspire hope", and "will listen instead, if they listen at all, to those who exploit fear".[97] With voters frustrated by exclusions, the attractions of "populists is that they give voice to the anger of the excluded" by pointing them to and fanning the flames of populist rage fuelled by various political, social and identity cleavages "revolving around nationhood, ethnicity, or religion", and on acute income and social class disparities.[98]

The United States of America (USA) – with a long tradition of populism, right-wing populism in particular, which started with the anti-communist movement, McCarthyism and later the Tea Party movement (Kazin 2017[1995]; Kalb 2018) – has thus not been spared by what Peter describes as a "tsunami" of populism.[99] It is not surprising that the USA has joined the populism bandwagon of the day. As Kazin argues and demonstrates with the examples of the depressions of the 1890s and 1930s and the financial collapse of 2008, at "times of systemic crisis, citizens almost inevitably look to figures who blame entrenched leaders while assuring 'the people' that they bear little or no responsibility for what has gone so wrong" (Kazin 2017[1995]: xiii). In his essay titled "The Pseudo-Conservative Revolt—1954", Hofstadter argued that the "populist culture" of the USA, in which "a responsible elite with political and moral autonomy" seemed wanting and where it was "possible to exploit the wildest currents of public sentiment for private purposes", it was "conceivable that a highly organized, vocal, active, and well-financed minority could create a political climate in which the rational pursuit of our well-being and safety would become impossible" (Hofstadter 2008[1965]: Chapter 2).

Much of the "political populism on both left and right" in the US "feeds on the forlorn stagnation of people at the bottom of the American economy", according to Brooks. This situation is compounded by the "steady decline of movement from and to the country, between states and even more locally" caused in part by "education policies that don't advocate or create opportunity to move to prosperous areas".[100] Education policy and equality in education have a very uphill battle to fight in the face of "redlining" which was practised by real estate agents like Donald Trump to segregate people by race into different neighbourhoods (Reid 2019). Notwithstanding the growing and low unemployment rate in the USA in 2016, many people felt economically excluded and (especially

93

working-class whites) blamed the "rising inequality over the past few decades on foreigners", according to Nye. With such unease among people, it is easy to mobilise opposition against immigration and globalisation, in favour of "economic populism", in addition to which, "a significant minority of the population also feels threatened by cultural changes related to race, culture, and ethnicity".[101]

Moisi describes Donald J. Trump as "America's reality-TV Mussolini". Trump is "not just a populist, isolationist politician; he is a caricature of one",[102] claims Moisi. Though Trump came across as a buffoon and did not accord reality the seriousness and gravity it deserves, he became a serious contender for the presidency of the USA in 2016. This was largely due to the fact that Trump, unlike most previous presidential contenders, "had a level of celebrity that meant he was already known to the vast majority of Americans". Regardless of how Trump was known, whether "as a buffoonish New York real estate developer with a history of splashy divorces and casino bankruptcies" or "as the cocky billionaire boss on *The Apprentice*", the important point was the fact that "everyone knew him, or at least thought they knew him" (Simpson and Fritsch 2019: Chapter 2). In her detailed account as participant in the first year of casting, Omarosa Manigault Newman discusses, among other things, how "*The Apprentice* was a branding opportunity for Trump, and nearly every task was self-promotional" (Newman 2018: Chapter 2).

"Trump's talent for showmanship" in the actual campaign, Coppins observes, "ensured that hardly a half hour passed on cable news all summer without his famous mug and more famous pompadour filling the nation's TV screens." In addition, as "the daily Donald show sucked up media oxygen, the rest of the Republican presidential candidates were left desperately gasping for air" (Coppins 2015: Chapter 24), and eventually falling off one by one until Trump, like a colossus, towered as the only candidate left standing for the Republican party endorsement for president. Newman finds parallels between the Trump campaign and *The Apprentice*, arguing that one "could liken the entire GOP primary season, from February to June 2016, to a season of *The Political Apprentice*, with Trump 'firing' his sixteen opponents one by one" (Newman 2018: Chapter 6). This, Pickard blames on the commercial imperatives that drive news organisations to popularise a dangerous politics by privileging profit over democracy (Pickard 2018), and that has given rise to activist fact-based journalism in defence of democracy (Russell 2018). Waisbord et al. report that "media tracking companies calculated that Trump had benefitted from almost five billion dollars of free media time" by the end of the 2016 election campaign, and that "Trump's presence boosted television ratings, especially for cable news companies that reported increased ratings and profits" (Waisbord et al. 2018: 30). As "a famous celebrity who was well-trained, from years of reality-television appearances, to perform before the camera", Zada argues that Trump was a "great TV" candidate, and that the "news organizations, with CNN leading the way, were crucial in elevating the man [Trump] to the presidency". Trump "promised to be the story that keeps on giving: a guaranteed four years of sensational and unprecedented headlines to help pull news organizations out of the financial gutter" (Zada 2021: Part 2). Barrett concurs, adding that from the outset of the campaign, Trump intuited that it was easier to buy or scare television executives and producers than politicians. Trump reckoned that "If he was good television, and he knew he would be", the television executives and producers "would give him billions in exposure while demanding little more than unpredictable conflict and controversy from him. They, too, he understood, believe his life is a movie and are competing, often on his terms, to sell tickets to it" (Barrett 2016[1992]: Foreword). Achter references a study by the Harvard Shorenstein Center, according to which "in his first 100 days as president, Trump was the topic of 41 percent of national news coverage, three times the coverage presidents usually receive during that time period" (Achter 2018). Indeed, it could be argued that Trump and his variant of populism have been a Santa Claus to journalism, elite commentators, the media (both mainstream and social) and scholars of democracy, with Trump adding an extra Christmas surprise present to the entertainment industries. As tribute to "the triumph of news market values as American virtues", Achter, reacting to CNN's Jeff Zucker that Trump made for great television, argued that "TV-loving Trump is a character in a drama that includes CNN, one who embodies and amplifies the neoliberal logics of for-profit news organizations – of conflict and incivility in the name of ratings and revenue". Trump and the media are mutually fascinated with each other. Achter sums up the synergy between Trump and cable television as follows: "Hero or villain, Trump draws viewers

95

and clicks, and that is both his goal and the goal of cable TV news" (Achter 2018). Trump, in this regard, could be compared to a heap of cow dung manure that enables the mushrooming of opportunity and content for media practitioners, cultural producers, academics and the big tech giants to flourish. Did it matter that he fell short of the empathy and compassion that had come to be expected of someone running for president? Trump drew and continues to draw his support "chiefly from working-class Republicans, who are attracted to his opposition to trade deals, his support for Social Security and Medicare, and his vilification of immigrants — a program similar to that of other nations' right-wing racist-populist parties with working-class support, such as France's National Front", Meyerson writes.[103]

In passing, it is worth asking of the news media the following questions: If coverage is predominantly driven by the need to increase ratings and profits, should it surprise the media that claim objectivity and factuality by giving equal weight to opposing viewpoints when media consumers feel "emotionally manipulated for ratings, subscriptions and clicks"? What happens in instances where the truth is far more complex than can be accounted for by a mere binary opposition of viewpoints? How does one counter the argument that it is in the interest of the news media to sensationalise, dramatise and exaggerate conflict, chaos, cleavages, fear, anger and hatred in news reports in order to stay in business? Could the prioritisation of profit over people and over reality, and/or "the systemic automation of human beings at the heart of the contemporary news machine" account for the tendency for the media to navigate towards and fixate on events that are mostly "outliers" or "exceptions and not the rule" in the everyday experiences of the societies and world we inhabit? (Zada 2021: Preface & Part 1). Lastly, how would the news media react to this conclusion by Zada – whose insider knowledge of how the media excels at "putting 'reality' together" (Schlesinger 1978) is not in doubt – that the media, in their "choice of stories and the extent of the coverage and significance attributed to them" seldom reflect "most of our day-to-day experiences"? Rather, Zada argues, just by covering the stories and covering them the way they do, the media not only create "a distorted picture of our reality", but also the implication that world as depicted by the media "*is* the world we physically inhabit every day", the media are involved in manipulating its consumers into taking seriously what it has put together as reality (Zada 2021: Preface). Like Schlesinger (1978), Zada argues that the media, by defining reality, however inadvertently, are able to alter that reality (Zada 2021).

Most Americans, Trump supporters included, who are experiencing spikes in violent crimes and killings, and who are victims of drug overdose and chronic dependency on opioids, just want to make America safe again – though one should hasten to add that this applies mainly to whites, as blacks (largely speaking), Hispanics, Asians, and native Americans have seldom felt "safe" in the USA. Drawing attention to the rapidly increasing death rate of middle-aged white Americans due to suicide and alcohol and drug use, Meyerson notices a correlation between this group and those that have become Trump supporters. Whilst these two groups cannot be equated to each other directly, Meyerson indicates, they have common roots: "a sense of abandonment, betrayal and misdirected anger".[104] Taub asserts that Trump, like other contemporary populists, has exploited a "fear of social change; fear of terrorist attacks and other physical threats; and the crisis of identity that many whites are experiencing as they struggle to maintain their position". Trump's populism, like most other kinds across Europe, Taub claims, is "the majoritarian backlash; the rage of those who now are slightly less powerful against the gradual erosion of their privilege".[105] Middle class and middle-aged white women are part of the fold, and Trump would not have been voted in were it not for them. This is, notwithstanding a characteristic with gender and sexuality in right-wing populist circles, of which Trump is a part, that is seldom favourable to women. It is all too common, as Dietze and Roth argue, for populist actors like Trump, to "conjure up the heteronormative nuclear family as the model of social organization, attack reproductive rights, question sex education, criticize a so-called 'gender ideology,' reject same-sex marriage and seek to re-install biologically understood binary gender differences" (Dietze and Roth 2020: 7).

The fears of middle class and middle-aged white women may not be voiced in the same in-your-face ways as the fears of some others, but they nonetheless determine how they vote. Fear and scare tactics proved to be very useful to Trump the politician (Woodward 2018; Hassan 2019; Rucker and Leonnig 2020; Woodward and Costa 2021).

"To defy Mr. Trump is to invite the president's wrath, ostracism within the party and a premature end to a career in Republican politics",[106] wrote Martin and Haberman in December 2019. According to Rucker, during "his five years on the national political stage, Trump has used fear to acquire and keep power", with "scare tactics" as "the hammer and screwdriver of his toolkit".[107] Unlike Tutuola's "The Skull" turned "The Complete Gentleman", Trump used fear, wrath and threats of ostracism to hang on to the illusion of completeness made possible by his activators in Republican politics. This Trump achieved by opting for the concentration of power in his person, thus amounting to borrowing without acknowledgment, and to eating without providing for being eaten.

Judah attempts to explain the rise of Trump in racial terms, with the argument that, "Hegemonic groups, as they shrink, are at their most vulnerable to populists"." This is what has happened to white Americans, with Trump weaponising the "Racial anxiety" that "is deep in white American ethnicity".[108] According to Angelo, during his 2016 presidential campaign:

> Trump harnessed his supporters' racial resentments regarding immigration and crime, took stances that were supported by predominately conservative White middle-Americans, targeted his appeals in a strategic way that tried to gain support from a virtuous middle, and claimed that those policies supported racial equality. He flirted with the far-right but eventually (symbolically) rejected their support, and lashed out against the media about whom he claimed misinterpreted his approach and lied about his stances to discredit him (Angelo 2019: 202).

While Trump is credited with recognising and taking political advantage of the fact that working-class voters are "hurting" and that his move towards more protectionist and isolationist politics would remedy that "hurting", Hutton warns that "destroying the international trading system is not going to bring [the America of the 1940s and 1950s] back". In Hutton's view, such policies are misguided, because "Trade and exchange are the foundations of our [American] civilisation" and "the more, the better".[109] In July 2018, Krastev wrote that, initially, Europeans were deluding themselves into thinking that Trump had a policy that mattered more than his tweets, and that the tweets could be ignored as inconsequential. They were wrong. To Krastev, "It was the tweets that really mattered in the end." He thinks that Europeans were finally being forced to realise that Trump's world had no place for allies.[110] And indeed, Trump's presidency turned out to be one of weakened alliances and shambolic diplomacy, with the outcome being, as Ioffe laments, "politicizing our embassies, alienating our allies, and decimating the ranks of the foreign service".[111] This has given the Biden presidency a new slogan: "America Is Back", as his administration set about rebuilding broken and strained relations with the wider world. But the slogan could also put the rest of the world on its toes, if understood as America, the global policeman or gendarme, is back.

Much has been written associating Trump's brand of politics with what Sullivan has described as "Trump's ugly, thuggish populism". Not dissimilar in Sullivan's estimation to any neo-fascist movement, Trump's populism advances not "gradually by persuasion" but by seeking to "transform the terms of the debate, create a new movement based on untrammelled emotion, take over existing institutions and then ruthlessly exploit events". Sullivan elaborates: Socrates' fear is realised, that tyranny is likely to be established out of democracy. Plato argues that the full ripening of democracy could see a tyrant making his move through the obedience of the mob that follows him. Sullivan asks prominently whether the Constitution would be able to constrain the realisation of this revelation visible through the rise of Trump. The founding fathers of the United States likely read Plato correctly and attempted to set up systems that would see to tyrannical, demagogical figures never quite attaining the power imagined because the technocratic systems are to be around every corner. Yet it seems Trump, from the "circuses of pro wrestling and New York tabloids, via reality TV and Twitter" has realised the fears of Plato and the founding fathers – and the walls built around democracy to tame the wildfires are possibly being torn down[112] (Sullivan 2021: Chapter 47). We would do well to realise that the climate Obama thrived in was also ripe for opportunists, which Sarah Palin[113] showed in 2008 through pride of her own ignorance. To Sullivan, Palin was "a John the Baptist for the true messiah of conservative populism, waiting patiently and strategically for his time to come". The dynamic in which Trump's "thuggish populism" cannot hold tune with the White House is no longer important; he changed the rules of the game he was unable to play[114] (Sullivan 2021: Chapter 47). Traverso is less inclined to categorise Trump as fascist, though he argues that Trump, as "an uncontrollable and unpredictable loose cannon", is much more of "a postfascist leader without fascism" (Traverso 2019: Chapter 1).

Trump's disregard for democracy notwithstanding, the founding fathers, some have equally argued, were not effusive enthusiasts of democracy either. According to Beres, those "founding fathers of America were not proponents of democracy and seemed to prefer that the common people have as little to do with government as possible, expressing a clear sense of anti-popular sentiments". Alexander Hamilton went as far as to say, "The People sir, are a great beast." Beres seems to share much of these sentiments in remarking as societal commentary that "we the people want comfort and easy wealth, but very little else". Thomas Jefferson made a tongue-in-cheek critique of the people, suggesting that 20 of the best geniuses from elementary schools be offered proper education, "raking rubbish" away annually. The sustained presidential nuance which praises and panders the American people without focus on individual responsibility will continue to realise the founding fathers' fear of democracy.[115]

Writing in May 2016, Johnson saw Trump's approach to economic policy as "classic populism" and his "Make America Great Again" slogan as "a political swindle" which "would undermine America's security, depress its economy, and destroy the financial system". To Johnson, "Make America Great Again" is no more than a lie told to win votes and one that will lead to certain destruction in the country and beyond. Trump's authoritarian, populist politics consisted in seeking to silence opponents "physically in the courts, and […] on Twitter".[116] *The Economist* saw Trump's populism as "a blow to civic nationalism".[117] For these reasons, Johnson urged for a rejection of Trump's candidacy in 2016 in order "to keep America and the world safe".[118] In *The Room Where It Happened*, Trump's former national security advisor, John Bolton, says that weekly intelligence briefings with Trump were not effective because Trump tended to outtalk the intelligence experts. He writes: "I didn't think these briefings were terribly useful, and neither did the intelligence community, since much of the time was spent listening to Trump, rather than Trump listening to the briefers" (Bolton 2020: Chapter 4; see also Rohde 2020: Chapter 15).

However, as Freeman suggests, drawing parallels between Trump's populism and the populism of Publius Clodius Pulcher of the Roman Republic, the populist forces Trump has unleashed are likely to remain very much alive, and to quickly find new champions, with Trump out of power.[119] In this sense, Trump could well be credited with, as Escobar argued following Trump's election victory in 2016, a victory compared to 9/11 for the shockwaves it sent through the nation and the world, having "managed to destroy the self-propelled myth of US institutional stability/predictability/ credibility because these were already hollow qualities".[120] To Krastev, Trump's victory made it "clear that we live in a moment when the fear of an uncertain future is a weaker mobilizing force than a disgust with the present". The victory signalled that "threatened majorities have emerged as a major force in Western democratic politics".[121]

In a long and detailed portrayal of Trump and his rise to power, Aitkenhead reflects on the political year 2016, comparing the 2010s to the 1930s and criticising the contemporary world for being "every bit as slow as our forefathers to recognise impending catastrophe". Brexit and Trump's election are portrayed as political earthquakes – unforeseen outcomes that upended the state of the world,[122] bringing to the fore the fact that unhappy white working-class voters were as, if not more, motivated by perceived cultural loss, related to concerns about immigration and ethnic change than they were by economic calculation (Goodhart 2017; Eatwell and Goodwin 2018). Geopolitically, however, Quah and Mahbubani argue that what unites Trump and Brexiters, "is not anger at being excluded from the benefits of globalization, but rather a shared sense of unease that they no longer control their own destinies". The "transatlantic axis that used to run the world" is fast losing his power, and "the sense of losing control is being felt by these countries' political elites and ordinary citizens alike". While "closing the income gap can help the poor" it is unlikely to "alleviate their anxiety".[123]

Fast forward. Not in any hurry to disguise his determination to see American history as white history, Trump has never emphatically discouraged support for the Confederacy and its legacy. Unsurprisingly, this reached an explosive point when he lost the 2020 presidential election. Unable to fathom himself as a loser even as he labels many who dare criticise him "losers" (O'Brien 2015[2005]: Introduction), Trump, the eternal winner who "never thinks of the negative" (O'Brien 2015[2005]: Chapter 2), came up with what Timothy Snyder, author of *On Tyranny: Twenty Lessons from the Twentieth Century* (2017), terms a "Big Lie". In the book, Snyder urges us to take history seriously. And if we were to, we would learn, from 20th century Europe for example, "that societies can break, democracies can fall, ethics can collapse, and ordinary men can find themselves standing over death pits with guns in their hands" (Snyder 2017: Prologue). In ten successive tweets on 7 January 2021, Snyder draws on the book to disabuse Americans of any misguided sense that the country's democratic heritage insulates them against tyranny and autocracy, and to explain how Trump's insistence that he had won the election despite the facts to the contrary, amounted to a big lie. According to Snyder:

> The claim that Trump won the election is a big lie. A big lie changes reality. To believe it, people must disbelieve their senses, distrust their fellow citizens, and live in a world of faith. A big lie demands conspiracy thinking, since all who doubt it are seen as traitors. A big lie undoes a society, since it divides citizens into believers and unbelievers. A big lie destroys democracy, since people who are convinced that nothing is true but the utterances of their leader ignore voting and its results. A big lie must bring violence, as it has. A big lie can never be told just by one person. Trump is the originator of this big lie, but it could never have flourished without his allies on Capitol Hill. Political futures now depend on this big lie. Senators Hawley and Cruz are running for president on the basis of this big lie. There is a cure for the big lie. Our elected representatives should tell the truth, without dissimulation, about the result of the 2020 election.

The big lie as appropriately captured by Wolff in *Landslide: The Final Days of the Trump Presidency* (Wolff 2021a), and who quotes Trump making the false claim on 6 January 2021: "We won. Won in a landslide. This was a landslide." This is echoed by Bender in *"Frankly We Did Win This Election": The Inside Story of How Trump Lost* (Bender 2021). Trump deflated attention from his strongman propensity by playing the victim. He "likened the U.S. election to one where despots in authoritarian regimes supplanted the rightful vote and replaced it with fake ballots in order to stay in power" (Wolff 2021a: Chapter 9). The big lie had been a long time coming, from when President Trump claimed after the 2016 election that he had won the popular vote, that there had been widespread fraud, with three to five million illegal votes for Hillary Clinton, and that his inaugural crowd was the biggest ever[124] (Miller 2018; Karl 2020; Rucker and Leonnig 2020; Leonnig and Rucker 2021). The big lie was followed by an appeal by Trump to his supporters to "stop the steal", and to fight as hard as they could to achieve this end, even if it meant "stop the count" of votes as well.

In populist fashion, Trump was ready to bypass and even to challenge existing institutions, structures, processes and procedures of democratic legitimacy and legitimation, if following them would mean losing the election. When Chris Krebs, Director of the Cybersecurity and Infrastructure Security Agency openly debunked Trump's voter fraud lies with a report that the 2020 "November 3rd election was the most secure in American history" and that there was "no evidence that any voting system deleted or lost votes, changed votes, or was in any way compromised",[125] Trump "terminated" his directorship by tweet, "effective immediately" (7:07 PM tweet, 17 November 2020).

If Trump indulged in legal challenges, it was in the hope that the partisanship of judges he had appointed in close coordination with the Republican party might come to his rescue. When the cases were not decided in his favour, and despite his Attorney General, Bill Barr, dismissing – in what amounted to a rare standing up to or contradiction of Trump in public by a close collaborator who had until then served as Trump's "hatchet man" by jeopardising the independence of the Department of Justice (Honig 2021) – his theories about a stolen election as "bullshit" and reporting that "we have not seen fraud on a scale that could have effected a different outcome in the election"[126] (Wolff 2021a: Chapter 5; Leonnig and Rucker 2021: Chapters 17, 18 & 19; Honig 2021: 195–219; Bender 2021: Chapter 18), Trump's reaction was to criticise the judiciary and Bill Barr (Leonnig and Rucker 2021: Epilogue). In an 8:14 AM tweet on 26 December 2020, Trump wrote:

The "Justice" Department and the FBI have done nothing about the 2020 Presidential Election Voter Fraud, the biggest SCAM in our nation's history, despite overwhelming evidence. They should be ashamed. History will remember. Never give up. See everyone in D.C. on January 6th.

In a 9:14 AM tweet on 18 December 2020, Trump urged Senate Republicans "to get tougher" and fight for the presidential election which he insisted he won, else they "won't have a Republican Party anymore". Appealing for gratitude and reminding Senate Republicans of one-good-turn deserves another, Trump tweeted at 6:08 PM on 24 December 2020:

I saved at least 8 Republican Senators, including Mitch, from losing in the last Rigged (for President) Election. Now they (almost all) sit back and watch me fight against a crooked and vicious foe, the Radical Left Democrats. I will NEVER FORGET!

When the Senate Republicans did not throw their weight behind his big lie, Trump accused "Mitch & the Republicans" of doing "NOTHING", instead of fighting "to the death" in what he qualified as "an act of war" – "an Election Rigged & Stolen", in an 8:00 AM tweet on 26 December 2020. In an 8:59 AM tweet on 29 December 2020, Trump accused the Republican leadership of wanting "the path of least resistance". He wrote:

Our leaders (not me, of course!) are pathetic. They only know how to lose! P.S. I got MANY Senators and Congressmen/ Congresswomen elected. I do believe they forgot!

In a 10:45 AM tweet on 4 January 2020, Trump wrote:

The "Surrender Caucus" within the Republican Party will go down in infamy as weak and ineffective "guardians" of our Nation, who were willing to accept the certification of fraudulent presidential numbers!

The growing reticence of Republican senators to embrace Trump's big lie was already pre-empted on 15 December when Mitch

McConnell, the Senate majority leader, albeit belatedly, congratulated Joe Biden and Kamala Harris. He said:

> Our system of government has processes to determine who will be sworn in on Jan. 20. The Electoral College has spoken. So today, I want to congratulate President-elect Joe Biden. [...] I also want to congratulate the vice president-elect, our colleague from California — Sen. Harris. Beyond our differences, all Americans can take pride that our nation has a female vice president-elect for the very first time.[127]

Increasingly losing faith in his Republicans to jump into his bandwagon of the big lie, Trump warned in a power-to-the-people-like 5:12 PM tweet on 5 January 2020:

> I hope the Democrats, and even more importantly, the weak and ineffective RINO section Republican Party, are looking at the thousands of people pouring into D.C. They won't stand for a landslide victory to be stolen.

On the morning of 6 January 2021, knowing that Vice-President Mike Pence was his last institutional trump card, Trump tweeted at 8:17 AM:

> States want to correct their votes, which they now know were based on irregularities and fraud, plus corrupt process never received legislative approval. All Mike Pence has to do is send them back to the States, AND WE WIN. Do it Mike, this is a time for extreme courage!

Reportedly, Trump, in a conversation, told Pence, "You can either go down in history as a patriot, or you can go down in history as a pussy"[128] (Wolff 2021a: Chapter 8).

Thus, having indicated to his militant supporters that he had little faith in the establishment and procedural democracy (Dean and Altemeyer 2020), it is hardly surprising that the supporters would want to mobilise themselves to overthrow the system and those defending it, even if this meant "hanging" his otherwise loyal Vice-President, Mike Pence. When Pence, in what Wolff describes as "a curiously novel moment in the Trump presidency" decided to stand up for himself as Vice President (Wolff 2021a: Chapter 8), Trump did not hide his disappointment. At 2:24:22 PM EST on 6 January 2021, Trump tweeted his disappointment with Pence:

> Mike Pence didn't have the courage to do what should have been done to protect our Country and our Constitution, giving States a chance to certify a corrected set of facts, not the fraudulent or inaccurate ones which they were asked to previously certify. USA demands the truth!

For not going along with his big lie to "stop the steal" by stopping the certification of the electoral college vote, indeed, by insisting that he would do his duty under the Constitution, Mike Pence had proved disloyal to Trump"[129] – something unpardonable to Trump, as Michael Cohen, Trump's former personal attorney depicts in his book, *Disloyal* (Cohen 2020). And Trump did not condone disloyalty, be it from an individual, an institution, the American Constitution, democracy or the USA itself (Leonnig and Rucker 2021: Chapter 8; Grisham 2021: Epilogue). This was a taxing expectation that led Cliff Sims, a special assistant to President Trump, to ask himself at one point, paraphrasing the Gospel of Mark, "*What does it profit a man to survive in Trump's White House but forfeit his soul?*" (Sims 2019: Chapter 8 italics in original). Dreher references Michael Kruse who quotes Trump saying: "I value loyalty above everything else—more than brains, more than drive, and more than energy" (Dreher 2020: Chapter 2), and as Sims discovered, "in Trump World, loyalty was mostly a one-way street", and everyone who did not share a last name with Trump was "disposable" (Sims 2019: Chapter 15). Stephanie Grisham, who resigned on 6 January 2021 over the siege of the Capitol by the Trump instigated mob,[130] after six years of devoted service to the First Lady Melania Trump as chief of staff and to Trump as communications director and press secretary, agrees, adding that, "most of the Trump family dismisses and cuts people from their lives on a whim", and "demand total loyalty, but they are loyal to no one" (Grisham 2021: Epilogue).

James Comey, FBI Director at the time Trump ascended to the Presidency, recounts how Trump demanded loyalty of him in these words: "I need loyalty. I expect loyalty", said Trump. "You will always get honesty from me," replied Comey. "That's what I want, honest loyalty," Trump told him (Comey 2018: Chapter 13). This attitude is summed up in another 6 January 2021 Trump tweet hailing the hard-core supporters that had stood and fought by him till the end, in defence of a well-deserved landslide victory unfortunately "stolen" by establishment Washington politicians with a history of treating them badly and unfairly:

> These are the things and events that happen when a sacred landslide election victory is so unceremoniously & viciously stripped away from great patriots who have been badly & unfairly treated for so long. Go home with love & in peace. Remember this day forever![131] (see also Wolff 2021a: Chapter 10)

As reported by Barbara Ortutay of the Associated Press, "Twitter immediately stuck a warning label on the tweet which continued the president's false allegations."[132]

If former Trump campaign spokeswoman Karina Pierson is to be believed, Trump's militant supporters had known all along "that both Republicans and Democrats were against we the people", leading them to conclude: "We are the Cavalry. No one's coming for us."[133] The reasoning being that, thenceforth, it was up to them to harken to the call of their President and only leader they could trust and rely upon to save America where elite democracy and the Washington establishment had failed them by selling out (Nance 2019: Chapter 10; Dean and Altemeyer 2020). Trumps' fantasy to maintain power by holding democracy to ransom had the widespread support of a steadfast base with whom he shared the same emotional zone and who credited him with messianic qualities. He could count on them even though he was "without a plan", had little "knowledge of how the government worked", would not listen to those who did, and was almost entirely without staff in the waning days of his presidency (Wolff 2021a: Chapter 8), when Trump "was isolated and vengeful" (Leonnig and Rucker 2021: Chapter 22). This sentiment was superbly captured by a post on 4 January on TheDonald.win website: "If Congress illegally certifies Biden," the post read, "Trump would have absolutely no choice but to demand us to storm congress and kill/beat them up for it."[134] Feeling betrayed by the legalities of a purportedly rigged democracy, pro-Trump posters justified carrying guns to Washington D.C. to "stop the steal" as follows: "Yes, it's illegal, but this is war and we're in a post-legal phase of our society".[135] This brings to mind a statement in Mary L. Trump's book, *Too Much and Never Enough*: "Although more powerful people put Donald into the institutions that have shielded him since the very beginning, it's weaker people than he is who are keeping him there" (Trump, M. L. 2020: 199). According to Mary Trump, the "need for affirmation" that draws Donald Trump to weaker people "is so great that he doesn't seem to notice that the largest group of his supporters are people he wouldn't condescend to be seen with outside of a rally" (Trump, M. L. 2020: 197). Trump is thus elite by cultivation and culture, and populist in political speech and public performance, even if not always in action and sociality.

With a bit of luck, Trump's big lie might have succeeded. A mob he instigated committed an insurrection that was carried out on live TV in his name and in a manner reminiscent of his hiring and firing of contestants on *The Apprentice*. In this instance he, the boss, was outsourcing the hiring and firing of members of Congress to a mob of his supporters energised by his menu of alternate reality. The mob was described by some media outlets as "ideologically-motivated violent extremists" and as Trump's "battalion of fascist tugs" armed with "perceived grievances fueled by false narratives".[136] The mob stormed the Capitol building on 6 January 2021 to disrupt or stop congress from certifying the electoral college votes confirming Joe Biden as President Elect. "Faced with a choice between their president and the Constitution, they chose Trump", argues Mounk.[137] The mob would have succeeded in overthrowing the legislative branch of government and in Trump taking over control of the state despite losing the election both in the popular and the electoral college votes (Wolff 2021a: Chapters 8; Leonnig and Rucker 2021: Chapter 21; Woodward and Costa 2021).

Trump and his hardcore base, which he fondly referred to as "my people", were like oxygen to each other. Like a shepherd of biblical proportions, he needed his people just as much as his people needed their president, even if unlike a shepherd Trump did not know much about his people beyond meeting them physically at his rallies, and virtually on social media and via Fox News and other right-wing media outlets. Mutually oxygenated one another would be made evident again and again in the course of Trump's presidency, especially during the Covid-19 dominated 2020 political campaign and his contestation of the outcome of the election. When the chips were down and his approval ratings low, Trump would turn to his rallies, which served "to boost his energy and mood" with a dramatic rendition of an idea, fantasy or nostalgia of an America he shared with his supporters, purified and protected from the messiness of its current state. The rallies made it possible for Trump's "aesthetic identity to be nurtured, sustained, and projected", thus ensuring that he made up for what he lacked "in coherent political philosophy or policy" with "aesthetic and stylistic performance, mediation, and circulation" (Young 2018). According to Sims, Trump exhibited great energy and stamina, adding that while "public speaking sucks the life out of most people, Trump's battery seemed to recharge itself on the energy of the crowds" that he was addressing (Sims 2019: Chapter 3). At his rallies, Trump was as much a power bank to his followers as they were to him.   Bender relates how Trump rallies perpetually:

> [...] attracted a coterie of political pilgrims who traveled across the country and camped outside arenas for days at a time for the opportunity to stand in the front row and, for ninety blissfully frenzied minutes, cheer on the man they credited with changing the country and, in many cases, their own lives (Bender 2021: Prologue).

As Wolff asserts, Trump and his hardcore support base or superfans mutually incited each other, leading to what Wolff categorises as a rare brand of populism:

> This was a real and exceptional sort of populism. He egged the fans on, and they egged him on. He knew nothing about government, and they knew nothing about government, so the context of government itself became beside the point. It was one-on-one, direct. He had charisma in the Christian sense (Wolff 2021a: Chapter 8).

Trump's charisma notwithstanding, Roberts-Miller argues that "charismatic leadership is not necessarily good for business, and its tendency toward authoritarianism makes it actively dangerous as a basis for democratic policymaking", given its expectations of "complete acquiescence and submission on the part of the followers", which is something that suits Trump authoritarian disposition, craving for unconditional loyalty and aversion to democracy (Roberts-Miller 2018). Together, Trump and his fans shared "his belief that he was a natural winner and Biden an obvious loser", and no election result would counter that as far as they were concerned. There was simply "no way Trump could lose" (Wolff 2021a: Chapter 1). If someone else won, to Trump and his hardcore supporters, the reason must be that "America had a broken and corrupt election system that was robbing people", Trump's "people, of their vote and their choice of leaders", particularly, "Of *him*" (Wolff 2021a: Chapter 11). Lest they be mistaken as exclusively made up of what Hillary Clinton famously labelled as "the deplorables", Nichols reports, "a detailed analysis [...] of those arrested for their part in the insurrection found that the January riot was a day-camp outing for middle-aged, middle-class Americans". To Nichols, this was "a bored 'lumpen-bourgeoisie,' a narcissistic and mostly affluent middle class of deep pockets and shallow minds who paid lip service to democracy but had no interest in it if the results of democratic elections offended them" (Nichols 2021: Chapter 5).

It did not matter that some of the Capitol attackers, as it soon emerged, did not vote in the election they tried to overturn.[138] What mattered was their conviction, however authoritarian and illiberal, that their will had been subverted by an entrenched bureaucracy and security state, the press, election rules and censorship by various big technology platforms.[139] Trump urged them to "fight like hell" and to "show strength" and take their country back or risk having a country no more. After Trump's persistent misrepresentation of the election, he claimed had been stolen, and mobilising his supporters to "stop the steal", the storming of the Capitol would have amounted to an unconstitutional power grab – by Trump known for his determination to win at all costs (Wilson 2020) – which the USA had traditionally tended to associate with "the third world" and with the strongmen in power that Trump admired throughout his presidency. In a tweet – "this is what you get when you steal an election" – Trump left few in doubt about where his sympathies lay with regard to the Capitol insurrection, which Congress, the media and the FBI qualified as "an act of domestic terrorism".[140]

To many the storming was an "attempted coup" by a mob Trump had summoned to Washington, exhorted into a frenzy and aimed like a loaded cannon down Pennsylvania Avenue. Trump did not hesitate to call the mob "patriots" and to reassure them with words of "we love you, you are special" (Leonnig and Rucker 2021: Chapter 21).

Patriotism is most certainly a word that has different meanings for different people of the political spectrum. Speaking to Anderson Cooper on CNN on 7 January 2021, Lt Alexander Vindman, Former European Affairs Director at the National Security Council, who testified against Trump at the first impeachment trial, said, "It was more like throwing hand grenades to hang onto power, not so much of a coup which is more methodical and planned." Whether an attempted coup or a throwing of hand grenades, the delusions that the mob dressed themselves in was all from the conspiracy theories that Trump and his enablers had dished out over the years, and especially since his capture of the Republican party (Muirhead and Rosenblum 2019; Stevens 2020). As Grisham, a former press secretary to Trump writes, "Just as his critics never wanted to give Trump credit for anything, we didn't want to give any credit to the critics who hated us. Even when they were right." Hence, not only did they who worked for Trump tie themselves "even more tightly to Trump and looked away", Trump became "the distant, erratic father we all wanted to please". The tendency for her became "to forgive his sins, forget his foibles, believe that he was better than outsiders were saying he was" (Grisham 2021: Introduction). "By ignoring all factual corrections, reversing all accusations, and branding all reality-based media as 'fake news'," Trump and his enablers have sought to "establish a false equivalence between trolling and truth" (Rauch 2021: 171). The ease with which content can be shared made possible by social media, means that, as Brooke rightly observes, regardless of intension, the "very act of sharing, even when the content is demonstrably false, serves to spread that falsehood almost as effectively" as spreading factually verified content (Brooke 2018).

Over and above Trump's usage of the term, as Zada aptly observes, "fake news" has become an "overhyped" catchphrase and "a trope", just like populism, I may add, that is "so used and abused, both in truth and deceit, that it can now refer to virtually anything". The danger in the proliferation of use and attribution of the label "fake news" is "the implication that, just because there is such a thing as 'fake news' all news that is not designated fake is therefore 'real'". While "fake news" is more usefully understood as "conscious deception operations" "designed to trick" media consumers and "involves stories deliberately made up to go viral", such falsehood should not blind one to "the more oblique, often inadvertent falsehoods that combine in piecemeal and collude with our perceptions to infect our overall picture of reality" that occur in the mainstream media, even when not labelled as "fake news" by Trump or any other critic. The distortion is compounded by the "limited ability" of "consumers to properly verify and contextualize the news" (Zada 2021: Part 1).

Some see Trump's contempt for democracy and institutions as the hallmark of his desire to cling to power, by demonstrating in no uncertain terms that, even in the world's foremost democracy, power ultimately lies with the real bullies of the playground. If a president has the right to appoint people who support his or her agenda and policies, why should anyone be critical of Trump's appointments if his agenda and policies are to grab democracy and institutions by the scruff of the neck, turn and twist them into compliance with his autocratic desires and "absolutist view of executive power"?[141] As Stephanie Grisham writes, when she noted that she would "still be working with the first lady, too" just before Trump officially hired her as White House press secretary and communications director, Trump told her: "But remember, I'm the only one who matters" (Grisham 2021: Photo Section). Arguing that Trump tried and largely succeeded "to turn himself into a king", Res rightly asserts that while in principle nobody is above the law, "Donald Trump has revealed that the democratic system in America is only as good as the person who is entrusted with preserving it" (Res 2020: Introduction). The conclusion by many was that Trump had acted as a madman, and as a despot. For purely selfish reasons, it would be argued, Trump pushed Americans to do more than pay lip service to democracy and to render its processes less ritualistic and honorific. In his mind, he threw open the curtains for the usually manipulated wider American public to see into the phoney and sterile enactment of American democracy by self-serving politicians in Washington, who do not hesitate to make evident that their own political fortunes are more important to them than the business of being truthful to democracy (Welfens 2019; Pfeiffer 2020).

Indeed, as Kakutani has argued, "the more clownish aspects of Trump the personality should not blind us to the monumentally serious consequences of his assault on truth and the rule of law, and the vulnerabilities he has exposed in our institutions and digital communications" (Kakutani 2018: 16). It could be argued as well – though some like Drezner (2020) would disagree – that Trump's toddling and clownery, are an essential tool in an elaborate technology of deception and diversion, purposely and strategically deployed to distract the masses and the media from paying attention to important causes and events, and especially to controversies pertaining to Trump and/or his administration. Be it in the form of pronouncements at rallies, or as tweets, retweets, posts and memes shared on Facebook, Instagram and other platforms, Trump's clownery and toddling could be seen as shadowing masks that diffuse and simplify social complexities and political controversies into slogans, catch words and phrases to be used to fuel political tensions, culture and identity wars, chaos, confusion and feelings of helplessness and abdication in the interest of power without responsibility or accountability. As Omarosa Manigault Newman remembers as contestant in the first season of *The Apprentice*, who later on joined the Trump campaign and followed him all the way to the White House, "Trump demanded respect and deference", and had little respect for those who "showed fear". "He loved conflict, chaos, and confusion", and "he loved seeing people argue or fight". And "whenever there was a disagreement or an argument, his eyes lit up" (Newman 2018: Chapter 2).

Anne Applebaum has argued that, with "the right conditions, any society can turn against democracy", adding that "if history is anything to go by, all of our societies eventually will" (Applebaum 2020: 14). Writing with prescience in October 2017, Polakow-Suransky argued that where and when "rapid immigration and terrorist attacks occur simultaneously – and the terrorists belong to the same ethnic or religious group as the new immigrants – the combination of fear and xenophobia can be dangerous and destructive". One should hasten to add that this of course, only makes sense in a discursive context in which terrorism is already configured as the exclusive domain of certain ethnic/religious groups. Maintaining that the threat to Western democracy was not from Islamists, Polakow-Suransky argued that "white nationalism" as an ideology "poses a significantly greater threat to Western democracies", predicting that white nationalists will "eventually seek to trample the rights of immigrants and minorities and dismiss courts and constitutions as anti-democratic because they don't reflect the supposed preferences of 'the people'".[142] "The bad few years that democracies have had is no reason to tout the virtues of dictatorship and authoritarianism," Patten cautions.[143] To Martinelli, far from being "anti-democratic" or a "pathology of democracy", populism is more of "a symptom of democratic pathologies" that "implies an illiberal version of democracy, bringing to the surface the constant tension between the two components of the 'democracy of the modern', the liberal and the democratic". Populism "tries to solve the tension between the two by exploding" the liberal and limiting the democratic (Martinelli 2016: 22–23). Whether the challenges facing liberal democracy are life-threatening or not, as Brooks reiterates, nothing in life is inevitable, "but liberal democracy clearly ain't going to automatically fix itself".[144]

Harvard economists Alberto Alesina, Stefanie Stantcheva and Armando Miano have acknowledged "the polarization of reality" in the USA as real and growing. Drawing on a paper written by these economists, Edsall points to growing evidence "that Americans are polarized not only in their views on policy issues and attitudes toward government and society, but also in their perceptions of the same, factual reality accompanying it".[145] Such polarisation – which is not exactly new in American politics, according to Hawkins and Hawkins (2018: 56–58) – Kakutani indicates, has tended to be amplified by technology as "highly flammable accelerants", which, in the form of social media, often "undermine trust in institutions" and make it "more difficult to have the sorts of fact-based debates and discussions that are essential to democracy" (Kakutani 2018: 119 & 132). Although, it should be added, as Leonnig shows in her study of the secret service – a study that depicts an institution "weakened by arrogant, insular leadership, promotions based on loyalty rather than capability, years of slim budgets, and outdated technology" – that the institutions are constantly in need of reimagination in order not to become paper tiggers or shadows of themselves, and must not take the trust of the American public for granted (Leonnig 2021: Author's Note). A shortcoming, particularly acute under the Obama and Trump presidencies was "an overworked staff and an overstretched budget". Under Trump whose security needs were particularly challenging and costly (Leonnig 2021: Chapter 27), Leonnig writes:

The Secret Service was stretched so thin protecting all these people that some Trump aides getting protection occasionally had to ride in their agents' personal cars. Senior officials were told to give the Secret Service two hours' notice if they needed a ride, because they couldn't take a car out for the whole day. The Secret Service simply didn't have enough working vehicles to go around (Leonnig 2021: Chapter 26).

This, Leonnig explains, has led to some embarrassing and dangerous blunders in presidential security (Leonnig 2021: Chapter 26). While Trump did little to address the budget constraints of the Secret Service, the fact of his frequent travels meant extra costs. Leonnig writes:

> By traveling so often to his clubs, Trump was vacuuming up the money of not just the Secret Service and other federal agencies that secured his trips, but of everyone: scores of Republican politicians, corporate VIPs, special interest lobbyists, and foreign delegations, all of whom flocked to follow him, seeking an audience to curry his favor and paying his business for the special access (Leonnig 2021: Epilogue).

Rohde sees the need for the FBI and CIA as "enormously powerful" organisations to be "vigorously monitored by elected officials, the courts, and the press". He recognises the "long history of abuse" by both organisations, as well as "the improper actions of the low-level FBI officials who wiretapped former Trump campaign advisor Carter Page". However, he disagrees with Trump's rather exaggerated "conspiratorial" allegations of a "deep state" that is politically motivated in a witch hunt against him and his administration. On the contrary, Rohde reiterates, in making such unsubstantiated claims, Trump was effectively "creating a parallel, shadow government filled with like-minded loyalists, without transparency, democratic norms, or public processes — a 'deep state' of his own" (Rohde 2020: Epilogue). "The term 'deep state' had risen in popularity online among conservatives who believed that bureaucrats within the national security establishment were purposefully undermining Trump's presidency" (Sims 2019: Chapter 11).

From the perspective of Trump's supporters (Dean and Altemeyer 2020), Trump's populist antisystem politics has not been taken lightly by the liberals, the deep state and the government in particular. As Continetti recounts, although by historical and constitutional standards "the people" elected Donald Trump and endorsed his programme of nation-state populist reform in 2016, the liberals opted instead for "an unprecedented revolt" against Trump's victory. The decision to launch a Special Counsel investigation into Russian interference with the election was perceived by Trump supporters as an attempt by the government to reverse the will of the people.[146] To Continetti, Trump:

> [...] forced the winners of the global economy and the members of the D.C. establishment to reckon with the fact that they are resented, envied, opposed, and despised by about half the country. But this recognition did not humble the entrenched incumbents of the administrative state".[147]

Such resistance was reason enough for Trump to seek to turn the tables, by investigating his investigators, using his powerful position as President to smoke out, discipline and punish his "perceived enemies" and "deep state" opponents[148] (Simpson and Fritsch 2019: Chapter 12; McCabe 2019; Nance 2019; Reid 2019: Chapter 6; Strzok 2020; Rohde 2020: Chapter 17; Toobin 2020). As O'Brien writes, "For Donald, fighting back and knowing your enemies was more than mere prudence. It was a way of being, even at the tender age of eighteen" (O'Brien 2015[2005]: Chapter 2). Not only did Trump love to have, and to fight his enemies, he liked beating his enemies to the ground (O'Brien 2015[2005]: Chapter 5). Ironically, Frum remarks, it is not the "deep state" as a whole that bothered Trump, only that which insisted on the rule of law as provided for constitutionally. For, "even as Trump defied the 'deep state' of the rule of law, his administration empowered the 'deep state' of economic monopoly and privileged favor-seeking", converting political power into economic benefit in the form of tax cuts for himself and his wealthy supporters, while leaving out in the cold, his fervent support base among others (Frum 2020: Chapter 6). Thus, if right-wing populism was driven in part by economic considerations, there was little evidence that Trump, in his tax policy, was living up to the expectations of his millions of working-class white supporters. In the absence of delivery on the economic front, it is hardly surprising that

Trump has found more fertile ground in the culture and identity politics of anger, fear, hate and scapegoating predicated on a racialised hierarchy of humanity.

Trump has not hesitated in using his overwhelming popularity with the Republican party base to discipline Republican politicians who have dared to contradict him or failed to do his bidding, a vindictiveness that has continued post his presidency, as he has maintained control of the party in which he claims an "enduring and unrivaled power" (Leonnig and Rucker 2021: Epilogue). Trump may have left the presidency, but as Wolff notes, "he absolutely believes he is the single most powerful political entity in the United States, holding the power to anoint or de-anoint any Senate or House member in a Trump state" (Wolff 2021a: Epilogue). He revels at and is energised by the "parade of Republican politicians flocking to Mar-a-Lago all spring to kiss his ring" and seek his endorsement, which he sees as proof of "the value of his stock". In Trump's words: "I don't say this in a braggadocious way, but if they don't get the endorsement, they don't win" (Leonnig and Rucker 2021: Epilogue).

Regarding Trump's power to punish and to redeem, Wolff conjectures that Trump's pardon of Steve Bannon in the final hours of his presidency, despite the latter's "frequent and public disloyalties" was "perhaps his only real act of forgiveness and magnanimity" (Wolff 2021a: Chapter 11). Leonnig and Rucker describe the Bannon pardon as the "most controversial", pointing to the fact that prior to the pardon Bannon "had been charged [...] with defrauding donors to a charity that had been established to privately fund the wall on the southern border" (Leonnig and Rucker 2021: Chapter 22). It is perhaps worth recalling, as Sims remarks, that "Bannon was a survivor", who "had weathered being on the outs with the President before", including "when he seemed to be taking too much credit for Trump's election victory". According to Sims, Bannon's "most valuable asset" was "the fact that he and the President had an ideological mind-meld on Trump's favorite issues—immigration, trade, and foreign affairs". Their kindred mindedness consisted of Bannon "ideologically aligned with the President and encouraging him to go with his gut, disrupt the status quo, and demand 'the establishment' get on board or get out of the way" (Sims 2019: Chapter 9). According to a tally shared by Leonnig and Rucker, by the end of Trump's presidency, "88 percent of pardons" by him had gone to "people who had personal ties to the president or who furthered his political aims" (Leonnig and Rucker 2021: Chapter 20).

Empathetic to Trump and his supporters, Brooks asks:

> [...] if you weaken family, faith, community and any sense of national obligation, where is that social, emotional and moral formation supposed to come from? How will the virtuous habits form? Naked liberalism has made our society an unsteady tree. The branches of individual rights are sprawling, but the roots of common obligation are withering away. Freedom without covenant becomes selfishness. [....] Freedom without connection becomes alienation.[149]

Brooks concludes that "Trump offers people cultural solutions to their alienation problem", drawing on history to argue that, "people will prefer fascism to isolation, authoritarianism to moral anarchy".[150]

McBain hails Trump's "knack for stoking the politics of fear, anger and racial resentment", as something that could do good by marking "the end of American optimism". She is of the opinion that "Faith in the American dream has persisted for too long, even as social mobility has stalled, jobs have disappeared and the population has sickened".[151] Brooks wonders the extent to which Americans fully grasp just how much "fear pervades our society and sets the emotional tone for our politics". He characterises the Trump era as "a time defined by fear" – a fear stoked by politicians, exacerbated by a very polarised landscape of media that either implacably criticises or blindly supports the populist strongman of a leader, and coming up from below "in the form of childhood trauma and insecurity". To Brooks, "Fear stokes anger, which then stokes more fear".[152]

MacGillis and ProPublica argue that to understand "why so many regular Americans were drawn to a man like Donald Trump," it is important to take seriously the reality of "less privileged white Americans" who "are in crisis". According to them, "the bitterness" which "Donald Trump has tapped into among white Americans in struggling areas is aimed not just at those of foreign extraction". The bitterness is equally "directed toward fellow countrymen who have become foreigners of a different sort, looking down on the natives, if they bother to look at all".[153] It is perhaps with allusion to this, that, Tierney argues, the lack of an external threat is part of the cause of current discord in the United States. "The existence of the other may be essential to shore up American identity and reinforce a sense of political exceptionalism." However, Tierney believes that the solution to the current discord is not to "yearn for an enemy to arise", or to "deliberately create one". Instead, he calls for US presidents to "rally people around a positive project", as "Americans need something to fight for—before they find someone to fight against".[154]

Brownstein maintains that many in Europe under the grip of conservative populism in 2016 viewed "Trump's rise less as an American singularity than the escalation of a trend toward defensive nationalism across the Western industrialized world".[155] Fukuyama suggests that the rise in populism be read as a failure of establishment politics and not necessarily as a failure of democracy in America. Instead, he suggests that the rise in populist-type candidates in American politics could be interpreted as proof that democracy is "working better than expected". Radical outsiders have been accorded preference by voters. Thus, Fukuyama contends, the question should not be why populists were able to make such gains in 2016 "but why it took them so long to do so", especially considering the socioeconomic plight of the white working class. This class has borne the brunt of "economic stagnation" together with an increase in death – nearly half a million people – related to suicide, drug use and crime.[156]

Sections of this population have for long been characterised as "white trash". Nancy Isenberg, in her book *White Trash: The 400-Year Untold History of Class in America,* explores in historical perspective the predicaments of often stereotyped, marginalised and stigmatised working class white Americans trapped in naturalised cycles of poverty that force them to waste their humanity away in a context which otherwise exudes abundance in resources and opportunities for much more than the purportedly meritocratic elites and propertied class. Throughout history, this category of Americans has tended to be perceived as losers and unwanted and as stagnant and expendable, hence the words "waste", "rubbish" and "trash" employed in their regard. In the 20th century "when the eugenics movement flourished" with interest on "thoroughbreds" and physical prowess, those who passed the litmus test for white trash "were the class of degenerates targeted for sterilization" in a manner akin to "inferior animal stocks" (Isenberg 2016: Preface). As Isenberg aptly observes:

> At all times, white trash remind us of one of the American nation's uncomfortable truths: the poor are always with us. A preoccupation with penalizing poor whites reveals an uneasy tension between what Americans are taught to think the country promises—the dream of upward mobility—and the less appealing truth that class barriers almost invariably make that dream unobtainable. Of course, the intersection of race and class remains an undeniable part of the overall story (Isenberg 2016: Preface).

In the concluding paragraph of the book, Isenberg writes:

> White trash is a central, if disturbing, thread in our national narrative. The very existence of such people—both in their visibility and invisibility—is proof that American society obsesses over the mutable labels we give to the neighbors we wish not to notice. "They are not who we are." But they are who we are and have been a fundamental part of our history, whether we like it or not (Isenberg 2016: Epilogue).

Even as Donald Trump declared himself a "supersized version" of it (O'Brien 2015[2005]), he acknowledged at the inception of his 2015 presidential campaign as well, that "The American dream is dead!" as he promised to "bring it back bigger and better than ever" and "make America great again!" (Reid 2019: Introduction). Trump's appealing negativity aside, Reid argues, "For millions of Americans, a President Donald Trump meant jobs and opportunity and a gaudy, joyous spectacle of gold-plated success" (Reid 2019: Chapter 5). The American Dream remains elusive, regardless of race, ethnicity, religion or gender. As Wylie observes, "A white man living in a trailer park doesn't see himself as a member of a privileged class, though others may see him that way just because he's white" (Wylie 2019: Chapter 7). Jessica Bruder's award-winning study, *Nomadland: Surviving America in the Twenty-First Century*, shows people in a state of chronic homelessness, living in mobile caravans without a place they can call home, even as they long for homecoming (Bruder 2017). In some cases, these are people "driving away from the impossible choices that face what used to be the middle class", people "who never imagined being nomads" (Bruder 2017: xii). For those trapped in homelessness amid the apparent abundance of the American Dream, Bruder argues, "survival isn't enough. [...] Being human means yearning for more than subsistence. As much as food or shelter, we require hope". They take to the road in caravans to keep elusive hope alive (Bruder 2017: xiii).

In *Hillbilly Elegy: A Memoir of a Family and Culture in Crisis*, J. D. Vance, who "grew up poor, in the Rust Belt, in an Ohio steel town that has been hemorrhaging jobs and hope" for as long as he can remember, shares "a passionate and personal analysis of a culture [...] of poor, white Americans" in crisis, and "what a social, regional, and class decline feels like when you were born with it hanging around your neck" (Vance 2016: Introduction and blurb). According to Alix Kroeger of BBC News, though "profoundly conservative" and someone who understood the reasons for Trump's rise, "Mr Vance was not a Trump loyalist", adding that the *Hillbilly Elegy* "became one of the touchstones of the Trump years: a portrait of the forgotten white working class, a key to the voters overlooked by the coastal elites".[157] These working-class white Americans belong to a highly polarised country (Klein 2020), one that makes them feel like *Strangers in Their Own Land*, to quote Arlie Russell Hochschild's aptly titled book on their predicament.

However, Trump would not have won the 2016 election had he relied exclusively on their vote. It is noteworthy, for example, that 53 per cent white women, across the class divide, voted for Trump,[158] who won the election by harvesting more electoral college votes, despite losing the popular vote to Hillary Clinton, by almost three million votes (Norris and Inglehart 2019: 331; Dean and Altemeyer 2020: Chapter 5). Hillary Clinton, on the other hand, won only 37 per cent of the white vote, compared to Trump's 58 per cent (Wilkerson 2020: 328). For the centrality of whiteness and white supremacist ideology to Trump's ascendancy to power, in addition to Trump's perceived commitment to undoing every Obama legacy,[159] Coates suggests we see Trump more appropriately as "America's first white president" (Coates 2017: Epilogue). Regardless of whether or not Trump identifies himself or is identified with white supremacy, there is evidence to the effect that Trump's "bigoted rhetoric emboldened white supremacists to step out of the shadows" (Leonnig and Rucker 2021: Prologue), not only in the US but globally (Geary et al. 2020).

A development that, according to Phiri, has in turn occasioned or fed into a "counter-discursive, restitutional cultural populism" in black communities that is not dissimilar in its risky "hierarchical and exclusionary, separatist iterations" to Trump's "apocalyptic populist discourse" propagated in the main by "mainstream, white society" and internalised and reproduced in the form of anger, fear, hate and stereotypical violence by the ordinary folks they enchant and fire up with deceptive promise of supremacy (Phiri 2020: 45).

What is perplexing about white working-class Americans to many of their compatriots on the left, Hochschild observes, is their loyalty to "the Republican Party and Fox News" which many see as family, despite the determined intent by the latter to dismantle "much of the federal government, cutting help to the poor, and increasing the power and money of an already powerful and rich top 1 percent". Notwithstanding feeling like strangers in their own land, these Americans seem convinced that government is bad for them and their interest, that it is "a power-amassing elite, creating bogus causes to increase its control and handing out easy money in return for loyal Democratic votes" (Hochschild 2016: ix; see also Kreiss 2018).

This point about left-behind white Americans is made, even though, as should be evident to even the most touristic of observers, whites do not enjoy a monopoly of being working-class or underclass, landless farmers and precarious workers in the USA,[160] nor are whites the only racial category disadvantaged by deindustrialisation, globalisation and broad income inequality in the country. Black and Latino citizens seem carefully gerrymandered into invisibility in the configuration of entitlement and the hierarchies of citizenship in right-wing populism (Coates 2017: Chapter 8 & Epilogue; Reid 2019). "Working-class men, most of whom are white and live in rural and exurban parts of the United States" may suffer more from what Brooks calls a "dignity crisis" among "people left behind by economic change", but they are not alone in being treated by government "as liabilities to manage rather than as human assets to develop".[161] Lind suggests an analytical approach that identifies two class-based political spectrums, "one for the college-educated managerial-professional overclass minority and one for the non-college-educated working-class majority of all races", with each having a "right", a "left" and a "center" of its own (Lind 2020: Chapter 5).

To Kaletsky, "people outside the workforce: pensioners, middle-aged homemakers, and men with low educational qualifications receiving disability payments" constitute the "main demographic groups behind the anti-establishment upsurge".[162] Buruma depicts contemporary right-wing populism in Europe and the USA as a "Status anxiety [that] is gripping white people throughout the West", and one that "is probably exacerbated by the rise of Chinese power and the sense that Europe and the United States are losing their global preeminence". He provides an example of how Trump mines such anxieties for political ends. Following a clash between peaceful protesters and a mob of mostly white supporters of his, "Trump declared that the mobs in Charlottesville included 'some very fine people'" on both sides. A second example was when Trump called Mexican immigrants "rapists". In doing that, Buruma believes, Trump "dragged racism into the political mainstream". Hence Buruma's conclusion that, "Once the most powerful person in the Western world incites mob violence, it is clear that the West, however one defines it, is in serious trouble."[163]

It is significant, Fuchs argues, that Trump, in his speeches, hardly mentions or criticises the exploitation of foreign workers or immigrant workers by American capitalists (himself included), who tend to subject such workers to "extremely low wages in order to maximise profits". Instead, Trump has regularly argued that "illegal immigrants are criminal and have negative impacts on jobs, wages, housing, schools, etc.". Such failure to condemn illegal exploitation of immigrants is hypocritical and betrays Trump's politics of scapegoating immigrants (Fuchs 2018: 139–140). It is equally hypocritical for Trump to be so virulently hostile to illegal immigrants in rhetoric and policy, when as Simpson and Fritsch write, "Trump's record revealed him to be a longtime, avid, and quite deliberate bulk consumer of illegal immigrant labor", as well as to have a "long record of recruiting workers from abroad and importing them to the United States" (Simpson and Fritsch 2019: Chapter 3).

It is curious that the Republican voters (harvested in the main from white working and middle classes who feel left behind or invaded by outsiders) would settle for someone like Donald Trump, a person who is said to excel in cold-heartedness and to be totally lacking in empathy and compassion, and known for his perfect record for never taking responsibility for anything, as well as for his capacity to downplay, blame shift, goalpost shift and spin his way out of reality (Kivisto 2017; Res 2020: Chapter 7 & Epilogue), not to mention his masochistic statements and behaviours. Stephanie Grisham, one of the longest serving senior members of staff in the Trump administration admits this was what she found "refreshing" about Trump. She adds that Trump "was bold and poked at convention. He challenged dumb rules that people had just lived with for no reason. He said things people thought but never said. He took positions that no Republican had ever taken, including some shared by Bernie Sanders" (Grisham 2021: Introduction). Yet, judging by adherence to "political correctness" or "cancel culture" and the spiral of silence it engineers (Dreher 2020; Rauch 2021), few Americans would disagree in public with presidential historian Michael Beschloss's sentiment that what the American public wants as president is someone with a heart so that even if he or she makes a mistake people would say it is not because of indifference on his or her part, but because the president is human. In other words, it is OK for a leader to not get it right,[164] as long as he or she has a heart.

Yet, being heartless seems insufficient to deter many people from voting Trump, as the 74,222,958 votes for him at the 2020 presidential election would attest. Hence the question, to what extent does political correctness, tolerance or accommodation that champions "sensitivity, community harmony, social tranquility, inclusiveness, multiculturalism" provoke even more discord and polarisation with its "increasingly righteous and indiscriminate enforcement of civility in society's discussions and debates" (Will 2013: xiv)? Put differently, how does one balance between the need for inclusion and the need for critical mindedness, open inquiry and freedom of expression of singularity and individuality of being and reason as attributes of an open society (Rauch 2013[1993], 2021)? In other words, how do we from our different entry and vantage points, get along by agreeing to disagree? How are we to ensure, as Dreher claims, that "'diversity,' 'inclusivity,' 'equity,' and other egalitarian jargon" are not simply "powerful mechanisms" created by the left or progressives "for controlling thought and discourse" and for marginalising "dissenters as evil" (Dreher 2020: Introduction)?

To Lozada, "Trump feels like an American hallucination" embodying "every national fixation in excess". Fiction and reality are intermingled. Lozada claims that the predictions of many literatures are realised in Trump (totalitarianism, borders, concentration camps, violence, lies, etc.), and that with the advent of Trump and his brand of populism, the American dystopian novel seems to be happening in America and elsewhere in the world.[165]

Ferguson attempts to understand the rise in the politics of populism in America with a focus on Trump supporting ageing white America – conservative and Republican in the main. He picks up on the tension between truth and fiction by comparing modern-day America to dystopian novels that predicted Nazi-like America. Ferguson looks beyond the explanation of the decreasing middle class in America and identifies an increased mortality rate among middle-aged white Americans, largely through drug overdoses (immediate or spanning time) and resulting in a 50 per cent increase in liver disease and other conditions. Deduced is that the "white underclass is not so much mad as hell as sick as hell". The two are not mutually exclusive. Written in 2015, Ferguson wrongly predicts that Trump will turn out to be fiction and "sanity will prevail" or "Trump will be beaten".[166] Sanity did not prevail, Trump won and his losing did not begin to take shape until the mid-terms in 2018, followed in 2020 with him losing to Joe Biden. Not being a gracious loser, Trump decided to fight like hell, using every tool in his autocratic toolkit, from disinformation to mobilising his steadfast supporters to storm the seat of constitutional democracy.

Trump's leadership of the Republican party and popularity with the Republican base should not imply that Trump is conservative in any major way, insists Dreher. To him, "Trump is a politician of the nationalist Right, but he is not a conservative in any philosophical or cultural sense".[167] If anything, Trump is the Republican party's Frankenstein who bulldozed his way into Republican politics in 2016, according to senator Harry Reed of Nevada, echoing Robert Kagan.[168] James concurs, linking Trump much more to what he terms "the nihilistic imposters" who have been acting in the name of conservatism.[169] Hence Krugman's conclusion that Trumpism may share the "racism and contempt for democracy" of European populism, "but European populism is at least partly real, while Trumpist populism is turning out to be entirely fake, a scam sold to working-class voters who are in for a rude awakening".[170] In this regard, Trumpist populism is similar to Trump University, as both are sold to consumers as tested and guaranteed to deliver success, but which on a closer look, have little more than good salesmanship going for them (O'Brien 2015[2005]).

Wallace writes about his grandfather, Henry A. Wallace (33rd Vice President of the US, 1941–1945), who "warned about hucksters spouting populist themes but manipulating people and institutions to achieve the opposite. They pretend to be on the side of ordinary working people", "paying lip service to democracy and the common welfare". But at the same time, those dissemblers who seek personalised power without responsibility "distrust democracy because it stands for equal opportunity". Wallace believes his grandfather "predicted President Trump",[171] for whom, as Pillar seeks to demonstrate in an article aptly titled "A President without a purpose", the presidency is nothing but "a huge ego trip for an extreme narcissist with a knack for demagoguery".[172]

Holden et al. have compared Trump to Spiro Agnew, who served as vice-president to Richard Nixon, and whose personal and political history is very similar to Trump's. Both are just as similar in their affinity for international antidemocratic strongmen and in how they harnessed anti-elitism, disregard for tradition and populism to rise to the top of the Republican party. "As unlikely national political leaders, both Trump and Agnew savaged the political norms of the day with their open hostility toward the media and their use of rhetoric, high and low, to brand their opponents." A noted difference between the two is that unlike Trump, who has attracted tremendous scholarship and a proliferation of books, there is very little published on Agnew in terms of scholarly books (Holden et al. 2019: Chapter 7).

Dowd has termed the Trump presidency as "all theatrics, all performance, all form with no content" with "his script" being "the only truth".[173] Trump does not hide the fact: "I'm a total act and I don't understand why people don't get it," he reportedly told Anthony Scaramucci (Rucker and Leonnig 2020: 191–192), whom Trump recruited briefly as communications director and charged with the important task of unmasking and ridding the White House of leakers to the press in the manner of the Pied-Piper of Hamelin. Scaramucci undid himself eleven days into the job after a media outburst in which he accused Trump's first Chief of Staff, Reince Priebus of plotting against him and of leaking (Sims 2019: Chapter 9). To Kellner, Trump is a "one-dimensional man" who is all about winning, who with his one-dimensional being has a "gigantic ego that must be fed with unlimited amounts of adulation, money, power, and attention" (Kellner 2016: 95). Drawing on *Surviving Autocracy* by Masha Gessen (2020), Szalai argues that:

> [...] the United States has been terribly unprepared for a figure like Donald Trump. Not because he came out of nowhere; if anything, he took advantage of a political system that was ripe for a demagogue, swollen already by money and the powers concentrated in the executive branch.[174]

With a penchant for what Masha Gessen refers to as "performing fascism".[175] Trump would seek to assert total dominance by personalising power and institutions and using a narrow and racialised nationalism of keeping America white through the merciless suppression of difference and opposition, along with the scapegoating of minorities.

Fukuyama claims that in the USA the Democrats' focus on identity politics has alienated many working-class white Americans,[176] who, as Brooks affirms, constitute the base of the Republican party and, in general, favour "closed trade, closed borders and American withdrawal abroad".[177] According to Fuchs, data from the 2016 election indicate that:

> [...] the typical Donald Trump voter is an older white man, who lives in rural America, is self-employed or a blue-collar worker, has a low level of education, has fears about immigration and economic decline, and is angry with the government (Fuchs 2018: 85).

It should be added, as well, the significant percentage of white middle-aged women who voted for Trump – making up part of the 53 per cent of white women who voted for him – without whom he could not have won.[178] Could Trump's appeal as an outsider to the perceived sterility of Washington politics have trumped Hillary Clinton's popularity even amongst women as the first woman nominated by one of the two main political parties to contest for the presidency? As Solana and Talbott argue, many working-class Americans, "especially in rural and blue-collar areas, are pessimistic about the future and nostalgic for a seemingly better past". Similar to

Europe, "there is widespread mistrust of elites and experts, and feverish enthusiasm for anti-establishment populists".[179]

Stephens points out, in an article titled "The perils of a populist paean to ignorance" that, under the grip of the populism of the moment, facts, science, the opinions of experts, reason and evidence are dismissed and replaced by prejudice, populism, majoritarianism, fear, anger, lies and ignorance. Stephen illustrates this tendency with the example of Michael Gove during the Brexit campaign, who, arguing that "facts were not as important as the feelings of the British voter" (Nichols 2017: 209), declared: "People in this country have had enough of experts." In light of such contempt and disrespect for expertise, Stephens asks when Mr Gove – a former education secretary – will be piling books onto bonfires. He goes on to predict that "soon enough, migrants – and Muslims especially – replace heretics and witches" to be metaphorically burned at the stake. Acknowledging that experts do also get it wrong, Stephens identifies that local communities receiving large numbers of migrants are coarsened into believing that "the remedy is a simple act of revenge".[180] It is ironic, to note in passing, that while Trump personally hated and repeatedly complained about the special counsel investigation led by Robert Mueller into Russian interference with the 2016 presidential elections to favour him (Toobin 2020), Trump did not hesitate to conduct witch-hunts of his own, especially against immigrants and various minorities that did not embrace his cause (McCallion 2019; Reid 2019), often mobilising and politicising his Justice Department, especially under Bill Barr as Attorney General, to do his bidding (Honig 2021). He is rich and powerful, yet so easily turns himself into the victim, just as other powerful and privileged elite feel victimised by the populism that he embraces. To be elite, it would appear, is to seek to turn the tables of victimhood on those truly deserving to be considered victims of the excesses of power and privilege.

Davies believes the revenge is targeted in the main at government as an overarching bureaucracy that is often detached from the local context and the felt needs of people on the ground. "One way to understand the rise of reactionary populism today," according to Davies, "is as the revenge of sovereignty on government." Far from "simply a backlash after decades of globalization", the revenge is against facilitators of such globalisation in the form of technocratic, multilateral political power that is increasingly divorced from local identities. Populists like Boris Johnson and Donald Trump – who thrive "on galvanising longstanding discontent and prejudice through inflammatory rhetoric and egregious falsehoods" [181] – in their "madness", with or without "method", refuse "to listen to inconvenient evidence, of the sort provided by officials and experts". [182]

To Buruma, it is a most dangerous idea to act, as is common in contemporary populism, as if "political parties are obsolete, and should be replaced by movements led by charismatic leaders who act as the voice of 'the people'", while treating "all dissenters" as "enemies of the people". [183] Such blanket condemnation of dissent is not different from the stigmatisation and accusation which autocrats and dictators find handy in silencing critics and instituting one-dimensionalism with Machiavellian decisiveness remindful of Mussolini and fascism (Kakutani 2018: 102–103; Martinelli 2016: 24). As Finchelstein indicates, "populists desperately need enemies of the people to confirm the fiction that they speak and act in the name of the national community" (Finchelstein 2017: Epilogue). Matters are compounded by the fact that "the self-defeating nature of populist policies" does not appear to "blunt their appeal" in "left behind places", writes *The Economist*. For this reason, *The Economist* appeals to "Mainstream parties" to "offer voters who feel left behind a better vision of the future, one that takes greater account of the geographical reality behind the politics of anger". [184]

Krugman has accused Trump of "fake populism", arguing that Trump only appears to be on the side of his overwhelmingly supportive "white working-class voters, who believed that he was on their side". Yet Trump's "real policy agenda" has not differed much from "standard-issue modern Republicanism" such as "huge tax cuts for billionaires and savage cuts to public programs, including those essential to many Trump voters". [185] In this sense, Krugman suggests that US Trumpism is "different" from European populism. "The campaign rhetoric may have included promises to keep Medicare and Social Security intact and replace Obamacare with something 'terrific', but this is not what happened following the election", as "policies [...] remained conservatively Republican". [186] The very idea that Trump wanted to replace Obamacare without a clear alternative elicited the following remark from Joe Biden: "I cannot comprehend the cruelty that's driving him to inflict this pain on the very people he is supposed to serve".[187] To Serwer, "The Cruelty Is the Point". The pleasure, delight and joy Trump and his enablers derive from inflicting cruelty and watching others suffer, Serwer argues, "is an adhesive that binds them to one another" in their "shared scorn for those they hate and fear: immigrants, black voters, feminists, and treasonous white men who empathize with any of those who would steal their birthright". The infliction of cruelty is meant to leave no one in doubt about where and with whom power lies, and who qualities for the rewards of citizenship: "Only the president [Trump] and his allies, his supporters, and their anointed are entitled to the rights and protections of the law and, if necessary, immunity from it. The rest [...] are entitled only to cruelty, by their whim" (Serwer 2021: Chapter 5).

The elites are like team A and team B of the same football club playing each other. Whether team A or team B wins or loses, the club can count on winning all the time. Put differently, the elites are like garbage entrepreneurs. Irrespective of whether they are producing or recycling garbage, they are there to ensure that nothing is left to waste. Not even waste. Nothing is too used to be used. Thus, when a section of the elites creates waste as it seeks to make economic and cultural capital, another retrieves and makes political and cultural capital out of the waste. Either way, the elites are winners, financially or politically, with neoliberalism or with populism. Just as the Washington elite and professional class are criticised for business-as-usual globalism and institutionalism at the disservice of the left-behind (Parmar 2017) "truly patriotic Americans", Trump the elite and his elite enablers and loyal flatterers, could be said to be milking the very same dispossessed and disenchanted left-behind for political capital. Whatever the form of capital, economic, political or cultural, it is the elites, through their monopoly of the power to manipulate symbols, to define and confine, who are most likely to be laughing all the way to the bank (be this a cash bank or a vote bank), leaving their victims high and dry. As if in a game of cards with a confidence trickster, it does not matter the card that ordinary Americans pick or the elite they play – neoliberalism or populism – because the left-behind are bound to lose. The game played by the elite is a zero-sum game that seems programmed, a priori, to always favour the elites, almost as if they alone matter. It serves up as fodder for the masses the rhetoric of democratic participation and the institutionalisation of opportunity as wallpaper over the cracks of elite opportunism.

Trump and Populist Strongmen Compared

It is impossible not to see parallels between Trump and other strongman leaders worldwide through the prism of authoritarianism, dictatorship and personalised rule. What marks Trump out as a reckless populist is his outright disrespect of US institutions and the Constitution to the extent that he tries to win elections by seeking unscrupulous foreign help from enemies of American democracy like Vladimir Putin and Xi Jinping, thereby conflating private interests and personal gain with national security interest and the public good. Like fellow strongmen elsewhere, Trump sought to draw sustenance from the surging lack of trust in either experts or politicians among ordinary Americans and thrived on divide-and-rule and on constructing and perpetuating the idea of external and internal enemies. Not unlike his fellow strongmen, Trump has sought to tame, silence or discredit media and journalists critical of him and to effusively endorse and seek endorsement from media outlets and journalists supportive of him while simultaneously harnessing social media as complementary or alternative channels for communicating with "the people" with less conventional mediation and filtration. To many a liberal elite writer and commentator, Trump and what some have termed his "reality TV authoritarianism" has cost the US its much-envied role as the global gendarme of democracy and seriously damaged its diplomacy.

Let's take a closer look.

In *The Plot to Betray America*, Nance writes and substantiates in great detail how "Trump has openly and loudly embraced his relationship with dictators and mass murderers", while equally making public, his "disdain for" America's "closest allies, long-standing security cooperation, and historic alliances" (Nance 2019: Chapter 14). Analysts have been quick to establish similarities not only between Trump and other populists in the West, but also with populists in regions of the world considered to be prone to authoritarianism, dictatorship and personalised rule (Fuchs 2018; Norris and Inglehart 2019; Applebaum 2020; Ben-Ghiat 2020; Dean and Altemeyer 2020). Kendall-Taylor and Frantz write on how democracies fall apart and why populism is a pathway to autocracy. They argue that:

> Post–Cold War populists such as Chávez, Putin, and Erdogan took a slow and steady approach to dismantling democracy. These leaders first come to power through democratic elections and subsequently harness widespread discontent to gradually undermine institutional constraints on their rule, marginalize the opposition, and erode civil society. [...] This strategy makes it hard to discern when the break with democracy actually occurs, and its insidiousness poses one of the most significant threats to democracy in the twenty-first century.[188]

Rachman highlights how the rise of Trump fits into a larger global trend at play since 2012. He believes that Trump "exhibits many of the characteristics" of a "crop of strongman leaders, including Messrs Putin, Xi, Erdogan, Sisi, Modi, Orbán and Duterte"[189] (see also *Journal of Global Faultlines* 2017; Kenny 2017).

For an insider view, Bolton, after serving as Trump's national security advisor, writes of "Trump's penchant to, in effect, give personal favors to dictators he liked", even if this amounted to "obstruction of justice as a way of life" or "appeasing our adversaries, totally contrary to our interests" (Bolton 2020: Chapter 14). Similarly, Trump expected foreign leaders to do him favours in turn, as evidenced by his "quid pro quo" or "this for that" phone call making US $400 million in security and military aid to the Ukraine contingent on a public pledge by President Volodymyr Zelensky to investigate Trump's political rival Joe Biden and his son, Hunter Biden, for which Trump was impeached (Bolton 2020: Chapter 14; Vindman 2021: Chapter 1), as well as by reports that China had offered Trump background information on Hunter Biden.[190] According to Bolton, at a meeting with Chinese President Xi Jinping at the Osaka G20 summit, Trump, "stunningly, turned the conversation to the coming US presidential election, alluding to China's economic capability to affect the ongoing campaigns, pleading with Xi to ensure he'd win". (Bolton 2020: Chapter 10). Where established channels of diplomacy and foreign relations were an encumbrance, Trump did not hesitate to bypass these, as the implementation of his attempts to tie Ukraine aid to investigations of his domestic political opponents illustrates. Private interests and personal gain were conflated with national security interest and public good (Burns 2019; Nance 2019: Chapter 13; Bolton 2020: Chapter 14).[191]

Despite vigorously rejecting the suggestion by Hillary Clinton during a debate in 2016 that he was a puppet of Putin's (Rauch 2021: 167), Trump was drawn to Putin in a "bizarre relationship" that, according to Simpson and Fritsch, begged the question "why was Trump so smitten with Putin, who seemed fond of Trump in return?" (Simpson and Fritsch 2019: Chapter 1). Putin, according to Bolton, thought he could play Trump like a fiddle.[192] Trump's bizarre relationship with Putin was noticeable during his campaign and throughout his presidency, leading to much speculation on what could account for the strong grip that Putin had on him (Simpson and Fritsch 2019; Wolff 2019: Chapter 13; Miller 2018; Nance 2019; Reid 2019: Chapter 6). In December 2019, Speaker of the House, Nancy Pelosi, implying that Putin had him under his thumb, declared that with President Trump, "All roads lead to Putin".[193] On his part, House Republican leader Kevin McCarthy, reportedly told colleagues in 2016: "I think Putin pays Trump".[194]

To many, Trump has littered the landscape with circumstantial evidence in this regard, amongst which reports that: "Trump revealed highly classified information to Russian foreign minister and ambassador" at an exclusive White House meeting in 2017;[195] went to "extraordinary lengths to conceal details of his conversations" with Putin from senior officials in his administration, after a meeting at the G20 summit in Hamburg, Germany in 2017, as well as after their Helsinki summit[196]; and endorsing and promoting fictional accounts by Russia to frame Ukraine as responsible for the hacking of the 2016 election that was blamed on Putin and Russia,[197] thereby making it possible for Putin to declare in turn, "Thank God [...] no one is accusing us of interfering in the U.S. elections anymore; now they're accusing Ukraine"[198] (see also Wolff 2019: Chapter 13). In the widely recognised global information wars, Stengel presents the US as playing more catchup than a leadership role, having largely lost the global battle against disinformation, which democracies are not particularly good at combating, given the principle of freedom of thought and expression that underpin their very existence, and in view of how government is ill-equipped to fight such battles. The spread of disinformation is accelerated by social media platforms on which popularity matters more than accuracy and truthfulness, and there are few barriers to and hardly any gatekeeping or fact-checking of content (Stengel 2019). Another reason why America is playing catchup in the disinformation wars, according to Stengel, is that these are wars that do not cost much in terms of equipment or sophisticated technologies. As he puts it:

> One reason for the rise in global disinformation is that waging an information war is a lot cheaper than buying tanks and Tridents, and the return on investment is higher. Today, the selfie is mightier than the sword. It is asymmetric warfare requiring only computers and smartphones and an army of trolls and bots. You don't even have to win; you succeed if you simply muddy the waters. It's far easier to create confusion than clarity. There is no information dominance in an information war. There is no unipolar information superpower. These days, offensive technologies are cheaper and more effective than defensive ones. Information war works for small powers against large ones, and large powers against small ones; it works for states and for non-state actors—it's the great leveler. Not everyone can afford an F-35, but anyone can launch a tweet (Stengel 2019: Introduction).

Brooks explains the rise of Putin to become "the most influential man in the world" and to bring about what has come to be known as "Putinism". To Brooks, Putin's influence is summed up by how successfully Putin has capitalised on "times of anxiety and distrust" to make a case for "clear centralized authority" rather than "dispersed, amorphous authority"; "to rally people around" his person rather than "an abstraction"; "to sell cynicism" rather than "idealism"; and "to sell us/them distinctions" rather than "tolerance for cultural diversity".[199] Just like Putinism, Trumpism has drawn its sustenance from the "nervous state" of Americans, who, as Moore indicates, "live in anxious times, no longer trusting either experts or politicians, fearful of terror, often dwelling in the past, unsure what the criteria for truth are in a world of alternative facts". Americans, she claims, "are viscerally geared up for imminent catastrophe". The resentment rife among Americans, Moore points out, "is the key emotion in the rise of populism. Nationalism does not arise unbidden but occurs when emotions such as fear, anxiety and […] loneliness can find no democratic voice".[200] We need societies that can listen, and that are configured and enabled to be responsive to the dynamism that characterises them and the world of which they are a part.

Trump has also been likened to Putin in their brands of populism which thrive on divide-and-rule, and constructs and perpetuates both the idea of external and internal enemies in their articulations of "we" versus the "other" (Hauser 2018). Putin is arguably the only leader in the world that Trump never tweeted or said anything bad about, even as Trump was notoriously foul-mouthed from his 2016 campaign, during his presidency and till he left the White House on 20 January 2021. During his presidency, Trump displayed perplexing veneration and "subservience to Putin's agenda and the continuing campaign of obstruction and coordinated lies", with several of Trump's closest aides opting "to go to prison for long prison terms rather than tell the truth to investigators" (Simpson and Fritsch 2019: Epilogue).

Comparing Trump and Putin, Feifer indicates that both leaders "took office with a populism that caught their opponents off guard, upending their countries' political establishments with culture wars that helped divide and conquer their critics. Their withering assaults on their critics have also prompted opponents to believe that their only course of action is to resist the regimes at all costs". Although Trump, unlike Putin, did not effectively shut down media critics during his presidency, he did not hesitate "to wish they go out of business",[201] often alluding to "journalism that he finds threatening or unflattering" (Kakutani 2018: 95). This invariably meant every media outlet apart from Fox News and other right-wing media were treated as "fake news media", with Trump inviting his supporters to boycott them (Nyamnjoh 2018b: 45–52; Hassan 2019: Chapter 6). Trump, as "a man who looks at the world through a mirror" (Kalb 2018: 147), Kalb argues, has convinced himself that "he is God's gift to America", and thus "erupts with a special fury whenever he reads, or is told about, stories he regards as unfairly negative". With the authoritarian instinct, Trump believes he is "entitled to a good press", so when "coverage, on TV and in print, becomes relentlessly negative, as it often has been for Trump, he feels he must find an enemy, a handy scapegoat". For maximum effect, he presents the critical media not as his personal enemies, but as "enemy of the people" (Kalb 2018: xvi).

As a White House insider serving on the communication team who knew Trump well, Sims points out that "behind the scenes, the relationship between the press and the White House was more complicated—and sometimes more incestuous—than either side wanted to admit". While "Trump sincerely held most members of the media in low regard", equally true, although he did not like to admit it, was the fact that "he also craved their approval". To Trump, "being the topic of conversation—whether positive or negative—was what really mattered" (Sims 2019: Chapter 13). To Sims, it was an understanding that served both parties well:

> To the public, Trump versus the press was a bitter war. But behind the scenes, it was much more like professional wrestling. The reporters needed Trump and his team to leak to them and give them information or they couldn't break news. By contrast, Trump and his team needed them to get information out, or misinformation, or serve as a powerful and effective political foil. They also served two almost completely separate audiences—the press often seemed to be writing stories to get clicks from the Trump haters while the White House used those same stories to rile up the media haters. *Wash, rinse, repeat* (Sims 2019: Chapter 13).

Trump and the media were thus like porcupines who threatened each other with their quills, but who were equally sufficiently self-interested to negotiate conviviality and accommodate one another for mutual survival.

The fact that: "Americans still get more news from television than from any other source"; that "the most-watched form of television news is local news, relied upon by 37 percent of Americans"; that the local television "market is dominated by the lavishly pro-Trump Sinclair Broadcast Group"; that cable television, the most important news type is "dominated by Fox News, now reinforced by the new Fox-on-meth One American News Network (OANN)"; and that a significant number of Americans get their news from social media platforms (Frum 2020: Chapter 1), means that Trump could afford to insult and ignore the mainstream media critical of him without jeopardising his relationship with his base and without having to give up on propaganda as his preferred mode of communication.

To Trump supporters for whom politics is first and foremost "about identity, and not rational decision-making", Kreiss argues, Fox News makes them feel less like strangers in their own land. It is like family, that "provides a sense of identity, place, and belonging; emotional, social, and cultural support and security; and gives rise to political and social affiliations and beliefs". Together with Trump, Fox News speaks to their desire to "be restored to their rightful place at the center of the nation", and to be emotionally released from "the fetters of political correctness" that have "dictated they respect people of color, lesbians and gays, and those of other faiths" in a land they consider theirs, and where their authority ought to be final. Hence, to Kreiss, Fox News is best understood not as an information channel but as an "identity media outlet" primarily. It is an identity outlet "not only for the Republican Party, but also whites more generally who perceive themselves as the victims of Christian persecution and reverse racism". If Fox News and related identity media outlets teach us anything, Kreiss contends, it is about the "power in the claim of representing and working *for* particular publics, quite apart from any abstract claims to present the truth" (Kreiss 2018: 94–99).

To Wylie, this identity and cultural prism explains why Democrats and Republicans may watch the same newscast and reach opposite conclusions. If Fox News is effective, it is in its capacity to graft "an identity onto the minds of viewers, who then begin to interpret a debate about ideas as an *attack on their identity*". "This in turn", Wylie argues, "triggers a *reactance effect*, whereby alternative viewpoints actually strengthen" the resolve of the Fox News audience "in their original belief, because they sense a threat to their personal freedom". The more criticism Democrats direct at Fox News for its programmes and indifference to facts, "the more entrenched the audience's views and the angrier they became". This, according to Wylie, would explain why Fox News "viewers could reject criticism of Donald Trump for saying racist things", by internalising "the critique as an attack on *their own identity* rather than that of the candidate". Beyond Fox News and its viewers, "an insidious effect" of such cognitive biases is that "the more debate occurs, the more entrenched the audience becomes" (Wylie 2019: Chapter 5, italics in original). This is explained in part, Wylie claims, by the fact that "the area of the brain that is most highly activated when we process strongly held beliefs is the same area that is involved when we think about who we are and our identity" (Wylie 2019: Chapter 7).

Trump, Carpini asserts, has exploited "the multiaxiality and hyperreality of the current information environment" which "creates conditions in which we are always just one click of a mouse or remote control away from information that contradicts what we just heard, read, or saw". It is an environment that "makes it easier for ideologically committed citizens to hold fast to their prior beliefs regardless of the facts; for less politically engaged citizens to be uncertain, dazed, and confused; and for political elites to exploit this situation" (Carpini 2018: 21). A rare disappointment with Fox News by Trump came on election night on 3 November 2020, when Fox News was the first television channel to project that Joe Biden had won in Arizona. As Leonnig and Rucker report, "Trump, who had been watching Fox, was livid. He could not fathom that the conservative news network he had long considered an extension of his campaign was the first news organization to call Arizona for Biden. This was a betrayal" (Leonnig and Rucker 2021: Chapter 16). It was, to put it differently, like being stabbed in the back by a trusted member of the family.

In a speech at the CIA following his inauguration, Miller writes, "Trump called members of the media 'the most dishonest human beings on earth' for refusing to acknowledge the "'million, million and a half people'" he said had attended his inauguration the previous day—an erroneous claim off by a factor of four" (Miller 2018: Prologue). Tweeting on 17 February 2017, barely a month into his presidency, Trump singled out for attack what he termed "The FAKE NEWS media", labelling them "the enemy of the American people". These included *The New York Times*, CNN, NBCNews, ABC and CBS. Disregarding the possibility that calling some media outlets "enemies of the people" "could incite violence", Karl reports, Trump "did not retract the phrase, and he certainly didn't apologize for it. He kept using it" (Karl 2020: Chapter 11; see also Reid 2019: Chapter 8; Gessen 2020: Chapter 15; Kessler et al. 2020: Conclusion; Rauch 2021: 174–184). "In Trump's book, apologizing was a sin, an admission of weakness" (Leonnig and Rucker 2021: Chapter 22).

Kivisto notes that "a standard part of Trump campaign rallies and in numerous tweets was to call reporters 'dishonest,' 'scum,' 'slime,' and 'liars'" (Kivisto 2017: 2; see also Robinson 2018), even as "Trump proved to be a ratings bonanza for television executives" (Kivisto 2017: 81). Of populism and the media in general, Manucci argues that "populist discourses are considered to fit the media-logic by providing controversial and newsworthy content, thus incrementing the visibility of politicians articulating populist discourses vis-à-vis mainstream politicians" (Manucci 2017: 467). To counter "Trump as an institutional obstacle for fact-based information to circulate and exchange", Robinson challenges professional communicators "to learn the best ways to manipulate social networks so as to build connecting and connected bridges instead of exacerbating rampant distrust that nurtures isolation and polarization" (Robinson 2018: 193).

Described as "digital demagogues" by Christian Fuchs, Trump and other strongmen politicians have harnessed superbly, smart new social communication technologies such as the internet, social media (especially platforms like Facebook and Twitter), big data analytics and cloud computing (Fuchs 2018). It could be argued that Trump, whom Douglas Kellner has described as "the *master of media spectacle*" (Kellner 2016: 1–5) with a genius for creating and manipulating the media spectacle for the interest of his business as well as for the politics of spectacle (Fuchs 2018: 165-257; Reid 2019: Chapter 8), found little reason to go beyond flogging the critical liberal media (or the "Lamestream Media" as he loved to call them in his tweets) in public and actually ban them because of the satisfaction he derived from coverage by right-wing media outfits and what he and his presidency had achieved in harnessing social media to do his bidding.

As Kakutani observes, Trump has been largely successful in keeping his bubble of supporters loyal thanks to "a solar system of ring-wing news sites orbiting around Fox News and Breitbart News.[202] Breitbart News was a right-wing website founded in 2005 as a "tool for reversing the flow of American culture" and reframing "American culture according to the nationalist vision of Andrew Breitbart". This was something Breitbart News sought to achieve under the senior editorship of Steve Bannon from 2012 through "cultural warfare" and "*informational dominance*—a data-powered arsenal suited to conquer hearts and minds in this new battlespace", in which he was ably and diligently assisted by Cambridge Analytica. "In this new war, the American voter became a target of confusion, manipulation, and deception. Truth was replaced by alternative narratives and virtual realities" (Wylie 2019: Chapters 1 & 4, italics in original). These right-wing media outlets have consolidated their hold over the Republican base, and in addition to the growth in use of social media, are able to serve as hubs connecting "users with like-minded members and supplies them with customized news feeds that reinforce their preconceptions, allowing them to live in ever narrower, windowless silos" (Kakutani 2018: 17–18). The silos create and experience their own realities and determine their own facts (Kakutani 2018: 88), thereby "rapidly shrinking" any common ground between Trump and his supporters and fellow Americans who do not necessarily share their beliefs, feelings and perspectives (Kakutani 2018: 106). As Wylie rightly observes, "The destruction of mutual experience is the essential first step to *othering*, to denying another perspective on what it means to be *one of us*." Creating and promoting echo chambers of social isolation that segregate our reality in the manner that Facebook, for example, tends to do with its gated communities of "homogenous Lookalikes" can only breed the sort of "mistrust" that yields "conspiracism and populism" (Wylie 2019: Chapter 12).

According to Rauch, epistemic bubbles form when coercive conformity corrupts a reality-based community, leading to a spiral of silence that stifles diversity and objectivity with "viewpoint monocultures". When this happens, those entrapped in "the bubble will perceive themselves to be engaging in vigorous contestation and criticism—unaware that what they are actually doing is confirming and re-confirming their shared biases" (Rauch 2021: 197). It is all about "selective perception", Sonnevend suggests. Not only do we tend to "hope that our beliefs are based on facts, rationality, and a nuanced balancing of conflicting expectations of reality", media scholarship, she points out, has established "the ubiquity of selective perception" that validates that "our desire to support our claims is so strong that we literally see only the evidence that confirms our established views" (Sonnevend 2018: 87). Sims, with reference to Trump, agrees, adding that, "Different people can witness the same events, hear the same words, and digest the same facts, and still walk away with dramatically different opinions on what it all meant.". Not only is Trump a peddler in selective perception, "Trump is almost always viewed through a distorted prism". Just as there is "a big market for Trump hatred", there is a big market as well for Trump lovers. He attracts both sycophants and haters, with each offering only "a glimpse of the real Donald Trump—the genius, the impulsive risk taker, the hothead, the insurrectionist, the hypocrite", but hardly "the full story" (Sims 2019: Author's Note). When does a good salesman turn conman in a context that tolerates and promotes the illusion that winning is possible as a zero-sum pursuit? Trump, like the good salesman he claims to be, and as an exemplary practitioner of Edward Bernays-like persuasive communication techniques, is aware that "we all desire something more from life than reason"; we desire "hope, prosperity, and dignity" even if only as a promise or a myth (Sonnevend 2018: 92). With such astute salesmanship, Trump has been able to persuade his followers to suspend reality and keep them glued to him with offerings of red meat in the form of a fantasy and rhetoric (Skinnell 2018a) or, as Sonnevend puts it, "a very powerful myth embodied in three key slogans 'Make America Great Again!,' 'We Will Drain the Swamp!,' and 'We Will Build a Wall!'" (Sonnevend 2018: 88). Hassan sees in this Trump's consummate mastery of mind control as a technique for cultivating and sustaining a cult-like following in which reason is suspended in favour of absolute loyalty to the cult leader (Hassan 2019). In addition to repetition and fearmongering which he employs to programme the beliefs into the conscious, Trump uses other cult tactics such as "lying, insulting opponents, projecting his weaknesses onto others, deflecting, distracting, presenting alternative facts and competing versions of reality" "to confuse, disorient, and ultimately coerce his followers" (Hassan 2019: Introduction).

Instead of conventional media censorship, Trump opted for trolling among other strategies (Marcotte 2018; Muirhead and Rosenblum 2019; Rauch 2021: 155–188). As Gessen argues, Trump has sought to dominate and neutralise the media, instead of controlling and supressing them. Thus, far from seeking to dictate reality from above, he has rather opted to render reality intangible. In addition, "Trump has exploited existing problems and weaknesses: dwindling trust in journalism, profit-driven media's reluctance to engage with substantive politics, and a tradition of extreme restraint in covering politics" (Gessen 2020: Chapter 15). Apart from what Schmidt and Haberman of *The New York Times* describe as a "Macabre Video of Fake Trump" shooting, assaulting and stabbing his critics and the media that was shown at a conference held by a pro-Trump group at Trump's National Doral Miami resort in October 2019 – a conference attended by his son Donald Trump

Jr.[203] – the closest Trump has come to curbing the flow of the critical or "Lamestream Media" has been to suspend White House News Conferences, and to seek to withdraw access for journalists perceived to be overly critical of him. In this regard, it could be argued that his authoritarian tendencies notwithstanding, Trump did not outrightly seek to eliminate the opposition media in order to exert exclusive control of information the way authoritarian leaders have done elsewhere (Pearce 2018).

However, to dominate the media, Gessen posits, "for his three years as president before the coronavirus pandemic", Trump "discontinued the practice of press conferences that are announced in advance, ensuring that experienced journalists are present and allowing journalists to prepare" (Gessen 2020: Chapter 15). Here is a 25 April 2020 tweet by Trump justifying a suspension of news conferences at the White House:

> What is the purpose of having White House News Conferences when the Lamestream Media asks nothing but hostile questions, & then refuse to report the truth or facts accurately. They get record ratings, & the American people get nothing but Fake News. Not worth the time & effort!

Equally, Trump managed to keep at bay critical voices at Fox News, by reminding them, when they dared to be critical, that he was "the golden goose" that "made them successful" by bring them high ratings. This was the essence of a tweet on 12 November 2020, when Fox News dared the join the "Lamestream Media" in suggesting that Biden had won the election. Trump twitted:

> @FoxNews daytime ratings have completely collapsed. Weekend daytime even WORSE. Very sad to watch this happen, but they forgot what made them successful, what got them there. They forgot the Golden Goose. The biggest difference between the 2016 Election, and 2020, was @FoxNews!

In terms of manipulating and manoeuvring the media to achieve populist ends (Krämer 2017; Roncarolo 2017), Trump, Kellner observes, has displayed fascinating masterfulness at creating and perpetuating "media spectacles", by which Kellner means:

[…] media constructs that present events which disrupt ordinary and habitual flows of information, and which become popular stories which capture the attention of the media and the public, and circulate through broadcasting networks, the Internet, social networking, smartphones, and other new media and communication technologies (Kellner 2016: 3).

Kellner argues that "media spectacles proliferate instantaneously" in a global networked society, becoming "virtual and viral" in some instances, "tools of sociopolitical transformation" in others, and "mere moments of media hype and tabloidized sensationalism" in some cases (Kellner 2016: 3). Little wonder, therefore, that in Trump world, the truth as an objective pursuit really does not matter, especially if it is likely to stand in the way of a good media spectacle. As Michael Cohen, his personal attorney and confidant for 10 years, has observed, Trump has regularly abandoned the truth in favour of falsehoods, which he knows perfectly well are false, "in exchange for news-cycle soundbites, and the media has fallen for it over and over and over". Trump thrives on exploiting divisive issues to his advantage. The more divisive an issue is, the better for Trump, as such issues are more likely to arouse strong feelings and keep his supporters loyal (Cohen 2020: Chapter 6).

Such divisiveness and perceived disdain for democracy and the ethics of right and wrong, along with vindictiveness have attracted criticism of Trump's self-engrossed, incompetent and disorganised authoritarian leadership style (Dean and Altemeyer 2020). Some have qualified his leadership style as "reality TV authoritarianism" modelled around "The Apprentice Trump", the reality TV show "that had propelled him to great fame" by selling him to viewers as "a consummate negotiator, a fearless dealmaker, and an unflinching evaluator of talent who forgot nothing" (Miller 2018: Prologue). Others have compared his leadership style to "McCarthy-era tactics", given Trump's proclivity for disorder and for falsehoods in his play of victimhood and the blame game through allegations of witch-hunts and McCarthyism (Kalb 2018; Miller 2018: Chapter 11; Achter 2018; Steudeman 2018; Nance 2019: Chapter 11; Dean and Altemeyer 2020: Chapter 1), and given the readiness among "so many of Trump's advisers […] to find someone or something else to blame for Trump's actions" (Leonnig and Rucker 2021: Chapter 22). These attributes all made for what Sims terms "a unique White House [...] with reality television stars and famous First Family members as senior staffers, billionaire industrial titans as Cabinet members, a multilingual supermodel for a First Lady, and a celebrity CEO as the President" (Sims 2019: Chapter 9).

According to former navy admiral, William McRaven, in a reaction to Trump's revoking of the security clearance of former CIA Director, John Brennan, Trump does not embody the qualities associated with the office of president, lacks the moral integrity to be a role model, fails to prioritise the welfare of others over his personal interests and has "embarrassed us in the eyes of our children, humiliated us on the world stage and, worst of all, divided us as a nation" through his actions[204] (Rucker and Leonnig 2020: Chapter 18). In their post-mortem book on the Trump presidency titled *I Alone Can Fix it*, Leonnig and Rucker (2021) explore Trump's leadership characteristics and examine their deadly ramifications in his final year in office. In sum, Trump's leadership style amounted to a display of:

> [...] his ignorance, his rash temper, his pettiness and pique, his malice and cruelty, his utter absence of empathy, his narcissism, his transgressive personality, his disloyalty, his sense of victimhood, his addiction to television, his suspicion and silencing of experts, and his deception and lies (Leonnig and Rucker 2021: Prologue).

Beyond Putin, Trump has been compared to other populist strongmen. One is Duterte. According to Bello, Philippine President Duterte as presidential candidate had a lot in common with Donald Trump the candidate. They were both political outliers and both known for using harsh and insulting language, and their candidacies were framed in terms of class conflict, even as they did not "buy into liberal values and liberal democratic discourse". To Bello, Duterte's "railing against corruption and poverty, his obvious disdain for the rich" and more importantly, "his coming across as 'one of you guys' that acted as a magnet to workers, the urban poor, peasants, and the lower middle class", was very much like Trump.[205] Arguelles explains the rise of Duterte as precipitated by a "widening gap between rich and poor, recurrent domestic economic crises, epidemic levels of corruption and failed attempts to significantly reduce criminality". In all of this, "Duterte is seen as a man of action" who "articulated the public's deep-seated feelings of precariousness and powerlessness using rhetoric they could relate to". And "When Duterte's campaign translates to perceived everyday safety, it is no wonder that drug-war murders have not met considerable resistance".[206] In terms of wealth, however, Duterte is not to be compared to Trump who remains very rich, even if the true size of his wealth is subject to continuous speculation, and his attacks on the rich elite of America is therefore hypocritical.

Another leader with whom Trump has been compared is Recep Tayyip Erdogan of Turkey (*Journal of Global Faultlines* 2017). To Akyol, Erdogan and Trump have in common the fact that Erdogan's supporters "see the American president-elect as a similar figure: an outsider who horrifies 'the elite' yet is able to win at the ballot box".[207] Another similarity, according to Cockburn, is that just like Erdogan has used his powers to weaken Turkish democracy, Trump may well do the same in the US. Cockburn points to "a surprising degree of uniformity in the behaviour of Trump and Erdogan" despite the very different political landscapes of the two countries. The same can be said of Trump and "populist, nationalist, authoritarian leaders who are taking power in many different parts of the world".[208] Trump and Erdogan reportedly exchanged favours during Trump's presidency, including when President Trump "assigned his attorney general and Treasury secretary to deal with" Erdogan's "repeated pleas to avoid charges against one of Turkey's largest banks",[209] which followed in the hills of Trump's 9 October 2019 letter to Erdogan seeking a ceasefire in Syria in exchange for "a good deal!" that would avoid "destroying the Turkish economy": "Don't be a tough guy, Don't be a fool", Trump urged the Turkish President, ending with the words, "I will call you later."[210]

Trump has also been compared to Boris Johnson of Britain. Cohen sees "striking similarities" between the two men, "and not just on the hair front".[211] To Cohen, these are:

> [...] two charlatans and narcissists with flimsy notions of the truth, utterly unprincipled, given to racist slurs, skilled practitioners of the politics of spectacle, manipulators of fear, nationalist traffickers in an imaginary past of radiant greatness, fabulists of reborn glory, with giant

145

holes at their centers where conscience and integrity went missing. So much for the leadership of the free world![212]

Trevor Noah, the South African host of the US-based satirical news programme, *The Daily Show*, from when Trump campaigned for the presidency to when he left office after losing the 2020 election, shot into prominence mainly through his capacity to compare Trump to African leaders such as Idi Amin, Muammar Gaddafi, Yahya Jammeh, Robert Mugabe and Jacob Zuma, showing how similar Trump was to these leaders in his penchant for dictatorship, autocracy, pomposity and braggadocio-ness.[213]

Equally, the South African political scientist, Roger Southall, has highlighted how similar Trump and Jacob Zuma are in how they, as deeply narcissistic and paranoid personalities, cleverly mobilise the status of outsiders to the establishment and conspiracy theorists to endear themselves with those supposedly left behind by the system, while personally inhabiting and promoting a world devoid of morality, as they crave and reward loyalty and impunity while punishing perceived enemies and those who dare to stand up for the truth. Both demand unconditional loyalty to them personally, which they price above any other commitment, including to the truth, morality, decency, party, the Constitution and country. For both, democracy, institutions and the Constitution are abided with only to the extent that these serve their personal interests narrowly defined and single-mindedly pursued, with or without caprice and contradictions. As Southall writes, being "half a world apart in ideology", does not seem to deter Trump and Zuma from inhabiting "a similar world of conspiracy, lies, threats and paranoia". Both are exceedingly adept at "providing explanations of their misfortunes to the socially insecure and economically vulnerable",[214] and at harnessing the popularity this generates to capture and personalise power all in the name of democracy.

Trump would end his presidency in a desperate quest to trump democracy by encouraging his hardcore and loyal supporters, whom he characterises as justifiably "very angry", to mob-storm the Capitol building to hijack the processes of counting electoral college votes democratically (Leonnig and Rucker 2021; Wolff 2021a). Trump's description of the insurrectionists as very angry is in tune with what Wahl-Jorgensen terms "an emotional regime of anger, driven by public displays of disaffection" which Trump has ushered into politics, and which he often displays in exclusionary fashion on behalf of those he narrowly considers as "the American people" while unleashing a contagion of anger amongst his supporters and non-supporters alike (Wahl-Jorgensen 2018).

Zuma would, after stepping down reluctantly and systematically refusing to cooperate with the Zondo Commission investigating state capture by the Guptas that he was widely perceived to have enabled, be sentenced to 15 months imprisonment by the Constitutional Court, for defying summons to appear before the Zondo Commission, which he accused of bias and labelled as a "slaughterhouse" and forum of "unsubstantiated and defamatory allegations" aimed at undoing him.[215] His imprisonment in July 2021 would occasion several days of violent mass protests and looting of shopping malls in Zuma's province of origin, KwaZulu Natal, as well as in Gauteng province – protests that the government labelled as an attempted insurrection, and that resulted in "more than 300 dead, and billions of rands lost in damage to infrastructure, the economy and business".[216] Just like Zuma, Trump has initiated or been the target of a mind-blogging number of lawsuits (Simpson and Fritsch 2019), his very latest suit being to sue Facebook, Twitter and Google, post his presidency, for banning him. Vowing to "to hold big tech very accountable", Trump said, "If they can do it to me, they can do it to anyone."[217] Could Facebook's decision soon after in October 2021 to change its company name to Meta have been motivated in part by a desire to break with a past of contentious complicity and strategic ambiguity towards Trump?[218] Christopher Wylie, a whistleblower who was banned by Facebook before Trump's ban, recounts his experience thus:

> When Facebook banned me, they did not simply deactivate my account; they erased my entire presence on Facebook and Instagram. When my friends tried to look up old messages I had sent, nothing came up: My name, my words—everything—had disappeared. I became a shadow. [...] (Wylie 2019: Chapter 12).

Trump may be a latecomer, but he is not alone in waking up to the realisation that the big tech companies concentrate far too much power than is healthy even for a market-driven democracy (Wylie 2019).

Trump's relations with North Korean leader, Kim Jong Un, went from initially tense and combustible, with Trump threatening "fire and fury like the world has never seen", if "Little Rocket Man" Kim did not disabuse himself of his keenness to test his nuclear weapons. The two leaders, like boys in a first-grade playground, exchanged explosive words, comparing the size and efficiency of their nuclear buttons. In a tweet on 3 January 2018, Trump, in a manner that brings to mind Drezner's book, *Toddler-in-Chief* (2020), complained:

> North Korean Leader Kim Jong Un just stated that the "Nuclear Button is on his desk at all times." Will someone from his depleted and food starved regime please inform him that I too have a Nuclear Button, but it is a much bigger & more powerful one than his, and my Button works! (Donald J. Trump (@realDonaldTrump) 3 January 2018).[219]

Kim Jong Un, who enjoyed a colourful history of name-calling with his American counterpart, threatened to call Trump "a senile dotard". The exchange kept politicians, the media, commentators and comedians preoccupied for some time with the question whether Trump could press the button. Trump's relationship with Kim Jong Un then moved to exchanging affectionate "love" letters which Trump readily announced for media effect, and to holding two submits, one in Singapore in 2018 and the second in Hanoi, Vietnam in 2019, qualifying both leaders as the first sitting heads of their respective countries to meet.[220]

Bandow remarks that where Trump ceases to be like other strongmen in power to whom he has been compared is in that he is someone who is "so little rooted in reality and so much dominated by personality".[221] Sims, as someone who served as Trump's special assistant for 500 days, concurs, adding: "Everything was personal to Trump—*everything*. In international affairs, he believed his personal relationship with foreign leaders was more important than shared interests or geopolitics" (Sims 2019: Chapter 6).

Compared to autocrats elsewhere "who are highly disciplined with a fixed ideology and party apparatus," Kellner argues that:

Trump is chaotic and undisciplined, viciously attacking whoever dares criticize him in his daily Twitter feed or speeches, thus dominating the daily news cycles with his outrageous attacks on Mexicans, Muslims, and immigrants, or politicians of both parties who dare to criticize him. Trump effectively used the broadcast media and social media to play the powerful demagogue who preys on his followers' rage, alienation, and fears (Kellner 2016: 24).

From an insider perspective, Sims alludes to "Trump's laissez-faire style" that sometimes led to "uncertainty about who exactly was in charge and empowered to do what." He admits that reporting on "Trump's 'chaotic' management style" during the early days of administration "was generally accurate" even if some were "somewhat overblown". As Sim's writes, "We were all figuring it out as we went along", given that there "were very few people on the original Trump White House staff who had any experience in the West Wing" (Sims 2019: Chapter 5). It did not help matters that Trump ran "the country much as he did his small family business—with a flat organization and a cast of advisers and hangers-on who rarely challenge his authority" (Kessler et al. 2020: Conclusion). The chaotic and impulsive approach to leadership steeped in self-protection and self-promotion did not deter Trump from insisting, in the course of his four years in power, that he was a very stable genius (Rucker and Leonnig 2020), that he alone could fix whatever was wrong with the USA, and through his actions, demonstrating that if democracy was perceived to be the problem by his steadfast supporters and himself, he had no qualms seeking to subvert it (Leonnig and Rucker 2021).

To Coates, Trump may not have a fixed ideology, but he is not ideology free as is often claimed. He asserts that Trump's "ideology is white supremacy in all of its truculent and sanctimonious power", adding that "In Trump, white supremacists see one of their own". Trump's "whiteness is neither notional nor symbolic but is the very core of his power", which is white supremacist in that it seeks "to ensure that that which all others achieve with maximal effort, white people (and particularly white men) achieve with minimal qualification". If with Barack Obama the message was that "in working twice as hard as white people, anything is possible", with

Donald Trump, the message became "work half as hard as black people and even more is possible" (Coates 2017: Epilogue).

Ben-Ghiat agrees, arguing that Trump has differed from strongmen who preceded him in one particular respect, namely, "his almost exclusive reliance on television for information about the world", with his "daily thoughts and moods" being "determined by what has just been said on shows he watches" (Ben-Ghiat 2020: Chapter 5). Beyond television, Trump has earned his place in history, albeit ambiguously according to Brooke, as America's "first social media president", just as did Obama before him as the country's "first internet president" (Brooke 2018). Trump successfully instituted government by tweet and by gesture, according to Gessen (2020: Chapters 4 & 13). When Trump joined Twitter in 2009, barely three years after the medium was launched, his aim, according to Oborne and Roberts, was to promote his personal brand, sell his books and generate publicity for his TV programme, *The Apprentice*. When he became a politician, he turned his embrace of Twitter into "a lethal political weapon" in reaching out directly and whipping up the feelings and entrenching the beliefs of millions of his followers who had turned their back on the Washington Establishment and its ideas of fact and truth. "He viscerally understood the power of this new medium to simplify complex ideas, to remove nuance and subtext and, above all, to remove any boundary between assertion and fact" (Oborne and Roberts 2017: Introduction). Ben-Ghiat adds:

> Twitter has been for Trump what newsreels were for the fascists: a direct channel to the people that keeps him constantly in the news. Dissected by pundits with the diligence of Communist-era Kremlinologists, Trump's tweets feature simple vocabulary and misspelled words, offering a curated sense of authenticity. Tweets have been his preferred propaganda delivery vehicles for falsehoods, and they have enabled him to distract attention from his corruption and policy failures. Designed for instant impact and encouraging feelings of omnipotence, Twitter is the perfect tool for an impulsive, attention-addicted strongman. "Boom. I press it, and within two seconds, 'We have breaking news'," said Trump of the effect of his tweets, like the March 2019 one that recognized Israel's claim of sovereignty over the Golan Heights and took US officials by surprise. (Ben-Chiat 2020: Chapter 5).

Sims provides the following example of a Trump tweet (7:52 A.M. on 29 June 2017) which President Trump personally described as "modern-day presidential", adding, "I'm not going to stop telling the American people what I think because it makes some people uncomfortable"(Sims 2019: Chapter 9):

> "I heard poorly rated @Morning_Joe speaks badly of me (don't watch anymore). Then how come low I.Q. Crazy Mika, along with Psycho Joe, came to Mar-a-Lago 3 nights in a row around New Year's Eve, and insisted on joining me. She was bleeding badly from a face-lift. I said no!" (Trump tweet, Sims 2019: Chapter 9).

Trump, who before and during his presidency, "constantly interacted online with his supporters, thus saturating the public debate with his presence", famously described himself as "the Ernest Hemingway of 140 characters" (Manucci 2017: 483). It could be argued that Trump's populist communication style (Skinnell 2018a; Young 2018; Steudeman 2018) has not only taken advantage of the changing media ecology of his time but also that his adeptness in the use of Twitter has offered him "a way of trying to hold responsiveness and responsibility together, while attempting to survive the impossible challenge of actually delivering what the people want within the framework of the constraints the economy imposes" (Roncarolo 2017: 401).

Autocrats elsewhere in the world have celebrated Trump's rise to power and his penchant for autocracy, disparaging comments about democracy and criticism of American state institutions and mainstream media interested in facts and objectivity. African strongmen in power take Trump as a licence for them to ignore the common weal with impunity. As Madeleine Albright complains, Trump's virulent criticism of American institutions and democratic processes has tended to comfort and provide excuses to those whom America would normally condemn for their anti-democratic practices. She elaborates:

> In my travels, I hear the same questions all the time: If the president of the United States says the press always lies, how can Vladimir Putin be faulted for making the same claim? If Trump insists that judges are biased and calls the American criminal system a "laughingstock," what

is to stop an autocratic leader like Duterte of the Philippines from discrediting his own judiciary? If Trump accuses opposition politicians of treason merely for failing to applaud his words, what standing will America have to protest the jailing of prisoners of conscience in other lands? If the leader of the world's most powerful country views life as a dog-eat-dog struggle in which no country can gain except at another's cost, who will carry the banner for international teamwork when the most intractable problems cannot be solved in any other way? (Albright 2018: 5–6).

Before Trump, America tended to claim a certain moral high ground in matters of liberal democratic legitimacy, which it almost instinctively felt was its duty to enforce around the world along with the idea and ideals of a free market economy, using it like an ideological and diplomatic whip to flog competing and conflicting systems of power and government into a ridiculous defensiveness (Burns 2019). With the advent of Trump, that disappeared, to the supreme satisfaction of many an autocrat the world over. Burns terms this "The Demolition of U.S. Diplomacy", arguing that "Trump is the gift that keeps on giving" for dictators, "a non-stop advertisement for Western self-dealing". He has rendered meaningless the idea of enlightened self-interest, the power of leading by example, and the very credibility of the US.[222] This is how Applebaum captures the demise in America's role as the global gendarme of democracy that came with Trump's election in 2016: "Instead of a nation that leads 'the citizens of democratic societies,' we are 'America First.' Instead of seeing ourselves at the heart of a great international alliance for good, we are indifferent to the fate of other nations, including other nations that share our values." Trump's America "sees no important distinction between democracy and dictatorship", she concludes (Applebaum 2020: 157). Insisting on "America First", Sims explains, was a determined departure by Trump from focusing "too much on lecturing other countries about how they should conduct themselves", and not prioritising America's strategic interests enough (Sims 2019: Chapter 8).

Trump's focus on a pointedly national "America First" agenda (Magcamit 2017) has suffered from his even narrower fixation with prioritisation of white America. As Dean and Altemeyer argue, Trump's isolationist outlook was "based on the belief that everybody else, friend and foe alike, was taking advantage of a patsy USA". It was an approach that invited Americans to keep everyone else perceived not to belong at a distance. Thus, it was hardly surprising, as we gather from the section below, that when Trump "learned in January 2020 that a new disease had broken out in central China, his first thought was probably, 'Good. That's going to hurt China,' and the last thing he would have thought of was that it could reach the United States", which he probably thought "would be stronger, more resilient, 'exceptional people' who would be an exclusion to the rule". Like Trump, his ardent followers would tend to think that "they were virus-proof too", and would resist wearing a mask in solidarity with a president who was ready to stand up to the virus as a sign of American exceptionalism (Dean and Altemeyer 2020: Chapter 6). Both Trump's "America First" and narrow prioritisation of white America have served to contradict his desire for global visibility and celebrity through slogans such as "Make America Great Again". Such greatness is hardly possible through delinking in a globalised world that challenges nativism and celebrates diversity.

In terms of branding, something one would have expected Trump to understand well, given his notoriety in the practice, the American brand, ironically, has suffered globally under Trump, who loves (in Trump with Schwartz 1987) to tout his deal-making and branding skills. On the other hand, given Trump's disdain for "restraints, particularly restraints on himself" and given his strongman ambitions, like Louis XIV, the Sun King of France who famously proclaimed that he was the state, it could be argued that Trump, seeing himself as America and America as Trump, conflated the American brand with the Trump brand. As Mercieca maintains, not only does Trump take "pride in his Sun King-like ability to decide what is and what is not", he "has lived his life as a Sun King of sorts – he has believed himself to be above the law, never permitting himself to be held accountable for his actions" (Mercieca 2018). Hence, Singh's suggestion that "Trump is better understood as brand marketing via opportunistic entryism" (Singh 2017: 8). For Trump, the brand is everything, affirms Coppins (2015: Chapter 1). And with regard to commodifying his personality, playing upon the unconscious desires of his consumers in lieu of rational arguments, using stereotypes and prejudices to kindle the flames of fear and hate he needs to prop up the value of his shares in the capricious stock market of public opinion, and generally promoting the Trump brand (Taveira and Nyerges 2016; Wingard 2018). And in terms of branding, it would appear even the name "Trump" is an anglicisation of "Drumpf" by his grandfather, Friedrich, or his father, Fred, according to Palash Ghosh. It would appear as well, that although originally an immigrant from Germany, Trump had reported, that his grandfather was, more appealingly, from Sweden (Reid 2019: Chapter 5). Trump probably had a much better story to tell for his four years as president. As someone "with unquenchable ubiquity", who "licenses his name for tidy fees" and imagines himself as a "supersized version" of the American Dream (O'Brien 2015[2005]: Introduction), how much has leasing or licensing his name "like a celebrity brand of cologne" (Reid 2019: Chapter 5) to –Trumpifying – America for four years as president contributed to his net worth?

Trump's Populist Leadership Style and the Covid-19 Pandemic

In this section, I argue that Trump's politicised handling of the coronavirus pandemic, seen through the prism of a populist leader who is more interested in winning than in governing responsibly and accountably, is a good illustration of the USA's failure to act as the pandemic policeman of the world. Instead of offering national and global leadership, Trump was more interested in finger-pointing and outsourcing blame to China and Europe and inciting fear of New Yorkers, the first state to be severely affected by Covid-19. Trump's refusal to wear the mask and politicisation of mask-wearing was a crude populist way of putting forward his image as a strongman leader and, by extension, that of an invincible USA. However, in both attempts, he failed. After politicising the virus, Trump went ahead to weaponise, electionise and partisanise it by disregarding racial and ethnic minorities who were dying in inverse proportions to their white counterparts, classifying them as Democratic Party lackeys and categorising them as less patriotic, if not outrightly unpatriotic. Far from offering effective federal level leadership, Trump resorted to playing the governors of blue states against their red-state counterparts by encouraging the latter to reopen, minimise lockdowns and mask wearing.

I argue that, granted the heightened interconnectivity of our times, other strongman politicians and leaders joined Trump in disregarding the enormous threat of the coronavirus, thereby aggravating the situation in their respective countries. Trump was so concerned about losing the elections that he unsuccessfully attempted to use the outbreak of the virus in his favour by attempting to override the Congress and Article II of the Constitution to postpone the elections. The section parallels Covid-19 and Trump by arguing that, like Trump, it fuelled fear of the other and prompted the closing of borders the world over. Trump's reckless handling of the pandemic resonates with his unremitting reminder that not everyone can be an American or deserves to be seen as an American and that even people who have thought of themselves as Americans can be de-Americanised as not-American, un-American, or anti-American.

Let's elaborate.

The handling of the coronavirus pandemic is a good illustration of the global ramifications of America's failure to take leadership under President Trump (Slavitt 2021; Abutaleb and Paletta 2021; Leonnig and Rucker 2021: Chapters 1–6 & 12), whose political calculus increasingly trumped science (Woodward 2020; Slavitt 2021; Trump, M. L. 2021). Initially, as Bob Woodward reports, according to the Center for Disease Control (CDC) Director, Anthony Fauci:

> [...] some of Trump's early decisions had been his finest hours—restricting travel from China (January 31) and Europe (March 11) and asking sick Americans to stay home and all to practice good hygiene with his initial "15 Days to Slow the Spread" (March 16) and then extending it for another 30 days (March 29). The president had stepped up to the task and had listened to Birx, Redfield, himself and others (Woodward 2020: 353).

Even when "Trump engaged in wishful thinking about the virus, musing it would disappear on its own", as long as "Fauci could correct the record on television", the situation was still manageable. It was when such television appearances by Fauci were limited that Trump's political calculus increasingly trumped science (Woodward 2020: 353; Slavitt 2021: Chapter 10). For Trump, it was always about playing down the severity of the coronavirus, in order not to create panic. "I wanted to always play it down," Trump told Woodward. "I still like playing it down because I don't want to create panic."[223] A 1:48 PM tweet on 29 March 2020 about his high ratings indicated that Trump was equally, if not more concerned about maintaining his approval ratings. It read:

"President Trump is a ratings hit. Since reviving the daily White House briefing Mr. Trump and his coronavirus updates have attracted an average audience of 8.5 million on cable news, roughly the viewership of the season finale of "The Bachelor." Numbers are continuing to rise …[224]

Another tweet read:

Because the "Ratings" of My News Conferences etc. are so high, "Bachelor finale, Monday Night Football type numbers" according to @nytimes, the Lamestream Media is going Crazy. "Trump is reaching too many people, we must stop him," said one lunatic. See you at 5:00 PM!

Trump has been said to run his presidency as a show – the Trump Show – of which he is creator, chief publicist, executive producer and star, tracking the ratings and the crowds, following the reviews, slamming critics but craving their approval (Karl 2020). And the show must go on. Not even Covid-19 could conspire to stop it. In tune with the depiction of him as a consummate showman, "Trump credited himself with turning government officials into household names" through his administration's capacity to attract media attention. As Trump himself put it, "'With Trump, everybody becomes a star. I'm the greatest star-maker in history" (Leonnig and Rucker 2021: Epilogue). "For a numbers-obsessed Trump" who "has spent his life in thrall to numbers – his wealth, his ratings, his polls", writes Parker, Trump was "uncharacteristically silent" when in May 2020 the USA "reached the bleak milestone" of "100,000 American dead from the novel coronavirus".[225] "The president chose not to honor the occasion", Leonnig and Rucker recount, adding that there was neither a "moment of silence or somber commemoration" nor an "opportunity for Americans, frightened by the relentless power of the 'invisible enemy,' as Trump had termed it, to grieve collectively" (Leonnig and Rucker 2021: Chapter 7).

Trump, increasingly impatient that the virus was not going away as he had hoped, instead of offering national and global leadership, was more interested in outsourcing blame to others, China in particular. He was equally keen on putting forward an invincible image of the USA, likening the coronavirus to a flu, overstating the preparedness of his country, and playing up his own personal invincibility. His domestic political calculous and re-election calendar seemed more important than timely and sustained efforts to contain the virus (Woodward 2020; Dean and Altemeyer 2020: Chapter 1; Frum 2020: Introduction). Initial reports that racial and ethnic minorities (black and brown people) were dying in inverse proportions to their white counterparts might have played a part in Trump's lukewarm response, as such racialised minorities tend to vote Democrat overwhelmingly, and are often categorised in Trump's perverse rhetoric as less patriotic, if not outrightly unpatriotic (Gunn 2018; Mercieca 2018). This was consistent with Trump's populism, which according to Young, "is overwhelmingly about brown and black and non-Christian and women and gay people enacting crime and taking your jobs and disrespecting our values and ruining America" (Young 2018). It is hardly surprising therefore, as Res remarks, that "Trump was happy to let people suffer with coronavirus as long as it was contained in the 'blue' states" and that "He was willing to let the elderly and infirm die if it avoided hurting his economy and his prospects for reelection" (Res 2020: Epilogue). This comes across as if Trump found getting re-elected more important than keeping alive Americans entrusted to him as president for protection by the Constitution.

The higher risk of dying from Covid-19 experienced by black, brown and indigenous populations in the US, at face value, reflects the inaccessibility of affordable and quality healthcare as well as systemic exclusion from other societal services and benefits. It also reflects their lowly positions on the hierarchy of socioeconomic and political visibility that neoliberalism and legacies of the institution of enslavement have enshrined and perpetuated even in camouflage.[226] In general, they may be citizens in principle and as prescribed under the Constitution, but, in reality, the benefits of citizenship that they derive or are able to activate successfully pale in comparison to their white counterparts (Trump, M. L. 2021: Chapters 5, 6 & 8). As Slavitt reports, "As of October 2020, one-third of all Americans over the age of 65 who have been hospitalized with the virus are Black, a rate almost four times higher than the rate for White people of the same age group" (Slavitt 2021: Chapter 7). Hence, the pertinence of former President Barack Obama's comment that a disease like Covid-19 "just spotlights the underlying inequalities and extra burdens" that black, brown and indigenous communities have historically had to deal with in the US.[227]

Even the wearing of masks was not something Trump recommended easily (Leonnig and Rucker 2021: Chapter 6; Trump, M. L. 2021: Chapter 4), not least because of the initial confusion and reticence that surrounded mask wearing even among medical professionals advising the White House (Abutaleb and Paletta 2021: Chapter 9), but also because it affected the macho image or "virility" of the tough strongman he wanted to be and portray to his mainly white, male, working class Republican support base (Ben-Ghiat 2020), who found such undiluted and brash masculinity particularly appealing. Urged to wear a mask, Trump insisted: "Wearing a mask is a sign of weakness" and "You look weak if you wear a mask" (Abutaleb and Paletta 2021: Chapter 9). Trump's hesitancy on mask wearing was also a political statement. As Slavitt notes, "when the president decided he would not wear a mask, it became a political statement whether to wear or not wear one" (Slavitt 2021: Chapter 6). The bandwagon effect, Abutaleb and Paletta argue, was "diminished trust" in institutions, state and federal leaders, the media and in one another, and a prioritisation of individual liberties over collective action culminating in an "unwillingness to make small concessions and sacrifices for the collective good" (Abutaleb and Paletta 2021: Epilogue). Furthermore, having repeatedly touted the economy as his strength, Trump was more interested in discouraging prolonged lockdowns and reopening the economy, even if this amounted to promoting livelihoods to the detriment of lives.

In a context of heightened interconnectivity thanks to social media and global consumer television, it is hardly surprising that soon, other strongman politicians and leaders the world over began to reason and act like Trump. Jair Bolsonaro, the President of Brazil and "Trump of the Tropics", for example, joined Trump in his repeated insistence that economies should reopen despite the enormity of deaths and continued surges in coronavirus infections. In their zero-sum approach, there was little investment in the imperative to focus both on saving lives by curbing the spread of Covid-19 and keeping economies alive in a responsible manner that does not simply throw Covid-19 a lifeline with sighs of resignation such as Trump's: "Something I don't like saying about things, but that's the way it is".[228] Earlier, Bolsonaro of Brazil, the second most coronavirus-afflicted country globally, after the USA, with over 1 million and 670 thousand infections, and nearly 67,000 Covid-19-related deaths as of 8 July 2020, had callously remarked as well, "I'm sorry, some people will die, they will die, that's life".[229] Covid-19 opportunistically preys on sociality, comparative disadvantages, pre-existing precarities and related physical frailties that feed from and into debilitating hierarchies of systemic inequality and poverty. A balance of the tension between saving lives and saving livelihoods is needed, while livelihoods lost can be regained, lives lost are lost forever.

It has been argued that had Trump taken up mask wearing personally and encouraged Americans unequivocally to wear masks, America's coronavirus-related death toll would not have been as devastating as it has turned out to be. Masks and the wearing of masks have been presented by health experts as a means of preventing the spread of Covid-19, and almost everywhere, masks have acquired a significance, symbolism and potency beyond the simple but important fact of their relevance in fighting Covid-19.[230] Despite Trump's very reluctant concession to be seen wearing a mask in public, he, contrary to the recommendation by the top US infectious diseases expert, Dr Anthony Fauci, that everyone should use masks, rejected mandatory masks nationwide, insisting: "I want people to have a certain freedom".[231] It did not seem to matter to Trump that Covid-19 was dictating its terms and daring anyone to defy it at their own peril.

In an apparent volte-face – of appearing to care at long last, in the hope, perhaps, that the electorate would forget his initial inertia and failure to rise to the occasion and provide leadership,[232] – on July 21 Trump claimed wearing masks a show of "patriotism"; warned that the coronavirus pandemic "will probably unfortunately get worse before it gets better"; appealed to everybody to "wear a mask, get a mask" when "not able to socially distance"; and admitted that masks "have an impact" and "an effect" regardless of one's attitude towards wearing them.[233] His position contradicted the urgency of the situation, with almost 7 million people in the USA having tested positive for Covid-19 and at least 200,807 having died from the disease by 23 September 2020.[234]

Trump may have reluctantly yielded on masks, but he still self-consciously believed mask wearing somehow diminishes one's masculinity. Such curious thinking would need unmasking in the same way that Trump set about unmasking those he criticised for wearing masks. On 3 September 2020 Trump mocked his opponent, Democratic party nominee, Joe Biden, for wearing a mask. As Paul LeBlanc of CNN reports, "Speaking to a largely mask-less crowd in Pennsylvania, Trump asked his supporters if they know 'a man that likes a mask as much' as Biden. 'It gives him a feeling of security,' the President said. 'If I was a psychiatrist, I'd say this guy has some big issues.'"[235]

Trump may have vacillated on masks, but Trump's impatience with science, especially with the slowness of the "expert" instances of validation of scientific results was palpable, including in his embrace of magical solutions and miracle cures (Slavitt 2021: Chapter 10). In his estimation, it amounted to unnecessary and almost conspiratorial gatekeeping and collusion with the Democrats. Leonnig and Rucker report that "Trump had long nursed this paranoia that the drug companies were going to try to screw him out of his rightful victory in delivering a vaccine to the American people", a feeling that was only compounded by the fact that Pfizer only announced on 9 November, its coronavirus vaccine with 90 per cent efficacy in clinical trials (Leonnig and Rucker 2021: Chapter 17). As he would insist in an interview after leaving office, Trump "pushed scientists at the FDA 'at a level that they have never been pushed before' to get vaccines approved in record time", affirming: "I think we did a great job on COVID and it hasn't been recognized" (Leonnig and Rucker 2021: Epilogue).

The situation was further complicated by allegations that even renowned and authoritative journals as the *Lancet* and the *New England Journal of Medicine*, are sometimes pressured to accept for publication papers with contested conclusions by "financially powerful" pharmaceutical companies interested in promoting or taking attention away from a particular drug.[236] The *Lancet* reformed its editorial policy three months after retracting a controversial peer-reviewed study it published in May 2020, "which concluded that Covid-19 patients who received the drug hydroxychloroquine were dying at higher rates", although "figures on the number of deaths and patients in hospital cited by the authors did not match up with official government and health department data".[237]

As president, Trump continued, with remarkable consistency, to promote and defend the use of hydroxychloroquine as a cure (Abutaleb and Paletta 2021: Chapter 11), retweeting a video of and praising a controversial Cameroon born Houston based medical doctor-cum pastor, Dr Stella Immanuel, who actively touted the efficacy of the drug and who is said to believe "demons cause illnesses".[238] Describing her as "very impressive", President Trump spoke of Dr Stella Immanuel as someone who had had "tremendous success with hundreds of different patients", adding: "I thought her voice was an important voice but I know nothing about her".[239] President Trump's endorsement of the unproven cure contradicted his own public health officials, including Dr Anthony Fauci, a leading member of the White House coronavirus task force, who maintained that "every single good study [...] has shown that hydroxychloroquine is not effective in the treatment of Covid-19", and "regulators warn it may cause heart problems".[240] Major digital-media companies probably did far more than Trump to counter the spread of the misinformation and conspiracy theories that were circulating faster than the coronavirus itself. The measures included "everything from promoting verified videos on YouTube to removing fake reviews of health providers on Google Maps to elevating public-health agencies in search results" (Rauch 2021: 153–154). In terms of Trumpian populism, an argument could be made to the effect that it was hardly in Trump's interests to join the liberal establishment and its chorus of scientific experts in their orchestration of pandemic fear, and further enhancing the feeling of being manipulated among his largely white working-class Republican supporters. Rather, Trump stood to gain, for however short a term, from being in solidarity with those inclined to see the pandemic as a catalyser deepening the conflict between the liberal oligarchs and the powerless patriotic American people whom he was fighting for.

Masks, just like Covid-19, were at the centre of American politics. In 2020, an election year, Tara McKelvey reported that the wearing of masks had "become a catalyst for political conflict, an arena where scientific evidence is often viewed through a partisan lens". While most Democrats supported the wearing of masks, most Republicans did not. The Republicans were following the lead of President Trump, whose reluctance to wear a mask was public knowledge, saying, for instance, that "it did not seem right to wear one while he was receiving heads of state at the White House".[241] Trump's exploitation of presidential power to settle political scores and secure political advantage against his opponents by denying them the necessary resources or deploying America's financial abilities to commandeer personal protective equipment (PPE), is largely seen to have encouraged the spread of the virus in the USA.

Trump's vacillations were condemned in general, including even from within the ranks of his governing Republican party. In "Fighting Alone", an opinion piece in *The Washington Post* of 16 July Larry Hogan, the Republican governor of the state of Maryland, criticised Trump for not providing timely federal leadership to mitigate the high number of Covid-19 related deaths in the USA. Governor Hogan regretted the absence of a nationwide coordinated effort in the early days of the coronavirus outbreak. "While other countries were racing ahead with well-coordinated testing regimes, the Trump administration bungled the effort",[242] Hogan wrote (see also Leonnig and Rucker 2021: Chapter 3).

To Joe Biden, Trump's Democratic party opponent for the presidency in the election, writing in July 2020, it was "long past due for President Trump to listen to somebody other than himself in how to fight this virus, because after six straight months of deadly mismanagement it is spiralling even more out of control".[243] To Jeremy Konyndyk, a senior policy fellow at the Center for Global Development who contributed actively to the US government response to Ebola in 2014, the Trump administration's response to the coronavirus was "one of the greatest failures of basic governance in modern times" – "a leadership failure of astounding proportions".[244] According to Leonnig and Rucker, "his fear of losing" was such that on 30 July President Trump suggested delaying the 2020 election. They argue that the "suggestion was laughable" as "dates of presidential general elections are determined by the Congress, with power enshrined in Article II of the Constitution", and no president in history, dating back to 1845 "has ever successfully delayed an election, not even in times of war" (Leonnig and Rucker 2021: Chapter 11). Given his strongman propensities, if any president had to try a postponement, Trump was a most likely candidate, especially as he was actively campaigning against mail-in ballots which would favour Democrats significantly (Honig 2021: 195–219). Just as it turned out to be the case.

Critical of leaders who have downplayed and sabotaged collective efforts to tackle the pandemic, UN Secretary General, Antonio Guterres, called for humility and global solidarity. He regretted the "total lack of coordination among countries" in response to the pandemic, criticising the world's biggest powers in particular for failing to work together, and thereby "creating the situation that is getting out of control".[245] South Africa invested in creative and innovative solidarity, as reported in *Business Insider SA*, by exporting 800,000 masks to Italy in the early days of Covid-19 in Europe, when no fellow European Union country would assist.[246] As Sanne van der Lugt remarks, Italian hospitals, running out of stock of medical protection gear and desperate, naturally "asked their European partners for help. However, the first reaction from the rest of Europe was to stockpile face masks and other equipment to help their own citizens and not one European country came to the rescue. Instead, it was South Africa that sent the first batch of face masks to Italy".[247] This early sign of North-South solidarity speaks to the sort of leadership that some Americans and the global community had hoped that Trump, drawing on the rich repertoire of past US leadership initiatives, would offer to his country and the world more generally.

Covid-19 was increasingly proving itself a humbling virus even for the high and mighty of politics, the rich and famous, and the most powerful and privileged. It caught up with Trump. On Friday 2 October 2020, President Donald Trump, "being 74, a man and someone categorised as obese" and "in a higher-risk category for Covid-19",[248] tweeted: "Tonight, @FLOTUS and I tested positive for COVID-19. We will begin our quarantine and recovery process immediately. We will get through this TOGETHER!"[249] (Leonnig and Rucker 2021: Chapters 14 & 15) offer a detailed account of how Trump contracted Covid-19, including the treatment he was administered by his medical team at Walter Reed National Military Medical Center close to Washington DC, and his attempts to manage the intersection between the proliferation of cases of Covid-19 and his re-election campaign. According to Wolff, Trump blamed his contracting Covid-19 on a close friend and adviser, Chris Christie:

Trump blamed getting COVID on Chris Christie, who would himself come down with the virus a few days later (and spend a week in the ICU). Christie had sat across from him at the debate prep table, and Trump had seen the spittle come out of his mouth and tried to duck from the droplets (Wolff 2021a: Chapter 1).

Two days after he was admitted for treatment at the Walter Reed, Trump sought to reassure the American public: "I came here, wasn't feeling so well, I'm much better now," he said. Later he added: "Over the next period of a few days I guess that's the real test. We'll be seeing what happens over those next couple of days."[250] Slavitt claims "the White House physician, Sean Conley, misled the public about the severity of the president's illness— describing it as mild, even as it worsened and doctors were pumping Trump with drug cocktails not yet available to the general public as well as a number of other powerful medications" (Slavitt 2021: Chapter 11).

Speaking on CBS Face the Nation, House Speaker Nancy Pelosi, a Democrat, was critical of the president's "anti-science" attitude to the virus, which she said was shared by Republicans in congress. She expressed hope that following his positive Covid-19 diagnosis, President Trump's "heart will be open to the millions of people who have been affected" and "signal that we really have to do better in preventing the spread of this virus".[251] Determined to continue downplaying the deathly virus, on Monday, 5 October, "feeling really good", Trump tweeted he would be releasing himself from the hospital later that day, with these defiant words: "Don't be afraid of Covid. Don't let it dominate your life. We have developed, under the Trump Administration, some really great drugs & knowledge. I feel better than I did 20 years ago!!"[252]

It was not until after he left office following the 2020 election, when it emerged that Trump and his wife, Melania, "were vaccinated at the White House in secret in January". Probably, with little to lose but all to gain as the head of the Republican party and Godfather of Republican politics after his post-election defeat, Trump re-emerged to encourage his supporters to present themselves for vaccination. If Republican politicians are in awe of his popularity with the party rank and file, it is only proper for those who make him powerful to be alive even if not in sustainable livelihood. The BBC reports Trump's television interview on vaccination thus: "'I would recommend it,'

Mr Trump said during an interview on Fox News Primetime on Tuesday [March 16, 2021]. 'I would recommend it to a lot of people that don't want to get it and a lot of those people voted for me, frankly.' He added: 'It's a great vaccine, it's a safe vaccine and it's something that works.'"[253]

Trump's handling of Covid-19 may or may not have cost him the 2020 presidential election, as both Trump and his Democratic opponents sought to capitalise politically on the virus (Slavitt 2021; Abutaleb and Paletta 2021; Leonnig and Rucker 2021; Wolff 2021a). In Trump's mind, Wolff writes:

> COVID was the way for the Democrats not only to ruin his beautiful economy but also to steal his election—by getting people who would otherwise not vote, the "low-propensity" voters, Democratic voters, to cast ballots (Wolff 2021a: Chapter 1).

> [...] the Democrats, seizing on the COVID excuse, had pushed for mail-in voting and had encouraged their people to use this new privilege, while the Republicans had discouraged it, and therein lay the Democrats' thin margin—and it would be thin. (Wolff 2021a: Chapter 3).

To Gessen, "COVID-19 was the perfect disease for the Trump era", in that, like Trump, "it fueled fear of the Other and prompted the closing of borders" the world over. Internally, when not "pointing the finger at China" or "blaming Europe", Trump was "inciting fear of New Yorkers". It was fear that "spawned, or exposed, dozens, perhaps hundreds, of mini Trumps" (Gessen 2020: Chapter 22; see also Abutaleb and Paletta 2021: Chapter 9).

This account of how Trump dealt with Covid-19 as president echoes Chandler's argument, informed by a study of Vladimir Putin and pension reforms in Russia, that "a strategy to court voters can impel [populist] leaders to postpone or delay important decisions". It echoes as well, Chandler's argument that populist leaders are likely to make social policy mistakes, because of their propensity to act on impulse and with little consultation, and to be reluctant "to undertake measures that might be unpopular with key constituencies" (Chandler 2020: 148–149).

Trump's approach also demonstrates the limits of a populism that is narrowly driven by the need to pander to the whims and caprices of a section of the population only, when as president one has taken an oath to protect and to offer leadership to all fellow compatriots, regardless of race, ethnicity, class, gender, sexuality, culture, religion or whatever other indicators are common currency in a given country. It is unfortunate, as Gessen observes, that "Trump never tires of reminding us that not everyone can be an American or deserves to be seen as an American, and that even people who have thought of themselves as Americans—culturally, socially, politically, and legally—can be declared not-American, un-American, or anti-American". Far from being inclusive or representative and accommodating, Trump has reduced his America to: "white, male, straight, besieged, aggressive". Blinkered by fantasies of "an imaginary past" for his supporters and constituents "in which their jobs and daughters were safe from brown-skinned immigrants", Trump, in his campaign for the presidency, promised to annihilate the threat of what he called "radical Islamic terrorism". The rhetoric, stated and insinuated, was all about purging Trump's white America of the obligation "to treat African Americans as equals", understand and accommodate women meddling in politics, and gay and transgender people advertising their sexual orientation and existence (Gessen 2020: Chapter 18).

Such narrowing of being and belonging together as Americans, made it possible for Trump to pay lip service to democracy. While every political community has the right to determine inclusivity, to behave autocratically in a democracy as Trump has done is to narrow the parameters of inclusivity and participation in a manner contrary to the principles and practices that lend credence to a democratic system of government. That amounts to eating one's democratic cake and having it. Covid-19 permitting.

Trumpism: The Real Deal or a Con?

In this section, I explore the extent to which Trump, the businessman and showman politician, has lived up to or fallen short of prevalent representations of him as a renowned dealmaker or a consummate conman who sells qualities that he possesses only in abstraction (Barrett 2016[1992]). Although showmanship as a pillar of American consumer culture would like to insist on the need to distinguish between "the show" and "the real person", as well as between pronouncement, intentions and enactments (Gunn 2018), there is no reason why we can appreciate these distinctive attributes as mutually complementary towards a compositeness of being. Intentional falsehood or artful deception are just as harmful as real deception in the eyes of those who are called upon to witness it, in real life or in movie theatres, which is why people react to the show with similar emotiveness that they would react to the same act in real life. As president, Trump did not live up to his own salesmanship that took him to the White House, which was the understanding that he would be the president of all Americans, responsible and accountable to the Constitution. Instead, his political leadership thrived on nativism, mainstreaming and normalisation of far-right ideologies and conspiracy theories, deceit, repeated lies, incivility and the demonisation of fellow citizens who fell below the radar of his narrow nationalism. In other words, Trump's manifest antipathy for racial and other minorities, disregard for conviviality, social cohesion and unity in diversity expected in a nation-state as an imagined community amounted to disappointment in his leadership among many who expected otherwise despite their political differences. Whether Trump's leadership is viewed as *Trumpocracy* or *Trumpocalypse* (Frum 2018, 2020), Trumpism is both the real deal and a con. Trump suggests that being cosmopolitan and transnational is uncharacteristic and incompatible with being American and being patriotic, thus neglecting incompleteness, mobility and history and failing to provide a much more creative and imaginative prism of dealing with those whose flexible mobilities tend to unsettle those who feel more grounded and more entitled to particular spaces and places.

Let's take a closer look.

O'Brien has described Trump as more of a showman and an entertainer than a businessman or a politician. As a businessman, Trump, was unlike most businesspeople in that he "was telegenic and quite willing to jump into the fray without a script". As a showman, Trump defied the tendency in some celebrities to behave like "cultural chameleons, changing hues willy-nilly or simply shedding personas like layers of skin as fans' passions shifted". Rather, Trump opted to "simply remaining very Trumpy, very himself, from the

1970s into the new millennium. He kept the suit, kept the tie, kept the hair in unusual configurations, and week after week, year after year, kept his tongue wagging in exactly the same way". This loyalty to the Trump style, O'Brien argues, meant that Trump, in his showmanship, "came across, blazingly, as the unreal real thing" (O'Brien 2015[2005]: Chapter 7). As a showman and businessman, Trump's "marketing talents" according to O'Brien, "are grounded in an actor's disciplined ability to always hit his mark, on cue, and an unwavering commitment to staying on message (the message being: Trump = Success, and Trump = Glamour)" (O'Brien 2015[2005]: Chapter 8). It is also a talent for "everlasting" ubiquity as proven by a media story, superbly captured by Larry King, introducing Trump as his guest at the CNN in July 1990 as follows: "Our guest is Donald Trump, who is an ongoing, endless, forever story, right? You're a forever story" (O'Brien 2015[2005]: Epilogue). How much of this style did Trump take along with him into the White House?

Norris and Inglehart (2019: 3) have described "Trump as a leader who uses populist rhetoric to legitimize his style of governance, while promoting authoritarian values that threaten the liberal norms underpinning American democracy". This is in tune with other descriptions of Trump (Frum 2018; Nance 2019; Anonymous 2019; Weyland and Madrid 2019; Dean and Altemeyer 2020; Karl 2020; Drezner 2020). To some commentators, Trump and democracy are a perfect mismatch; they see him as "a strongman menacing democracy". Others have labelled him "a xenophobic and racist demagogue skilled at whipping up crowds", and to others he is "an opportunistic salesman lacking any core principles" (Norris and Inglehart 2019: 3), but who craves a world addicted and dependent on his every whim and caprice. In his branding and salesmanship, Trump, according to Leonnig and Rucker, has to his credit, an "extraordinary capacity to say things that were not true" with a straight face and the complete conviction of a consummate salesman:

> He [Trump] always seemed to have complete conviction in whatever product he was selling or argument he was making. He had an uncanny ability to say with a straight face, things are not as you've been told or even as you've seen with your own eyes. He could commit to a lie in the frame of his body and in the timbre of his voice so fully, despite all

statistical and even video evidence to the contrary. (Leonnig and Rucker 2021: Epilogue).

Trump craves the limelight, and makes no secret of it. Sims, his former assistant at the White House, observes, following the circulation of a study of dubious scientific credentials in the West Wing of the White House, "proclaiming Donald J. Trump the most famous person on the planet", Trump dreaded obscurity more than he did death or failure or loss. Sims elaborates:

> Unlike most human beings, his greatest fear wasn't death or failure or loss. It was obscurity. If he was noticed, he mattered. And he didn't much care if the attention was good or bad, as long as it wasn't indifferent. Mentions in the press had long been his oxygen. Another "Page Six" scoop, another breath. A Time magazine cover, a shot of adrenaline. He spent his adult life keeping the brand going, whatever it took. He couldn't just own a nice hotel, but the most beautiful hotel ever built. He couldn't have a difficult divorce, but the most sensational ever to hit the tabloids. He couldn't just have a popular TV show, it had to be the most highly rated in history. He couldn't be a good president, he'd have to be as great—greater, even—than Lincoln. The most famous person in history? Of course he was. Donald J. Trump wouldn't settle for anything less (Sims 2019: Author's Note).

While Trump craves and lives by and for media attention, Sims argues, with interesting illustrations (including the cases of Steve Bannon and Anthony Scaramucci), that "Media attention in Trump World is a double-edged sword", and "when a staffer's media coverage detracted from the Boss, it could prove disastrous". Trump valued nothing "more than a loyal, effective surrogate who will go toe to toe with an aggressive interviewer and not give an inch", but what he could not stand were staffers who became "drunk on the attention and adulation" they harvested from the media (Sims 2019: Chapter 9).

In what some may be very critical of in Trump as the unprincipled person, the salesman and the politician, others find an irresistible attraction and have been drawn to his leadership style, even when in certain cases, this has meant going against their own core principles and value system (Skinnell 2018a; Young 2018; Steudeman 2018).

Like him or hate him, Trump, like populism, has been able to impose himself as a phenomenon for public debate, which he has shaped remarkably, drawing on his carefully cultivated repertoire of persuasive communication skills and astuteness at adopting and adapting the media ecosystem to serve his ends. By flooding the news cycle with a tsunami of tweets, often chaotic and confusing pronouncements, Trump has somehow, to the surprise of many an observer often managed to outsell many of his competitors for the limelight in public debate and media attention, while rendering some so exhausted and gasping for breath that they have been rushed to ICUs for political oxygen. Trump's capacity to take a loyal and significant portion of the public into his confidence and hold them captive through his ability to engineer spectacle and manufacture consent using his media agenda-setting wizardry would be the envy of many a confidence trickster. With such a commanding presence in public affairs, national and global debates and conversations, it is hardly surprising that studying Trump has caught on in academia, with some, like anthropologist Michael Taussig, suggesting a new area of inquiry – "Trump Studies"[254] – "with a distinctive political and theoretical imperative" (Brabazon et al. 2019: 4).

As someone who has repeatedly touted his deal-making skills, Trump's Trumpism rightly attracts curiosity. Is it the real deal or a conman's trick? And if the latter, for how long could Trump get away with the con? In *Authoritarian Nightmare: Trump and His Supporters*, Dean and Altemeyer provide an insightful discussion of Trump using the "Conman Scale" which "was developed in 1996 to explore the thinking of people who might want to become authoritarian leaders" (Dean and Altemeyer 2020: Chapter 3). In *The Art of the Deal*, Trump volunteers this advice:

> You can't con people, at least not for long. You can create excitement, you can do wonderful promotion and get all kinds of press, and you can throw in a little hyperbole. But if you don't deliver the goods, people will eventually catch on. (Trump with Schwartz 1987: 60)

How faithfully has Trump lived up to his own advice in salesmanship? Not much. In his political leadership, Trump has thrived on nativism, mainstreaming and normalisation of far-right ideologies and conspiracy theories, deceit, repeated lies and incivility through the appropriation of social media and manipulation of mindsets (Waisbord et al. 2018; Mudde 2019; Hassan 2019). His leadership style is full of antipathy for racialised people and disregard for conviviality, interdependence, social cohesion and a sort of unity in diversity expected in a nation-state as an imagined community. This is the case, even though his commitments, over and above being very personal, are narrowly tailored to suit the collective whims and caprices of the political, economic and cultural elites.

In spite of his (purported) deal-making skills, Trump lost a second presidential term because of his lack of concern for people of colour, support for far-right groups and poor handling of the Covid-19 pandemic. Some would add that Trump, the deal maker, should have found wriggle room to avoid impeachment, not to mention being twice impeached (Toobin 2020; Wolff 2018, 2019, 2021a; Rucker and Leonnig 2020; Leonnig and Rucker 2021; Bender 2021). Interpreted in terms that highlight the ambiguity in populist appropriation of "the people", twice impeached meant that twice, regardless of Trump's overwhelming popularity with his Republican party and base, the people's constitutionally recognised representatives had, in their majority, found Trump guilty of betraying the national interest and the people of the nation by acting as if he was above the law. Impeachment meant that Trump had lost the political and legal legitimacy to govern (Rohde 2020: Chapter 19). Nonetheless, there is a certain "Trump appeal" that still makes him popular, even after his impeachments and electoral defeat in 2020.[255] He continues to wield phenomenal power within the Republican party and is able to mobilise party structures at the grassroots and in Congress to discipline and punish those who dare cross him, including fellow Republicans in the House (10 out of 197), who voted to impeach him, and in the Senate (7 out of 50), who were ready to convict him, following the mob insurrection he mobilised and urged to march on 6 January 2021 to the Capitol building to overturn the outcome of the election. This practice of detecting and discrediting perceived enemies or non-loyalists dates back to when "A network of conservative activists, aided by a British former spy, mounted a campaign during the Trump administration to discredit perceived enemies of President Trump inside the government".[256]

Trump's craft at manipulating communication technology, particularly social media, and everybody around him through repeated lies constitutes the source of his popular appeal. In addition, it is important to factor in how Trump's political opponents have also emboldened him and made his case more appealing to the populace than theirs. Globalisation and liberal ideologies sustained by the Democratic party continue to make the party unpopular in more conservative circles and thus strengthen the party's opponents, no matter how lunatic such opponents may be. Even as Trump is perceived as the most extreme epitome of such lunacy, he is able to contain revulsion against him among Republicans by playing up the perceived left-wing extremities of politicians such as Bernie Sanders and Alexandria Ocasio-Cortez, ignoring concerns of African Americans and Native Americans, criticising socialism, Asians and LGBTQI+ communities, scapegoating immigrants and badmouthing women and others that have been stereotyped in conventional, conservative and white Christian religious circles.

Republicans and Democrats have voters on whose loyalty they can count. According to Wilkerson, in terms of the most loyal voters, "white evangelicals are to Republicans what African-Americans are to Democrats, though each makes up a minority of the total electorate" (Wilkerson 2020: 329). Although Trump's support among white Evangelical Christians – who saw him as "the strongman the Christian right had long been waiting for" even as he was hardly more than a "baby Christian" (Posner 2020: Introduction) – is overwhelming (Posner 2020), as discussed below, his support among religious groups is hardly limited to white Evangelical Christians. Americans of other races and religious persuasions are likely, on matters such as tolerance towards sexual freedoms and reproductive rights for example, to share more with Republican ideologies and Trumpism than with left-wing liberals and Democrats. Hence, it is hardly surprising that Trump has greater support in Texas and Florida, two states in America which are heavily populated by Latino immigrants from Central and South America and the Caribbean, though Trump appears to despise and oppress them in his rhetoric and constant stigmatisation of immigrants and "shithole countries". So, it is not only white conservatives that provide refuge and support to Trumpism but also conservative Catholics, including in Latino immigrant communities, which, ironically, have been among the most afflicted by Trumpism. Similarly, many Asian Americans who are scared by Democrats' proclaimed or perceived liberal dissemblance, double-standards, dominance and failure to protect traditional fundamental values such as marriage between heterosexual people and the traditional family, are likely to vote for Trump despite themselves. Curiously as well, and driven by the same reasoning, Trump enjoys much support in many a "shithole" country in Africa, where, as Dion Forster observes, US style evangelicalism is alive and well, even with Trump gone from office. Trump's African supporters may not have voting rights in the USA, but many of them actively prayed for Trump to win the 2020 election. [257] Such Christians, in the US, Africa and elsewhere see Trump as a necessary evil, and a case of the rejected stone becoming the corner stone. The perception that liberals and Democrats accommodate and accept some social practices traditionally considered deviant and unacceptable by society and mainstream religious bodies, as well as the sense that liberals and Democrats attempt to force or even impose such practices into the mainstream, has helped embolden the Republican position and Trumpism at the extreme. As Ivanka Trump would put it:

> Perception is more important than reality. If someone perceives something to be true, it is more important than if it is in fact true. This doesn't mean you should be duplicitous or deceitful, but don't go out of your way to correct a false assumption if it plays to your advantage. (Trump, I. 2009: Introduction).

With these considerations in mind, it could be argued that Trump is both the real deal and a con.

Trumpian politics narrowly limits recognition and representation for the disaffected mainly to his white Republican base. Hillary Clinton, during the 2016 presidential campaign, famously referred to Trump's base as "a basket of deplorables", and it did not help her campaign that this label was taken out of context in the reporting that followed. Kivisto provides a background and context that is missing from much of the reporting, which is worth citing in detail here:

> In a speech delivered at the LGBT for Hillary Gala in New York City on September 9, 2016, Hillary Clinton characterized Trump voters in part in terms that drew a firestorm of criticism from many of those very supporters. What became the takeaway for many in the media and

for the Trump camp was when she said that "you could put half of Trump's supporters into what I call the basket of deplorables. Right? The racist, sexist, homophobic, xenophobic, Islamophobic — you name it." But the critics failed to take her comments in context or in their entirety. In terms of context, she was responding to Trump's "latest outrageous, offensive, and inappropriate comments" and reacting to what she cast as a "volatile political environment," prefacing her categorization as being "grossly generalistic."

But what was missing from most reporting on the speech was what she went on to say, which was that in another basket there were "people who feel that the government has let them down, the economy has let them down, nobody cares about them, nobody worries about what happens to their lives and their futures, and they're just desperate for change." She went on to say that, "Those are people we have to understand and empathize with as well" (quoted in Holan 2016) (Kivisto 2017: 35–36)

In context or out of context, it is still problematic for Hillary Clinton to call her fellow citizens and electorate "deplorables", a term reminiscent of other derogatory referents used throughout history to naturalise poverty and suggest that this group of white Americans were trash, rubbish or waste fit to be forgotten or left behind like debris, if not quite simply sterilised to make way for the supremacy of the superior breed of a master class (Isenberg 2016). If elected, she would have been their President and would have to have their wellbeing in mind. And if she failed to rise to the call of being the president of the "deplorables" as well, she would have been blamed in the same way that Trump has been blamed for failing to be the president of those he repeatedly disparages as "immigrants", "Muslims" and "the radical left", among others.

Quinn compares Donald Trump to Andrew Jackson, who, like Trump was seen by many as "a populist hero", and points to the "similarities in their confrontational natures, blunt talk and fiery tempers". To Quinn, "It is fascinating how the intellectual elites of Jackson's time had the same level of contempt for the common man as the arrogant ruling elite have for the 'deplorables' inhabiting the towns and hamlets of flyover America today". Quinn's article reads like a celebration of Jackson – and, by extension, of Trump – and Quinn uses harsh language to describe Trump's opponents.[258]

Given his talent for making things unintelligible, Trump, to some, may not be capable of intellectual thought, and his awareness and grasp of history may be superficial. Indeed, if one takes Mary Trump's word for it, "Donald [Trump] today is much as he was at three years old: incapable of growing, learning or evolving, unable to regulate his emotions, moderate his responses, or take in and synthesize information" (Trump, M. L. 2020: 197). However, according to Egan, Andrew Jackson's influence on Trump is undeniable. Not only did Jacksons' portrait hang in Trump's office, but Jackson also "is often called a populist, the first people's president. Jackson was also an unapologetic slave owner" and "To many Native Americans, Jackson is just short of Hitler — a genocidal monster".[259] Notwithstanding, Steve Bannon – Trump's anti-globalist yet global in scope, anti-EU and anti-secularist chief political strategist and advisor who was known to have Trump's ear for quite some time (Fuchs 2018: 133–137), and who it was suspected "could use American power like a crowbar to pull the EU apart"[260] – frequently cited Jackson as a role model for President Trump.

Zakaria's comment on liberal attitudes toward Bannon as a threat to democracy is worth bearing in mind here. To him, many on the left fear Bannon's "white nationalism", and the possibility that this could "prove seductive and persuasive to too many people". For this reason, Zakaria concludes, Bannon's detractors have resolved not to "give him a platform, and hope that this will make his ideas go away". But ideas are stubborn, and would not simply disappear with denying their authors or those who harbour them a platform. On the contrary, Zakaria argues, "by trying to suppress Bannon and others on the right, liberals are likely making their ideas seem more potent". All they need is appraise themselves of the failed "efforts of communist countries to muzzle capitalist ideas".[261]

Egan argued, as Trump ascended to the presidency, that the "fate of the republic may hinge on how much Trump decides to emulate the slaveholding, Indian-hating, Constitution-violating man staring at him from that portrait in the Oval Office", adding, "Jackson is too close for comfort".[262] The Jacksonians who see similarities with Trump, according to Mead, share the conviction that the "role of government in the US consists in fulfilling 'the country's destiny by looking after the physical security and economic well-being of the American people in their national home—and to do that while interfering as little as possible with the individual freedom that makes the country unique'". [263] As Drezner explains, for Jacksonians, American exceptionalism is seen "not as a function of the universal appeal of American ideas, or even as a function of a unique American vocation to transform the world, but rather as rooted in the country's singular commitment to the equality and dignity of individual American citizens". [264] Trump, in Walt's estimation, is seeking to reverse the trends of the early 1990s, when American elites "fueled a dangerous overconfidence" among themselves, with the belief that "they had the right, the responsibility, and the wisdom to shape political arrangements in every corner of the world. That vision turned out to be a hubristic fantasy". [265] Trump's ambitions may be far from shaping the affairs of the world in the interest of America and its constitutional values, but they certainly are all about bending everyone, American and foreign alike, to Trump and Trumpism as the best brand and the best value system ever.

In light of Trump's propensity for demagoguery – fuelled by a "worldview of simple truths and falsehoods" and rhetoric of victimhood, scapegoating and reversal "centered on the preservation of a conception of American identity rooted in whiteness, masculinity, and heteronormativity" (Steudeman 2018) – and strongman populism (Ben-Ghiat 2020), in October 2016, Diamond reflected on what would happen if a demagogue or strongman were to rise to power in the US, a feat Trump achieved shortly after. Diamond observed that Trump "has increasingly embraced the rhetoric and logic of the extremist far-right in American history", and called Trumpism "modern-day McCarthyism". Diamond pondered then what is still being considered in 2021 after Trump left the presidency though still having a solid grip on the Republican party: "It is now not only fair but necessary to ask whether those in Donald Trump's party who fail to denounce his democratic disloyalty are not themselves doing great damage to American democracy". [266] Categorising Trump's Republican party as "a cult" that has aided and abetted Trump's vandalisation of facts with shameless impunity, Rich predicts that the truth about his enablers and defenders as strategically located powerful co-conspirators – "The Trump Toaders", as he calls them – would out. [267] As Balz puts it:

Being a Republican during the Trump presidency demands much. He is quick to anger at any Republican who strays from absolute loyalty and at times has sought to punish those who have. Few have had the wherewithal to question him, and they have generally paid a price. Their examples have shaped the behavior of others in the party.[268]

Trumpocracy is how Frum characterises Trump rule (Frum 2018), which is infused with populist and nativist rhetoric, and by Trump's autocratic urges, and his plutocratic policies.[269] It is significant that as President-elect, Frum observed, that Trump was keener to reach out to populists in Europe than to anyone else. "President-Elect Trump received Nigel Farage, the former leader of the UK Independence Party, before he met British Prime Minister Theresa May. Before Bannon joined the Trump campaign, he promoted the Dutch politician Geert Wilders and France's Marine Le Pen on his Breitbart.com website. Hungary's authoritarian prime minister, Viktor Orbán, claimed to have been granted a call with President-Elect Trump in November before the president of France" (Frum 2018: 156).

Trumpism, according to Tierney, is "a brew of nationalist, populist, anti-establishment, anti-'expert', anti-globalist, protectionist, 'us versus them', and most of all, anti-immigrant sentiment". Tierney acknowledges that, although this movement did not begin with him, Trump has "embraced and shaped the mood so profoundly that it's possible to brand the movement with his name". Tierney discusses commonalities between Trumpism(s) in different parts of the world and attempts to explain the sentiments that tie it all together. To him, the "glue that binds Trumpism together is anti-immigrant sentiment and fear of the 'other'".[270]

Tengjun has a slightly different take by arguing that: "Trumpism is created and built by him alone. Yet Trumpism doesn't equal isolationism as Trump is not an isolationist, but mainly a conservative." Such conservatism, domestically, "emphasizes the role of tradition, language and culture in social cohesion" and "is different from modern conservatism or liberalism". Tengjun makes a case for Trumpism to be taken seriously. "No matter what disputes Trumpism causes and how long it can last or even the possibilities of a step down," writes Tengjun, "we should realize that Trumpism has come into being and may be the reality that we need to face for a long time."[271]

To Pfeiffer, Trumpism is nothing but "billionaire-funded racial grievance politics" or "plutocracy in populist clothing". Put differently, Trumpism, he argues, is a "political playbook" that: finds nothing objectionable in promoting "racial division to turn out the base"; condoning and encouraging lying with reckless abandon; treating the press as the enemy of the people; being more interested in personalised power than in the will of the people; indulging in propaganda as a preferred mode of communication; and a determination to win at all costs (Pfeiffer 2020: Chapter 1; see also Kalb 2018). Frum terms Trumpism an "infinity fraud" or "a scam that exploits the trust of people who feel something in common with the fraudster" (Frum 2020: Introduction). Pfeiffer predicts that Trumpism will outlive Trump, simply because it unites two halves that are core to Republican conservative politics, "the billionaires and the bigots". He elaborates that upon attaining power, not only did Trump opt "to keep the racist rhetoric and inflammatory tweets that endeared him to the base, but he also decided to adopt the policy agenda of the donor class". This embrace of apparent contradictory options, was Trump's indication to the party that "they could have their racism and their tax cuts, too". Pfeiffer sees in this union "the core of Trumpism—billionaire-funded racial grievance politics". Trump has "united the billionaires and the bigots", a union that will outlive Trump "because they need each other to maintain their political power" (Pfeiffer 2020: Chapter 1).

Frum agrees (2020). To curb Trumpism and engineer the return of light and "inaugurate a new and better order in which justice would triumph at last over injustice", Frum in *Trumpocalypse*, calls for major progressive "reforms of the process of government" to "enhance the efficiency of government, improve the integrity of elections, and strengthen the national state" and ensure "reconciliation and nation-building" in earnest (Frum 2020: Introduction). Those who seek restoration have far more in common with those who seek transformation than is ever provided for by the divisive politics of fear and hate.

In Dionne's perspective, not only does the country need both restoration and transformation, but polarised citizens must also rise above mistrust of one another's motives and their squabbles to restore valued democratic norms and begin the process of healing the social and economic wounds that inspired Trump to the presidency (Dionne 2020). This requires abandonment of fantasies of victimhood left and right, and the mass production and circulation of fear and hate that has had the effect of demonising instead of embracing a living-togetherness at the service of social and economic justice (Samuels 2016; Reid 2019; Steudeman 2018; Sinn and Harasta 2019; Barber 2020).

During Trump's presidency, his administration seemed to suggest that being cosmopolitan and transnational is uncharacteristic and incompatible with being American and being patriotic. A position that did not necessarily deter him personally from pursuing private business interests such as running golf courses and erecting Trump Towers outside of the USA (Simpson and Fritsch 2019: Chapter 2 & 3; Reid 2019: Chapter 1 & 2).[272] Buruma discusses Stephen Miller, a foremost proponent of such thinking and Trump's adviser on immigration – who was associated with some of Trump's barbaric, sadistic and spectacularly cruel mass deportations and the caging of immigrant children at the Mexican border – and Miller's use of "cosmopolitan" as an insult. Buruma draws parallels to how the term was used as an anti-Semitic code-word by Stalin and pre-war fascists. He observes that "One of the oddities of the Trump administration" was that several of its leading representatives had "revived traditionally anti-Semitic rhetoric, even though some of them, like Miller, are Jewish." Buruma argues that Miller's use of "cosmopolitan" may refer both to "Muslims and the liberal urban elites", and he concludes that Miller was probably unaware of the broader history of the term[273] (see also Guerrero 2020: Chapter 12). Guerrero details the extent to which Stephen Miller and Donald Trump are "hatemongers" at the service of "the white nationalist agenda", using the contentious issues of border and immigration control to demonise migrants and fuel the flames of racism, xenophobia and polarisation among Americans. They knew the value of outrage only too well, and the more upset and numb their opponents grew, the stronger their supporters became (Guerrero 2020).

David Glosser highlights the hypocrisy in Miller's immigration approach, from the perspective of an uncle, in an article titled "Stephen Miller Is an Immigration Hypocrite. I know Because I am

His Uncle". Describing Miller as part of a "family with a chain immigration story" that started from Belarus, Glosser writes, "I have watched with dismay and increasing horror as my nephew, an educated man who is well aware of his heritage, has become the architect of immigration policies that repudiate the very foundation of our family's life in this country." Glosser calls upon "free Americans, and descendants of immigrants and refugees", to exercise their "conscience by voting for candidates who will stand up for our highest national values and not succumb to our lowest fears".[274]

Indeed, not only does everyone in America, with the exception of Native-Americans, have a more recent history of mobility that took them directly or through their forebears from other geographies far and near to the USA, President Trump is a noteworthy example of someone who is married to more recent immigrants, and who was actively facilitating the naturalisation of Melania's parents as his tough policies against "chain migration" were being implemented. This is how Reid captures the double standards and contradictions with regards to Trump:

> There was tremendous irony in Donald Trump being the avatar for this broad rejection of newcomers. Two of his three wives had been immigrants, and Melania's immigration status when she arrived in the United States remained an elusive story to pin down. Her parents and sister joined her in America through the same "chain migration" Trump so vehemently derided. And Trump's own paternal grandfather, Friedrich Drumpf, arrived in the 1890s from Bavaria at sixteen years of age without papers and without speaking English (Reid 2019: Chapter 1).

Taking incompleteness, mobility and history seriously would provide a much more creative and imaginative prism of dealing with those who come after us, or those whose flexible mobilities tend to unsettle those who feel more grounded and more entitled to particular spaces and places. With humility comes conviviality.

Arguing for a nuanced approach sensitive to the predicaments of both insiders and outsiders, host communities and immigrants, Kaufmann expresses the view that to want "to keep a country ethnically and racially 'pure' is racist". However, to seek "to slow down an ethnically different inflow so as not to disrupt radically the sense of ethnicity and nationhood of large numbers of people is not, on a dictionary definition, racist – though it becomes so if the reason for restriction is hating or fearing the newcomers". [275] Patten concurs, affirming that there "is nothing wrong with nationalism when it is simply a celebration of a country's best values, traditions, and history," but warns that, once "kindled, nationalism can easily rage out of control, consuming all moderating structures and leaving communities – and entire countries – at the mercy of even more dangerous arsonists".[276] Kaufmann draws attention to the reality of the contemporary world in which "borders are secure but populations are in flux". In is a context in which "Few wish to restrict citizenship to the ethnic majority, but many are uncomfortable with a wholesale transformation of their societies – even over generations".[277]

The challenge thus becomes how to reconcile the imperative of mobility needed to activate one's potency and efficacy through encounters and relationships with equally mobile others, while at the same time maintaining an acceptable and healthy recognition and representation of dignity in identity and identification as an essential reality that is simultaneously a permanent work in progress. It is to such a challenge that Kakutani refers, with reference to American leaders who have "viewed America as a work in progress – a country in the process of perfecting itself". Among such leaders Kakutani names Abraham Lincoln, Martin Luther King Jr. and Barack Obama, but he warns, as did Dr King, that "progress is neither automatic nor inevitable" but requires "continuous dedication and struggle" (Kakutani 2018: 22–23). It is hardly a secret, argues Mary Trump, that as a country born of and sustained by multiple traumas, "America is a deeply imperfect country—a country that has never actually been a democracy for all of its people, just for a privileged majority—but it always had the potential to become that hoped for more perfect union" (Trump, M. L. 2021: Introduction). Gessen agrees, adding that until the Trump presidency, "Republican and Democratic presidents regularly reminded the American public that the country's democracy was a work in progress, that its guiding principles were a set of abstract ideals that continued to be reinterpreted" (Gessen 2020: Chapter 16). Indeed, whether in America or elsewhere, as William Taylor, a Trump appointed Charge D'Affairs and acting ambassador at the US Embassy in Ukraine and witness at the first

Trump impeachment trial writes, "strengthening and protecting democratic values is a constant process, requiring persistence and steady work by both officials and ordinary citizens".[278]

Kaplan compares Trumpism to "Caesarism", which "is roughly characterized by a charismatic strongman, popular with the masses, whose rule culminates in an exaggerated role for the military". He contends that with the election of Trump in 2016, America was moving in this direction.[279] It should be noted, however, that though Trump was fond of the military and of co-opting some high-profile military officers to serve in his administration, the military came together and gave advance notice that it would not support Trump's attempt to overturn the 2020 election results.[280] It was the military's line in the sand to Trump as their commander in chief. In addition, former defence secretaries, all 10 of them still living, in an opinion piece they jointly authored, urged against any attempt to involve the military in the "dangerous territory" of "election disputes".[281]

If as president, Trump was "the toddler-in-chief" (Drezner 2020) and "the bad boy" of American politics, the military was not there to encourage and collude with him in his tantrums, caprice and fantasies, but to ensure that the age-old institutions and processes of American constitutional democracy survived his stormy passage and wreckage. This, one gathers, from reading about how the Chairman of the Joint Chiefs of Staff, General Mark A. Milley, went about his interactions with Trump in *I Alone Can Fix It: Donald J. Trump's Catastrophic Final Year* (Leonnig and Rucker 2021: Chapters 8 & 22) as well as in *Peril* (Woodward and Costa 2021: Prologue, Chapters 26, 47, 50, 53 & Epilogue). As Bender reports, at the opening of the US Army's museum on 11 November 2020, Milley, in the presence of Trump's acting defence secretary, Chris Miller, stated categorically: "We do not take an oath to a king or a queen, a tyrant or a dictator", and "We do not take an oath to an individual" (Bender 2021: Chapter 18). Trump's former defence secretary, James Mattis, affirms that "Donald Trump is the first president in my lifetime who does not try to unite the American people—does not even pretend to try. Instead, he tries to divide us".[282] Another former general, John Kelly, Trump's former chief of staff, reportedly told friends: "The depths of his [Trump's] dishonesty is just outstanding to me. The dishonesty, the transactional nature of every relationship, though it's more pathetic than anything else. He is the most flawed person I have ever met in my life."[283]

Notwithstanding these and related urges to do the right thing, Trump broke with the country's 230-year legacy of the peaceful transfer of power when he rallied his devoted supporters – who, like him, were driven by an authoritarian impulse (Dean and Altemeyer 2020) – around his big lie of a stolen election and incited them to disrupt the counting of electoral college votes[284] (Wolff 2021a: Chapter 11; Bender 2021: Chapter 18). As the editorial board of the *Wall Street Journal* put it, "He [Trump] has refused to accept the basic bargain of democracy, which is to accept the result, win or lose. It is best for everyone, himself included, if he goes away quietly".[285] Trump was behaving like an aggressive and stubborn salesman who would not take no for an answer, and who could not bring himself to fathom another salesman – one for whom he had little regard – clinching the deal.

Trump is a "decadent leader" under whom the Republican party has "gone from being the party of Reagan to the party of Trump", Kaplan maintains. Contrasting the two, he situates Reagan as "a conservative internationalist", and Trump as "a populist nationalist". Furthermore, Reagan "represented national revival" while Trump represents "national decline".[286] By implication, while Reagan was an impetus and an inspiration for Republican politics, Trump's decadence risks taking the Republican party down the drain with him. With time, Cohen asserts, "Trump has ended up being a highly erratic, obnoxious version of the Republican normal".[287]

As "an antisystem outsider" Trump, according to Taub, has perfected the art of beating the system, extracting as much mileage from it as anyone could possibly do, and thereby raising the appeal of "antisystem populist parties in Europe, such as the National Front in France, Syriza in Greece and the Five-Star Movement in Italy".[288] By so doing, Trump has, according to Kaletsky, increased the possibility of a "contagion" of populism across Europe and the world.[289] Trumpism has found such rapid traction among strongmen in power or seeking power, populist and non-populist alike, that many have openly and proudly identified with him. Jair Bolsonaro of Brazil has been nicknamed the "Trump of the Tropics" and Lee of South Korea as "Korea's Trump".[290] Others have just been emboldened by him and his indifference to the moral high ground that America used to claim and exert in international relations on matters of accountability and responsibility for politicians and the business world.

While *The Washington Post* reportedly labelled Jeff Sessions the "'Intellectual Godfather' of Trumpism" (Sims 2019: Chapter 6), Michael Wolff (2018: Chapter 8) suggests that a more appropriate term for Trumpism is Bannonism, which, according to Wylie, was characterised, inter alia, by a commitment to fundamental societal change by "breaking everything", by fracturing the "big government" and "big capitalism" "the establishment" to liberate the American people and their destiny from the tyranny of "the administrative state" (Wylie 2019: Chapter 7). According to Wolff, it was initially Steve Bannon, when he became Trump's campaign manager in 2016, who espoused the virtues of isolationism and a commitment to working-class, rural American Republicanism and convinced Trump to take seriously this segment of the population to win voters. Trumpism with a distinctive Bannon flavour is also about whiteness in America, if not white supremacy, lest whites be reduced to playing second fiddle in a country they perceive as first and foremost theirs. To white Americans, if the country does not belong to them by birth, it certainly does by inheritance from their forebears who turned the tables of territorial ownership on the indigenous Native American populations they conquered, while taking advantage of the labour of enslaved African-Americans. Trumpism appears to at least pay lip service to the cause of disaffected whites and to encourage them to blame, for their predicaments, counterpart populists to the left of what Trump loves to refer to as "the Democrat party".[291] It is significant how under Trumpism, the popular white supremacists found the opportunity to voice deep thoughts and stage symbolic acts in much more daring ways than was evident in administrations much more in tune with conventional liberalism (Coates 2017; Reid 2019; Nance 2019; Geary et al. 2020).

Clark echoes some of these concerns, arguing that "a corrupt, arrogant, and hideously out-of-touch establishment lies teetering on the brink". Unlike 100 years ago, the gap between rich and poor is "truly staggering", and it is worthy of note, Clark proposes, that "it's the populist right – and not the left – that's making all the headway". He faults "the liberal-dominated western left of today" for shying away from "proletarian rebelliousness", and for failing to embrace "working-class populism and positioning themselves at the forefront of anti-establishment protests as Lenin and the Bolsheviks did in 1917".[292]

There is no escaping the expectation, Nye argues, that "Policy elites who want to support globalization and an open economy will clearly need to pay more attention to economic inequality, help those disrupted by change, and stimulate broad-based economic growth."[293] The super-rich may not hate all populists, but "just those who refuse to make them richer", as Chakrabortty claims, however, if they want to carry on with capitalism, the super-rich and the rich "will need to give up their winnings and cede some ground".[294] "There is a dawning recognition", as Beckett points out, "that a new kind of economy is needed: fairer, more inclusive, less exploitative, less destructive of society and the planet". He welcomes the emergence of a network of thinkers, activists and politicians in Britain and the US who "have begun to seize this opportunity". Not only are Britain and the US in many ways the most capitalist Western countries they are also the ones where the problems of capitalism are starkest, according to Beckett. The network "are trying to construct a new kind of leftwing economics: one that addresses the flaws of the 21st-century economy, but which also explains, in practical ways, how future leftwing governments could create a better one".[295]

According to Rutherford, the populist right in North America and Europe attracts more sympathy than the progressive left. The aggressive pursuit of liberal globalism has exacerbating inequalities that have jeopardised class interests and rekindled interest in nationalism and kindred social identities as people shop for security and confidence "in order to stand up for themselves and challenge powerful interests". Rutherfold is categorical, in the case of Europe and North America, that "the populist right" not "the progressive left", "speaks for those who feel dispossessed" and that "is winning the arguments between nationalism and cosmopolitanism, national sovereignty and global governance, and particularism and universalism".[296]

If the American empire is showing signs of decline, Steigan argues, instead of bemoaning the fact that people are "turning their back on the globalism they have preached for decades" and "turning instead to populist politics and are so 'reactionary'", the globalists should rather accept blame. For "it is the globalists who are playing Russian

185

roulette. It is their system that has made us so extremely vulnerable".[297] Populism is thus portrayed as those who have traditionally and quietly borne the brunt of the ill-thought policies of capitalism's global ambitions and of globalisation gone wild finally rising up to say, "enough is enough!" (Judis 2016).

Faced with growing white populism championed by Trump, Buruma expected, "civil-rights groups, NGOs, students, human-rights activists, Democratic members of Congress, and even some Republicans" to "do everything in their power to push back against Trump's worst impulses". As a raw, untamed and supremely self-absorbed impulse, the advent of Trump as a significant, dangerous, divisive, capricious and tantrum-throwing force in American politics is enough for long-dormant political activism to "erupt into mass protest, with resurgent liberal idealism breaking the wave of right-wing populism".[298] Some would point to the phenomenal rise of congresswoman Alexandria Ocasio-Cortez and her causes such as the Green New Deal, which Republicans are keen to label socialist or left-wing populist, as evidence in this regard. In addition, worthy of note are various movements from Black Lives Matter to the MeToo movement that have championed the causes of persons and groups marginalised or oppressed because of their race or gender or sexuality. According to Invernizzi-Accetti and Steinmetz-Jenkins, "the American left has asked itself tough questions about what it must do to respond" to Trump's rise, since his election in 2016. The American right needs some soul searching of its own about its future in a genuine democracy. They believe that Christian voters are well placed to "play a key role in moving the right away from the likes of Trump" and in the interest of democracy.[299]

Some, according to Smith, see right-wing populism in the USA as a re-emergence by dominant white males who temporarily lost their power to Barack Obama for eight years. Smith cites Halifu Osumare who expresses this sentiment in these words: "I think that Barack Obama was such a rupture in the master narrative of the white, wealthy male being the only possible leader for this country, the original sin of America erupted with Donald Trump and we had permission for the violent racist past to re-emerge." Trump's blatant and latent racism – working in tandem with his base – seems to have been baked into the cake of exclusionism. Smith also cites Timothy Snyder who says: "I think the eight years of Obama were in large measure a kind of self-congratulatory illusion instead of the very tough remaking of politics that probably had to happen if we weren't going to get a Trump."[300]

Kivisto stresses the importance of inserting Trumpism within the long history of an "American identity [that] has been the product of identity politics from the founding of the Republic, when it was determined that [enslaved persons] were to be excluded from the benefits of citizenship" and to understand that "in that long history, it has always been the disadvantaged and marginalized that have had to" struggle against their individual and collective stigmatisation (Kivisto 2017: 69).

Populism by progressive or liberal forces such as championed by Bernie Sanders (Judis 2016: Chapter 3; Parmar 2017) and movements like Black Lives Matter and MeToo in the USA, Europe and beyond, usually focuses on challenging systems of patriarchal violence and exclusion erected and/or perpetuated by strongmen politics along with their authoritarian variants of populism in which the systematic erosion of women's rights and heteronormativity are normalised (Grewal 2020). It calls for a more inclusive deracialised and depatriarchalised liberal democracy, free of gerrymandering and related disenfranchisement gimmicks (Abrams 2020; Reid 2019), which gimmicks, Kakutani observes, favour Republicans. Republicans "launched a concerted effort after Obama's election in 2008 to gain control of state governments, which are in charge of drawing (or redrawing) congressional districts" (Kakutani 2018: 109).

Left-wing populism is more amenable, at least, in the case of the USA, to freedom of movement for people, cultures, religions and things, tangible and intangible, across borders, and is more likely to appeal to the younger than it is to older generations. Stephens argues that the decade, from 2010, "has been fundamentally shaped by the technological creations of the young, in the form of social media and mobile apps; by the mass migrations of the young, from Africa and the Middle East to Europe and from Latin America to the U.S.; by the diseases of the (mostly) young, notably addiction and mental illness; and by the moral convictions of the young, from the #MeToo and Black Lives Matter movements in the U.S. to mass demonstrations from Cairo to Hong Kong".[301]

Edwards makes a clear distinction between what he terms "constitutional populism" – "a strain of politics that runs from

Goldwater to Trump" – which "has helped to shape the politics of American conservatism and its chosen political instrument, the Republican Party" and "Populism on the Left, as personified by Senator Bernie Sanders and Congresswoman Alexandria Ocasio-Cortez", which has "socialist, secular, globalist, and utopian roots". Edwards further explains that the silent, moral or forgotten Americans awake to constitutional populism are characterised by "a respect for the Founders and the founding documents, a less intrusive federal government, a balanced budget and a reduced national debt, a code of law and order that favors the victim and not the criminal, and a strong national defense". Furthermore, this group of Americans, according to Edwards, as if in contrast to other Americans, who do not love America, which they consider "exceptional", are "protective" of America's "Judeo-Christian heritage and historic symbols like the American flag". Such Americans are "more conservative when times are good and more populist when the times are not so good" but always look to "the Constitution" as their "political compass".[302]

Kazin recognises Bernie Sanders and Donald Trump to represent competing variants in the American populist tradition. However, he points out that unlike past populist leaders such as Andrew Jackson, Father Charles Coughlin and George Wallace, both Tump and Sanders lack "a coherent, emotionally rousing description of 'the people' they claimed to represent" (Kazin 2017[1995]: xiv). Using Bernie Sanders as a consistent representation of left-wing populism, Kazin elaborates that what passes for left-wing American populism "directs its ire exclusively upward: at corporate elites and their enablers in government who have allegedly betrayed the interests of the men and women who do the nation's essential work". Their concept of "the people" is "based on economic interests" and shies away from "identifying themselves as supporters or opponents of any particular ethnic group or religion". As part of "a broadly liberal current in American political life", they subscribe to and promote a version of civic nationalism that champions fundamental equality of all human beings, promote the inalienable rights to life, liberty and the pursuit of happiness for all and sundry, and militate for a democratic government that draws legitimacy from the will of the people. "Sanders advanced this type of populism in nearly every speech he delivered during his campaign for president [in 2016]"

(Kazin 2017[1995]: xiii). The exclusive focus by left-wing populism on the economic interests of the people, however inclusive, could be seen by some as leaving much to be desired by giving the impression that being human can be reduced to economics alone. It begs the question of how people that are economically happy, with guaranteed livelihoods, cope with a world that insists on solidarities informed by differentiation along lines of race and ethnicity, geography and class, gender and sexuality, age, culture, religion, education and other non-economic but salient social categories.

Kazin maintains that although similar to Sanders's populism in its blame of "elites in big business and government for undermining the common folk's well-being and political liberties", Trump's populism is different in that its "definition of 'the people' is narrower and ethnically restrictive". This has "For most of U.S. history, [...] meant only citizens of European heritage— 'real Americans' whose ethnicity alone afforded them a claim to share in the country's bounty." Those like Trump, who subscribe to this ethnically restrictive populism believe in conspiracy theories or allegations that "there is a nefarious alliance between evil forces on high and the unworthy, dark-skinned poor below—a cabal that imperils the interests and values of the patriotic (white) majority in the middle". Kazin explains the "suspicion of an unwritten pact between top and bottom" as deriving from a belief in "racial nationalism" that conceives of America in ethno-racial terms, in which "the people" derive their solidarity and kinship from common blood and skin colour and an inherent belief in their fitness for self-government (Kazin 2017[1995]: xiii–xiv). In other words, being born to rule and not to be ruled. This belief in a unifying, standardised, routinised and shared Europeanness of being American persists and is actively perpetuated and capitalised upon by politicians and others despite the lived existence to the contrary. The politicians who, like Trump, subscribe to this belief in the superiority of the European origins and breed of being American, unlike Sanders, believe that life and being human are larger than livelihoods, even as they capitalise on and control access to such livelihoods with contrived regimes of power and privilege. Trump, Trumpism and kindred variants of racial nationalism believe that economics, its centrality notwithstanding, cannot be divorced from identity and identification as part and parcel of being human and American.

Racialised class and caste chasms and breeding are central considerations in how identities are claimed and denied in the US (Wilkerson 2020). This leads Isenberg to ask rhetorically: "If the republic was supposedly dedicated to equality, how did the language of breeds appeal as it did?" Hence her conclusion that speaking of breeds has been a way of justifying, even among those who celebrate the superiority of being European-American, "unequal status among white people" and "the best way to divide people into categories and deny that class privilege exists". To categorise someone as a part of breed means that that person cannot control who he or she is nor can he or she avert his or her appointed destiny. According to such eugenics which seeks to establish analogies between humans and animal stocks, breeding determines who rises and who falls. It is a fate neither democracy nor the American Dream can do much to change (Isenberg 2016: Epilogue). This is an important point echoed by J. D. Vance in his argument that a generic Europeanness of origin is not enough for a truly inclusive solidarity if ethnicity is insinuated out of the picture. A generic shared Europeanness of being American is too overly simplified to account for those who fall through the cracks of respectable whiteness. According to Vance, although they are Europeans without doubt, the fact of hierarchies of Europeanness means that "Americans of Scots-Irish descent who have no college degree", for whom "poverty is the family tradition" and whom fellow "Americans call […] hillbillies, rednecks, or white trash" cannot take for granted the privileges and power conferred by being white in principle (Vance 2016: Introduction).

Another distinction between Sanders and Trump comes from the fact that unlike Trump, Sanders does not claim to be the only one who can put things right in America or in his party and is willing to accept, however reluctantly, the outcome of elections even when these go against his candidacy. While they share a rhetoric of anti-elitism, it does not translate into anti-pluralism for Sanders or the claim that he is the only one who can speak on behalf of "the people". He lays no claim to being a stable genius, having good genes or being the only one who can put things right in America. The highly problematic aspect of Trump's brand of populism is that everyone who disagrees with him can be declared un-American in a heartbeat and thus denied their status as being part of "the people". It is this ideology of exclusion – of absoluteness or completeness – that many find so distressing in the anti-pluralists of the current populism moment. There is no in-between, no compositeness, no larger picture – only neat categories one can either fit into permanently or fall out of irredeemably. This amounts to a disregard for the very conviviality and interdependencies that make a nation-state possible as a permanent work in progress, in which consensus, even when initially imposed by the dominant ethnicity, is open to review and renegotiation with changing demographic and related configurations.

Optimistically, Bradford DeLong sees the end of the road for white male political dominance in Europe and North America. As he elaborates, the "period of white males' political dominion in Western democracies is coming to an end [...] at a time when economic populism is replacing technocratic management, often with white males turning to nativism in response to the destruction of their jobs and livelihoods by the impersonal forces of globalization". He draws attention to the fact that, across countries, "the old order won't give up without a fight", which is to be expected. What is certain however, he posits, is that "the caste-like privilege of white males is doomed", and what we should be preoccupied with henceforth "is how best to realize newly available opportunities for human betterment, for the benefit of all".[303]

If white male power has dominated for so long, Van Reybrouck claims, it is mainly because it has successfully "undermined the democratic process by relying on a dangerous practice of 'electoral fundamentalism'" that reduces the meaning of democracy "to voting in elections and referendums".[304] Far from being the desperate kicks of a dying horse, the upsurge in white embrace of national or cultural populism in the USA and the West, speaks to how deeply entrenched ideas, beliefs, practices and aspirations for a world of caste and racialism still are despite the doctrine of equality and rights for which liberal democracy has distinguished itself and with which it has sought to reassure outcasts (Wilkerson 2020).

Writing in 2016, Rodrik remarks that the biggest surprise regarding the rise of populism is that it had taken so long to manifest in this form, when signs were visible even two decades ago – with mainstream politicians unwilling to offer remedies for insecurity and inequality. Now the politics of anger has produced new populist demagogues. Two types of political cleavage are prominent as part of this politics of anger. One is based on identity (nationhood, ethnicity, religion) and the other on income and social class. Trump takes on the former and Sanders the latter. Both create an "other" towards which to direct anger. Moderate politicians would do well to take note and start offering real solutions that leave room for hope.[305]

Fisher and Taub argue that the dynamic, "sometimes known as a majority with a minority complex, is thought to be a major factor in the rise of right-wing populism in Europe, religious nationalism in Asia, and white nationalist terrorism in the United States and New Zealand". They argue that, "Conspiracies about foreign influence or minority birthrates are often driven by fears of a much more real change: a loss of status." Yet, such fears and efforts by majorities aimed at maintaining power and privileges unduly are at variance with modern democracy, which, as they put it, "demands that minorities be granted equal rights and opportunities, which can feel like a threat to majorities' traditional hold on power. Fears of existential, sectarian conflict can be self-realizing".[306]

Konstandaras makes the point that "Populists may play the system to gain power, but if they continue to undermine it, they will either destroy their nation, or it will destroy them".[307] Müller agrees that "populist parties are primarily protest parties and that protest cannot govern, since one cannot protest against oneself", but points to important nuances. He postulates that it is equally illusory to claim that populists in power would stop blaming the elite, as the latter have the real or imagined possibility to act behind the scenes, making it easy for populists in power to credibly continue to behave as victims (Müller 2016: 41–42). This is a point which Trump, in his four years as president, repeatedly validated through his serial claims of victimisation and witch-hunts.

Smith cautions against what he terms "the tyranny trap" in his discussion of the "decline in the status of honor and ambition" in the United States, and the need to guard against a form of postconstitutional rule that combines elements of traditional kingship with populist demagoguery and charismatic leadership. Smith maintains that men who are unproductive and cannot see beyond the personal in their ambitions for power are "a permanent challenge to a constitutional order" and "cannot be retrofitted for life in a republic". To Smith, Abraham Lincoln "was thinking of the dangers of potential usurpers, would-be Napoleons who would transform a republic into their own personal empire". Lincoln's "apprehensions, then as now, were fully merited".[308] This line of thinking is similar to Baker's, who laments losing the America he knew, the America that served as his north star, when Trump was elected in 2016. An election Baker describes as "a desecration, a foolish and vindictive act of vandalism". He protested Trump's election: "We don't want to accept this, because we cannot accept that the people, at least in the long run of things, can be wrong in our American democracy. But they can be wrong."[309]

As president, Trump would prove he was not beyond vindictiveness either. At a bi-partisan national prayer breakfast meeting following his impeachment acquittal by the Senate in February 2020, with Mitt Romney being the only Republican senator voting "guilty", Trump indicated he would not take lightly those he believed had wronged him and his family. He said: "I don't like people who use their faith as justification for doing what they know is wrong. Nor do I like people who say 'I pray for you' when they know that that's not so." Hinting at the retribution that would follow he said, "So many people have been hurt and we can't let that go on." Romney had justified his vote with: "My promise before God to apply impartial justice required that I put my personal feelings and biases aside."[310] Soon, reportedly, Trump began "to target perceived enemies over impeachment",[311] leading Peter Baker to caption: "Instead of Reconciliation, a Promise of Payback."[312]

In an act widely perceived as retribution and as a chilling and frightening message to US officials insisting on self-censorship, passive obedience and the imperative of supreme loyalty to the president and not necessarily to the USA or the constitution[313] (Frum 2020: Chapter 4), Trump "ousted Lt. Col. Alexander Vindman from his post on the National Security Council and recalled U.S. Ambassador to the European Union Gordon Sondland" both "key impeachment witnesses".[314] In the case of Vindman, he and his also "abruptly fired" twin brother, "were escorted from the White House as part of Trump's payback."[315] Vindman recounts in his book:

> On Friday, February 7, I was working on emails and the last-minute handoffs when the NSC director for resource management entered my office abruptly, accompanied by one security officer. She gave me the spiel: "Please step away from your computer, leadership has determined

your services are no longer required. Pick up any personal effects. You will be escorted from the building." (Vindman 2021: Chapter 11).

Escorting him out of the White House was apparently not punishment enough, as the president wanted him denied the promotion, he knew he deserved, in the army. Eventually, when it was apparent even to him that his promotion would not come under the Trump presidency, he announced his retirement from the army, having reached the conclusion that the "army and the entire Defense Department, it appeared, were not above conducting sham investigations in order to please this commander in chief" (Vindman 2021: Chapter 12). He blames the end of his military career on "a campaign of bullying, intimidation, and retaliation" (Vindman 2021: Epilogue). Other retaliations would follow, including the dismissal of Joseph Maguire, the acting director of national intelligence, for having "privately briefed a bipartisan group of key members of Congress, as the law required, on intelligence—specifically that Russia was interfering in the 2020 election and had developed a preference for Trump" (Leonnig and Rucker 2021: Chapter 3).

In a 4:57 PM tweet on 7 February 2020, Trump appeared to doubt Romney's religiosity with the words: "Every Republican Senator except Romney, many highly religious people, all very smart, voted against the impeachment hoax." At a Trump rally in Manchester, New Hampshire, following the impeachment, a rally at which Trump attacked Democrats and Romney, the crowd chanted "Lock her up!" about Nancy Pelosi, the Democrat Speaker of the House of Representatives, the suggestion being it was either the Trump way or no way for American democracy, institutions and Constitution. The signal was clear: America = Trump, and America – Trump = 0. Leonnig and Rucker provide ample evidence of this in their book on Trump's last year in office, reiterating that Trump "cared more about himself than the country" throughout his presidency. "Whether managing the coronavirus or addressing racial unrest or reacting to his election defeat, Trump prioritized what he thought to be his political and personal interests over the common good" (Leonnig and Rucker 2021: Prologue). Some would see in such attempts at the personalisation of power, institutionalisation of autocracy and lip service to patriotism, democracy and rule of law, the makings of a "Banana Republic", which is "un-American".[316]

Reportedly, Trump proceeded to place "Loyalists in Key Jobs Inside the White House While Raging Against Enemies Outside".[317] These and related developments were what Masha Gessen meant in November 2016 by this excerpt from an imagined address by Hillary Clinton when she lost to Donald Trump:

[….] We are standing at the edge of the abyss. Our political system, our society, our country itself are in greater danger than at any time in the last century and a half. The president-elect has made his intentions clear. We must band together right now to defend the laws, the institutions, and the ideals on which our country is based.[318]

Gessen underscores the importance of institutions in maintaining democracy, and the need for active citizen engagement in safeguarding the institutions that make democracy possible, and in fighting off autocracy and all those who would prefer little beyond cosmetic or face powder democracy (Gessen 2020).

Stiglitz is persuaded that instead of a commitment to safeguarding the "enormous increases in standards of living" that have come about since the enlightenment, and instead of resolving to "discover and address our prejudices", Trump has made no secret of seeking "to reverse all of that". To Stiglitz, Trump's active interference with or "rejection of science, in particular climate science, threatens technological progress. And his bigotry toward women, Hispanics, and Muslims […] threatens the functioning of American society and its economy, by undermining people's trust that the system is fair to all". Stiglitz sees Trump's "true objective" as being "to enrich himself and other gilded rent-seekers at the expense of those who supported him". Writing in 2017, Stiglitz called for Americans to take "action" against Trump.[319] Elliot reports that, asked "whether he really thinks Trump is a fascist, Stiglitz says: 'I certainly think he has those tendencies.'" Stiglitz adds, "We have never had a president who day after day lies and is unaffected by it. […] I think the other thing you have seen with some of these fascist leaders is using 'us versus them' as a way of dividing society."[320] Cornel West refers to Trump as "a gangster in character and a neo-fascist in content", in a resolute commitment to speak the truth and bear witness on the travails of the poor in the face of Trump era repression, economy with the truth and betrayal of working people (West 2017: 27).

Fuchs provides additional voices (including Noam Chomsky and Cornel West), elements and substantiating events on the debate about whether Trump is a fascist. For example, dissemblance and economy with the truth become effortless, and transparency loses its value (Fuchs 2018: 118–129). As the saying goes, if you tell a lie often enough you start to believe it, and so do those who follow you blindly. As someone schooled at salesmanship, Trump has mastered the idea of repetition with conviction and a straight face. He repeats things over and over again in the belief that if he says something long enough, people will start believing it (Muirhead and Rosenblum 2019: 52–54; Wolff 2021a: Chapter 9).

Kivisto draws on Jason Stanley in *How Propaganda Works*, to argue that:

> [...] the goal of the outright lies and factual distortions, which are often easily refuted, is to have the cumulative effect of changing the way people perceive the world. Authoritarian rulers rely on propaganda to create an alternative reality, a post-truth world in which ultimately the people come to view the leader as the only source of truth (Kivisto 2017: 83–84).

As someone with still vivid memories of the fascism she experienced as a child, escaping from Czechoslovakia to London for refuge and subsequently relocating to the USA, Madeleine Albright warns about stalling democracy in the US and globally. In *Fascism: A Warning*, she argues that fascism (both as an ideology and as a means of seizing and holding power), like every other human creation, can always be reinvented. Its demise, just as the achievements of liberal democracy, must not be taken for granted. She writes: "IF WE THINK OF FASCISM as a wound from the past that had almost healed, putting Trump in the White House was like ripping off the bandage and picking at the scab" (Albright 2018: 4–5, caps in original).

"Though 'fascism' generally evokes images of jack-booted thugs and mass rallies," argues Stanley, "fascist movements first politicize language. And, judging by the arguments and vocabulary now regularly used by mainstream politicians and thinkers in the US and Europe, their strategy is bearing fruit." He goes on to argue that "far-right populists" such as the US "alt-right", authoritarians and, indeed, fascists "have been self-consciously waging a battle of words in order to win the war of ideas."[321]

Cockburn argues that although "fascist leaders and fascism in the 1920s and 1930s were similar in many respects to Trump and Trumpism", there are some differences. German and Italian fascism, for example, "had additional toxic characteristics, born out of a different era and a historic experience different from the United States". These included "aggressive and ultimately disastrous wars". Trump, Cockburn affirms, "on the contrary, is a genuine 'isolationist' without a war to his credit yet",[322] even if, as would happen the waning days of his presidency, with an insurrection against democracy and the peaceful transfer of power that would be blamed in a large measure on him.

Far from fanning the flames of cultural wars, Carafano suggests a way forward that deemphasises a clash of civilisations à la Samuel Huntington and prioritises more thinking "about how the interaction between authentic civilizations can be the glue that binds the human community together [...]". He urges America to play the role of "a powerful voice in that conversation", for, "a modern civilization" gains legitimacy from "its capacity to respect and improve the human condition".[323]

On the other hand, Roberts comes to Trump's rescue with the argument that Trump has been victim of wild and unsupported accusations or illegal Russian connections since his campaign for president. The unjustified accusations orchestrated by "the national security state and its liberal media" went all the way to Trump's impeachment.[324] The persistent persecution, Robert argues, is because Trump is perceived as a threat to the "American National Security State". Trump's detractors would stop at nothing until Trump is "broken and/or removed as President of the United States", Roberts predicted in 2017. This, to him, was a sign that "Once again democracy in America is proving to be powerless."[325]

As Bradatan remarks pertinently, "Genuine democracy is difficult to achieve and once achieved, fragile". To her, "Fundamentally, humans are not predisposed to living democratically". Yet, it is worth remarking that "the democratic idea has come close to embodiment a few times in history — moments of grace when humanity almost managed to surprise itself". Bradatan prescribes "a sense of humility" as an essential ingredient for the emergence of democracy.[326]

There is enough evidence to argue that in the USA, the left-behinds (not always clearly defined) or those with the fear of being left behind are the reason why, as a populist leader, Trump, during his 2016 campaign and throughout his presidency, resorted to slogans such as "America First" and "Make America Great Again". This has led Sierakowski to argue that with Trump's election, it is all too clear that "illiberal idiocy is steadily replacing liberal democracy as the ruling doctrine of Western [...] politics today".[327] As Stephens points out, behind the use of these slogans:

> Mr Trump is proposing in effect the dismantling of the global architecture established by the US at the end of the second world war. The underlying assumption is that the Pax Americana has been an entirely altruistic venture, an international order gifted by a generous US to an ungrateful world.[328]

To Auerswald and Yun, it is important to understand why "Nativist, nationalist rhetoric — 'Make America (or Whatever Other Country) Great Again' — appeals". They argue that the appeal of such rhetoric lies in "it promises to restore the rightful economic and cultural stature of 'common people' in relation to a decadent urban intelligentsia". Auerswald and Yun maintain that "people in rural, remote places have been disproportionately losing not just jobs and opportunities but people, elementary schools and confidence in the future" in the past decade. It is unsurprising, they argue, that in the face of such "general decline, populists' promises to revive dead or dying local industries are understandably welcome".[329] It used to be the case that voters would ask for much more carefully thought-out policy options, but that seems to have ceded to hollow rhetoric laced with the right anxieties, fears, hate, stereotypes and scaremongering, with or without the encouragement of the incendiary rhetoric, tweets and Facebook posts of a charismatic leader (Skinnell 2018a).

Churchwell sees another meaning in "America first". The slogan, she indicates, has a long history, "one deeply entangled with the country's brutal legacy of slavery and white nationalism, its conflicted relationship to immigration, nativism and xenophobia". The "complex and often terrible tale this slogan represents" has often been "lost to mainstream history" Churchwell argues, "but kept alive by underground fascist movements". Other people aware of this deplorable side of America's history also quickly see through the slogan and recognise it for what it is. Churchwell shows that the Ku Klux Klan used "America first" as a motto. She suggests that Trump may have inherited eugenicist ideas from his father and hints that this legacy may have played a part in influencing his choice of slogans.[330]

Some of Trump's tweets during his presidency were not only provocatively xenophobic, they tended to be divisive and to question the citizenship and nationality of fellow elected politicians he perceived to be not quite American. Here is an illustration Trump tweeted in a series of tweets on 14 July 2019 about "Democratic Congresswomen of color":

> So interesting to see "Progressive" Democrat Congresswomen, who originally came from countries whose governments are a complete and total catastrophe, the worst, most corrupt and inept anywhere in the world (if they even have a functioning government at all), now loudly [...] and viciously telling the people of the United States, the greatest and most powerful nation on earth, how our government is to be run. Why don't they go back and fix the totally broken and crime infested places from which they came. Then come back and show us how [...] it is done. These places need your help badly, you can't leave fast enough. I'm sure that Nancy Pelosi would be very happy to quickly work out free travel arrangements![331]

According to Silverstein, the tweets "almost certainly" referred to "a quartet of newly elected non-white Democratic congresswomen who have been outspoken critics of the president and his administration". Three of them – "New York Rep. Alexandria Ocasio-Cortez, Michigan Rep. Rashida Tlaib and Massachusetts Rep. Ayanna Pressley – were born and raised in the U.S. The fourth, Minnesota Rep. Ilhan Omar, came to the U.S. from Somalia when she was 10 and became a citizen when she was 17".[332]

Alexandria Ocasio-Cortez reacted with tweets of her own, on 14 July 2019:

> Mr. President, the country I "come from," & the country we all swear to, is the United States [...]
> You are angry because you don't believe in an America where I represent New York 14, where the good people of Minnesota elected

@IlhanMN, where @RashidaTlaib fights for Michigan families, where @AyannaPressley champions little girls in Boston.

You are angry because you can't conceive of an America that includes us. You rely on a frightened America for your plunder. [...]

This brings to mind a key question at the heart of the polarisation in contemporary American politics: What to do with Trump and the Trump voters who cannot be persuaded, shamed or embarrassed "into listening to the better angels of their nature" by taking seriously "diversity, inclusion, and liberal values" (Wilson 2020: Introduction) instead of Trump's zero-sum nationalist populism that rejects the traditional limits and boundaries of American political contests (Wilson 2018, 2020)? Trump, as Wilson notes, is "a crafty animal, and he knows that four women of color who aren't pure 'Mericans like the MAGA base are a fantastic foil" (Wilson 2020: Part 4).

To George Conway, husband of Trump's senior counsel and communication expert, Kellyanne Conway, Trump's tweets about the congresswomen were conclusive. "Trump Is A Racist President", was the title of his op-ed in *The Washington Post*. As a former supporter of Trump, Conway had not come to this conclusion lightly. What he considered "just as bad" as the fact of Trump's racism, was the deafening silence of Trump's Republican enablers. As Conway recounts, even when Trump's "Naivete, resentment and outright racism" were glaring, this was met with "virtual silence from Republican leaders and officeholders". It was not "good enough" when "the nation's ideals, its very soul" are at stake to use the fact that their silence is because "they fear his wrath", "knowing how vindictive, stubborn and obtusely self-destructive Trump is".[333]

With very few exceptions (Leonnig and Rucker 2021; Wolff 2021a), if Republicans have dared to criticise Trump, his furies, capriciousness, tantrums and related inadequacies (Wolff 2018, 2019; Drezner 2020), they have tended to do so anonymously (Wolff 2019: Chapter 17; Reid 2019: Chapter 3), a trend exemplified by the Trump administration senior official who authored an editorial announcing: "I Am Part of the resistance Inside the Trump Administration" fighting to steer the president away from his "self-destructive impulses",[334] and who would subsequently publish a book *A Warning*. In the book, Anonymous presents Trump as someone who is "unfit for his job", unable to focus on governing and "prone to abuses of power, from ill-conceived schemes to punish his political rivals to a propensity for undermining vital American institutions". Anonymous affirms that, "a toxic combination of amorality and indifference" resulted in Trump's failure "to rise to the occasion in fulfilling his duties" (Anonymous 2019: Introduction).[335] Leaking to the press, according to Grisham whose book discusses the theme at length, was "the biggest sin of all in the Trump administration" (Grisham 2021: Introduction). As Sims, a former special assistant to President Trump admits, it is not always evident whose best interests are served by anonymous leaks, and the infighting and backstabbing that went on in the inner circle of Trump World (Sims 2019: Chapter 8). As an insider who had the courage to write and publish in his own name, "unlike the many leakers in the White House", Sims confesses:

> We leaked. We schemed. We backstabbed. Some of us told ourselves it was all done in the service of a higher calling—to protect the President, to deliver for the people. But usually it was for ourselves. Most of us came to Washington convinced of the justice of our cause and the righteousness of our principles, certain that our moral compasses were true. But proximity to power changes that. Donald Trump changes that. The once clear lines—between right and wrong, good and evil, light and darkness—were eroded until only a faint wrinkle remained (Sims 2019: Author's Note).

The imperative to respect duly constituted authority, albeit one with a loose sense of right and wrong, good and evil, light and darkness was a constant challenge at every level of the Trump administration. As Woodward and Costa report, even top military officials usually renowned for their loyalty to the president as their commander in chief found themselves facing serious ethical quandaries. A case in point was chairman of joint chiefs of staff, General Mark Milley, who, thinking that Trump was suffering a mental decline, had bypassed Trump and sought to reassure China and others in previously undisclosed phone calls in October 2020 and January 2021 that stability was assured and the US would not start a war even if the "routinely impulsive and unpredictable" President Trump ordered an attack in the waning days of his presidency, in a desperate move to "create a crisis" and "present himself as the savior, and use the gambit to win reelection". Two days after the 6 January

2021 storming of the Capitol, Milley sought to reassure his rattled Chinese counterpart, chief of the Joint Staff General Li Zuocheng, with words such as: "Things may look unsteady", "But that's the nature of democracy, General Li. We are 100 percent steady. Everything's fine. But democracy can be sloppy sometimes." According to Woodward and Costa, "Milley had misled" his Chinese counterpart, as on the contrary, "Milley believed January 6 was a planned, coordinated, synchronized attack on the very heart of American democracy, designed to overthrow the government to prevent the constitutional certification of a legitimate election won by Joe Biden" (Woodward and Costa 2021: Prologue).[336]

That some senior Trump administration officials were eager to have a conventional, disciplined and competent White House was not in doubt, even if how they went about ensuring this might be questionable. Chief of Staff John Kelly is one such example, as evidenced by the telling accounts of two staffers – Omarosa Manigault Newman and Cliff Sims – in their respective books after being pressured to leave the White House: *Unhinged: An Insider's Account of the Trump White House* (Newman 2018) and *Team of Vipers: My 500 Extraordinary Days in the Trump White House* (Sims 2019). According to Sims, one of Kelly's first orders of business on becoming chief of staff "was to choke off all direct access to the President" in his role as "Trump's self-appointed babysitter", and in a manner that was "vindictive, unhinged, and prone to abuse [of] his power" (Sims 2019: Chapter 15). Newman expressed similar concerns when Kelly ordered her out of the White House. Her book was one of the earliest published, non-anonymous, insider accounts into the Trump administration. According to Newman, Kelly was "so vague" about her crime, insisting her departure from the White House was because of "serious integrity violations" on which he refused to elaborate, claiming their discussion "nonnegotiable". She deduced her dismissal should have something to do with the alleged existence of a tape, from her days as one of only two African American contestants in a cast of sixteen for the first season of the reality TV show *The Apprentice*, of Trump using the "N-word" (Newman 2018: Prologue).

There is a moral question, however, Braun argues, for a Trump administration officer to decide to resist a Trump policy instead of resigning, especially a policy in response to a campaign promise, since it could be argued that "the American people, indirectly at least, had participated in making this decision", given that "Trump did not usurp power, but was democratically elected", and that "by winning the election, the American people had given him a mandate to implement what he had promised" (Braun 2021: 3). This is a point echoed by Anthony Scaramucci, who very briefly (11 days only) served as President Trump's communications director. Here is an excerpt from an CNN interview of Scaramucci:

> "There are people inside the administration that think it is their job to save America from this president," he said, with great insight, on CNN. "Okay, that is not their job. Their job is to inject this President into America so that he can explain his views properly and his policies so that we can transform America and drain the swamp and make this system fairer for the middle- and lower-income people" (Scaramucci cited in Sims 2019: Chapter 9).

The Constitution is not exactly helpful, beyond brushstrokes, on the qualities it wants in a president. As Singh rightly points out, "the Constitution stipulates only that presidents be 35, born in the United States and a citizen; wisdom, knowledge and irony are not formal prerequisites" (Singh 2017: 12). Neither does the Constitution disqualify narcissists, liars, bigots, sexists, xenophobes, homophobes or racists, to name just a few things that Trump has been accused of. To some, the fact that the Constitution is cursory on the qualities of a president does not mean that they are short on their expectations of one. Barbara Res, for example, who worked with Trump for 18 years long before he became president, insists that a "U.S. president has to know how the government works, commit to following the Constitution, and be willing to stand as its preeminent defender", as well as "put the people's needs and interests before his own". Far from rising to these and related expectations by letting the presidency change him, Trump changed the presidency. "He didn't rise to the office; he brought it down to his level" (Res 2020: Introduction).

Like Coates (2017: Epilogue), Gessen has labelled Trump's presidency, "a white male supremacist presidency", especially after Trump "drew an equivalency between the KKK and neo-Nazis on the one hand and their opponents on the other" after violent confrontations between the two groups in Charlottesville, Virginia, over removal of a Confederate statue (Gessen 2020: Chapter 17; see also Sims 2019: Chapter 10; Serwer 2021: Chapter 6). To Nance, "Trump's brand of 'populist' extremism is anything but popular" (Nance 2019: Chapter 12). Instead of seeking to unite the various shades of Americans around a shared project, Trump:

> […] has successfully parlayed the inner hatred of his followers on many subjects, particularly his anti-immigrant theme in which he claims to speak for what he calls the "silent majority's" expressions of unhappiness with the "other." Instead of celebrating America's strength through assimilation and cultural diversity, he has embodied a public loathing of immigrants. He first equated white neo-Nazis, white nationalists, and Ku Klux Klansmen with legitimate protesters in 2017, at the Unite the Right rally in Charlottesville, Virginia, and then in 2019 he doubled down and claimed they were actually innocent of the violence (Nance 2019: Chapter 12).

These and other "sins" by Trump detailed by Nance, who describes Trump as a "self-appointed 'king'" and a "modern American tyrant", lead him to assert, "unequivocally", that "Trump is unfit to be a ruler of the just people of the United States precisely as stated in the Declaration of Independence" (Nance 2019: Chapter 15; see also Reid 2019: Chapter 4).

Harnessing popular discontent to whip up nationalism, chauvinism and xenophobia, as Pillar contends regarding the Brexit vote in Britain, often goes against the interests of the common people.[337] The situation is often exacerbated, Brooks indicates, by the propensity among "populists [to] dehumanize […] people into the moronic categories of 'the people' and 'the elites'".[338] To Müller, "democracy requires pluralism and the recognition that we need to find fair terms of living together as free, equal, but also irreducibly diverse citizens" and thus "The idea of the single, homogeneous, authentic people is a fantasy", especially in a context where populists tend to treat "political opponents as 'enemies of the people' and seek to exclude them altogether" (Müller 2016: 3–4). Some wonder if Trump, who rose to office through the power of fantasy, may himself be a fantasy, yet his rhetoric and manipulation of the truth has ramifications in the real world (Skinnell 2018a; Hassan 2019). With

Trump, reality and fantasy play cat and mouse with such dizzying regularity that one loses sense of what is what.

Anti-populists may have a point when they argue for the need to acknowledge, as Mouffitt claims, the "many overlapping, competing characterisations of 'the people' in society" and that the collective or group identities often summoned by populists in their bid to oppose the people and the elite are in any case "only ever made up by individuals [...] as the primary actors in political struggles". And anti-populists may be right "to defend a world of free markets and free movement of peoples, as well as acknowledging the important role of transnational economic and political bodies in our globally interdependent era".[339]

However, the answer to populism and whatever dangers it poses is not necessarily anti-populism. Anti-populism may enjoy an intuitive appeal, especially given the increasingly divisive and volatile nature of politics and public debate, which some attribute, rightly or wrongly, to the upsurge of populism. The divisiveness and volatility are such that make many yearn for civility, maturity and deliberation. As Mouffitt asserts, anti-populists subscribe to an idea of politics beyond the confines of "referendums, plebiscites and forms of direct democracy". Their idea of politics is one in which political engagements are "relatively rational" and in which "politicians debate one another, hopefully finding consensus by convincing the other side with the strength of their arguments". They see politics not as "a battle of passions" but rather as "something of a puzzle to be solved". The emphasis for them is in being "sober, mature and graceful" in their politics, as opposed to "the allegedly immature, kneejerk and sensational politics of populists".[340]

Mouffitt cautions, however, that such anti-populism must not fall prey to the same contradictions, ambiguities and propensity to homogenise for which it criticises populism. For anti-populism to valorise consensus in an unproblematised manner, or to call for a new way, amounts to little more than rehabilitating and rebranding what populists are mobilising against. To use political stability, unity or urgency of getting along as an excuse, amounts to a ploy to sacrifice effective recognition, representation and participation for those who dare to conspire against the status quo. It is too simplistic for anti-populists to claim, a priori, that they are "concerned with the capital-T Truth" as opposed to populists whom they "cast as peddlers of lies, manipulating people's emotions, playing on their basest fears and whipping up hysteria" with "fake news".[341]

Mouffitt rightly observes tha, both populists and anti-populists fall short of what is conducive for the times. Both "are driven by a nostalgia for days gone by". On the one hand, "Populists seek a simpler imagined time, where jobs were plentiful, national sovereignty was intact and borders were stronger." On their part, "Anti-populists, too, are stuck in the past, imagining a time of consensus politics, a supposedly sane and rational period where consensus reigned, and representatives worked together to solve political problems for the greater good."[342]

The question both populists and anti-populists have to answer is, thus, one of how to recognise and provide for the reality of incompleteness as a permanent attribute of being and becoming liberal, democratic or whatever other configuration to which humans are drawn in their creative imagination. Within the framework of incompleteness, nothing is sacrosanct. Social and political orders are subject to contestation and renegotiation with time and in accordance with the imperative for inclusivity. It is a framework in which pluralism is a permanent pursuit beyond tokenism.

If pluralism is what a given society seeks, it can be facilitated by media that are neither anti-elite nor anti-populism. One does not have, a priori, to be anti-something to be for something. Pluralism and its ambitions of collective memory informed by shared history, disruptions and transformations[343] can be facilitated by media that carefully avoid the pitfalls of co-optation, wittingly and unwittingly, through a balanced, plural and discursive approach of its own (Krämer 2017). It would make a difference if Trump were effectively putting America first (Magcamit 2017), but as Steil writes, what is striking about Trump's "America First" foreign policy "is not that it places American interests first. It is the misguided way in which those interests are being defined".[344] Gvosdev sums it up as follows: "in essence, Trump is offering a new deal: American-led globalization with Trumpian characteristics". He characterises it as "a more mercenary, nakedly transactional approach", a gamble by Trump vis-à-vis those who "want American power and leadership to preserve and sustain the liberal order" on which they depend. In adopting this position, Grovdev speculates, Trump, the dealmaker, was hoping that "the U.S. market—and U.S. leadership" would remain "too attractive to too many states". The hope was that the reprioritisation would, in the end, carry the day with most countries, however reluctantly, taking "the revised offer". [345] To what extent was Trump's option for "America First" a transactional ploy by an astute dealmaker? And to what extent was it simply undisguised populist nativism?

To Fared Zakaria, "America First" was more than just a negotiating strategy on Trump's part. "Amid the parochialism, ineptitude and sheer disarray of the Trump presidency," writes Zakaria, "the post-American world is coming to fruition much faster than I ever expected." [346] As he sees it, "under the Trump administration, the United States seems to have lost interest, indeed lost faith, in the ideas and purpose that animated its international presence for three-quarters of a century".[347] Hudson agrees that the "end of America's unchallenged global economic dominance has arrived sooner than expected", and points to Trump as "the catalytic agent" that has accelerated the coming about of a break that "has been building for quite some time, and was bound to occur". Hudson contends that by bringing about the "break up the American Empire", Trump has succeeded in doing what, "No left-wing party, no socialist, anarchist or foreign nationalist leader anywhere in the world could have achieved." Hudson goes on to explain exactly how – and in great detail, focusing mainly on financial transactions – the end of America's monetary imperialism has come about.[348]

To Cockburn, "Self-absorption by any country leads it to take a skewed and unrealistically optimistic view of its place in the world", and the US, just like Britain and others who have opted for the current "populist nationalist wave" is "likely to pay a high price for political miscalculations" and especially for "the excessive expectations" generated by such populist nationalism,[349] which is understood to be "more right wing than traditional conservatism".[350] Mills and Rosefielde recognise that "Trump has touched America's raw nerve, and the problems he senses are real". Ordinary Americans are in their right to be frustrated with a foreign policy is biased in favour of cosmopolitans at their expense. Hence, Mills and Rosefielde propose what they consider a "sane" and more people-oriented foreign policy dictated by "democratic nationalism". Under such a policy, America is likened to "a large family in which the needs of members of the family should not be sacrificed to those of people abroad or to the interests of establishment insiders in the US" (Mills and Rosefielde 2017: v–viii).

Commenting on the effect of the rise and proliferation of populism and narrow nationalism in the West in general, Stephens argues that both phenomena have rendered:

> The West [...] rudderless. To be rudderless puts you at the mercy of elements. The elemental forces of politics today are tribalism, populism, authoritarianism and the sewage pipes of social media. Each contradicts the West's foundational commitments to universalism, representation, unalienable rights, and an epistemology built on fact and reason, not clicks and feelings. We are drifting, in the absence of mind and will, toward a moment of civilizational self-negation.[351]

The paucity of admirable qualities in contemporary political leadership leads Brooks to the pessimistic conclusion that these days, to elect a leader, "you generally have two choices: a sensible, establishment figure who is completely out of touch", or "an incompetent populist outsider".[352] In terms of incompetence and mendaciousness, there is no better populist than Trump, whom Walt characterises as "an incompetent vulgarian in the White House".[353] To Gessen, "Trump's incompetence is militant. It is not a factor that might mitigate the threat he poses: it is the threat itself" (Gessen 2020: Chapter 4). "Trump is an infantilist", according to Brooks, who explores how "Immaturity is becoming the dominant note of his presidency, lack of self-control his leitmotif." Brooks contends that Trump is "the all-time record-holder of the Dunning-Kruger effect, the phenomenon in which the incompetent person is too incompetent to understand his own incompetence". Wren-Lewis thinks that the media are making matters worse instead of acting as safeguards against incompetence. He explains that "when a large part of the media encourage rather than expose acts of incompetence, and the non-partisan media treat knowledge as just another opinion, that safeguard against persistent incompetence is put in danger".[354] The result, Brook contends, is that, "We've got this perverse situation in which the vast analytic powers of the entire world are being spent trying to understand a guy whose thoughts are often just six fireflies beeping randomly in a jar."[355]

If history is anything to go by, Gessen maintains, Trump has had some illustrious predecessors at limited ability, education and imagination. Gessen suggests that "a careful reading of contemporary accounts will show that both Hitler and Stalin struck many of their countrymen as men of limited ability, education and imagination — and, indeed, as being incompetent in government and military leadership". Both men were propelled to power "in a frighteningly complex world" by "the blunt instrument of reassuring ignorance". Gessen contends that, "The rejection of the complexity of modern politics [...] lies at the core of populism's appeal." It could be argued that it is "Mr. Trump's insistence on simplicity that makes him want to rule like an autocrat".[356] Gessen proposes six rules for surviving in an autocracy, namely: Rule #1: Believe the autocrat; Rule #2: Do not be taken in by small signs of normality; Rule #3: Institutions will not save you; Rule #4: Be outraged; Rule #5: Don't make compromises; and Rule #6: Remember the future[357] (Gessen 2020).

Quoted by Durden, Beppe Grillo, a former comedian and leader of the populist Five Star Movement in Italy, responds to criticism of Trump and other populists like himself by arguing that "the amateurs are the ones conquering the world and I'm rejoicing in it because the professionals are the ones who have reduced the world to this state".[358] As Zakaria recounts, to Grillo, Trump's appeal is in being "against political correctness" and, like Trump, Grillo's party is undeterred by labels of sexism and populism.[359] Skinnell describes Trump as "a self-styled fearless speaker – unafraid to tell it like it is, unbeholden to the political elites" (Skinnell 2018b). Fukuyama concurs, calling Trump "the perfect practitioner of the ethics of authenticity that defines our age" and hailing Trump for playing "a critical role in moving the focus of identity politics from the left, where it was born, to the right, where it is now taking root", by "taking on political correctness so frontally" (Fukuyama 2018: 119). Rauch attributes the heights in influence attained by Trump, Breitbart News and Russian Troll farms in part to political correctness and its tendency to shut down debate, critical engagement and freedom of expression with contrived conformity, censorship and intimidation (Rauch 2021: 14).

As Wieviorka explains, "Voters express their lack of trust in political actors by eliminating the ones they feel they've seen too much of; they hope that newcomers, supposedly anti-establishment, will be able to do better." It is a logic which accounts for the success of nationalist, far left, and extreme centre populisms.[360] The logic accounts as well, for why Trump's "base sticks with him through scandal". As Brooks indicates, they stick with him "because it's not just about him; it's a movement defined against the so-called ruling class". In this regard, Brooks thinks "Trump may not be the culmination, but merely a way station toward an even purer populism".[361]

What sets contemporary right-wing populism apart in Europe and the USA, in particular, and makes it such an easily recognisable movement, one could argue, is that it has an additional component of "identity chauvinism", in terms of being centred around (a) ethno-nationalist sentiments and/or (b) white men's feeling of losing their long-held power and privilege. Value conservatism is also often part of it. The core of right-wing populism can be summed up as nostalgia for supremacy and sovereignty ("America First"), a longing to return to former glory ("Make America Great Again") and a time where "common people" (white people, men, the ethnic majority) were in charge and did not have to deal with too much social and economic discomfort and cultural impurities perceived to be primarily caused by the inflow of "undesirable populations" from historically marginalised groups within or from migrants coming from other geographies, other ethnicities and other races. Therefore, it is hardly surprising that Trump's "Make America Great Again" has attracted a growing number of supporters, especially among middle- and working-class white voters, with whom it resonates particularly strongly, as Moak argues[362] (see also Mercieca 2018).

As detailed by Hawkins and Hawkins, Trump's "voters are disproportionately white, male (especially among crossover Democrat voters), older (65+ years), Protestant (especially Evangelical), less educated, blue-collar workers or serving in the military, and/or rural" (Hawkins and Hawkins 2018: 54). From 62,979,879 votes in 2016, Trump's support at the 2020 presidential election rose to 74,222,958, even though he lost to Joe Biden, ultimately, who had 81,283,098, i.e., seven million more votes, and won 306 electoral college votes to Trump's 232 votes.

As such, right-wing populism is a highly exclusionist movement, almost always with a specific in-group and often – but not always – a particular enemy (the definitions and boundaries of the in-group and enemy group vary from context to context). Right-wing populism may or may not include white supremacist ideology; for example, Modi in India – where a white population is not a significant demographic and ethnicity, religion and patronage are more important indices for differentiation – has been characterised as a right-wing populist, but his populism is based on Hindu nationalism (Kenny 2017). Put differently, populism may coincide with but is not confined to categories such as race, ethnicity, geography, class and gender. Sometimes, it is a blend of all of these categories, mobilising them in various combinations to maximise their potency for the opportunistic politics of the populist leaders in particular contexts.

Whatever the brand of populism at play, Patten expresses his discomfort with the situation in Europe, where "too many are easily deluded into believing that there is a simple solution" to migration into Europe. "Build walls. Send them all home. Stop the world, we want to get off". He cautions that "Neither America nor Europe should abandon their policies to the populists' dangerous virtual reality. Theirs is not the world we live in or a world we should want to live in. It is a fictional world, but with none of the bearing on our problems that attracts generation after generation of readers to Tolstoy's work". Patten contemplates the nature and limits of power by linking Trump and Tolstoy's views on power. America is viewed in terms of its initial economic successes as the new world was established, making America "one of the greatest success stories in world history". Donald Trump is all the more dangerous because of this, as he taps into an imaginary fantasy, a dangerous virtual reality, a fictional world where the building of walls and "sending people back home" will reignite the previous successes. Slogans signalling, "we want to control our own lives and our own borders" fail to recognise that this is not a real solution to Europe or America's immigration "crisis". Patten suggests that the rebuilding of states and reasons to live in them is the only real solution, and therefore "neither America nor Europe should abandon their policies to the populist dangerous virtual reality".[363]

Following up in 2018, in an article titled "Tough times for the tough guys", Patten writes: "Shares in strongman leaders seem to be falling", as Xi Jinping's personality cult faces "growing criticism", Putin's Russian economy is "moribund" and Trump is implicated in the commission of a federal felony by his long-time lawyer and "fixer", Michael Cohen.[364] Solomon echoes the predicaments of strongmen leaders with the argument that walls such as Trump's on the border with Mexico "are concrete symbols of exclusion, and exclusion is seldom a diplomatic move". "In the end, xenophobia is a vulnerability masquerading as a fortification".[365] To *The Economist*, "the gravest risk to the free world since communism" is one in which "the politicians with momentum are those who argue that the world is a nasty, threatening place, and that wise nations should build walls to keep it out".[366]

In the case of the rise of Donald Trump in American politics, his style and approach to populism have been basically and systematically to school and mobilise his supporters and ultimate defenders to be hostile to the establishment, and to established rules, procedures and processes, which he has categorised either as a swamp that needs draining, or as part of a well-orchestrated "deep state" or the "administrative state" meant to take away rights and freedoms from ordinary folks by concentrating power in the hands of corrupt federal politicians and self-serving bureaucrats in Washington to the detriment of states and local communities. There is little equivocation whom ordinary folks are to Trump in the racialised hierarchy of Americanness that propels him (Judis 2016: Chapter 3; Reid 2019: Chapter 10; Rohde 2020; Dean and Altemeyer 2020). It is a style characterised by Richard Hofstadter (2008[1965]) as "paranoid", and by Peter Strzok (2020) as hostile to the professionalism and commitment to the truth with which the FBI and the US intelligence community have imbued their agents in their efforts to defend American democracy against foreign interferences.

To promise is not necessarily to deliver, especially with populism, and Trump has not been an exception (Hawkins and Hawkins 2018). As satirical comedian John Oliver of *Last Week Tonight* so aptly summed it up: "Trump has in no way drained the swamp; what he has done is drain the phrase of its original meaning".[367] "Instead of fulfilling his campaign promise to 'drain the swamp,'" writes Walt, "Trump dug it wider and filled it deeper". This has led the USA to fall out of the ranks of the top 20 "least corrupt" nations into the category of "a country to watch", according to Transparency International. Walt mentions that "Corruption and other forms of elite malfeasance also nourish populist anger".[368]

Trump has cultivated an attitude of scepticism among his followers, against a perceived widespread conspiracy by so-called liberals and the liberal media (Muirhead and Rosenblum 2019). This has positioned him as the only credible source of information and truth. To keep his followers permanently animated and glued to him, "Trump excels at treating the past as raw material to be sculpted into whatever claims serve his interests", according to Smith. Trump sees history as "infinitely malleable" and independent of facts, and thereby takes licence to "tell stories, and create our reality".[369] Sooner or later, the truth means little to people inundated with lies. Hence, some have argued that Trump's lying and shredding of every standard of decency imaginable are designed to unwire the face of American democracy in the interest of Trump's self-aggrandisement and self-preservation. "Trump's proclivity for exaggeration and falsehoods [...] made it harder for him to build popular consensus even for his most successful actions" (Kessler et al. 2020: Conclusion). And as he encountered resistance, his lying and lies grew bigger and bigger, culminating in questioning the outcome of the 2020 election to the point of whipping up anger and violence in some of his hardcore supporters to mob-storm the Capitol where the election results were being validated. According to Sims, who served as Trump's special assistant at the White House, Trump, in his "single-mindedness" or "hedgehoggishness", believes "that creating chaos gives him an advantage, because he's more comfortable in the mayhem than anyone else" (Sims 2019: Chapter 7). Indeed, as Woodward and Costa maintain, not only is Trump "Eager to use fear to get his way", but he also sees "real power" in terms of how much fear he is able to instil in others, and relishes the fact that he provokes rage: "I bring rage out. I do bring rage out. I always have. I don't know if that's an asset or a liability, but whatever it is, I do," Trump told them (Woodward and Costa 2021: Epilogue).

Some commentators have seen such scepticism to facts, institutions and expertise as destructive of certain established political traditions and value systems (Nichols 2017, 2021; Kakutani 2018). Institutions being only as good as the individuals who work in and lead them, Trump's Republican party and presidency cannot be better than who Trump is, some have argued (Stevens 2020). Rauch writes about the disintegration of American politics and political institutions during the 2016 presidential elections as "chaos syndrome", where chaos becomes the new normal. Rauch uses the metaphor of disease to describe the fallout in party politics, which has led to a scenario where candidates for leadership positions are usually not party loyalists but independents, swinging to and fro to gain support for the party brand. Political parties no longer have "intelligible boundaries or enforceable norms" to contain "renegade behaviour". Rauch explains that this is due to the "demoniz[ation] and disempowering [of] political professionals and parties" (the political middlemen), as well as ideological polarisation, the rise of social media and the radicalisation of the Republican base. Middlemen were demonised from all sides. "Progressives accused middlemen of subverting public interest; populists accused them of obstructing peoples' will; conservatives accused them of protecting and expanding big government." Rauch forefronts the value of compromise and calls for a return of the "establishment" – professional middlemen and middleman institutions, who, despite not being perfect, still brokered and "brought order from chaos" and protected the political system from excess populism. Anti-establishment nihilism should not be accommodated but rather abandoned[370] (see also Rauch 2021: 79–85).

The election of Trump in 2016 seemed to have marked a watershed moment for populism, especially in the West (Traverso 2019; Mudde 2019). The election of Emmanuel Macron in France and related events in 2017 "led many to wonder if the populist politics that defined 2016" were "being met by an equal and opposite force in 2017". The Project Syndicate editors present the argument that Trump "may have inoculated Europeans against the contagion of right-wing populism".[371] Traverso (2019) provides more meat, context and nuance to the situation in France, with interesting comparisons between the variants of populism of Marie Le Pen of the National Front and Macron's.

Conman or real deal dealmaker? Trump succeeded in mesmerising the world by being some of both, but mainly the former. He is the real deal when it comes to threatening democracy, and to whipping up dreams of economic, cultural and political autonomy among his supporters at the grassroots, while giving his enablers in Congress and among the business elites cause to keep doing what they do best: defend political and fiscal conservativism, and demonstrate loyalty without equivocation to Trump and Trump only.

Part III

The Role of Media and Digital Technologies in the Upsurge of Populism

We are living in an age that seems almost post-truth in its acceptance of mistruths and untruths and the totalitarian propensities this occasions in how we claim right and wrong or the moral high ground with the "us" versus "them" lines of absolutism we draw in the sand of our social interactions. What is the role of the media, digital technologies driven social media in particular, in Trump's birth, proliferation and resonance as the embodiment of a phenomenon associated with the upsurge in narcissism and populism both as cause and catalyst? What do social media's growing relevance and usage tell us about ourselves as producers, consumers and contesters of Trump, populism and the spiral of ever-diminishing circles of inclusion? Moreover, even for those of us that stood on the other side of the world cringing at Trump and his laughable lying and callous disregard to civility or decorum, we were also the consumers and contesters that flamed his upsurge and created the Trump monster and baby blimp in active collaboration with Twitter, Facebook and related platforms and fantasy spaces. Indeed, we assembled Trump and launched him like a rocket, both those of us that accepted and laughed off his lies and braggadocio, respectively. We brought him down, crashing into dismemberment, when we realised his dangers, cancelled him, or otherwise used him for our political, economic, commercial and cultural benefits. Even the most ordinary among us were complicit with the providers of social media fantasy spaces and owners of media empires that milked Trump for sustenance and celebrity, even when we did not necessarily laugh all the way to the bank as they did from featuring Trump as a billionaire-producing king of spectacle. Whether accidental or intentional, our collective response to Trump's insatiable thirst and hunger for attention – good or bad – through his fascinating ability to manipulate and manoeuvre the attention merchants (Wu 2016), makes mini-Trumps of us all and contributes to sustaining and reproducing the cultures of which he is a formidable salesman.

In the face of dwindling regard for expertise, the elusiveness of truth has combined with relativism gone wild to generate an infinity in the proliferation of silos and echo chambers. The embrace of the idea that a good story (defined through the number of hits or likes one receives) is better than the truth, especially when such stories are rewarded by the platforms that accommodate and promote them, has given credence to the belief that facts come in different shapes and sizes, are negotiable, and produced and made available along with their alternatives to sovereign consumers shopping round the clock for them, to pick and choose as they see fit. The world has been exposed to flexible facts and truths in such abundance in a moment where conspiracy theories and news traditionally gathered in tune with journalistic canons are quoted side by side and where leaders are playboys, schooled in the very art of deception and uncontained narcissism. When are these toddler deceivers and dissemblers self-consciously master manipulators and manoeuvrers? Furthermore, when are they, seemingly unaware of their own deceptive finesse, playing someone else's game of trickery and manipulating algorithms without knowing? Who are the faces behind the masks at this time of the coronavirus pandemic? When has wearing a mask become both fashionable and imperative? Wittingly or not, to what extent could Trump and many of his populist interlocutors, friends or foes, be said to have managed to change the fabric of democracies with infusions of populism and narcissism? It may be too soon to measure Trump's populist impact, but his contribution to keeping the psychology and sociology of narcissism in command is not in doubt, as evidenced throughout this book.

Equally worth contemplating is the impact to social truth of the intersection between social media and populism *à la* Trump. To what extent could it be argued that social media have both enhanced and disrupted the articulation of Trumpian populism? Granted, nothing collective is possible without a shared sociality, a shared idea of right and wrong, or shared ethics of belonging and relating or practising whatever we claim to be our professions. What room is there for moving beyond polarisations and forging conviviality? Could social media as fantasy spaces or flexible zones of imagination contribute towards such an imperative for more inclusive citizenship and belonging? Put differently, to what extent are Trump and his supporters (74,222,958 of whom voted for him during the 2020 election) and Biden and his supporters (81,283,098 of whom voted for him in 2020), along with those who are supporters of neither, ready to harness the positives of the media and social media fantasy spaces they share and frequent towards a common, inclusive social truth that reinfuses the "United" in the polarised, uncivil and troublingly traumatised "States of America" on the brink of "the precipice" (Trump, M. L. 2021: Chapter 7)? As with the rest of this book, I invite you to read these reflections through the prism of incompleteness articulated in the general introduction.

The Media and Social Media as Magic Multipliers in Trumpian Populism

Trump's use of the media to extend himself and his potency has lots of parallels with how Tutuola's characters, such as "The Skull" and the Drinkard, use what Tutuola refers to as *juju* to acquire the powers of self-activation for their efficacy in action and interactions with others. As argued elsewhere (Nyamnjoh 2019), the idea of digital technologies making it possible for humans and things to be present, even in their absence, and absent, even in their presence, is not that dissimilar to the belief in what is often labelled and dismissed as magic that lends itself to a world of infinite possibilities. A world of presence in simultaneous multiplicities and eternal powers to redefine reality. The new magic multipliers – or technologies of instant availability and reachability, with a propensity to facilitate narcissism, self-indulgence and the keeping up of appearances, which Trump has harnessed to good effect – are the internet, the cell phone and the smartphone. Without these wizardries of these magic multipliers, Trump, who has often portrayed himself as a victim of witch-hunts by Democrats and liberals, would not have survived or prevailed for long as President, given his two impeachments.

Paradoxically, although averse to being thought of as incomplete, Trump, like everyone else schooled to uncritically endorse and reproduce the ideology of autonomy as a zero-sum pursuit, implicitly recognises incompleteness even when not owning up to it. In their relentless quests for ways of enhancing themselves through relationships with other humans and using their creativity and imagination to acquire magical enablers such as digital technologies that can extend themselves in their delusions of grandeur. The reality of incompleteness is true of technologies of self-extension as well, in that these technologies equally need activation by other technologies to be effective. Hence the need to constantly lubricate relations with the supplier of one's technology – manufacturer, software maker, service or platform provider, or whoever has supplied one the technology – which is almost always accompanied by strict instructions to be followed scrupulously.

These interconnections and interdependencies, even when unstated, suggest the ubiquity of incompleteness. They work in favour of perception and an approach to life, sociality, encounters and relationships that are cognizant of the importance and centrality of charging, discharging and recharging. This recognition should be humbling for those who insist on completeness, in that one can only stay permanently charged if one is in splendid isolation, disconnected, aloof and inactive. Even then, one's charge risks leaking or wasting away (draining itself out unproductively for lack of interactivity), and with that, one's life eventually also drains away with little to bequeath to society and the world, which have given so generously to one. To be social and in relationship and interaction with others requires and simultaneously makes it possible to charge actively, discharge and recharge oneself and others involved. Discharging within relationships is not a wasteful exercise as it entails charging others (energy expended is not necessarily energy depleted), just as recharging entails drawing from the charge of (or being energised by) others. Symbiotic relationships and sociality are full of charge, discharge and recharge. As long as one loses one's charge to others in a social relationship, that cannot be considered sterile leakage or wastefulness, as long as recharge or reactivation is possible. In a world where incompleteness is a characteristic of both humans and the technologies to invent, imagine and reimagine themselves, everything is possible, and think the unthinkable is currency thanks to the circulation of charging, discharging and recharging.

How does Trump's relationship with the media and social media compare with this reality? In what follows, I seek to show how the media and social media, in particular, magically catapulted Trump to power, promoting Trumpian populism in all its ramifications. I further illustrate how Trump, the narcissistic businessman, politician and President, has used conservative media outlets such as Fox News to fan conspiracism by prioritising proceeds over the populace, extravaganza over proof, sensationalism and dissension over the pursuit of common aspirations, thereby ridiculing US democracy's supposed historical loyalty to factuality and harmony in heterogeneousness. I also argue that despite Trump and his supporters' rationalisation of his misdeeds with whataboutism and scuttlebutt, and the turning of his flaws into virtues and strengths, with the use of social, multi-, and conservative media, the last straw on Trump's populism was two tweets on 8 January 2021. One praised the Capitol's attackers as "patriots", and another declared he would not attend Joe Biden's inauguration on 20 January 2021. The banning of Trump permanently from Facebook, Instagram and Twitter – who had enabled him all along, as insider whistle-blower accounts such as Christopher Wylie's indicate (Wylie 2019) – on the same day was a testament to the wisdom that every strongman is only as powerful as his enablers or technologies of self-extension. The section concludes by contrasting the garrulous autocratic Donald Trump of the USA, whose motormouth removed him from the White House after just four years, with the taciturn autocratic Paul Biya of Cameroon, whose struggling voice and reticence have kept him in power for a whopping 39 years. This insinuates, perhaps, that our global celebration of incompleteness dictates that the Global North may as well have something to (un)learn from the Global South when it comes to autocracy.

In neoliberal democracies where incompleteness is acknowledged only in principle, if at all, the liberal and populist elites alike manipulate facts, evidence, information, media and reality to maintain control by promoting polarisation and hierarchies of citizenship and belonging deliberately caricatured into "us" and "them", "insiders" and "outsiders", "winners" and "losers", "nationals" and "immigrants", "natives" and "settlers", "patriots" and "villains", "the people" and the "elites", "good" and "bad". It should not deter from the fact of manipulation, whether the justification or rationalisation used is meritocracy, patriotism, culture, economics or all of these combined. In these contexts of stark dichotomies and stubborn chasms, the disruptive effects of the mainstream and social media play a massive role because they set agendas and can easily be manipulated for advantage (political, cultural, economic and otherwise) and/or nihilistic opportunism. Rarely have these tendencies been so pronounced with such dire consequences than during Trump's administration and its politics of divide and rule and zero-sum games of power.

Social media has been the most exquisite breeding ground for Trump's lies, untruths and alternative truths. Just as a vampire shuns light and needs blood to activate itself into life and generate potency, Trump is lifeless without media coverage and the truthless canopy of darkness that insulates him. Daily and without stop, Trump is charged up by the media, discharged by the media and recharged by the media, without which he is helplessly deflated and demotivated. It does not matter whether the media coverage he receives is supportive or hostile, good or bad, factual or fabricated, as long as there is media attention. Quality matters less than quantity and frequency. Equally, the media have over the years relied on Trump as a superman of spectacle and ratings generating machine to attract enough advertising to stay in business and stay ahead. As ably captured in *The Art of the Deal*, Trump has learnt to take advantage of the media's hunger for a good story, and for sensationalism, outrage and controversy (Trump with Schwartz 1987: 56). In this regard, just as Trump is charged up, discharged and recharged by the media, so too are the media in turn charged, discharged and recharged by Trump. They may quibble and quarrel and appear at daggers drawn in public, but they cannot have enough of each other. They are mutually entangled and interdependent, even if their public rhetoric is one of autonomy of action and distance from each other. This speaks to the predicament of late capitalism, where everything is reduced to monetary and economic value. The neoliberal capitalist world thrives on monetising everything, including the subversion of canonised human values. Such tendencies of neoliberalism, it could be argued, undermine human freedom and conviviality, as it publicises and endorses inequality and excess – knowingly in many cases – for economic reasons. The challenge is how to see it for what it is, the trivialisation of socio-cultural interests in favour of economic considerations.

As for populism, Trump is proof of free media as a facilitator of populist political promise. However, what stands out the most is how alternative channels like social media are taken as authoritative news sources by Trump supporters and detractors alike. Whilst conservative or right-wing news sources like Fox complement Trump's social media constituents by making themselves a source of opinion and beliefs towards imagining and reimagining community and belonging beyond the desire for objective truth shared with those one would love to see and relate to as outsiders, even when the latter are, legally and sociologically, part of the fold. Additionally, as an astute manipulator and dissembler, Trump manages to attract sustained media coverage by repeatedly portraying himself as a victim of the liberal media and his supporters as victims of political correctness or cancel culture. He uses such claims of victimisation as an excuse for his Twitter rampages which are easily and often factually proven to be lies, and conservative media have been quick to defend rather than reprimand Trump's mistruths, which are worked to reinforce the idea that there is no such thing as objective, neutral, value-free and non-partisan media. All media are part and parcel of the cultural communities and echo chambers that lend them credibility and keep them in business, economically, politically and culturally.

Trump's allegations of victimhood keep the media, regardless of whether critical or supportive of him, preoccupied with his tweets and nonstop agenda-setting complaints. In this way, Trump not only dominates the news cycle but succeeds in transforming news and information of public relevance into a reality TV show not dissimilar to *The Apprentice*, and with him as the producer and the main act. The normalisation of lying and economy with facts under Trump and his loyal enablers in the media has blurred the lines between truth and untruths (Achter 2018; Kessler et al. 2020), just as it has deepened the cleavages and polarisation among Americans. Ironically, the same platforms (Facebook and Twitter in particular) that enabled the lying Trump to troll for years with impunity were the ones to, in the end, withdraw his magical powers by banning and fact-checking him. This, it could be argued, reflects the fact that social media fall far short of the often-touted capacity to foster socio-cultural reformation of the world to incorporate creativity and acceptability as well as promote inclusiveness in working towards a relatively better human community. Social media operators, arguably, are driven more by interest in fame, money and power than they are necessarily opposed to tramping Trump, whose narcissism suits their communication model superbly well.

Might Trump have had a longer reign if he had followed the example of the strongman of Cameroonian politics, President Paul

Biya, who desperately seeks a very royal and personalised leadership at the highest level of state? The latter has survived as head of state for over 39 years by monopolising the state-owned media while censoring critical privately owned media, in addition to staying wilfully quiet on burning issues of national interest. Like Trump, Biya has been hesitant, personally, about mask-wearing since the outbreak of the coronavirus pandemic. Reportedly, Biya was pictured wearing a mask in public twice only: first, during his sister's burial and again on Monday, 16 August 2021, as he returned to Cameroon "after weeks of a private stay in Geneva, Switzerland".[372]

Equally explored below is how news media and the digital media-driven communication environment gave impetus and scale to conspiracy theories and various forms of misinformation and propaganda under Trump. In conflict with professional journalistic traditions and expectations of factuality, accuracy, honesty and impartiality, Trumpism is strategically designed to challenge conventional wisdom, news values and canons by presenting "alternative facts" and introducing radical relativism to appeal selectively to citizens supportive of his endeavours, while simultaneously enraging and further alienating those opposing them. This often happened in ways that were detrimental to effective policy and the quality of democracy as conventionally understood and pursued. Particular attention is given to how Twitter as an alternate public sphere fuelled infotainment and Twitterstorms and concealed the truth numerous times. Trump's refusal to acknowledge debt and indebtedness, his hauteur and authoritarian attitudes and prejudices against outgroups complicated these pathologies and complicities. Even as powerful magical enablers, Twitter, Facebook and related social media platforms used by Trump to enhance himself and extend clout and control mostly tended to work only partly because, suddenly, their potency fizzles out for one reason or another. In the case of Trump as the most powerful man in the world, in his capacity as the President of the USA, this took long in coming but, finally, it did when Trump was de-platformed following his foolhardy pursuit of completeness and insistence on winning the 2020 election despite objectively having lost it. Following the ban, Trump's internet presence slid into irrelevance, exposing his perpetual state of incompleteness, even as he continued to ignore it.

Let's take a closer look.

If Trump is "The Skull" who became and for long sustained the image of "The Complete Gentleman" by borrowing without acknowledging and tenaciously refusing to recognise and/or settle his debts, his most distinguished enablers by far – greater than his supportive father and the financial institutions that were complicit in the production and propping up of what some have preferred to call a "Frankenstein Monster" – have been the media in general and social media in particular. He has employed the media to manipulate and manoeuvre public opinion in a manner that would have humbled Edward Bernays, famous among the founding fathers of American-type public relations and propaganda. Like Bernays who believed that reality was not quite reality if not mass mediated, Trump could be said not to believe he exists unless he is reading about himself in the papers, watching TV coverage of him, tweeting and reading and retweeting tweets and mimes about himself and having Facebook and Instagram posts about him brought to his attention as fodder (Nyamnjoh 2018b; Achter 2018). Indeed, Trump reportedly preferred televisual forms of ingesting information. As Wolff recounts, during Trump's four years as president, "What was on television left a greater impression on him than what was said to him, or what intelligence he received, or what facts were known." Trump's aides, whose success with Trump also depended on how well they did on television, claimed that "he had a kind of hyper-video sensitivity, with a keen recall of image and sound" (Wolff 2021a: Chapter 4).

According to Nicholas, when under increased pressure with few trusted aids to serve as a "pressure-release valve for him to air grievances in private", Trump tended to resort to "a tweetstorm" to vent himself. At such lonely moments, Trump tweeted more than ever, and spiked "his public appearances with profanity and name-calling", in frenzied performances.[373] To keep his existence activated on a daily basis, in addition to tweeting every now and then, Trump, during his presidency, reportedly spent "at least four hours a day, and sometimes as much as twice that, in front of a television, sometimes with the volume muted".[374] Taveira and Nyerges argue that Trump and the American populism on the waves of which he rode to prominence, depend immensely on propaganda as a means of self-promotion and commercial branding, even as both Trump and populism defend themselves in opposition to the "conventional state-based organs of 'propaganda'" upon which they depend. This makes Trump less singular, special or unique. Rather, he is more "wholly a part of the system that he decries", and "he would be nothing without the propaganda on which both public institutions and the private individual rely". Both the "demagogic personality" and "the faceless bureaucrat", though apparently at daggers drawn, "each provide an alibi for the other, protesting, unsuccessfully perhaps, against their essential sameness" (Taveira and Nyerges 2016: 10).

Unlike Bernays who was credited with some measure of acting in accordance with principles, an ethics and even a conscience, many have argued and substantiated abundantly, as evidenced in this book, that Trump has been able to go overboard because he had none of these guardrails associated with Edward Bernays. Without scruples, Trump has borrowed and enhanced his personal power as a businessman, a politician and a president by using the media and taking advantage of the policies and ownership of media platforms that prioritise profit over people, and spectacle over evidence. Or that prioritise sensationalism and divisiveness over the pursuit of a common purpose and a higher loyalty to truth and to unity in diversity.

In certain cases, especially with Fox News and related outlets where infotainment has been prioritised over and above the pursuit of objective truth or "evidence-based, dispassionate, and fair-minded" journalism (Rauch 2021: 20) as understood in conventional journalism à la Carl Bernstein and Bob Woodward (Bernstein and Woodward 1974; Woodward 2018, 2020),[375] the understanding that truth, knowledge and objectivity must not be allowed to kill a good story has played into Trump's hands in incalculable ways, especially in view of his propensity to lie without relent (Stelter 2020; Cohen 2020; Rauch 2021: 155–188). In evidence, "rank-and-file Republicans who watch Fox are far more loyal to Trump than those who do not", according to Sargent.[376]

In a repeatedly fact-checked and debunked but resilient quote in social media, allegedly published by *People Magazine* in 1998, Trump, in response to a question on running for president, was quoted to have said: "If I were to run, I'd run as a Republican. They're the dumbest group of voters in the country. They believe anything on Fox News. I could lie and they'd still eat it up. I bet my number would be terrific."[377] This stubborn defiance of fact-checking reminiscent of a Trump lie speaks to the challenge of fact-checking Trump so pertinently expressed by Masha Gessen in the following terms:

> [...] while the lying is repeated, fact-checking is administered only once. The lie dominates in the public sphere. Worse, the fact-checking articles themselves, appearing soon after the lie is uttered in public or on Twitter, serve as a gateway for the lie's entrance into public consciousness. Worse still, this particular gateway has a way of placing the lie and the truth side by side, as though the facts were a matter of debate. Then one of the sides of the debate drops the conversation while the other continues pounding the subject. Arguments are often lost this way (Gessen 2020: Chapter 13).

> Trump repeats his false statements after they have been fact-checked by the media and, in many cases, contradicted by officials in his own administration—and it is this repetition that gives Trumpian lies much of their power (Gessen 2020: Chapter 14).

The force of repetition of falsehoods is the charge they generate to power Trump through the claims he stakes to completeness. Through repetition, lies are made to appear as true to persons with a deep-seated confirmation bias, making the internalisation of lies easy, possible and seamless. The lies, in other words, are his magic for taming efforts at rendering him an ordinary player in a game where the only thing that counts is winning and winning absolutely. What is the purpose of the truth if all it does is blunt one's killer instincts in a zero-sum context? In addition, beyond Trump and his fixations with absolute victories, it is worth recognising that, driven by a need to belong to a community of shared values and practice than by a quest for objective truth, and especially when such truth threatens "our personal prestige or group identity", it is hardly surprising that, as Rauch argues with the example of a congregation, "When facts challenge the belief, the congregation will defend its faith by denying the facts" (Rauch 2021: 33–34). Despite our tendency to claim the country, we, as humans, are not terribly gifted at acting rationally or taking facts seriously when doing so would hurt our instinctive predispositions. Or rather, when we place an order for rationality, it does not come unaccompanied by emotions and feelings (Ioanide

2015). This explains the justification for the ritual of repeating lies – festering emotional confirmation biases. Politicians and businesses know this only too well, which is why advertising, public relations and political campaigns invest much more in emotion and feelings than in reason and rationality. The rational consumer is not good for business and politics (Nyamnjoh 2018b), and politicians who privilege rational arguments over and above mobilising affects and passions, do not stand much chance with their counterparts who whip up and make political capital of emotions. As Mouffe argues with inspiration from Spinoza, "ideas are only powerful when they meet affects" and, "to displace one affect, you need to build a stronger affect" more than you do rationality.[378]

We understand just how powerful as enablers the media have been to Trump, when some platforms decided to cut off his communicative power, thereby beginning or accelerating the process of his deactivation from "The Complete Gentleman" to "The Skull". An imagined image of the "Donald Trump balloon" or "Baby blimp" – "The 6m-high (19.7ft) inflatable blimp" depicting Trump "wearing a nappy and clutching a mobile phone" that "was flown over Parliament Square" "as part of a protest against" President Trump's "working visit to the UK in July 2018"[379] being deflated springs to mind.

Trump's incompleteness became apparent, so to say. The "free" media coverage that he had enjoyed until then had enabled Trump to thrive, just as his ability to deliver nonstop sensationalism and entertainment in controversy and braggadocio had enabled his enablers to thrive. With the power of free media coverage on his side, Trump has, in his populist style, been able to ignore nearly two-thirds of Americans either because they are liberals, ethnic, religious, gender or sexual minorities, or because they vote Democrat. In this way, he has used the media to whip up fear and hate among his mainly right-wing white support base, targeted at groups such as blacks, Hispanics, Muslims, Jews and women. In addition to his distaste for liberal media institutions such as CNN and MSNBC, Trump has cultivated a particular dislike for female journalists. The extreme negatives were his way of making his communicative style generative of news as spectacle even at the risk of carnage (Wingard 2018; Young 2018; Steudeman 2018; Brooke 2018).

According to Michael Cohen – long-time loyal personal attorney, confidant, consigliore and "adopted son" to Trump, who turned disloyal and testified against him in the House of Congress (Cohen 2020: Foreword) – the media was by far the biggest factor accounting for Trump becoming president. Even more importantly, it was free media coverage for which Trump did not pay a penny. All the other contributing factors were secondary. Cohen elaborates:

> [...] if you want to understand how Donald J. Trump became president, you have to grasp the essential fact that by far the most important element wasn't nationalism, or populism, or racism, or religion, or the rise of white supremacy, or strongman authoritarianism. It wasn't Russia, or lying, or James Comey, though all of those forces were hugely influential. It wasn't Hillary Clinton, though heaven knows she did all she could to lose the election.
>
> No. The biggest influence by far—by a country mile—was the media. Donald Trump's presidency is a product of the free press. Not free as in freedom of expression, I mean free as unpaid for. Rallies broadcast live, tweets, press conferences, idiotic interviews, 24-7 wall-to-wall coverage, all without spending a penny. The free press gave America Trump. Right, left, moderate, tabloid, broadsheet, television, radio, Internet, Facebook—that is who elected Trump and might well elect him again. (Cohen 2020: Chapter 11)

Although the majority of Americans do (Gessen 2020: Chapter 13), Trump's followers are not necessarily getting their information from the mainstream media, with the exception of Fox and OAN, both of which are said to normalise conspiracy theories that Trump and his supporters propagate and believe in but that serve to delegitimate democracy (Muirhead and Rosenblum 2019) by erasing the "distinction between truth and lies" (Gessen 2020: Chapter 13). Trump followers get information from alternative channels and sources such as social media.

In general, people tend to filter out what they do not want to hear and to navigate towards what they believe in and what makes them feel good. With what Muirhead and Rosenblum refer to as "the new conspiracism", the bar is set low enough to make it possible to reason that: "If one cannot be certain that a belief is entirely false, with the emphasis on *entirely*, then it might be true—and that's true enough."

According to this logic, they argue, "Even if it's not totally true, there's something there." Hence, their observation that "The new conspiracists do not necessarily believe what they say. But they do not disbelieve it either" (Muirhead and Rosenblum 2019: 43). Not only is Trump the embodiment of the new conspiracism, Muirhead and Rosenblum argue, "Populism and conspiracism come together in Trump in a way that is hard to unravel" (Muirhead and Rosenblum 2019: 64–65).

Trump has often succeeded in portraying himself as the victim of liberal media orchestrated witch hunts, hoaxes and "fake news", which, according to Hawkins and Hawkins (2018: 64–65) comprised the largest category of his tweets two years into his presidency. Trump did not need to actually indulge in clamping down on the media at the risk of his action being counter-productive. As someone who demands utter and complete supplication, Trump has been fortunate to have a captive audience of supporters in Fox News viewers who "do not watch alternative outlets of information" and are "exposed only to right-wing media venues for information" (Kivisto 2017: 85). With devoted enablers at Fox News such as Sean Hannity, Lou Dobbs, Laura Ingraham, Tucker Carlson and Jeanine Pirro, Trump could mount attack after attack on "fake news media", their "hoaxes" and "witch hunts", knowing that the attacks would be picked up by his army of spin doctors and amplifiers (Kalb 2018; Wilson 2018: Chapters 10 & 13; Reid 2019: Chapter 8; Wolff 2019: Chapters 2 & 11; Sims 2019: Chapter 13; Hassan 2019: Chapter 6; Stelter 2020).

Indeed, Trump's relationship with various Fox News hosts was so close, that Hannity was reported to basically have a desk at the White House,[380] and Carlson to dictate Trump policy on issues.[381] Labelling it the "Hannity-Trump marriage" or "the marriage of a reality-TV show" President "to a talk show host", Wilson remarks of the symbiotic relationship between Trump and Sean Hannity of Fox News:

> The president of the United States is addicted to an endless stream of praise from a shallow, dangerously stupid man. That same dangerous, stupid man feeds America's president a constant flow of conspiracy nonsense, uncritical praise, and uninformed opinion. It's a disaster in every way but the ratings (Wilson 2018: Chapter 13).

The relationship between Trump and Hannity was so complicitous that (Wolff 2019: Chapter 11), as Costa, Ellison and Dawsey report:

> The phone calls between President Trump and Sean Hannity come early in the morning or late at night, after the Fox News host goes off the air. They discuss ideas for Hannity's show, Trump's frustration with the ongoing special counsel probe and even, at times, what the president should tweet, according to people familiar with the conversations. When he's off the phone, Trump is known to cite Hannity when he talks with White House advisers.[382]

Such interdependence and conviviality between Trump and the media, and certain sections and players thereof in particular, drive home once again, the importance of seeing power through the prism of incompleteness and the relationships of mutuality in self-activation and self-extension we do not credit enough when we are schooled to fish for individuals and autonomous action as if these were the only modes of operation possible. That Trump and the media mutually enabled and extended each other throughout his presidency is not in question. Without the media, Trump would not exist as we know him, let alone winning the election, becoming president and apparently lording it over everyone in the manner of a tantrum-throwing toddler.

The fact of the possibility of informal channels of government and policy making, such as that between Trump and Hannity, suggests how ill-equipped for or simply indifferent to conventional and institutionalised mechanisms of power, responsibility and policy Trump was when he campaigned and won to become 45th President of the USA (Wilson 2018: Chapters 10 & 13; Benen 2020; Drezner 2020: Chapter 8). Arguing that the Republican Party has become "a post-policy party" and that this is especially so under Trump, Benen reports in *The Impostors*:

> By Inauguration Day, Trump and his team were so unprepared for the transition of power that they were reduced to asking several dozen senior Obama administration appointees to remain in their jobs, not because Republican officials approved of their work, but because the incoming administration wasn't yet properly equipped. The services of

Obama's people were required for the continuity of governmental operations. This included, among others, positions related directly to national security. On January 18, 2017, Foreign Policy magazine reported that Trump was poised to enter the White House "with most national security positions still vacant, after a disorganized transition that has stunned and disheartened career government officials" (Benen 2020: Chapter 1).

It was commonplace for Fox News and other conservative media outlets (Rush Limbaugh, Breitbart, etc.) to rationalise or explain away Trump's deeds and misdeeds, lies, dishonesty, failures and embarrassments, going even as far as normalising and trivialising these with whataboutisms, if not simply turning his flaws and weaknesses into virtues and strengths (Nyamnjoh 2018b: 45–52; Nance 2019: Chapter 11; Reid 2019: Chapter 8; Hassan 2019: Chapter 6; Cohen 2020: Chapter 11; Rauch 2021: 174–184). According to Rauch, if Trump and his echo chambers lie, it is to blur in the public psyche the distinction between truth and falsehood. He elaborates as follows:

> Trump and his media echo chambers were normalizing lying in order to obliterate the distinction, in the public realm, between truth and untruth. They were practicing the hallowed (if infamous) art of disinformation. They lied in trivial ways, when there was no point in lying except to show contempt for truth, as when Trump claimed rain had not fallen on his inauguration. They lied in grandiose and fantastic ways, as in their months-long disinformation campaign claiming to have won an election which Trump had demonstrably lost (a campaign which ended only when he was impeached for inciting a violent insurrection). They lied without distinguishing between truth and falsehood or between big lies and small lies, because their goal was to denude the public's capacity to make any distinctions at all (Rauch 2021: 8).

Fox News, renowned for being "too Trumpified" and for its "nothing-to-see-here approach to Trump scandals", [383] Stevens argues, constitutes a major part of a huge "machinery of deception" which Republicans have erected. He highlights the rise and place of Fox News in Republican politics and draws parallels with the election of Donald Trump, thus:

Fox News is unique in American media history as serving more like the in-house propaganda arm of a strong-man dictator than operating by the accepted norms of professional journalism. But Fox News did not spring fancifully into being as the creation of a former political consultant named Roger Ailes with the help of an immigrant who failed to assimilate American values, Rupert Murdoch. For decades a certain percentage of those who called themselves conservatives had been cultivating a country within a country, a sort of virtual secession from the United States of America. Like Donald Trump's election, Fox News was both an inevitable conclusion and an accelerant (Stevens 2020: 108).

Democrats, on the other hand, are in general, very critical of Fox News, and would rather keep their distance from the network, even during election campaigns when candidates seek to maximise coverage and outreach. When a candidate opens up to Fox News, as did Democrat Senator Elizabeth Warren in May 2019 as presidential candidate, it is usually with caveats. In several tweets (11:03 AM, 14 May 2019), Warren shared her opinion of Fox News and justification for why she had decided to welcome the network to her events thus:

Fox News is a hate-for-profit racket that gives a megaphone to racists and conspiracists – it's designed to turn us against each other, risking life and death consequences, to provide cover for the corruption that's rotting our government and hollowing out our middle class.

Hate-for-profit works only if there's profit, so Fox News balances a mix of bigotry, racism and outright lies with enough legit journalism to make the claim to advertisers that it's a reputable news outlet. It's all about dragging in ad money – big ad money.

But Fox News is struggling as more and more advertisers pull out of their hate-filled space. A Democratic town hall gives the Fox News sales team a way to tell potential sponsors it's safe to buy ads on Fox – no harm to their brand or reputation (spoiler: It's not).

Here's one place we can fight back: I won't ask millions of Democratic primary voters to tune into an outlet that profits from racism and hate in order to see our candidates – especially when Fox will make even more money adding our valuable audience to their ratings number.

I am running a campaign to reach all Americans. I take questions from the press and voters everywhere I go. I've already held town halls in 17 states and Puerto Rico – including WV, OH, GA, UT, TN, TX, CO, MS & AL.

I've done 57 media avails, and 131 interviews, taking over 1,100 questions from press just since January. Fox News is welcome to come to my events just like any other outlet. But a Fox New town hall adds money to the hate-for-profit machine. To which I say: hard pass.

Warren's conditional gesture of welcome to Fox News was criticised, including by some media figures, who were of the opinion that she should not have turned down the opportunity of a town hall with Fox News.[384]

As for Trump, in addition to Fox News and other conservative media outlets, he surrounds himself with people and nimble enablers who are ready to bend over backwards to the point of contortion to do his bidding, even when such loyalty is clearly self-destructive and a disservice to the greater good, national interest or what James Comey has termed "a higher loyalty" (Comey 2018).[385] Trump brands all as liars who dare contradict him and treats as a liability all those who hesitate to lie for him (Wilson 2018; Cohen 2020; Bolton 2020; Trump, M. L. 2020; Stevens 2020; Rohde 2020; Dean and Altemeyer 2020). According to psychologist Mary L. Trump, his niece,[386] Trump lies because he can, because the truth does not serve him and because no one holds him to account. She traces Trump's flexible relationship with the truth back to her grandfather who treated him as he could do no wrong and supported him with money, power and connections everywhere. To her, Trump is deeply insecure and wants to prove he is always the best. He is only concerned about himself, and his lack of truth has put him in a bubble. He is fundamentally a racist. He thrives in chaos and division[387] (see also Sims 2019; Kessler et al. 2020). Mary Trump's depiction of Trump reminds one of "The Skull" à la Tutuola, and how vulnerable and inadequate he must have felt before he went on to borrow body parts to make him look good and be the perfect gentleman. I can only imagine the making of present-day Trump from all sorts of borrowings, from childhood into his 70s, and how it must feel like to seek to sweep under the carpet of ambitions of completeness, the fact that he is who he is thanks to others, from his parents to his supporters and voters, through various social, economic, cultural and political institutions, his workers and collaborators and the media, both conventional and social. He can only remain propped up by generating and sustaining a "Tower of Lies" – to draw on the title of a book by Barbara Res, who worked for and closely with Trump for 18 years, and "who knew Donald very well" – that masks the fact of his debt and indebtedness as "a self-made man" beyond what he owes financial institutions. As Res remarks, Trump was good at hiring the best people and quick to take credit while avoiding blame, but "The bigger he got as a name, the smaller he got as a person" (Res 2020: Introduction).

Michael Moore concurs fully with Mary Trump's depiction, labelling Trump as "a consistent, absolute, unrelenting, fearless, and professional liar. A serial liar. A factually proven liar". [388] To Thurman, in an article titled "God hates a lying tongue", Trump lies for two primary reasons: "First, he lies to prop himself up, to make himself look better in other people's eyes than he is in reality." Secondly, "Trump lies to be mean, to sadistically tear other people down and make them feel small." Although Trump lies for many other reasons, Thurman believes, "his narcissistic desire to make himself look good and sadistic desire to demean others are the two most powerful motivations behind his tenuous relationship with the truth" (Thurman 2020: Chapter 2). To Skinnell, "Trump lies because lying works, plain and simple"; in business and politics alike, Trump has "known that lying sells" (Skinnell 2018b). Describing Donald Trump as "the most mendacious president in U.S. history", Glenn Kessler, Salvador Rizzo and Meg Kelly, the fact checker staff of *The Washington Post*, who documented over 16,000 falsehoods by Trump during his presidency until January 2020, have published the most comprehensive yet of President Trump's "most egregious and important" "falsehoods, misleading claims and flat-out lies" (Kessler et al. 2020: Introduction & Chapter 1) aptly titled: *Donald Trump and His Assault on Truth* (Kessler et al. 2020). Apart from Trump's big lie about winning the 2020 election, Trump is mostly known for "a constant stream of exaggerated, invented, boastful, purposely outrageous, spiteful, inconsistent, dubious and false claims". "One hallmark of Trump's dishonesty", Kessler et al. note, "is that if he thinks a false or incorrect claim is a winner, he will repeat it constantly, no matter how often it has been proven wrong". Far from being embarrassed for lying, Trump's approach was to dig in and double down, in an effort to replace the truth with one convenient to him, especially as his lying and constant repetition of falsehoods appeared to endear him to his supporters, rather than turning them off or making them disbelieve him (Kessler et al. 2020: Introduction & Conclusion). As Kessler et al. conclude:

> He [Trump] misleads about things both big and small; he seizes on flimsy, conspiratorial claims if they fit with his current position; and he is unconcerned about contradicting himself from day to day. He gets many of his facts wrong, no matter how important or sensitive the venue. And he attacks his opponents with outrageously false claims and hyperbolic rhetoric (Kessler et al. 2020: Conclusion).

Sometimes the falsehoods are too much and too costly even for steadfast supporters, home and away.

Across the Atlantic, even a staunch Trump supporter like Piers Morgan, a columnist with the UK *Daily Mail*, was forced to end his 15-year friendship[389] with Donald Trump, after Trump unfollowed him on Twitter for daring to be critical when Trump suggested that people with Covid-19 could ingest or be injected with bleach as a cure. At the time, Piers Morgan's Twitter account was among a privileged 47 that Trump followed, compared to Trump's over 88.7 million followers. In his repost, Piers Morgan called on Trump to "stop warring with the media" and reminded him of these words of President John F. Kennedy about freedom of the press: "Without debate, without criticism, no Administration and no country can succeed. That is why our press was protected by the First Amendment – the only business specifically protected by the Constitution – not primarily to amuse and entertain, not to emphasize the trivial and the sentimental, not to simply "'give the public what it wants'" but to inform, to arouse, to reflect, to state our dangers and our opportunities, to indicate our crises and our choices, to lead, mould, educate and sometime even anger public opinion." Piers Morgan concluded with: "If you want the press to show you respect, then start showing them some."[390]

Donald Trump is an addict for the spotlight and sees the media as the way for him to satisfy his addiction. He believes he can steer the conversation and coverage, even in the liberal media which he regularly criticises as fake and unreliable (Muirhead and Rosenblum 2019: 59–78). Trump basks in the spotlight even if this is Bob

Woodward's perilous torchlight, as evidenced by the 17 interviews he had with Woodward in preparation for Woodward's 2020 book, *Rage*, in the hope of promoting positive coverage of his case in the book – especially in light of elections coming up in November 2020. Trump needed some positivity amid the Covid-19 pandemic, the handling of which by Trump and his administration was highly criticised. It must have jolted Trump with rage that, despite his investment in time and effort to give Woodward his side of the story in his own voice and words, Woodward concludes *Rage* with a sentence that reads: "When his performance as president is taken in its entirety, I can only reach one conclusion: Trump is the wrong man for the job" (Woodward 2020: Epilogue).

In a 9:02 pm tweet on 9 October 2020, Trump reacted to Woodward thus:

> Bob Woodward had my quotes for many months. If he thought they were so bad or dangerous, why didn't he immediately report them in an effort to save lives? Didn't he have an obligation to do so? No, because he knew they were good and proper answers. Calm, no panic!

In his ambitions of supremacy and completeness, Trump is obsessed with status and rankings, and Bob Woodward, not Sean Hannity or anyone in the Fox News firmament, is the ultimate indicator of status in the conventional media world of objective fact-based journalism. Not only was Bob Woodward uncompromisingly objective in *Rage* about Trump's imperviousness to facts and the truth, he also did not mince words in the media interviews he had following publication of the book. To Woodward, the president has a moral responsibility to the wider population and not just his partisan supporters. Trump may not have invented highly volatile partisanship, but he channelled and nurtured it. The risk of going down in history as the person who levelled democracy against the people is enormous for Trump, who does not demonstrate that he understands the country he was elected in 2016 to govern. Trump assumed power not only to break norms but to smash them; and he resorted to lying, thus forsaking his basic duty to tell the truth and protect Americans. He makes decision on impulse and says the cruellest and crudest things, which is unbecoming of anyone, let alone the president. Even after his time in office, when some degree of retrospection and benefit of the hindsight were expected, asked about his responsibility to be honest as president, Trump still insisted: "'I want to be somebody that's optimistic for our country. I think it's very important'" (Leonnig and Rucker 2021: Epilogue). As Rucker and Leonnig document, Trump's moral and leadership failure is not only challenging the Constitution but also putting the dagger in the Constitution, a document he has reportedly remarked, reads "like a foreign language" and is "very hard to get through [...] without a stumble"[391] (Rucker and Leonnig 2020: Chapter 3).

As Omarosa Manigault Newman remembers from her time with Trump on *The Apprentice*, "Donald is not a big reader. While working with him side by side on my own briefings, I'd come to understand that he read at an eighth- or ninth-grade level." She believes that as President, not only did Trump "never read from beginning to end any of the major pieces of legislation, policies, or even some of these executive orders that he [...] signed", he relied on senior advisors to "spoon-feed him five to ten bullet points about the legislation and forgo any discussion of the complexities". In his business as well, Newman claims, "Donald has always relied on his charisma, his street smarts, and trusted advisers to tell him what was in the paperwork" (Newman 2018: Chapter 11).

It must be refreshing for those Americans still committed to being trusted with the basic facts of their circumstance, however traumatising, to hear Trump's successor, President Biden, insist as follows about how to communicate with the American public on when the coronavirus pandemic would be over: "'We don't know' is a perfectly acceptable answer" said President Biden. "Let's give it to people straight" (Slavitt 2021: Preface).

Mostly, it does not matter to Trump whether the coverage he craves is positive or not as long as there is coverage. Some commentators have observed that it does not matter what is said at a Trump rally; it is the ritual of attending it that matters to those who attend them religiously. The rally offers spiritual and magical protection for those who attend. Trump's rallies are not political events only but also religious rituals (Bender 2021). Media coverage for Trump is as important as oxygen is for those who cannot breathe. Thus, in reality, far from hating the media as he often claims on TV and Twitter, Trump loves and is obsessed with the media. He is a creature of television, of which he is a voracious consumer. He cannot have enough of the media. He has his own personal personality, and he has his media personality.

Michael Cohen, who "For more than a decade [...] was Trump's first call every morning and his last call every night" as Trump's personal attorney and confidant, refers to Trump's personal personality as: "the real real Donald Trump – the man very, very, very few people know". According to Cohen, this personality is not the same as his projected public persona as "the billionaire celebrity savior of the country or lying lunatic, [...] the tabloid tycoon or self-anointed Chosen One, [...] the avatar @realdonaldtrump of Twitter fame" (Cohen 2020: Foreword). Outside of reality TV, Trump's status as a billionaire is open to speculation. In the words of his biographer, Tim O'Brien, "Evaluating Donald's riches was like trying to bottle smoke", given Trump's "overly generous and malleable definitions of being a proprietor" of real estate. Questioned on the truthfulness of his stated net worth of property, Trump replied: "My net worth fluctuates, and it goes up and down with markets and with attitudes and with feelings, even my own feelings, but I try." (O'Brien 2015[2005]: Introduction).

In addition, Trump has his reality TV personality as in *The Apprentice* (Kellner 2016: 7–12; O'Brien 2015[2005]: Chapter 1; Newman 2018; Reid 2019: Chapter 5). According to Patrick Radden Keefe of the *New Yorker*, although the series creators knew that Trump was "a fake", they created a personality, worlds apart from the "skeezy hustler who huddles with local mobsters", and much more akin to "a plutocrat with impeccable business instincts and unparalleled wealth—a titan who always seemed to be climbing out of helicopters or into limousines" (cited in Dean and Altemeyer 2020: Chapter 3).

It must therefore have been a most devastating blow for Trump, like immediately sending him to an ICU gasping for oxygen in a time of Covid-19, when his favourite social media platforms, Twitter and Facebook, decided to ban or deplatform him permanently, following the insurrection by the mob that stormed the Capitol under his instigation and his refusal to accept the fact that he had lost the 2020 presidential election (Wolff 2021a: Chapter 11; Leonnig and Rucker 2021: Chapter 21). Those who had so gleefully assembled and propped up the Trump social media monster, reading the changing tides, were just as keen to disassemble the monster. It was all like a game of inflation and deflation driven primarily by putting profits over people until the very threshold of the profit motive was threatened by a moral imperative that not even the market in its consummate greed as creed could be indifferent to any longer. Before the ban, the closest Twitter had come to censoring Trump was to fact-check him, which was the case in May, when Trump tweeted:

> There is NO WAY (ZERO!) that Mail-In Ballots will be anything less than substantially fraudulent. Mail boxes will be robbed, ballots will be forged & even illegally printed out & fraudulently signed (8:17 AM 26 May 2020 tweet).

Twitter marked the tweet with: "Get the facts about mail-in ballots." It was the first time ever, that Twitter had fact-checked President Trump, Dwoskin reports.[392] Trump retorted: "@Twitter is now interfering in the 2020 Presidential Election. [...] Twitter is completely stifling FREE SPEECH, and I, as President, will not allow it to happen!" (7:40 PM 26 May 2020).

The Twitter ban, with effect from 8 January 2021, cited "the risk of further incitement of violence". Twitter cited two tweets posted earlier that day by Trump, one praising his supporters as "patriots" and another declaring he would not attend Joe Biden's inauguration on 20 January – reportedly the first president in 152 years not to attend a successor's inauguration – as violations of its rules against glorifying violence. Twitter concluded that the tweets "were highly likely to encourage and inspire people to replicate the criminal acts that took place at the U.S. Capitol on Jan. 6, 2021", a reference to the storming of the Capitol by a mob of Trump loyalists".[393]

As Trump's former personal attorney, Michael Cohen, writes, "President Trump controlled all the levers of the Commander in Chief and all the overt and covert powers that come with the highest office in the country". Trump "also possessed a cult-like hold over his supporters, some of them demonstrably unhinged and willing to do anything to please or protect the President". Cohen was only too aware "how committed these fanatics were", because until he turned disloyal, he used to be "one of them: an acolyte obsessed with Donald J. Trump, a demented follower willing to do anything for him, including, as I vowed once to a reporter, to take a bullet" (Cohen 2020: Foreword).

By finally deciding, even if only after the attempted insurrection at the Capitol, to ban Donald Trump permanently, Facebook, Instagram and Twitter were at long last yielding to the call of the moment: the need to deactivate the Frankenstein monster that they had helped create and prop up for over four years. Intended or not, Trump "The Complete Gentleman" whom they had propped up had, unlike "The Skull", manoeuvred to stay permanently activated in order to continue to enjoy without responsibility and regard for the desires and rights of others the potency of the magic of the social media platforms. Some have linked Trump's behaviour on Twitter to that of a drunk driver, even as Trump is known not to drink alcohol.

Here is how Brian Williams of the 11th Hour on MSNBC reacted to the ban of Trump by Twitter: "The man [Donald Trump] who said he could not have won the election without Twitter has been tossed off Twitter. His cell phone has been rendered mute and ineffective." Put differently, the forces that had activated Trump to extraordinary levels of potency to achieve his ends for four years had, with the press of a button, deactivated him in equal measure. How Trump would cope without Twitter, his "greatest megaphone" is open to speculation. Twitter's magic multiplier capacity to compress time and space, activate presence in multiple spaces and places at the same time, as well as its addictiveness and infusion of delusions of grandeur, had made a truly larger than life extremely powerful noise-making machine of Trump for 10 years.

Writing in 2016, when Trump was still campaigning for the presidency, Kellner characterised Trump's relationship with Twitter thus:

> Twitter is perfect for General Trump who can blast out his opinions and order his followers what to think. It enables Businessman and Politician Trump to define his brand and mobilize those who wish to consume or support it. Trump Twitter gratifies the need of Narcissist Trump to be noticed and recognized as a Master of Communication who can bind his warriors into an on-line community. Twitter enables the Pundit-in-Chief to opine, rant, attack, and proclaim on all and sundry subjects, and to subject TrumpWorld to the indoctrination of their Fearless Leader (Kellner 2016: 9).

After analysing 1,815 tweets by Trump, with a focus on "authoritarian personality" in Trump's online behaviour, Fuchs concludes, inter alia, that:

> Trump uses Twitter to present himself as a boss, strong leader and authority. The language used is very self-centred and narcissistic. He uses the first-person singular ('I', 'me') much more frequently on Twitter than the first-person plural. Twitter's brevity, speed, individualism and its structure for the accumulation of acclamation (via 'likes' and 'retweets') supports Trump's use of it as a communication tool for authoritarian leadership. Trump uses Twitter for continuously repeating nationalist slogans, above all that he will 'make America great again', which is supported by the use of hashtags such #MAGA, #AmericaFirst or #MakeAmericaSafeAgain. Trump constructs average Americans as an in-group who are under constant threat from immigrants, refugees, criminals, terrorists, foreign forces and the political elite. He uses Twitter for communicating that there is a conspiracy against America that aims at destroying it (Fuchs 2018: 250–251).

Furthermore, Trump, in his tweets, tends to portray Americans to be "under attack" and as a people who "have to struggle for existence". In his nationalism, Trump "constructs a joint political interest of capital and labour" in a manner that "deflects attention from class structures being at the heart of social problems" (Fuchs 2018: 251).

Trump's tweets as president stood at over 11,000 by 2 November 2019, with more than half of them – 5,889 – consisting of attacks, according to Shear et al. of *The New York Times*.[394] Trump is adept at projecting "political dualisms between friends and enemies" in his Twitter communication. "Negative references to individuals and groups strongly outweigh positive ones" and "His main scapegoats, whom he frequently attacks on Twitter, are the liberal media, Democratic politicians, immigrants, refugees, criminals and Islam." On the other hand, Trump has tended to reserve "his main positive references on Twitter" to "his family, Fox, the American people, the police and the military" (Fuchs 2018: 251), and – until the mob attack on the Capitol in which some Trump supporters threatened to "hang Mike Pence" for having "dared to defy Trump's order to violate the

U.S. Constitution in an attempt to overturn the results" of the November 2020 election" (Bender 2021: Introduction) – to Vice President Mike Pence as well.

In addition, Trump considers among "his friends, whom he follows on Twitter" "right-wing journalists and media", especially those associated with Fox News (Fuchs 2018: 251), a cable news channel owned by Rupert Murdoch, whom Michael Wolff compares with Trump, including in the following words: "If on one end of the rich scale there is Donald Trump, all mouth and affect, calling attention to himself, on the other end is Rupert Murdoch, shadowy and scowling, all head and no affect, his personality largely hidden from view" (Wolff 2008: Chapter 2). Trump draws a clear distinction between friendly media and enemy media, and uses Twitter to constantly characterise his enemies in a negative manner as "crooks", "disgusting", "failing", "dishonest", "biased", "bad", "terrible", "fake", etc. (Fuchs 2018: 251). Trump cherishes the fact that "Twitter's structure of 140-character messages does not allow for arguments". This "allows his friend/enemy propaganda to work through negative affects instead of arguments". It permits him to use "generalising synecdoches for presenting his enemies as unitary groups of bad people" (Fuchs 2018: 251). In sum, Fuchs argues, "Trump presents himself as a great little man on Twitter, a strong leader who is one of the people" (Fuchs 2018: 260).

Jordan Hollinger has described the Trump presidency as "the first Twitter-based presidency" and shown just how reliant on and effective with Twitter and social media Trump was in mobilising and staying in touch with his supporters, as well as in setting the agenda and influencing and shaping debates and events.[395] Cowls and Schroeder concur, arguing that Trump's skilful agenda-setting use of Twitter enabled him to dominate the mainstream media to the detriment of other candidates and, together with populism, contributed in a major way to his electoral victory in 2016 (Cowls and Schroeder 2018). Speaking of Trump as "a great story" which the media did not seem to have enough of, Michael Cohen writes, "By five a.m. every day, he'd created the news cycle with his stubby fingers sending out bile-flecked tweets attacking anyone or everyone" (Cohen 2020: Chapter 11). Humphrey, who has analysed Trump's tweets, believes that on Twitter, Trump "was especially potent as narrator-in-chief of his own political life", which combined well with "his repetitive rhetorical style" to account for "his power to rally a loyal base".[396]

In March 2021, it was reported that former President Trump, who pledges "always and forever [to] be a champion for the American people",[397] was planning an imminent social media return with a platform of his own, one that "will be the hottest ticket in social media" and would "completely redefine the game", according to Trump's adviser, Jason Miller, speaking on Fox News.[398] This was in line with the widely shared view "in the Trump White House that he was one of social media's most valuable assets, and that he would like nothing better than to share, monetarily, in that value" (Wolff 2021a: Chapter 9). The announcement was followed by the launch of a new "communications platform" that publishes content "straight from the desk" of former President Trump. But if reports are anything to go by, Trump's internet presence is fast sliding into irrelevance, with online talk about him plummeting to a five year low barely five months after he left office.[399] For Trump not to be popular on the internet is not to benefit from the latter's capacity to ensure that "a single digital act could partially occur in countless physical locations simultaneously, or an action in one place could result in effects in another place" (Wylie 2019: Chapter 12). It is thus hardly surprising that Trump closed "his beacon of freedom" website barely a month after its launch,[400] and in what he termed was a move to defend First Amendment rights, Trump, in July 2021, "filed three separate class-action lawsuits in federal court in Florida against the tech giants and Facebook's Mark Zuckerberg, Twitter's Jack Dorsey and Google's Sundar Pichais".[401] Starved of the magic multiplier potential and relatively less fleeting nature of these social media platforms, Trump must miss the limelight he craves, which could explain why in October 2021 he announced in anticipation the launch in 2022 a "Truth Social" media app by the Trump Media and Technology Group, a newly formed company.[402] O'Brien had this to say of Trump in 2005: "Being in the spotlight was what Donald enjoyed most, what he did best, and, unlike the average businessman, he was willing to do cartwheels to stay there" (O'Brien 2015[2005]: Chapter 1).

It is equally possible that Trump may be gradually weaning himself from his Twitter feeding bottle – arguably "one of Trump's most prized possessions" (Sims 2019: Chapter 3) –if this report by Bender, following an interview with Trump at Mar-a-Lago, post the Trump presidency is anything to go by. In the interview, Trump tells Bender that he is "glad to be off Twitter", adding that the statements he now releases for public consumption are "much more elegant" (Bender 2021: Epilogue). Bender finds this declaration somewhat stunning, and as possibly "the biggest change" by Trump since leaving the presidency. Bender quotes Trump as follows:

> "It's really better than Twitter because I don't do the stupid retweets that people don't like—the retweets are the ones that get you," Trump said. "And I saved a lot of time. I didn't realize you can spend a lot of time on this. Now I actually have time to make phone calls, and do other things and read papers that I wouldn't read. And with me, if I put a comma out of place or I accidentally misspelled a word, it was like the world coming down." (Bender 2021: Epilogue).

When Trump got into trouble or found himself in a pickle, he did one thing on teleprompter, almost always under duress, for his advisers, and one thing for himself on Twitter and social media, his communicative platforms of choice for everything, including dog-whistle politics. With Twitter, his lies could travel halfway round the world, making waves before the truth had time to put on its shoes. As Turner argues, not only did Twitter enable Trump and his craving for authoritarian individualism to make the world look chaotic and dangerous, but it also inserted him at the centre of the storm, thereby betraying Twitter's anti-authoritarian promise (Turner 2018). But now that these platforms have been withdrawn, Trump is considerably isolated at his palace at Mar-a-Lago where Republicans hungry for power have to physically travel to be fed, blessed and graced by his presence. But there is talk of looking for alternatives that would reactivate his capacity for presence in simultaneous multiplicities.

The jury is still out on the extent to which it could be claimed that the Trump of 2016–2020 has been the creation or Humpty Dumpty of social media algorithms (Wylie 2019) that, according to senator Michael Bennett, have largely served to divide Americans and jeopardise democracy (Bennett 2019), even if without destroying its foundations (Hawkins and Hawkins 2018; Miller 2018; McCallion 2019; Nance 2019; Stengel 2019; Weyland and Madrid 2019; Wolff

2021a). What is certain, Rauch indicates, is that Trump demonstrated such "efficacy in the epistemic sphere" of trolling and disinformation that, by the time he left office, "he had succeeded in unmooring half or more of his party from its sense of truth and falsehood, even of right and wrong". The Republican party under Trump was characterised by confusion and chaos and in a world apart, one governed by alternative facts (Rauch 2021: 173–174).

Lest we underestimate the transformative nature of algorithms on culture, Christopher Wylie, whose insider knowledge of the world of algorithms makes him an authority, argues that not only do algorithms have the capacity to transform cultures, but they can also "redefine the experience of existence". He attributes largely to "engagements" that are algorithmically reinforced "our outrage politics, call-out culture, selfie-induced vanity, tech addiction, and eroding mental well-being". Although as users "we want to feel like we are in control" and "like to think of ourselves as immune from influence or our cognitive biases", the reality is that algorithms are excellent at targeting and soaking us in content to keep us clicking. It is the same marketing strategy used by "industries like alcohol, tobacco, fast food, and gaming [who] all know we are creatures that are subject to cognitive and emotional vulnerabilities". Ours is an illusion of choice "if our choices are monitored and filtered for us" by algorithms that are programmed to "shackle us to histories that we prefer to move on from". Without privacy, "our power to decide who and how we want to be" – the power to grow and to change as we see fit – is lost, and with it our ability to be tolerant and to accommodate our creative diversity as humans (Wylie 2019: Chapter 12). It is thus an irony that the algorithm potential for big tech companies to embrace and promote incompleteness, interconnections and conviviality is not being fulfilled by social media operators who are more interested in curbing the enthusiasm of users for genuine freedom and networking for inclusivity across frozen divides and rigid hierarchies of citizenship, being and belonging to shared spaces and places.

In Cameroon, over the years since 1982, as the longest serving president in Africa, Paul Biya, has proven himself as a communication genius by largely maintaining a dead silence when he is most expected to speak to address burning issues. He leaves it to his surrogates to do the speaking on his behalf, often in the form of speculation about his intentions, motives and what he would have said, as if he were voiceless, dumb, dead or non-existent in human form. By so doing, Biya has invariably succeeded in allowing problems to resolve themselves, for which he has often then proceeded to take credit, and to outsource blame entirely onto others, his opponents and surrogates included (Nyamnjoh 2005). Trump on the other hand, has proven his genius not through silence, but through a skill at making the most noise and rattling away nonstop, seeking, like a weaver bird, to outtalk everyone else everywhere, to divert attention, to systematically turn the tables on the truth and truth seekers. Both Biya and Trump have nursed and pursued ambitions of completeness, using different trajectories in communication styles. Trump's victories have come from his ability to exhaust and panel-beat into compliance everyone who thinks differently. The most tenacious among his detractors he seeks to flatten in the fashion of Tom and Jerry violence. Truth is delicate, fragile, vulnerable and needing of constant tending and protection. This, it could be argued, is because the ontologies of truth and human nature are on opposite directions – colliding on each other for supremacy. It has found it difficult to cope with the sheer magnitude of Trumpian distractions. Biya – who could even make a case for being a man of the people given that nothing is impossible in Cameroon as a country united by ethnic ambition and difference (Nyamnjoh 1999), and in view of his over 35 years at the helm of the tellingly named omnipresent and omnipotent Cameroon People's Democratic Movement – is still in power. Trump has come and gone, albeit reluctantly. Trump and Biya appear as polar opposites who have the media in common, and who have manipulated the latter in different ways to influence public opinion and assert their power. Had Trump enough interest in world affairs to know of Biya's staying power, he might have reached out to him for tips. Do Biya and his leadership style offer a template for strongmen seeking to capture, personalise and royally wield power for 39 years and more? For students of autocratic power, it is well worth taking a closer look at Paul Biya as a very royal president in a purported democracy, who in the era of social media, does not even have to pretend to be publicly and physically present and active to exercise power. And if he so desired, Biya could seek out the services of spyware and malware manufacturers, in order better to monitor and contain dissidents and critics (Nyamnjoh 2019).

Trump, Social Media and the "Pandemic of Narcissism"

It could be argued that if Trump is the Frankenstein monster of American democracy, he, his creators and worshippers have a lot to thank America's culture of narcissism for, a culture that has reached pandemic proportions with the invention, adoption and proliferation of social media. Trump has repeatedly been categorised as a narcissist. Reading and listening to commentators, one cannot help wondering about the extent to which Trump is an exception, or not, among Americans. Christopher Lasch's book, *The Culture of Narcissism: American Life in an Age of Diminishing Expectations*, published in 1979 when Trump was in his early 30s, suggests that Trump's narcissistic preoccupation with himself, far from being an exception, was a national trend during his youth, and the foundation of what he and others in his generation have become to greater or lesser degrees. It was not uncommon to self-promote (in the lone ranger manner that one is encouraged to do in one's resumes and annual performance reviews for example) through winning images, as a substitute for self-cultivation, competence and substantive, measurable achievements. The rise of consumerism gave legitimation to propaganda and advertising in a manner that watered down the value of truth, credibility and a sense of history, and with this came the practice of politics as spectacle (Lasch 1991[1979]).

Thus, it could be argued that Trump's infantile illusions of omnipotence, inability to recognise others as independent beings with desires of their own and not merely as projections of his own desires, addiction to self-branding, incapacity for loyalty or gratitude except towards himself, inauthenticity, indifference to the truth and to history, and his understanding of politics as spectacle are informed both by personal psychological and cultural factors (Lasch 1991[1979]: 237–249). Being a dependent Drinkard, who deludes him- or herself of autonomy and of being self-made *à la* Tutuola, is not only a psychological condition, but also a socially cultivated reality as well. The fact that somehow Trump's disposition is so strongly rooted in American culture and times would account for his resonance and staying power, despite sustained public criticism by the media and by political foes and friends.

Lasch's description of what he terms "the new narcissists" echoes much of what I have read of Trump as a narcissist. According to Lasch, the new narcissist is haunted by anxiety and not by guilt. His or her ambition or goal is not so much "to inflict his own certainties on others but to find a meaning in life". The new narcissist may be liberated from "the superstitions of the past", he or she doubts even the reality of his or her own existence. "Superficially relaxed and tolerant", the new narcissist "finds little use for dogmas of racial and ethnic purity but at the same time forfeits the security of group loyalties and regards everyone as a rival for the favors conferred by a paternalistic state". He or she is "Fiercely competitive" in his or her "demand for approval and acclaim", and tends to distrust competition because he or she associates competition "unconsciously with an unbridled urge to destroy". The new narcissist harbours "deeply antisocial impulses" even as he or she extols cooperation and teamwork. He or she "praises respect for rules and regulations in the secret belief that they do not apply" to him or her. His or her acquisitiveness and limitless cravings are driven not by a need to "accumulate goods and provisions against the future", but by the urge for "immediate gratification" to a life in "a state of restless" and "perpetually unsatisfied desire". Without little or no vested interest in the past, it is hardly surprising that the narcissist has no interest in the future either (Lasch 1991[1979]: xvi).

Kakutani draws on Lasch to add that a narcissist is prone to "intense feelings of rage, a sense of inner emptiness, fantasies of omnipotence and a strong belief in [his] right to exploit others". Additional tendencies may include being "'chaotic and impulse-ridden,' 'ravenous for admiration but contemptuous of those he manipulates into providing it,' and inclined to conform 'to social rules more out of fear of punishment than from a sense of guilt'" (Kakutani 2018: 62).

If Trump is a narcissist, who cannot tolerate criticism and who is preoccupied, inter alia, by "an anxious concern with the impression one made on others, a tendency to treat others as a mirror of the self" (Lasch 1991[1979]: 239), he is in good company in a 21st century of liberal elites characterised by obsessive narcissism (Samuels 2016; Nichols 2021: Chapters 3 & 5) or "the unhealthy preoccupation with the self to the exclusion of all else—and especially to the exclusion of other human beings—tempts us away from thinking about the needs of other people and to see them only as objects in relation to our own happiness" (Nichols 2021: Chapter 3). As Wolff demonstrates, Trump's unabashed, relentless and unquenchable thirst for attention to enhance his public profile and renown are a trait shared by many other high profile "social climbers" or seekers of fame, celebrity and notoriety. Contemporary social climbers or narcissists are, as Wolff observes, as much creatures of as they are creations of the media, which simultaneously glorifies and keeps them in check (Wolff 2021b). According to Díaz – inspired by American sociologists Jean Twenge and Keith Campbell's book *The Narcissism Epidemic* (2009) – the 21st century is marked by "a pandemic of narcissism, for which there is no vaccine".[403] Building on Lasch (1991[1979]), Twenge and Campbell (2009) have detailed "the relentless rise of narcissism" in American culture, noting the increase in the number of narcissists, and the growing tendency among non-narcissistic people to be "seduced by the increasing emphasis on material wealth, physical appearance, celebrity worship, and attention seeking" (Twenge and Campbell 2009: 1–2). According to Twenge and Campbell, the narcissism epidemic is a mass producer of phoney realities and grandiose fantasies, with destructive consequences for society. Narcissism's destructive consequences include "aggression, materialism, lack of caring for others, and shallow values", they maintain (Twenge and Campbell 2009: 9). Hence their argument that:

> American culture's focus on self-admiration has caused a flight from reality to the land of grandiose fantasy. We have phony rich people (with interest-only mortgages and piles of debt), phony beauty (with plastic surgery and cosmetic procedures), phony athletes (with performance-enhancing drugs), phony celebrities (via reality TV and YouTube), phony genius students (with grade inflation), a phony national economy (with $11 trillion of government debt), phony feelings of being special among children (with parenting and education focused on self-esteem), and phony friends (with the social networking explosion). All this fantasy might feel good, but, unfortunately, reality always wins. The mortgage meltdown and the resulting financial crisis are just one

demonstration of how inflated desires eventually crash to earth. (Twenge and Campbell 2009: 4).

In a country where to be phoney and to fantasise and live in fantasy spaces are celebrated and actively encouraged to compete with and even to challenge reality (Wu 2016), why should there be such discomfort and brouhaha with a president who has so ably embodied the magic of the phoney and the make-believe? A president who has vigorously refused to live a lie by sticking to the true culture of the USA: narcissism, as opposed to the political correctness of keeping up appearances? Trump's narcissism feeds from and fuels the prejudices, stereotypes, violence, hate, anger, collective narcissism and fantasies of superiority of his largely white Republican support base.[404]

The narcissism pandemic, Díaz elaborates, is driven in part by an idiotic obsession with "ephemeral fame" that, like the coronavirus, spreads "much more quickly and efficiently" around the world, thanks to the internet and social media networks, which make is possible for fantasies to trump reality or for imagined reality to double as the really real. Questers after fame, however ephemeral, are fascinated with their ability to capture the attention of others by getting their faces and utterances reproduced on millions of smartphones just as they are validated by clicks. Accordingly, "The number of followers gives them the false illusion that their actions have garnered ironclad support", as in "some insane way, they view these followers as accomplices who approve" of their words and/or deeds, however despicable.

Boczkowski and Papacharissi write of "the emergence of a digital culture that combines high levels of top-down algorithmic power concentrated in the hands of a few corporations with equally high levels of bottom-up insurgency capabilities distributed among a myriad of individual and collective actors" (Boczkowski and Papacharissi 2018: 5). Facilitated by the internet and its ability to confirm the beliefs, preconceptions and biases of those drawn to it (Nichols 2017, 2021; Stengel 2019), predictive algorithms and datafication have risen to assume the status of penultimate celebrity creators in a manner that promotes surveillance and eludes accountability (Wu 2016; Lanier 2018; Wylie 2019; Dreher 2020: Chapter 4; Rauch 2021). As Lanier argues, it is difficult to "remain autonomous in a world where you are under constant surveillance and are constantly prodded by algorithms run by some of the richest corporations in history, which have no way of making money except by being paid to manipulate your behavior" (Lanier 2018: Introduction). Engineered to access extremely granular personal naturally occurring real life data of social media users and to commodify lives, identities, attention and behaviour, social media algorithms that track and quantify every scroll, every movement and every like, seem configured to prioritise the popular and the trending rather than that which is accurate or deemed important (Wylie 2019). As Rauch maintains, the "metrics and algorithms and optimization tools" are "sensitive to popularity but indifferent to truth", and even to meaning, since they lack understanding of the content they are disseminating (Rauch 2021: 125–126). However, as Wylie observes, although when taken in isolation each like is "almost always too weak to predict anything on its own, when those likes were combined with hundreds of other likes, as well as other voter and consumer data, then powerful predictions could be made" (Wylie 2019: Chapter 6). Unlike in the pre-internet world when fame used to be "tied to word of mouth" or "recorded in art, books, radio, press, and television", in the 21st century, fame is mostly generated "on social networks", where "A single click, and a relevant story can travel the world in seconds, bringing any anonymous character to fame, regardless of merit." This mechanism has two sides to it, as it can also help amplify legitimate voices that have been marginalised. Not that this is necessarily the intention, but it is sometimes the effect. Even as it eludes control, Díaz argues, "the algorithm is generous, in the sense that it invites a lot of people onto the catwalk of popularity, at the cost of making it increasingly ephemeral".[405]

In their supposed generosity, Kakutani argues, "Facebook, Twitter, YouTube, and many other sites use algorithms to personalize the information" they deliver to users, "information customized on the basis of earlier data they've collected" about us as individual users of their platforms, often too consumed by clicking passively away at options to be conscious of the personal data we are instinctively feeding the platforms. If these platforms appear to be unbiased, the reason may be because they are programmed to reproduce the biases of those who use them (Kakutani 2018: 116). From "what we click on and what other people similar to us click on", algorithms are able to build virtual avatars of us and to feed us whatever our avatars want more of. It does not matter that "no one understands why we see what we see" and that "no one knows exactly what anyone else is seeing" (Rauch 2021: 132). As Rauch observes, "one of the things our biases do is blind us to our biases" by making us "think we are most rational and feel we can be most certain when we are in fact most mistaken and most deceived". (Rauch 2021: 27–32). The more common and seemingly intuitive our biases are, the greater the likelihood that we may not recognise just how irrational they actually are (Wylie 2019: Chapter 4). As humans, we "are equipped with some of evolution's finest mental circuitry to protect us from changing our minds when doing so might alienate us from our group". Our brains have configured themselves to protect our worldview and our sense of identity and prioritise our basic instincts to survive. And if this takes responding more to social and group dynamics than to our intellect, so be it. Something need not be rational to make sense to us from the perspective of self-preservation through bonding with others with whom we share a common set of values. Thus, "to keep us in good standing with our tribe", we are ready to believe anything, "even if that requires denying, discounting, rationalizing, misperceiving, and ignoring the evidence in front of our nose" (Rauch 2021: 27–32). To "outsource our interpretations of reality, and even our perceptions of reality, to our social groups and personal networks", comes naturally to us as humans, Rauch argues. Equally true is our instinct to freeze the humanity of others whom we perceive to be outsiders or strangers to our identity bubbles and comfort zones, be these defined by race, ethnicity, class, gender, age, culture, religion or any other social category of distinction and differentiation (Rauch 2021: 71). Yet, it is worth taking a closer look at the intricate messiness of our lived experiences that point to interconnections and interdependences which defy neat categories and our tendency to take for granted rigid binary oppositions.

Stengel illustrates how algorithms confirm our biases thus: "If you like Rachel Maddow or Tucker Carlson, the algorithm will give you content that reflects your political persuasion. What it won't do is give you content that questions your beliefs" (Stengel 2019: Introduction). Customisation as a form of surveillance, behavioural control and crystallisation of biases (Stengel 2019), exemplifies Trump's media use and relations superbly. As a media addict, Trump has excelled at persuasive techniques, ranging from what he has termed "truthful hyperbole" that plays to "people's fantasies" and encourages people who "want to believe that something is the biggest and the greatest and the most spectacular" (Trump with Schwartz 1987: 58) – as "Hyperbole brings an underlying truth to the surface that the factual truth can't quite describe" (Skinnell 2018b) – to trolling (Marcotte 2018; Rauch 2021: 155–188), which has the effect of driving people nuts, cracking them up or making them livid (Sims 2019: Chapter 3), semantic infiltration,[406] and relentless attack, denial, distancing, discrediting, delegitimation, deflection and diversion of others, from political opponents to the media and beyond. He surrounds himself in a bubble of echo chambers, from right-wing media like Fox News and One America News Network (OAN) to Twitter, Facebook and Reddit, that feed from and into the fodder he generates in a cyclical network of charge, discharge and recharge. According to Smith, OAN for example, a relatively obscure network, has endeared itself with Trump by compensating for "its lack of clout or viewers by covering every Trump utterance, recycling conspiracy theories, downplaying Russian threats, bashing the mainstream media and championing the 'Make America Great Again' agenda". As Smith aptly observes, this is an excellent example of how Trump "cuts both ways" as media commentator. On the one hand, Trump derides "mainstream outlets as 'enemies of the people'" at the same time as "he champions those that offer flattering coverage" and offer him unlimited coverage. In the 2016 presidential election, OAN was the first channel to carry Trump's "campaign speeches live and in full", a practice that continued during Trump's presidency, where "not even Fox News broadcasts every [Trump] speech uninterrupted".[407] Nate White, quoted by Michael de Groot, describes Trump, who trolls for media oxygen and visibility, even when his news is not newsworthy:

> Trump is a troll. And like all trolls, he is never funny and he never laughs; he only crows or jeers.
>
> And scarily, he doesn't just talk in crude, witless insults – he actually thinks in them. His mind is a simple bot-like algorithm of petty prejudices and knee-jerk nastiness.
>
> There is never any under-layer of irony, complexity, nuance or depth. It's all surface.[408]

What is amazing is how algorithms help multiply with dizzying velocity and ferocity the prejudices and nastiness of Trump as a "most superior troll" (Rauch 2021: 169) or King Troll,[409] other trollers (Watts 2018; Nance 2019; Rauch 2021: 118–188), and "entire industries based on selling bad ideas to the public and charging them for the privilege of being misinformed" online (Nichols 2017: 115). Optimised for advertising with its propensity to prioritise emotion over knowledge and the truth, the internet, Rauch maintains, has proven to be "ideally suited to disinformation campaigns on a previously impossible scale" (Rauch 2021: 161–162). The endlessness of the reruns and reactions generated across various mediascapes, nationally and globally, is impressive indeed. Yet, this is equally worrying in contexts of disinformation, where, as Rauch indicates, a "key to the success of any disinformation campaign is to trigger repetition and amplification in the target society's own media and political ecosystems" in a manner that generates "Epistemic helplessness—the inability to know where to turn for truth" (Rauch 2021: 165–166). Rauch elaborates:

> If you cannot be sure at any given time whether you are being manipulated or scammed, then the natural way to protect yourself is to assume that you are always being scammed, or to hunker down with online friends in your own private version of reality, or to take a demagogic politician's word for it (Rauch 2021: 169).

Whatever the importance one attributes to algorithms, however, Laterza reminds us of the need to not lose sight of the fact that in and behind the algorithms are humans, lest we credit algorithms with agency over and above that of those who create and manipulate them (Laterza 2021: 127). Put differently, algorithms are only as clever and manipulative as their creators, and since creativity does not occur in a cultural vacuum, algorithms inherit the original sins and virtues of their makers (Lanier 2013, 2018). As Burke reminds us, the histories of technologies and information systems are first and foremost human histories (Burke 2018). Those of us enabled and propelled by algorithms and the desire for ephemeral fame could easily get carried away by our "narcissism epidemic" (Twenge and Campbell 2009), but as Lasch reminds us, the "world does not exist merely to satisfy our own desires; it is a world in which we can find pleasure and meaning, once we understand that others too have a right to these goods" (Lasch 1991[1979]: 242). It is thus to be regretted that social media may not be as much of enhancer choice or agency, as they tend to make believe. According to Wylie, social media tend rather "to narrow, filter, and *reduce* choice to benefit creators and advertisers", by herding "the citizenry into surveilled spaces where the architects can track and classify them and use this understanding to influence their behavior". This, he argues, is much more of a "subversion" of democracy than the promotion of freedom of choice (Wylie 2019: Chapter 12). Nichols argues that liberal democracy's need for patience, tolerance and perspective are not well served by the mere "ability to send and receive unfathomable amounts of data", for the human mind is pushed "beyond its capacity for reason and reflection" by the "constant ability to see into the lives of our neighbors, to compare ourselves to strangers, to be in constant contact with the entire planet day and night". By making "experiences immediate, instantaneous, and local", hyper-connectivity "overloads our ability to process information and irrationally heightens our sense of danger". A consequence is a proliferation of "depressed, anxiety-plagued wrecks who believe that they are hip-deep in danger and misery". This in turns "helps to make ordinary citizens easy prey for the comforting lies of disinformation, as well as for the reassuring sense of false intimacy created by virtual communities to which many people now feel more loyal than to friends or families" (Nichols 2021: Chapter 5). In other words, social media defy the logic of in-person social-bound conversation, where incompleteness finds relevance in a circuit of talking and listening, as opposed to talking at, talking on and talking past the other. Social media are exceedingly good at enabling their users to prioritise talking over listening.

Noting that "Narcissism led Trump into politics, but a politics driven less by public purposes than his own inner needs for public affirmation" (Fukuyama 2018: 99), Fukuyama argued in 2016 that Trump was "a singularly inappropriate instrument for taking advantage of the reform moment" that the "electoral upheaval" which catapulted him to power represents. [410] Put differently, notwithstanding the momentous election upheaval, Trump, driven by inner needs and not public service, would not be able to live up to the significance of the moment. Trump is incredibly talented and clever at steering the conversation, however, he is seen by many as incapable of much more than making noise and creating distraction, focusing mainly on keeping his base outraged.

Keeping people outraged demands an open and constant effort to defy and deny reality with "intentional falsehood", gaslighting, hyperbole and controversy the way Trump and his staff have excelled at with the help of social media as "a tool of distraction rather than edification or engagement" (Brooke 2018). Trump has come to be understood as totally fact free, something very understanding in the world of advertising and salesmanship, where the emphasis is on the positives of what one is selling rather than on any objective or factual truth in relation to what is being sold. In consumer capitalism consumers are consumed by branding, advertising, salesmanship and public relations as persuasive forms of communication. Like anyone cultivated to earn distinction in salesmanship, Trump is a prisoner of his lies, something that makes him destructive not only to other salesmen and saleswomen competing for a foothold in the marketplace of American public opinion, but also to himself in that, by sheer fact of repetition ad nauseam, he ends up believing his own salesmanship as the only reality possible.

His niece, Mary L. Trump, a psychologist and author of a highly critical book on Donald Trump, titled *Too Much and Never Enough: How My Family Created the World's Most Dangerous Man*, believes that:

> Donald's ego has been and is a fragile and inadequate barrier between him and the real world, which, thanks to his father's money and power, he never had to negotiate by himself. Donald has always needed to perpetuate the fiction my grandfather started that he is strong, smart, and otherwise extraordinary, because facing the truth— that he is none of those things—is too terrifying for him to contemplate (Trump, M. L. 2020: 15).

Mary Trump describes her uncle as someone not easily blackmailed as he is devoid of shame, has no humility and has been rewarded for bad behaviour all his life. He knows the difference between right and wrong, but if it benefits him there is no wrong. What is important to him is that people think that everything is fine. For him, the only thing that matters is that he is winning for the moment.[411] Mary Trump's description of her uncle would pass for any salesman who is truly good at his job, for whom what really

255

matters at the end of the day, is that an item was sold, and not so much whether hyperbole was employed to persuade the buyer. And if the following depiction by Mary Trump of her visit to the Trump International Hotel in Washington DC on 4 April 2017 is anything to go by, Donald Trump, the product, is the only thing that matters to Donald Trump the salesman – a sort of Holy Trinity of God the Father, without God the Son and God the Holy Spirit:

> My room was also tasteful. But my name was plastered everywhere, on everything: TRUMP shampoo, TRUMP conditioner, TRUMP slippers, TRUMP shower cap, TRUMP shoe polish, TRUMP sewing kit, and TRUMP bathrobe. I opened the refrigerator, grabbed a split of TRUMP white wine, and poured it down my Trump throat so it could course through my Trump bloodstream and hit the pleasure center of my Trump brain (Trump, M. L. 2020: 6).

O'Brien provides intriguing details on how Trump became a ubiquitous "highest-quality brand" in Trump's own words, and gained celebrity status by licensing his name to everything imaginable nationally and globally for a fee (O'Brien 2015[2005]). Dean and Altemeyer recount how Trump fell in love with publicity as a teenager, when his name was featured in a local newspaper for a base hit that helped win a baseball game. Thrilled to see his name in print, Trump exclaimed: "'It felt good seeing my name in print,' he said. 'How many people are in print? Nobody's in print. It was the first time I was ever in the newspaper. I thought it was amazing.'" (Dean and Altemeyer 2020: Chapter 2).

Trump, Miller writes, has been good at "slapping his brand on a motley array of products, including menswear, steaks, vodka, and get-rich-quick classes at Trump University", since he embarked on *The Apprentice* reality television show. As Miller notes, Trump's "search for partners willing to pay millions merely for the use of the Trump brand", while shielding him "from virtually all the financial risk" made it possible for Trump to promote his name and brand nationally and globally. Such global ambitions for the Trump brand put Trump "in business with multiple individuals and companies suspected of money laundering, political corruption, and other categories of fraud" (Miller 2018: Chapter 4). It sounds like impulsive personal branding and self-promotion with reckless abandon for which the only limit possible to conspicuous consumption is the exclusive celebrity superstardom and God-like supremacy of Donald J. Trump the person himself (Kellner 2016: 13–18). In this regard, Donald J. Trump is the penultimate embodiment, epitome and symbol of America's "culture of narcissism" (Lasch 1991[1979]) and "narcissism epidemic" combined (Twenge and Campbell 2009; Wu 2016: Chapters 17–19).

As psychologist Tony Schwartz, co-author of Trump's famous *Trump: The Art of the Deal* book states, "Donald Trump is an empty vessel, he is a black hole. He spent his whole life trying to fill that hole. That is the essence of Donald Trump". To Schwartz, the worst thing in the world for Trump is to feel like a loser. Having grown up feeling that he was not good enough, Trump has spent a lot of his life trying to prove himself to his daddy, even long after the latter passed on. To Schwartz, Trump had learnt a vital albeit self-destructive lesson from a father who had schooled him never to accept that he lost, never to admit mistakes, and always to declare victory even when it was overwhelmingly the case that he had lost[412] (see also Kivisto 2017: 13–21; Kellner 2016: 29–40; Dean and Altemeyer 2020: Chapter 2). According to Michael Cohen, someone who knew Trump more than many people in his intimate circles, "To Trump, life was a game, and all that mattered was winning" (Cohen 2020: Foreword). Omarosa Manigault Newman, another person who knows Trump well, agrees: "Donald likes winners. He likes people who make him money and get him attention and headlines" (Newman 2018: Chapter 4). To Trump, a "killer instinct" is the stuff of which winners are made, and winners are kings (Sims 2019: Chapter 8; Res 2020: Introduction). Cliff Sims, who also knows Trump well, writes of how Trump's father used to equate being a killer with being a king, something which had become "deeply engrained" in Trump's psyche from childhood (Sims 2019: Chapter 8). With winning being a zero-sum game in Trump's world, the one who outkills every one of his or her competitors becomes king of the jungle. If life as a game is an extension of the American Dream, in which there are no losers but only different gradations of winners, then Trump could be said to embody what it means to play the game of life aggressively by beating everyone on the way to top of the Mount Rushmore of the American Dream. Ultimately, if the American Dream is, unlike *The Apprentice*, not about zero-sum pursuits that culminate in absolute winners and absolute losers, but all about living and letting live through eating and being eaten, then investing and prioritising the killer instinct and a culture of killers is hardly going to deliver that dream for the majority, let alone everyone. Winning does not have to be absolute to be meaningful, just as recognising and providing for less successful and less entitled nationals, citizens and immigrants does not imply losing out to them, in a context where life is all about the circulation of debt and indebtedness.

Apparently, the traits which Trump has come to embody superbly are explained in part by books Trump and/or his father read as young men. *The Power of Positive Thinking*, by Norman Vincent Pearle, a pastor "known as 'God's salesman' for his hawking of the prosperity gospel", was one such book, admired by Trump's father. As Kakutani writes, "the young Trump would internalize the celebrity pastor's teachings on self-fulfillment and the power of the mind to create its own reality". A second book, a novel, *The Fountainhead* by Ayn Rand, was, according to Kakutani, admired by Trump for "her transactional view of the world, her equation of success and virtue, and her proud embrace of unfettered capitalism". Of particular resonance with "Trump's own zero-sum view of the world and his untrammeled narcissism" was Rand's argument in favour of "selfishness [as] a moral imperative" and that "man's 'highest moral purpose' is 'the pursuit of his own happiness'" (Kakutani 2018: 66), sometimes driven by the misunderstanding that happiness can be found in isolation. To Stephen Colbert, Trump is a multi-headed spineless creature that lives off the fears of others, and does not care if fellow Americans live or die of Covid-19 or racism as long as he wins.[413] As Kakutani observes, "If a novelist had concocted a villain like Trump – a larger-than-life, over-the-top avatar of narcissism, mendacity, ignorance, prejudice, boorishness, demagoguery, and tyrannical impulses [...] – she or he would likely be accused of extreme contrivance and implausibility" (Kakutani 2018: 16). To Wilson, in *Everything Trump Touches Dies*, life is stranger than fiction, for, Trump is a curse and effectively "the avatar" of Americans' "worst instincts and darkest desires as a nation" (Wilson 2018: Introduction).

For Trump to be rational, reasonable and inclusive would imply owning up to reality and taking facts seriously, beyond simply seeing himself as a salesman for Trump and Trumpism. It would imply, as well, disabusing himself of a vision of "the world as a dark, dangerous place teeming with enemies out to get him", claims Schwartz.[414] Even the most consummate of salesmen and saleswomen are expected to switch off every now and then, take breaks and reconnect with loved ones, friends and social networks, for shared emotions, moral truths and refreshing one's skills at other forms of communication over and above persuasion. The president is a salesman for all and sundry, and not only for a select few or for himself. If the pain of the working classes cuts across racial, ethnic, geographic, gender, sexual and age divides, how can one stay faithful to the truth and still make political capital out of racial, ethnic, geographic, gender, sexuality and intergenerational cleavages?

To address the disparities and disproportionateness in access to resources, power and privilege in society, one has to be ethical and truthful to the fact that the lives of all and sundry who are adversely affected matter, and so does their dignity. To pick and choose among the suffering and the marginalised is to be opportunistic and to play identity and cultural games with genuine human predicaments. As Toni Morrison would say, "If you can only be tall because somebody is on their knees, then you have a serious problem".[415] In this regard, populism, in the hands of an opportunistic self-absorbed, one-dimensional man of a politician like Trump (Kellner 2016: 95), is incompatible with truth, science, honesty, integrity and humility. As evidenced by some who have known Trump intimately or closer than most (Trump, M. L. 2020; Cohen 2020), it is what one gets from the propped-up "Complete Gentleman" who is in no hurry to acknowledge the fact of being made by others beyond his base, who refuses to service his debts and who systematically ignores the debt collectors sent his way, determined as he is to pass for "The Complete Gentleman" that he is not.

But then, Trump and his fellow Republicans could argue that they do not need to be popular beyond their narrowly construed base and constituency where they have traditionally exercised their salesmanship if voter suppression, an antiquated electoral college system and flirting with what Stacey Abrams has termed "the compelling nihilism of authoritarian populism" can keep them in power without having to compromise and dilute their cultural and political values by unnecessarily opening up to outsiders within (Abrams 2020: Introduction). They are all about putting power in the hands of those who believe that government is the problem and expertise overrated (Nichols 2017, 2021). In this regard, if Trump's contestation and outright refusal to concede to Biden as winner of the 2020 election is anything to go by, fair and impartial elections are unacceptable if they fail to deliver anticipated victories. They must be contested, at all costs, with lies and unsubstantiated allegations of irregularities, fraud and rigging if need be. And it doesn't or shouldn't matter if such contestation gravely endangers the security of the country and its institutions of government. The personal power of the strongman or supreme salesman is, according to such a logic, more important than the integrity of the democratic system in which every vote that counts should be counted.

Equally writing in 2016, Lozada agreed with Fukuyama that Trump was singularly unqualified to harness the rising mass discontent of the mostly white working-class Republican base, arguing that it was ironic that Trump who "personifies that very pseudo-aristocracy of wealth that has long shunned the white working class" should draw his greatest support from it, especially because "Trump amassed his fortune as a real estate developer, when land and property for so long have marked the red lines between rich and poor".[416] Applebaum agrees, pointing to two populist speeches by Trump – his inaugural speech and a speech on "Western Civilisation" delivered in July 2017 in Warsaw – speeches that contrasted between "the people" and "the powerful" forming the foundation of freedom and the corner stone of patriotism, "as if Trump himself were not a wealthy, powerful elite businessman who had dodged the draft and let others fight in his place" (Applebaum 2020: 154).

Many among the Republican intelligentsia hoped that the euphoric embrace of Trump was a temporary bout of "collective insanity", especially given the "abundance of evidence that Donald Trump, the 45th President of the United States, has the emotional and intellectual range of a misbehaving toddler" (Drezner 2020: Conclusion). Trump's critics, according to Shenk, believe that "entrusting the Republican nomination to a reality television star turned populist demagogue has been a disaster for their cause and their country" and that "Whatever Trump might be, he is not a conservative."[417] Rick Wilson, a Republican strategist, is one such critic, to whom "Trump lacked the moral and personal character to be the leader of the free world, to make the most consequential decisions, and to hold the lives and security of millions of Americans in his hands" (Wilson 2018: Introduction). Precisely for this reason, in July 2018, Buruma wondered:

> At what point are democracies truly in danger? What was unimaginable only a few years ago – a US president insulting democratic allies and praising dictators, or calling the free press "enemies of the people," or locking up refugees and taking away their children – has become almost normal now. When will it be too late to sound the alarm? [418]

He argues that "Donald Trump may not be a reincarnated Hitler, but Republicans' acquiescence in every step he has taken away from civilized democratic norms is ominous."[419]

Tracing America's route to possible fascism, Kagan, writing in 2016, notes extreme party loyalty (on the part of Republicans) and ambition in following the leader at the top. Combined with fear of dismissal, such extreme party loyalty and ambition could easily result in a fascist America under Donald Trump, a man who values loyalty more than expertise or the truth, even as he fancies the idea of himself as the truth, the law and the state. Trump would rather embrace lawlessness and chaos than be subjected to the rule of law in which winning is far from guaranteed for him. He has no organising principles beyond himself – needing loyalty without giving any in return. Anyone who is not with him is against him and must pay for it. Tyrant leaders are less about policy and more about stronghold. They purport to speak in the name of the people even as they are busy destroying the institutions that make democracy possible and life meaningful for the people. The movement to the top has been a play on "fears, vanities, ambitions and insecurities". The leader plays on these elements so that those that support him rise with him, and others are left behind, facing certain political death or life in the political doldrums.[420] As Frum maintains, "Trump collapses all politics into one question: for him or against him, regardless of what he does, regardless of anything the supporter might previously have believed. Formerly normal Republicans are zombified" (Frum 2020: Chapter 4).

"Donald Trump has led an enabled life", claim Dean and Altemeyer, who proceed to detail who Trump's enablers have been. It is a long list that spans from his father through Mark Burnett of *The Apprentice*, the likes of Roger Stones and Michael Cohen, to Republicans in Congress and many more, including those believed to have facilitated his 2016 victory through hacking and online disinformation campaigns (Dean and Altemeyer 2020: Chapter 11; Wilson 2018). Some have wondered why the Republicans in the House and Senate have succumbed to being reduced to the role of spineless enablers, water carrying lackeys and shoe-shiners for President Trump throughout his presidency, placating his unhealthy, undemocratic obsession (Wilson 2018, 2020; Frum 2018, 2020). While some have tried to rationalise or excuse it away, Stevens reasons that the Republican party and Republicans must bear the blame, for, far from being "strange or unexpected", Trump "is the logical conclusion or "a natural product of the seeds of race, self-deception, and anger that became the essence of the Republican Party" over the last fifty or so years. "Trump isn't an aberration of the Republican Party; he is the Republican Party in a purified form" (Stevens 2020: 4). According to presidential historian Jon Meacham, the reason Republican senators did little about Trump's excesses is because of the devotion, ferocity and never-shrinking demographic base of support for Donald Trump among the Republican rank and file. That said, Meacham thinks the Republicans in Congress who support Trump blindly are on the wrong side of history.

Boot regrets that, "as talk-radio hosts and television personalities have taken over the role of defining the conservative movement that once belonged to thinkers like Irving Kristol, Norman Podhoretz and George F. Will" the Republicans' relationship to the realm of ideas has of late "become more and more attenuated". This, Boot traces back to the Tea Party which came into existence as a vehicle and champion for "a populist revolt against what its activists saw as out-of-touch Republican elites in Washington".[421]

Barack Obama agrees, explaining why, in the eyes of the grassroots supporters of the Tea Party, he and his administration shouldered some of the blame. In *A Promised Land*, he acknowledges that "the Tea Party represented a genuine populist surge within the Republican Party", and that it "was made up of true believers, possessed with the same grassroots enthusiasm and jagged fury" which Sarah Palin's supporters exhibited during the election campaign in which she ran as vice-presidential running mate for John McCain. Obama claims he understood some of the anger, "even if I considered it misdirected". For one thing, he argues, his predecessor, President Bush and establishment Republicans had done little to address the plight of "Many of the working- and middle-class whites gravitating to the Tea Party" who "had suffered for decades from sluggish wages, rising costs, and the loss of the steady blue-collar work that provided secure retirements". The precarities of these communities had been compounded by the financial crisis, that had steadily worsened the economy with him in charge, "despite more than a trillion dollars channeled into stimulus spending and bailouts". To Obama, "For those already predisposed toward conservative ideas, the notion that my policies were designed to help others at their expense—that the game was rigged and I was part of the rigging— must have seemed entirely plausible" (Obama 2020: 405, Chapter 17).

Indeed, it is worth noting how much of what is currently associated with Trump and Trumpism, including conspiracy theories, insults and hate, was already quite evident with the Tea Party. Here is an excerpt from *A Promised Land*:

> As had been true at Palin rallies, reporters at Tea Party events caught attendees comparing me to animals or Hitler. Signs turned up showing me dressed like an African witch doctor with a bone through my nose and the caption OBAMACARE COMING SOON TO A CLINIC NEAR YOU. Conspiracy theories abounded: that my healthcare bill would set up "death panels" to evaluate whether people deserved treatment, clearing the way for "government-encouraged euthanasia," or that it would benefit illegal immigrants, in the service of my larger goal of flooding the country with welfare-dependent, reliably Democratic voters. The Tea Party also resurrected and poured gas on an old rumor from the campaign: that not only was I Muslim, but I'd actually been born in Kenya and was therefore constitutionally barred from serving as president. By September, the question of how much nativism and racism explained the Tea Party's rise had become a major topic of debate on the cable shows—especially after former president and lifelong southerner Jimmy Carter offered up the opinion that the

extreme vitriol directed toward me was at least in part spawned by racist views (Obama 2020: 405–6, Chapter 17).

Trump and Trumpism have indeed been a long time coming. Sarah Palin and the Tea Party, like John the Baptist, had thoroughly prepared the way for the coming of Trump as the unlikely "Messiah" (not from the conventional breed of politicians just like Jesus the son of a carpenter) for conservative values and nativism that would "Make America Great Again" through a frenzy of unravelling and ever diminishing circles of inclusion.

Anti-intellectualism in American life pre-dates Sarah Palin and Trump's Republicanism, as Richard Hofstadter's 1963 book, *Anti-intellectualism in American Life,* illustrates. So does the paranoid style in American politics that right-wing extremists like Palin and her Tea Party and Trump and his variant of the Republican Party have championed, a style and politics driven far more by the wish to destroy than by a desire to conserve (Hofstadter 2008[1965]). Trump and his populist followers have built on Palin's Tea Partyism's ever-diminishing criteria for inclusion as a bona fide American, and predilection for conspiracy theories, fear and hate mongering. In their dramatisation of victimhood or fantasies thereof in opposition to liberals and their "fancy" world and lifestyles (Samuels 2016; Young 2018; Steudeman 2018; Wingard 2018), Trump and his populist associates have developed a style of talking that often contradicts the truth of their very own personal successes as part and parcel of the elites of whom they are critical.

Among the ever-regressive criteria for inclusion discussed by Jay Nordlinger in an article titled "How Populists Talk", two are particularly illustrative of the continuities between Palin and Trump. Nordlinger quotes Republican Congressman Jim Jordan saying: "'The Republican Party is no longer the wine-and-cheese party. It's the beer and-blue-jeans party". [422] She also quotes Republican senator John Kennedy from Louisiana, who declares to Sean Hannity of Fox News:

I think the American people are so tired, so tired, of being lectured by the managerial elite: the politicians, the media, the academics, the corporate phonies, the tuna-tartare crowd who live in the expensive condos with the high ceilings and the imported art on the wall, who think they're better than the American people. [423]

Elite cosmopolitan tastes, mannerism, lifestyles, behaviours and practices are caricatured and disparaged as a way of disqualifying any credentials they may have and/or claims made to be able to speak on behave of "the American people", who in turn are represented as belonging to a completely different world, one frozen in time and space, and with values and behaviours that defy time, mobility and encounters with difference.

Commenting on the "toxic populism" of Josh Hawley, another Republican Trumpian senator, Peter Suderman shares excerpts of pronouncements by Josh Hawley, who has repeatedly: "decried the progressive overlords who hold the commanding heights of American politics, tech, academia, and culture, who he says have joined together to rule over a vast Middle American public that does not share their values". For example, Suderman quotes Hawley saying: "'Elites distrust patriotism' [...] 'and dislike the common culture left to us by our forbearers.' They 'look down on the common affections that once bound this nation together: things like place and national feeling and religious faith.'" According to Hawley, although the founders of America "built a new republic governed not by a select elite, as in the days of old, but by the common man and woman, grounded on the premise that it is the common man and woman who are the noblest of citizens", today the country has been taken over by a "'cosmopolitan consensus' that prioritizes 'social change over tradition, career over community, and achievement and merit and progress' and global integration over family and national loyalties". He is suspicious of "government by unelected elites who are confident they know better than the American people, that they know better than the Constitution" insisting "that they should be in control". [424] As Suderman observes, these critical pronouncements against the elites are:

[...] more than a little bit ironic, given that Hawley is, by almost any definition, an elite himself. A graduate of both Stanford University and Yale Law School, he went on to be a Supreme Court clerk for Chief Justice John Roberts before his 30th birthday. From there, he worked as a lawyer in private practice, a teacher at the prestigious St. Paul's

School in London, and an associate professor at the University of Missouri School of Law. Along the way, he wrote articles for the conservative policy journal *National Affairs* and a scholarly book, based on his graduate thesis, on the life of President Theodore Roosevelt, published by Yale University Press.[425]

Trump, as Boot claims, "is as much a symptom as a cause of the [Republican] party's anti-intellectual drift". He urges the party "to rethink its growing anti-intellectual bias and its reflexive aversion to elites. Catering to populist anger with extremist proposals that are certain to fail is not a viable strategy for political success".[426] But, as Tony Schwartz, co-author with Trump of *Trump: The Art of the Deal*, claims, Trump has no emotion except anger and rage, which he combines to good effect with a constant diet of lies, disinformation, fake news and propaganda to activate and sustain his supporters. Trump's ascension to power within the Republican party and as president has rendered "mainstream" "the extremist views of his most radical supporters – their racial and religious intolerance, their detestation of government, and their embrace of conspiracy thinking and misinformation" (Kakutani 2018: 26). As Nichols explains, "In Trump, Americans who believe shadowy forces are ruining their lives and that any visible intellectual ability is itself a suspicious characteristic in a national leader found a champion" (Nichols 2017: 213). Trump's ascendancy has harnessed, reinforced and accelerated the currency in Republican and American politics of what Stenner terms "the authoritarian dynamic" and the racial, political and moral intolerance it engineers (Stenner 2005), creating and attracting authoritarian followers to fuel and propel the authoritarian reflexes of their narcissistic leader (Dean and Altemeyer 2020).

As Kagan contends, it is not enough for a politician to make political capital of the plight of the poor and the sidestepped by playing "on all the fears, vanities, ambitions and insecurities that make up the human psyche". Politicians have to provide meaningful, workable and lasting solutions in the interest of the nation-state as a common project.[427] This is significant, Mitcha argues, because "Beneath the popular resentment and frustration bubbles a longing for a vanishing sense of community, mixed with an often deeply felt democratic impulse to reclaim ownership of the state." To Mitcha, "be it 'illiberal democracy,' 'populism,' or (from the extreme Left) 'neo-fascism''', these terms all describe attempts to "grapple with the same truth: The weakening of the consensus that the nation-state should remain paramount in world politics lies at the base of the deepening political crisis in Western democracies."[428]

Rodrik echoes these concerns for the nation-state, maintaining that the present-day "populist revolt [...] reflects the deep rift that has opened between the worldview of the global intellectual and professional elites, and that of ordinary citizens. [...] Yet the intellectual consensus that brought us to this chasm remains intact". The problem, Rodrik believes, lies "in elites' attachment to a globalist mindset that underplays and weakens the nation-state". To Rodrik, nation-states are without doubt essential for ensuring "economic prosperity, financial stability, social inclusion and other desirable objectives". Rodrik cautions against the dangers of tinkering with the nation-state without ensuring that provisions are made elsewhere for improvements in governance.[429]

Even defenders of the nation-state must wake up to the reality of transnational operators – from global corporate conglomerates to hackers, spyware and malware creators, algorithms and social media platforms such as Facebook and Twitter and WhatsApp and Instagram – and the fact that the nation-state is not as sovereign in determining what crosses into and out of its borders as it used to be prior to the proliferation of pandemics of accelerated, often flexible and invisible, mobilities and the compression of time and space facilitated by advances in technologies of radical and sometimes narcissistic self-activation, self-extension and self-multiplication (Watts 2018; Wylie 2019; Nyamnjoh 2019).

Pro-establishment and anti-establishment elites alike are keen to attract the media, both conventional and social, to do their bidding, knowing well the invisible power of algorithms to bring and deny visibility (Wu 2016) – all of which results in spiralling out-of-control zero-sum games of superiority and entitlement. Yet, as it becomes increasingly evident, such ambitions of dominance are ultimately doomed if they fail to recognise and accommodate beyond tokenism those who have competed poorly or not at all, for whatever reason. The future cannot afford to be one where everyone is expected to fend for themselves with the help of magic multipliers to which equal access is far from guaranteed.

Desperately Seeking Conviviality in a Digitally Mediated Post-Truth USA

As demonstrated here, informed arguments are increasingly rare, and disdain for evidence is commonplace even as media and political actors championed by Trump and Trumpism are all about the American people, patriotism, democracy and the Constitution. As some have suggested, Trump may be toddler-like in his beliefs and strategies, but this does not seem to be a major hurdle to his populist bandwagon of ever-diminishing circles of inclusion and what it means to be American and belonging to America. The Republican party collectively decided that there are no objective truths, but culture wars, and simultaneously held on only to their social facts and conservative white bubbles of sociality in the main. Civility and conviviality have been in the firing line. Evangelical support for Trump is an interesting piece of the puzzle, as Trump has made no secret of his zero-sum winner-takes-all approach to being and belonging in an America where God, to be relevant, must cut his generosity and pretensions to inclusivity and universality of humanity radically down in size to accommodate white nationalism and nativism exclusively (Geary et al. 2020). Trump has prioritised Evangelical concerns such as law and order, justice, immigration and abortion, yet engaged in all the sins they deem deadly – an irony of this Trumpian support base (Posner 2020).

Suppose both the populists of the right and the left are about recalibration and bringing back to the centre "the people", whom they perceive to have been marginalised, sidestepped and diminished economically and culturally by the neoliberal economic and political elites. In that case, it means that populists in contemporary America are united by the idea of "the people", even if who exactly they choose to include in their shopping basket of "the people" might be the subject of much contestation given the polarisations. What would it take to focus more on "the people" and their shared predicaments, regardless of whether their ideologies, populism-wise, are right or left inclined, regardless of their racial, ethnic, geographic, class, gender, sexual orientation or generational differences? If Americans were to agree on unity in diversity and on people being people over and above their ideologies and socially cultivated differences, and if they were to be less cynical about living-togetherness being all about partisan and racial conflict and antagonism, what would it take to overcome post-truth and its unproductive compartmentalisations of reality? What would it take to engage in conviviality informed by the humility of incompleteness? In seeking conviviality, could the way forward be in polling all the relativisms into a crucible of possibilities that seek to balance competing social truths that bring into conversation heartfelt truth with factual truth by acknowledging, interrogating and creatively negotiating towards accommodating and building on their intersubjectivities? What would the US have to do to overcome post-truth braggadocio politics, the politics of polarisation, the industrialisation of deceit and the role of digital technologies therein?

What follows, dwells on the extent to which digital technologies have fanned the embers of post-truth braggadocio politics, the politics of polarisation and the industrialisation of deceit. I argue that liberal, representative democracy is being wrecked by a conflict between the less educated majority and the highly educated minority because digital media has offered the majority access to the media as accelerants of freedom of expression, albeit often more constricted than recognised by those who embrace and celebrate digital media. Drawing on available literature, the section demonstrates how maniacs of post-truthism, polarisation and deceit like Donald Trump and his supporters have striven to benefit from the less-educated minority's access to digital technology, defining and confining US citizenship and democracy through binary oppositions. These binaries are visible in US real-life politics where people, especially Trump and his supporters, define Americanness in terms of friends and enemies of Trumpian populism, thereby nurturing a seething cauldron for spin warriors aggressively willing to lie, proliferate Trumpian populism's alternative facts and defend the "America First Caucus" (Skinnell 2018b).

As it is argued here, it is worth bearing in mind that in a busted society with a busted belief in the truth, one person's reality becomes another's fake news, fake science, fake history, fake culture, fake religion, fake patriotism, fake citizenship, fake democracy or fake election results. Little wonder then that Trump and his supporters, including even religious groups such as the white Evangelical Christians, refused to recognise Biden's victory. The section concludes with a call for conviviality, which, as argued, is achievable in a digitally mediated post-truth society by actively encouraging a more inclusive sense of community with shared truths, through a systematic effort at rehumanisation of those frozen out, often a priori, of the narrow confines of our social, cultural and political bubbles and echo chambers. With shared stories and interactions that are less focused on absolute winners and absolute losers, it should be possible to reflect the complexities and nuances of what it means to be an American individually and collectively, through living and letting live, and by embracing and celebrating incompleteness.

Let's take a closer look.

"Liberal, representative democracy", Møller reminds us, "is mired in a clash between the less educated majority", on the one hand, and "those with higher education", on the other. Digital media and the possibilities they have multiplied for social networking "have sharpened this confrontation by offering the majority something they didn't have before: access to the media with the possibility of setting the agenda". "The outcome", Møller believes, "will be determined by how well democracies tackle two major problems connected with social networks", namely, the problem of guaranteeing privacy, and the problem of assuring "citizens that social networks are theirs and it is up to them to prevent fake news".[430]

With a focus specifically on the USA, Tom Nichols, in his book *The Death of Expertise*, laments that "principled and informed arguments" are increasingly rare if not outrightly missing in American democracy, where experts and expertise are actively resented and persistence in being "misinformed", "uninformed", "aggressively wrong" and in believing "dumb things" is in vogue (Nichols 2017: x–xiii). With the availability of the internet, social media and related information and communication technologies, one would have expected a more knowledgeable citizenry (Nichols 2017: 40–69; Rauch 2021: Chapters 5 & 6). But the reality, as Nichols observes, is a paradox: "Never have so many people had so much access to so much knowledge and yet have been so resistant to learning anything." Nichols argues that "plummeting literacy and growth of willful ignorance is part of a vicious circle of disengagement between citizens and public policy". Americans increasingly "know little and care less about how they are governed, or how their economic, scientific, or political structures actually function". Yet, their equally growing sense of entitlement and unrealistic expectations of the political and economic system can only produce further alienation and discontent (Nichols 2017: 217–218). In a presentation of his book in *Foreign Affairs*, Nichols reiterates his argument that, "Americans have reached a point where ignorance—at least regarding what is generally considered established knowledge in public policy—is seen as an actual virtue."[431] Among other things, says Kakutani, Nichols highlights that the "protective swaddling environment of the modern university infantilizes students" and "suggests that today's populism has magnified disdain for elites and experts of all sorts, be they in foreign policy, economics, even science". This is exacerbated by the existence of echo chambers that result in what Nichols calls the "backfire effect".[432]

Trump and his administration have been repeatedly associated with having a fraught relationship with science and evidence-based information. To draw on Kakutani, the Trump administration has been "predicated upon the violation and despoiling of truth, upon the knowledge that cynicism and weariness and fear can make people susceptible to the lies and false promises of leaders bent on unconditional power" (Kakutani 2018: 11). The administration has "undermined" reason and "tossed [it] out the window, along with facts, informed debate, and deliberative policy making", just as it attacks science and "expertise of every sort – be it expertise in foreign policy, national security, economics, or education" (Kakutani 2018: 23).

Indeed, as Kakutani maintains, upon assuming office, the Trump administration soon became "the very embodiment of anti-Enlightenment principles, repudiating the values of rationalism, tolerance, and empiricism in both the policies and its modus operandi – a reflection of the commander in chief's erratic, impulsive decision-making style based not on knowledge but on instinct, whim, and preconceived (and often delusional) notions of how the world operates" (Kakutani 2018: 27–28). The inverse, but mutually inclusive of the enlightenment principle, is equally true – wantonly discarding the divine and metaphysical world, leads to privileging materialistic and humanistic approach to epistemology. This makes human beings more arrogant and prouder in a post-truth world – characterised by truth as relativistic.

Arguing that Trump's maturity is much more that of a petulant child than of a man in his seventies, Drezner believes Trump is more appropriately regarded as a Toddler in Chief than a Commander in Chief, and that this calls for greater oversight, in view of the phenomenal powers of the modern presidency. Drezner details the widespread perceptions of Trump as a toddler and toddler analogies associated with him, not only among media, comedians and political rivals critical of Trump, but also in Trump's closest circles and among those within his administration (staffers, allies and advisors) and support base who wanted him to succeed as president. Drezner's book, *The Toddler-in-Chief*, consists mainly in providing evidence "that President Trump's behavior closely matches that of a small, bratty child", and that this is cause for worry, given that Trump, as the President of the USA, was "the most powerful man in the free world", and that as a person, Trump seeks to defy all obstacles to his pursuits of self-gratification (Drezner 2020: Introduction).

To Drezner, not only did Trump as President, unlike most toddlers have "the power to say no to his caregivers", it also became apparent that not having "the disciplinary authority that parents and caregivers possess", White House staffers faced "limited options in keeping the Toddler in Chief out of trouble" (Drezner 2020: Chapter 8). In other words, "Trump being a toddler was dangerous because of the deterioration of the guardrails that constrain the raw power of the presidency". The consequences for Americans have been collective exhaustions. In Drezner's words, "living through the chaos of the Toddler in Chief has turned most Americans into the mental equivalent of exhausted parents". Yet, Drezner insists, to expect Donald Trump to "grow up" or "to mature is indulging in make-believe" (Drezner 2020: Conclusion). And no one is better at make-believe than Donald Trump.

Compelling and richly substantiated though Drezner's argument is, and even as Drezner dismisses as "absurd" the idea that Trump is "a master political strategist" (Drezner 2020: Conclusion), it should be added in passing, however, that Trump, like a true toddler perhaps, has sought to prove just how special toddlers are in terms of being smart and strategic. Toddlers appear to be toddling, but somehow understand that adults do think they are dumb, and really make mincemeat of adults. Trump seems to have understood that he was and is still dealing with adults who imagine him as a toddler, naïve and inexperienced. It is not surprising that he has used his populism bandwagon to run circles round the supposed adults of the

Washington political establishments. This is perhaps the reason why we need to start taking toddlers more seriously, and desist from zero-sum logics of adult winners having everything their way. There is need for adults to understand toddlers and not seek to domesticate them at all costs. As a populist, Trump could argue that it is hardly surprising for the political establishment to think and seek to relate to anyone who does not conform or rise to their institutionalised processes, logics and yardsticks of meritocracy, as a toddler, condescension not dissimilar to that shown the masses who vote for them. Drezner concludes his book by critically reviewing and engaging this and related counterarguments to his toddler-in-chief thesis on President Trump.

Trump and his administration believe that it is possible to ignore or, better still, delete inconvenient evidence, which they have done by pumping into mass circulation in industrial volume of fake news, fake science, fake history, fake Americans on Facebook, and fake followers and "likes" on social media, all with the active assistance of Russian troll factories (Kakutani 2018: 12–13) that "spread propaganda, harass dissenters, flood social networks with misinformation, and create the illusion of popularity or momentum through likes, retweets, or shares" (Kakutani 2018: 131–132).

Nichols clarifies that what is going on is far from being the same as "the traditional American distaste for intellectuals and know-it-alls" and warns that Americans "are moving beyond a natural skepticism regarding expert claims to the death of the ideal of expertise itself" (Nichols 2017: x). He argues that this is dangerous for democracy, because "In the absence of informed citizens, for example, more knowledgeable administrative and intellectual elites do in fact take over the daily direction of the state and society." In addition, "populism actually reinforces this elitism" (Nichols 2017: 217).[433]

As Davies recognises, "the authority of facts has been in decline for quite some time" and facts indeed are in crisis. He points to the "combination of populist movements with social media" as "responsible for post-truth politics". The growth in social media has afforded individuals with "growing opportunities to shape their media consumption around their own opinions and prejudices, and populist leaders are ready to encourage them".[434] As Kakutani contends, seeking to diminish the possibility of objective truth by overly dramatising the centrality of subjectivity has meant "the celebration of opinion over knowledge, feeling over facts – a development that both reflected and helped foster the rise of Trump" (Kakutani 2018: 63).

Yet, as Rauch suggests, it is incumbent on any society to provide the yardsticks or principles "for raising and settling differences of opinion", by determining "what is the right way, or at least the best way, to make decisions as to who is right (thus having knowledge) and who is wrong (thus having mere opinion)". He recommends the principle of "Checking of each by each through public criticism" as "the only legitimate way to decide who is right" (Rauch 2013[1993]: 5–6), or how to constitute knowledge from information and facts from arguments (Rauch 2021).

To some degree, it could be argued, the distaste for expertise is also a recognition of the limits of expertise and the need to decolonise knowledge by rendering it popular. For knowledge to be a truly collective product and of collective value, there is need to recognise that everyone is a knower of their experience and thus a contributor to the collective knowledge piggy bank. In the absence of a consensual truth and shared sense of right and wrong, if there is not space for diverse voices and experiences to be heard, what would democracy amount to? It is easy to understand how those schooled to be knowledge consumers much more than they are knowledge producers could become frustrated with expertise that is sometimes decontextualised and narrowly developed and applied to fulfil self-interested ambitions or the whims and caprices of a few who wield economic, political and cultural power. A healthy dose of scepticism and critical spirit is necessary. Equally paramount is for the entire population to engage with ideas and truth, and not merely outsource this to specialised institutions and individuals, whatever the justification of professionalisation.

If people spend their time only thinking about how to get food on the table or make ends meet at the margins, or how to furnish their house or make their yard look beautiful, there will be little time, energy or inclination left for engagement on issues. Yet such engagement is necessary for participatory democracy disabused of the tokenism convenient for the power elite. Like a plant, democracy needs to be nurtured, regularly and with intentionality. It cannot thrive on its own. As Levitsky and Ziblatt remind us, democracy dies by degree and often at the hands of elected leaders who subvert the very process that brought them to power while pretending to be acting in defence of democracy (Levitsky and Ziblatt 2018).

Steven, a long-time Republican who laments the Trumpism to which the party has fallen, acknowledges that "Large elements of the Republican Party have made a collective decision that there is no objective truth", which means contesting the possibility of facts existing independently of the opinions one holds of them (Stevens 2020: 105). In this regard, it could be argued, the Republican Party has become bedfellows with many a left-wing liberal and many an academic in the humanities who have long problematised and questioned the idea of an objective truth. Stevens adds: "Republicans have built a political ecosphere that thrives on deceit and lies. It is an industrialized sort of deceit that is unique to the Republican Party," which for decades, "have been conducting an experiment to determine how many control rods of truth could be taken out of a civil society's core reactor of truth without creating a meltdown." Steven insists "It didn't start with Trump, but Trump may prove to be the meltdown" (Stevens 2020: 107).

Americans would mostly agree that fake news predates Trump. Lobbyists and lobbying are a staple on the country's political menus. Many would recall, for example, lobbyists[435] and conservative think tanks (Dunlap and Jacques 2013), well before Trump, that manipulated public opinion, saying climate change did not exist or was not human made. Before that, lobbyists and lobby politicians tried to convince the public to be wary about evolutionism because such scientific truth contradicts the existence of God and the supremacy of Divine Truth.[436] Trump, however, like a champion jockey, has mastered the art of riding the fake news horse to victory. Trump is the embodiment of something in the American culture and the American psyche, if one could speak in such general and homogenising terms. He epitomises the tendency to want to bury one's head in the sand like an ostrich, to not face obvious truths, which might disrupt the way one sees the world or one's lifestyle. It is a tendency to let oneself be beguiled. Underpinning the tendency is a culture that prioritises salesmanship over and above the contents, substance or quality of what is actually be sold. With such a tradition, is it surprising that thousands (if not millions) of people can be beguiled by Trump's "Big Lie" into thinking that the 2020 election was "stolen"?

The successes of populist politicians on the right and left relate to the "post-truth" politics of politicians that feed on voters' suffering, weaknesses and fears. If one considers Christian Evangelicalism as a religion of the heart that cautions against a celebration of the mind, as Hofstadter (1963: 128, Chapters 3 & 4) suggests, one can easily understand why Trump has enjoyed overwhelming popularity with and enthusiastic support among white Evangelical Christians throughout his presidency. [437] As Sims remarks, the "alliance between Trump and evangelicals was powerful, and both sides reaped the political benefits" (Sims 2019: Chapter 10). Warning them against the purported dangers posed by Muslims and undocumented immigrants, and asking for Christians to unite and assert their power to fight off being placed under siege, Trump, as Du Mez demonstrates, has found unlikely bedfellows since 2016 in white Evangelicals ready to betray principles for short-term transactional authoritarian pursuits. Drawn to Trump's populist appeals, Du Mez substantiates how, "white evangelicals demonstrated a preference for rejecting political compromise, for strong, solitary leadership, and for breaking the rules when necessary" (Du Mez 2020: 18).

Kivisto highlights the "sense of victimhood" that "runs deep among these people", a feeling compounded by "the conviction that those on the left see them as gun-toting, Bible-thumping, racists, sexists, and ignoramuses". Driven by a sense of victimhood "even though they are better off economically than many Americans", they have hardened their hearts against "the well-being of those in their midst who are less well-off" (Kivisto 2017: 64). "[W]hite Evangelical Protestants—whether defined by affiliation, self-identification, or belief and behavior—represent the religious core of American populism," Guth concludes in a study of evangelicals and populism in the USA. This is the case, Guth affirms, "not only on legitimate issues of domestic economic and social policy (such as redistributionism, trade, and abortion), but in attitudes potentially more threatening to democratic values, such as countenancing rough politics, favoring a 'strong leader,' attacking religious or ethnic 'outgroups,' and opposing political compromise" (Guth 2019: 29).

The Evangelicals, happy with the positive things the administration accomplished on matters dear to them – matters such as , were very generous with their support for Trump (Posner 2020). As Posner puts it, "The vast majority of white evangelicals are all in with Trump because he has given them political power and allowed them to carry out a Christian supremacist agenda, inextricably intertwined with his administration's white nationalist agenda" (Posner 2020: Epilogue). Such uncritical endorsement, Barber would argue, does not serve the cause of love and justice for the rejected across America's racialised inequalities and poverty, nor does it serve to reconstruct and preserve the heart and soul of American democracy (Barber 2020). Even when it has been clear that he is loyal to no institution or higher authority than himself, the Evangelicals have stocked faith in Trump, leading some like Posner, to characterise their determination to "worship at the altar of Donald Trump" as "unholy" (Posner 2020). This was the case when in December 2019 *Christianity Today*, a magazine founded by Billy Graham to "help evangelical Christians interpret the news in a manner that reflects their faith", in an editorial by Mark Galli, its editor in chief, condemned Trump's controversial phone call with the Ukrainian President, and called for his removal from office.[438] An excerpt of the editorial read:

> [...] The president of the United States attempted to use his political power to coerce a foreign leader to harass and discredit one of the president's political opponents. That is not only a violation of the Constitution; more importantly, it is profoundly immoral.
>
> [...]
>
> Trump's evangelical supporters have pointed to his Supreme Court nominees, his defense of religious liberty, and his stewardship of the economy, among other things, as achievements that justify their support of the president. We believe the impeachment hearings have made it absolutely clear, in a way the Mueller investigation did not, that President Trump has abused his authority for personal gain and betrayed his constitutional oath. The impeachment hearings have illuminated the president's moral deficiencies for all to see. This damages the institution of the presidency, damages the reputation of our country, and damages both the spirit and the future of our people. None of the president's positives can balance the moral and political danger we face under a leader of such grossly immoral character.
>
> [...]

To the many evangelicals who continue to support Mr. Trump in spite of his blackened moral record, we might say this: Remember who you are and whom you serve. Consider how your justification of Mr. Trump influences your witness to your Lord and Savior. Consider what an unbelieving world will say if you continue to brush off Mr. Trump's immoral words and behavior in the cause of political expediency. If we don't reverse course now, will anyone take anything we say about justice and righteousness with any seriousness for decades to come? Can we say with a straight face that abortion is a great evil that cannot be tolerated and, with the same straight face, say that the bent and broken character of our nation's leader doesn't really matter in the end?[439]

In a series of tweets on 20 December 2019, Trump criticised the magazine for having a "socialist/communist bent" and for preferring "a Radical Left nonbeliever, who wants to take your return & your guns, than Donald Trump". He affirmed: "The fact is, no President has ever done what I have done for Evangelicals, or religion itself!" (tweets, 7:12 AM & 1:18 PM 20 December 2019). In a Facebook post titled "My Response to Christianity Today", Franklin Graham sided with Trump, claiming: "my father […] Billy Graham would not agree with their opinion piece. In fact, he would be very disappointed". According to Barnhart of *The Christian Post*, nearly 200 evangelicals also criticised *Christianity Today* "for questioning their Christian witness" in their perceived unconditional support for Trump.[440]

Babones explains that "Trump did not portray himself as the preserver of the faith, whether that faith be religious or party-based". What Trump did instead, was to ask that "people put their faith in him, personally". To Babones, Trump, as a narcissist and a populist is not an authoritarian because "you can't be an authoritarian when the only authority you recognize is yourself" (Babones 2018: Chapter 4).

Trump's insulting and braggadocio tweets, lack of humility and pride, divisive and dysfunctional politics, reputation as "a pathological liar" and tenuous relationship with "truth" in general, though scathingly criticised by some evangelicals (Sider 2020a; Du Mez 2020), are easily ignored, dismissed, forgiven, or even encouraged by his base. Trump's instrumentalisation of religion was demonstrated during the Black Lives Matter George Floyd protests in Lafayette Square in Washington on 1 June 2020, when President

Trump stood in front of St. John's Episcopal Church, lifted up a Bible and had pictures of himself taken (Hoover 2020; Leonnig and Rucker 2021: Chapter 7). In a statement, on the President's use of the church and the Bible, presiding Bishop Michael Curry said, President Trump, in so doing, "used a church building and the Holy Bible for partisan political purposes".[441] The controversial episode was explained away by the majority of his Evangelical Christian support base, with whom Trump enjoys unwavering endorsement over and above voting for him at elections. On The Brian Kilmede Show of 3 June 2020, President Trump claimed: "Most religious leaders loved it. I heard Franklin Graham this morning – thought it was great. And I heard many other people think it was great. The church leaders loved that I went there with a Bible."

Backing Trump and Trumpism is considered a worthwhile investment by supportive Evangelicals. They are compensated by Trump's disregard for rationality, scientific thought and expertise, which resonates with the anti-intellectualism with which Evangelical Christians are generally sympathetic. Among the deeper causes of their alliance(s) with Trump, Guth includes the fact that "white Evangelicals share with Trump a multitude of attitudes, including his hostility toward immigrants, his Islamophobia, his racism, and nativism, as well as his 'political style,' with its nasty politics and assertion of strong, solitary leadership" (Guth 2019: 32).

They equally appreciate the fact that, Trump "may be mendacious, malicious, bigoted, and unpresidential, but at least he says what he thinks" and, unlike identity politics on the left, which has "tended to legitimate only certain identities while ignoring or denigrating others, such as European (i.e., white) ethnicity, Christian religiosity, rural residence, belief in traditional family values, and related categories", Trump has, by throwing political correctness out of the window, sought to reassure his mainly working-class supporters that their identities and values, often "disregarded by the national elites", do matter and matter more than identities and values championed by liberals and the national elites (Fukuyama 2018: 119). As Fukuyama remarks:

> Rural people, who are the backbone of populist movements not just in the United States [...] often believe that their traditional values are under severe threat by cosmopolitan, city-based elites. They feel

victimized by a secular culture that is careful not to criticize Islam or Judaism, yet regards their own Christianity as a mark of bigotry. They feel that the elite media have put them in danger by their political correctness (Fukuyama 2018: 120).

As Wehner acknowledges, "for many evangelical Christians, there is no political figure whom they have loved more than Donald Trump". Wehner characterises as "among the most mind-blowing developments of the Trump era", the "enthusiastic, uncritical embrace of President Trump by white evangelicals". Support for Trump is in part motivated by the "grievances and resentments" many Evangelicals feel for being "mocked, scorned, and dishonored by the elite culture over the years". These Evangelicals saw in "Trump […] a man who will not only push their agenda on issues such as the courts and abortion", and who "will be ruthless against those they view as threats to all they know and love" (Wehner 2020: Chapter 9). In other words, the sustained promotion perceived permissiveness and sexual revolution, characterised by liberal sex education, and subsequent marginalisation of the Bible in American intellectual and progressive circles has had the effect of pushing some Evangelicals to even equate Jesus with a demagogue – in soteriological matters.

It is noteworthy that while some readily likened Trump to the anti-Christ, Evangelical Christians saw in him a messiah and the Chosen One, deserving of adoration even to the point of idolatry or what Horton calls "the cult of Christian Trumpism"[442] (Sider 2020a). As Dean and Altemeyer argue, Trump's support among Evangelical Christians remained unshaken by his lack of knowledge of the Bible and of Christianity, as well as by knowledge of how many deadly sins he was guilty of. (Dean and Altemeyer 2020: Chapter 8). They write:

> Of the seven deadly sins (lust, gluttony, greed, sloth, wrath, envy, and pride), Trump might get a pass on sloth if you count watching cable news as working. Otherwise, he had plainly reveled in sin for most of his life and delighted in it like a pig rolling in muck (Dean and Altemeyer 2020: Chapter 8).

During his presidency Trump effectively prioritised the evangelical policy concerns of "ending abortion, restricting immigration, protecting gun rights, limiting government, and, more recently, the disdain for science and the denial of climate change" (Wilkerson 2020: 330). Notwithstanding the touted agenda of protection of life, a contentious case could be made to the effect that the abortion agenda is linked to desires for male control in society. It could also be linked to other agendas, such as the desire for more white babies at times of changing demographics, and rising concerns among whites who fear being outnumbered in a context where, as Abrams demonstrates, despite gerrymandering and voter disenfranchisement, democracy is still a game of numbers (Abrams 2020).

As Hofstadter explains, among the Evangelicals, "Since the affairs of the heart are the affairs of the common man, and since the common man's intuition in such matters is as good as—indeed better than—that of the intellectuals, his judgment in matters of religion should rule." It is assumed that in case of a conflict between religion and science, it is the public who should decide, and not the intellectuals, the scientist or the expert who tend to rely overly on diplomas and college degrees (Hofstadter 1963: 128, Chapters 3 & 4). In other words, subjectivity and intuition matter more when dealing with affairs of the heart than science and objective truth.

Fowler suggests that "Trump may think he has a great relationship with God, but one can genuinely question if God thinks he has a great relationship with Trump" (Fowler 2020: Chapter 6). A question, one should add, which is certainly beyond the capacity of empirical science or investigative journalism to answer. It is worth acknowledging though, if the Bible is anything to go by, that God loves all His children, without exception. God aside, Pieper and Henderson provide "10 Reasons" why "Christians Should Reconsider Their Support of Trump": Trump's "lack of compassion"; his "appeals to fear and anger"; the fact that "He lies – a lot"; "He is hostile to women"; "He speaks about his daughter in a disrespectful and sexualized way"; "He does not attempt to love his enemies, but instead cultivates antagonism"; "He does not model sacrifice or altruism"; "He doesn't seem to care about the poor"; and "His love of money is more apparent than his love of God or others" (Pieper and Henderson 2020: Chapter 7). Whatever the benefits of supporting Trump may be, these must not trump the need for evangelicals and people of faith in general, to "embody moral and intellectual integrity", Wehner argues. [443] Hence Sider invites Christians to rise beyond the deep political divisions that have led to "destructive gridlock" among politicians in Washington, by embracing greater ecumenism undiluted by partisanship, and by acting their "political engagement in such a way that non-Christians are attracted to our Lord" (Sider 2020b: Afterword). The call to resist exclusionary populism in favour of dignity, justice, diversity and inclusive participation through narratives of truth and hope than of fear and hate is global (Sinn and Harasta 2019).

Davies observes that Trump's support in the USA is most concentrated in areas with high levels of physical suffering and rising mortality rates. Emotional politics is a part of this. Today's emotional politics is an inverse of that of the 1960s which attempted to draw on peoples' pleasures; today it draws on peoples' pains. Technology and social media are largely seen as a culprit in people making identity from their pains. Beyond the question of whether social media is good or bad is how social media behaviours spill over into real life, especially given the capacity of digital media to "operate at any scale of interaction, from the most intimate to the most public". Social media is based on binaries like "one/zero, follow/unfollow, like/unlike", as well as "'blocking' and 'muting'". These binaries are now visible in real life politics where people define in terms of "friend/enemy" – a breeding ground for populist politics. Private pain can be utilised successfully for public reform, by "turning private pain into protest". [444]

Seaton, Crook and Taylor find parallels between "the post-truth era" and "aspects of the dystopian world of Orwell's Nineteen Eighty-Four". These parallels include a "willingness to believe one thing one day, and one thing another" and social media's encroachments on privacy. "There has been a long drift away from rational beliefs", argue the three authors, "that we have watched too passively. Mistrust in facts was sown by the insistence on creationism and climate change denial by politicians and in many US churches. But it's not just America". [445]

On the contestations around truth and facts, William discusses how President Trump "dresses up useful lies as 'alternative facts' and decries uncomfortable realities as 'fake news'", adding that "Trump's playbook should be familiar to any student of critical theory and philosophy. It often feels like Trump has stolen our ideas and weaponized them".[446]

Karl, in his capacity as a front row journalist covering the Trump White House as correspondent for ABC News, provides substantiation of how Trump and his aides (press secretaries – Sean Spicer and Sarah Sanders – in particular) went about producing and seeking to force feed Americans with alternative facts, while simultaneously sowing doubt in their minds about their lived truths and trusted channels of transmission and articulation (Karl 2020: Chapters 9 & 19). Sims provides a rare insider account of how the story of Trump having the largest inaugural crowd ever was concocted behind the scenes to please President Trump who would not accept that Obama had a much larger inaugural attendance than him, and how collectively embarrassed they were as the new White House press team for kicking off with such glaring disservice to facts and evidence (Sims 2019: Chapter 4). When Karl reminded Trump of a campaign promise in 2016 to "always tell the truth", Trump's response was: "Well, I try. I do try. I think you try too. You say things about me that aren't necessarily correct. I do try, and I always want to tell the truth. When I can, I tell the truth." With Trump's attitude to the truth, Karl argues, "it shouldn't be surprising to hear a casual disregard for the truth from those charged with speaking for a president who seems to have an aggressive disregard for the truth" (Karl 2020: Chapter 19).

Kellyanne Conway, a senior counsel to Trump and first female campaign manager to win a presidential race, is credited with coming up with the phrase "alternative facts" (Carpini 2018; Skinnell 2018b; Kessler 2020: Conclusion). According to Rucker and Leonnig, none other than George Conway, Kellyanne's husband, believes she:

> [...] deserved—a lot of credit for guiding Trump to victory. She tried to hone his populist message to appeal to a broad group of voters, including the working-class union members peeling away from Democrats and well-heeled, establishment Republicans more than mildly suspicious of Trump. She was his spin warrior, sparring with news anchors at all hours of the day to seemingly wash away Trump's troubles (Rucker and Leonnig 2020: 74).

Trump acknowledges Kellyanne Conway as having "played a crucial role in my victory" and as "a tireless and tenacious advocate of my agenda" who "has amazing insights on how to effectively communicate our message".[447] Wilson depicts Kellyanne Conway as someone: "Aggressively willing to lie, then to deny she lied, then to deny that she denied she lied about lying." During her time at the service of Trump, Conway was "routinely wheeled out to defend the usual panoply of indefensible acts, colossal errors, grand and petit corruptions, and the rest of Team Trump's daily catalogue of disasters", and was "magnificent in turning a substantive interview into a Gordian knot of lies, evasions, misstatements, and distractions" (Wilson 2018: Chapter 14).

The rise and proliferation of "alternative facts", falsehood, propaganda, fake news and conspiracy theories coincides with the surge in new forms of populism and a nationalism of ever diminishing circles of inclusion (Muirhead and Rosenblum 2019). According to Feldman, it is populism and nationalism aimed at appealing to whites and whiteness, trapped in a racialised hierarchy of whiteness with, purportedly, whites of "Anglo-Saxons political traditions" as the "America First Caucus".[448]

As Michiko Kakutani demonstrates in *The Death of Truth*, these developments have also witnessed, inter alia, the decline and fall of reason and respect for reality; the rise of subjectivity and a fixation with me, myself and I; the embrace of social media and the filters, silos, tribes, culture wars; and attention deficits that social media promotes and on which it feasts (Kakutani 2018). The blurb of Kakutani's book captures the post-truth moment of Trump's America superbly in these words:

> We live in a time when the very idea of objective truth is mocked and discounted by the US president. Discredited conspiracy theories and ideologies have resurfaced, proven science is once more up for debate and Russian propaganda floods our screens. The wisdom of the crowd has usurped research and expertise, and we are each left clinging to the beliefs that best confirm our biases (Kakutani 2018: Blurb).

A consequence of this, according to Kakutani, is the dangerous blurring of "the lines between fact and opinion, informed argument and blustering speculation", such that renders ignorance fashionable (Kakutani 2018: 35).

Kakutani provides evidence on how the decline that has made the truth "an endangered species" in America and the West began decades ago, has multiplied and originates on both the left and the right, and combines "to elevate subjectivity over factuality, science and common values" (Kakutani 2018: 7 & Blurb). It is a case of relativism gone berserk and, ultimately, of sterility in unproductive zero-sum games of being and belonging impoverished by their lack of nuance in claims and denial of personal and collective identities. Civility, humility, sociality and humanity get eaten up or tossed in a trash bin in a never-ending game of ever diminishing circles of authenticity and bona fides.

A fractured society begets a fractured belief in the truth, as one person's reality becomes another's fake news, fake science, fake history, fake culture, fake religion, fake patriotism, fake citizenship, fake democracy or fake election results. A fragmented society is one without a cohesive essence, one always at risk of implosion, one far from working to pull together what subjectivities would keep asunder. Such a fractured and fragmented society contents itself with what David Foster Wallace describes as "a kind of epistemic free-for-all in which 'the truth' is wholly a matter of perspective and agenda" (cited in Kakutani 2018: 43). Drawing on George Orwell, Kakutani warns that a society in which "truth is so fragmented" runs the risk of opening itself up "for some 'Leader, or some ruling clique' to dictate what is to be believed: 'If the Leader says of such and such an event, "It never happened" – well, it never happened" (Kakutani 2018: 55). This is precisely what Trump was expert at – cancelling out inconvenient truths.

Trump poured gasoline on the social and political fractures of American society. Trump "exploited the partisan divides in American society", Kakutani reiterates, "appealing to the fears of white working-class voters worried about a changing world, while giving them scapegoats he selected – immigrants, African Americans, women, Muslims – as targets for their anger" (Kakutani 2018: 51). It was a case not of uniting against a common external enemy, but of identifying and dealing with one's enemies within.

The fact that "Trump lied reflexively and shamelessly" about his scapegoats, in a context of magical multipliers such as Twitter,

Facebook and other social and mainstream media platforms, had the cumulative effect of the "hundreds upon hundreds of lies" he pumped into nonstop circulation, coming "together to create equally false story lines that appealed to people's fears" (Kakutani 2018: 80). Again, there is an added insight to be gained from seeing this promiscuity in lying from the vantage point of the activation, self-extension and potency Trump sought through them in his ambitions of completeness. Beyond his "torrent of lies", Kakutani maintains, Trump has been able, in his use of language, to corrupt the use of words to the extent of exchanging "the language of democracy and its ideals for the language of autocracy" by demanding "allegiance not to the U.S. Constitution but to himself" and expecting "members of Congress and the judiciary to applaud his policies and wishes, regardless of what they think best serves the interests of the American people" (Kakutani 2018: 94). With allegiance ultimately to Trump and not to the Constitution of the country, Trump did not need to adopt the title of king or monarch to be effectively one.

"Call it what you want: relativism, constructivism, deconstruction, postmodernism, critique," William argues, "The idea is the same: Truth is not found, but made, and making truth means exercising power. The reductive version is simpler and easier to abuse: Fact is fiction, and anything goes." [449] If power and privilege are instrumental to making truth, the fragmentation of truth allows the powerful and the privileged to put together the puzzle pieces in a way that suits them. Gray is critical of those who rush to conclude that "voters are no longer interested in facts or arguments". He observes that "'post-truth politics', like 'populism', is a term mostly used by liberals who cannot face up to the self-defeating effects of their inordinate ideology". He echoes the argument that Europe's ruling elites are to blame for the populist backlash that their pursuit of "the ultra-liberal project of a borderless continent in which national identities count for little" has unleashed. [450]

Das suggests that the word "populism" might not tell us as much as we think it does. He claims that "Populism is an oxymoron", since the very idea of democracy is inherently about "popularity, with a majority or, at least, the sizeable support needed for political power". Instead of falling into the trap of "imprecise labelling, an examination of the underlying factors is more useful". To Das, such underlying factors that militate in favour of populism include: the labour market, terrorism and immigration, loss of sovereignty and cultural identity, anti-elitism, and, not least, nostalgia.[451]

It should be possible to actively encourage a more inclusive society by opening up and ensuring recognition, representation, resources and dignity for the debris, rejects, disenfranchised, dispossessed and left behinds of liberalism, globalisation or whatever other form modernisation and civilisation takes, while at the same time ensuring that the fears, angers and frustrations of those affected and inflicted are not unduly exploited by opportunists and nihilists "who want to make the case for offensive or debunked theories, or who want to equate things that cannot be equated" (Kakutani 2018: 73).

Observing that the Trump era has been one in which "there is no past and no future, no history and no vision—only the anxious present", Gessen rightly questions the extent to which hopes, dreams and ideals are possible "where there is no shared reality". Similarly, no political community is possible "where there is only the self-obsessed and endlessly self-referential president" (Gessen 2020: Chapter 16) in the manner of "The Skull" turned to "The Complete Gentleman" who refuses to all acknowledge his debt and provide for the circulation of debt and indebtedness. It takes more than one person, however man-mountain he is, to build a community of shared interests and sociality. A shared social reality constitutes social truth (Rauch 2013[1993]), which presupposes a shared consensus and trust achieved through robust debate and exchange of ideas in all freedom, or contrived and imposed by gatekeepers of palatability and kindred instances of legitimation.

As Stengel argues, the claim that "the truth is under attack is a beautiful phrase", but it does not diminish the challenge of multiple and competing truths. To recognise and provide for the fact that "people have their own truths, and these truths are often at war with one another", and that "it's impossible to stop people from creating falsehoods and other people from believing them" (Stengel 2019: Introduction), might be a good starting point to the process of forging an inclusive and shared truth with the communities of which we are a part, and ultimately, in a global or universal process of ever-increasing circles of belonging. Truths that are shared across divides in political communities and universally are still possible, even if in one's current existence one has reason to be sceptical. Indeed, people have sometimes easily yielded to the idea of "an objective reality", especially a *social* reality, when in fact a social reality does not exist independently of human perception. Social knowledge is always in flux and is constantly informed by and hinged upon by one's background and relational context, including factors such as race, ethnicity, culture, geography, class, sex, gender identity, sexual preferences, morality and ethics, and more.

The question is thus not one of eliminating relativism but, rather, one of disabusing it of nihilism and making it fruitful in carefully negotiated and delicately navigated inclusive and participatory consensus-building processes. To share a truth is not necessarily to embrace objectivity, phoney or otherwise; it is to be committed to the truth of one's subjective experiences as part of a community of practice informed by shared convictions, aspirations and rules of engagement, not capricious fantasies of victimhood and/or superiority. To share a truth requires believing in something not because this sounds good or tells an uplifting story about one, but because it reflects things as they are from the vantage point that we individually and collectively experience them in earnest and all honesty.

Itself the product of past struggles and negotiations, social truth cannot rest on its laurels, as it is open to constant interrogation and renegotiation, with changing circumstances and in tune with a world in permanent motion. As Brooks notes in a review of Rauch's *Constitution of Knowledge*, shared social truths spring to life from a society's ability to tell complex stories with maturity and honesty in which: "opposing characters can each possess pieces of the truth, stories in which all characters are embedded in time, at one point in their process of growth, stories rooted in the complexity of real life and not the dogma of ideological abstraction".[452] West concurs that social truth defies the logic of "uncritical deference to dogma" and "blind obedience to doctrine" and repression (West 2017). Put differently, social truth is always incomplete.

To speak of citizenship and belonging in whatever form is to imagine and construct a living-togetherness that takes seriously the reality of interconnections and interdependencies. One is and becomes a citizen through relationships with others, relationships that are institutionalised in one form or another. No institution, however carefully thought through from the outset is perfect, hence the need to humbly (and even enthusiastically) embrace incompleteness. There is power in incompleteness as a prism – through which to perceive life and live our creative ingenuity. Let us individually and collectively be ready to open up and accommodate those we may have left behind, consciously or inadvertently. Let us appreciate the enriching potentialities of new encounters – made possible by the reality of our dynamism as people and the dynamic world in which we seek to live, and hopefully, let live.

Concluding Thoughts

Writing about Trump and populism is no easy feat. Equally challenging is how to conclude an unfolding story. Nevertheless, one of the advantages of taking incompleteness seriously is that it encourages one to disabuse oneself of expectations of finitude. This book has explored numerous contributions and conversations from multiple sources on democracy, populism, citizenship and belonging through the frame of incompleteness, focusing on Trump and the present-day United States of America. This discussion essentially invokes the figure of Trump as the populist avatar. It grounds the discourse on and around populism through the prism of incompleteness in two ways.

First, it argues that at the core of populism is a pursuit of completeness. This, in the American context, is evident in a resurgent nationalism preoccupied with the purity and purification of the constitution of "the people", which is often presented in racial, class and ethnic terms. It foregrounds hierarchies of Americanness through affective dispositions like patriotism, loyalty, fear and attitudes towards expertise, science and rigid prescriptiveness about meritocracy that tends to serve the college-educated and narrow elite circles, to the detriment of the multitude. In addition, in its encounters with global others, populism (especially the right-wing Trumpian variant, as opposed to the left-wing variant of Bernie Sanders) eschews conviviality by asserting the primacy of "America First" in opposition to the perceived globalism of the liberal American elites and the present-day immigrants perceived to have benefitted from elite laissez-fairism.

As such, one of the things taken for granted in this illusory quest for completeness through the standardisation, routinisation, simplification and linearity of identity is the idea of the nation as a coherent and stable entity that is divorceable from histories of its constitution and reconstitution through various kinds of mobilities and unequal encounters. A key argument is for rethinking the nation-state as a composite entity that is fundamentally incomplete and thus a permanent work in progress, as a feature that should be celebrated rather than perceived as a threat to its overarching coherence.

In discussions of democracy, citizenship and belonging, therefore, populist discourses of completeness are illusory because they articulate belonging as a zero-sum game undergirded by ever-diminishing circles of inclusion. It is illusory in a historical and sociological sense, for it relies on the erasure of histories of mobility which have entertained diverse possibilities of nativisation and the very compositeness of being individuals and cultural communities.

Liberal democracy is equally another locus of discourses of completeness in addition to the idea of the nation. Many arguments against populism are biased because they endorse the superiority and/or universality and sacrosanctity of liberal democracy and the elite forms of governance it inspires. In this regard, populism is critiqued because of its danger to liberal democracy, which is presented as the only possible perfect form of government. A form of government, the nimble-footed meritocratic elite proponents of which assume, should become a global currency to be adopted without adaption or equivocation.

The centre of American democracy and America as a nation-state cannot hold in a context where populism and liberalism present themselves as zero-sum options beyond impeachment. Hence, the invitation to embrace conviviality is informed by the humility of recognising and providing for the universality of incompleteness and mobility.

Shopping with an Incompleteness Shopping Basket

I propose using imagery from shopping – as food for thought, on Trump, populism and citizenship, understood through the prism of incompleteness. I know names and labels are helpful, and that some readers would like to have a name for those who see incompleteness as a threat. Some of you might even wish to call them *solipsists*. Some might suggest that we could call those who do not perceive incompleteness as a threat *ubuntuists*, but I hesitate to name. Just as names can be helpful, they can equally be limiting. Incompleteness as a framework is all about being helpful without the trappings of confinement.

The disavowal or denial of incompleteness and interconnection is very much at stake, and thus these items are useful in our shopping baskets. Objectively, everyone is extended and distributed, but one of the issues for someone like Trump seems to be a refusal to acknowledge it. As we have seen, Trump seems more than comfortable with who he is as a person cultivated to appreciate and relate to others and the world purely through the prism of winners and losers. He combines both the psychology and culture of narcissism, in his determined refusal to see or own his own incompleteness even when it is staring him in the face. Even from Mar-a-Lago since leaving the White House, as journalists who have visited and interviewed him acknowledge, Trump still thinks he is the greatest US president of all time. Trump might be a supersized version of a thoroughbred in the psychology and culture of narcissism, but Trump is not alone. Hence the questions: Why do we not pause and try to live in our incompleteness? What about completeness is so attractive? What compelling lies are we telling ourselves, psychologically, sociologically and anthropologically, that lead us as individuals and collectivities to opt for fantasies and illusions rather than face the truth of ourselves as modest beings without required humility?

From the abundance of psychological and psychoanalytical accounts of him broached in this book, the challenge with personalities like Trump (and by extension systems such as neoliberalism and the local and global elites that prop them up) is a disavowal in the psychoanalytic sense of always being subconsciously aware of the shortcoming (in their view) and therefore lashing out at their inability to be autonomous. To take the Drinkard example that we started off with in our discussion of incompleteness, part of the issue seems to be the denial of dependency, not merely the dependence on the worker or the palm-wine tapster in Tutuola speak. They cannot bring themselves to contemplate even the most basic of truths, for example, that they were born, like anyone else, and thus, that they are expected, at the very least, to recognise the creative processes that predated their existence and their consciousness of themselves as beings.

How do we judge someone like Trump or the Drinkard? Some of you might derive from my discussion of the Drinkard, in the introduction to this book, the idea that the problem is the Drinkard's lack of gratitude and recognition of the other. A sentiment not dissimilar to how Trump has been characterised in much of the bumper harvest of literature that has been churned out on him. Yet, if the Drinkard had been appreciative and recognised the harvester, would he be absolved of the inequities and hierarchies that remain between the leisure class and the vulnerable worker: national or immigrant, working-class or middle class, black, white, Native-American or Latino? Would it change much, if, as some are likely to insist that the Drinkard deserves some credit for at least realising that he was in fact incomplete? The answer to both questions is quite simply no.

Populism would not be contained simply by a trickle-down munificence of the elites, neoliberal or otherwise. Nor can populist demagoguery deliver democratic pluralism through rhetoric alone and in the hope of naming and shaming the technocratic managerial elite out of their rigid monopolisation of institutionalised political, economic and cultural power (Lind 2020). There is need to rethink relations informed by completeness and its psychology of disavowal, to provide for a fulsome, universal and permanent recognition of incompleteness and interdependence in a manner that, while not necessarily ending inegalitarian relations of production and leisure, cultivates a consciousness, to inform practice, on the fluidity of power and privilege.

Thus, incompleteness it not merely about acknowledging interdependence, providing for gratitude and discouraging disavowal and denigration, because this does not guarantee the end of simultaneously thinking and relating in ways that reproduce subordination and exclusion. It is about (re)configuring the world and relations around incompleteness as the central organising principle. Such an organising logic would ensure that institutions and structures of sociality are imbued with new meaning beyond current orthodoxies such that incompleteness, extensibility and composition are not confined to the voluntary embrace of individual social actors.

Clearly worth its place in your shopping basket, I presume, is the fact of just how popular populism has become. The problem with the popularity of populism is that scientific precision in how the concept is employed as an analytical category has been drowned out by the value-laden and incredibly imprecise usage to which the term has been subjected (Singh 2017; Urbinati 2019). It is frequently used in politics as an affront, and everyday media discussions reveal the term to be especially opalescent, covering everything from "pub talk" to demagoguery by a "demagogue" as "an unscrupulous master of often bombastic rhetoric who manipulates the crowd for his own ends" with "empty promises or idle flattery" and to the detriment of the common good (Bartlett 2020: 6–11).

Even though populism seems to be everything and nothing, it, like Trump, is an indication that the nation-state, or whatever other political community, is not to be taken for granted. Rather, communities of people are best understood as permanent works in progress, in a spirit of incompleteness. It is thus of significance that the rise of populism seems to coincide with the resurgence of nationalism, which thrives by making a meal of liberalism and those, elites in the main, for whom crossing borders and cultures and mingling and comingling with perceived strangers have become second nature, and a privilege in flexible mobility that few beyond elite circles can afford.

Equally worth considering for your shopping basket is the argument that populism, be it right-wing or left-wing, feeds on and is fed by often unproblematised distinctions between the elite and the popular. Arguments against populism are skewed because they are mostly garnered by a belief in the superiority and/or universality of liberal forms of democracy and governance. In view of the fact that the drivers or propellers and peddlers of populism are often drawn from the ranks of the elites, there is need to beam the flashlight of scrutiny on the nebulous and often unproblematised indicators of excellence and meritocracy to which elites resort in their distinctions and hierarchies of humanity, credibility and legitimacy, which tend to depict the popular as inferior and populism as a distraction.

It is worth remembering that at the heart of this shopping spree is a curiosity with Trump and how he harnessed populism to exacerbate the propensity to claim and deny citizenship in ways that jeopardise the reality of a nation-state as a composition and extension of incompleteness. This book establishes parallelism between Trump and populist strongmen globally, who are united in their effortless embrace of a style and rhetoric of conspiracy, lies, threats and paranoia. Like strongmen elsewhere, and despite America's history, credentials and self-representation as a beacon and globalising template of democracy, Trump did not hesitate to opportunistically explain, highlight and exacerbate the misfortunes of the socially insecure and economically vulnerable and harness the popularity generated by mass discontent in American society, to the ironic delight of his mainly conservative white Republican base. Among his support base are evident simmers of anger, hate and fear – of being replaced, culturally and economically, by others (mostly blacks and Hispanics) perceived to be less authentic and less deserving Americans and citizens. Although the country in principle is an elective democracy in which every citizen who attains the age qualifies to vote, Trump has schooled his supporters to think and relate to fellow Americans as if their citizenship was undesirable and improper, and their vote worthless or at best, inferior (Reid 2019; Abrams 2020; Frum 2020: Chapter 5; Wolff 2021a).

This is exemplified by the speech Trump delivered at Mount Rushmore on 3 July 2020, which Leonnig and Rucker characterise as "an extraordinarily divisive speech to mark a holiday of national unity". In the speech, Trump differentiated between patriotic and bona fide Americans whom he labelled "the American people" and with whom he identified, and those (Black Lives Matter and others protesting the brutal killing of George Floyd by a policeman) whom he qualified as an "angry mob". The mob, he claimed, were running "a merciless campaign to wipe out our history, defame our heroes, erase our values, and indoctrinate our children". Trump made a point of distancing the "angry mob" from the ranks of those he identified with as fellow and patriotic Americans and the values and legacies he believed were under attack. The reasoning was simple. No one could seriously expect to be considered American by Trump and his supporters if they acted un-Americanly by seeking to "tear down statues of our founders, deface our most sacred memorials, and unleash a wave of violent crime in our cities". Trump warned that the proud and strong "American people" were far from "soft and submissive", and that they "will not allow our country and all of its values, history, and culture to be taken away from them" (Leonnig and Rucker 2021: Chapter 10). It is important to compare and contrast Trump's speech touting patriotism, heritage and law and order in reaction to the Black Lives Matter protests, with Trump's extraordinarily accommodating reaction to the mob of his supporters who violently stormed the Capitol building. When the violence was at his service and beck and call, Trump was all for it, but when it sought legitimate justice for those repeatedly treated as inferior citizens and less than human, Trump's hostility was not in doubt.

Equally worth retaining is how savvy Trump, as a narcissist and in his populism, harnessed the power of social media, Twitter and Facebook in particular, which have played a significant role in the upsurge of populism globally. Given how much Trump has been extended by the media, and how especially adept he has been at manipulating the media to achieve his ends, both in business and in politics, it is worth following more closely what becomes of him after the ban by platforms such as Twitter and Facebook. In June 2021, Facebook clarified that its ban of Trump was for two years, effective from 7 January 2021 to 7 January 2023, adding that Trump will be held to "a strict set of rapidly escalating sanctions", for any violations upon his return.[453]

Trump slammed the decision by Facebook, characterising it as "an insult to the record-setting 75M people, plus many others, who voted for us in the 2020 Rigged Presidential Election". It is very Trumpian to highlight how many people voted for him, and stop at that, as if the other section of the population who voted differently does not exist or account. Trump added that Facebook "shouldn't be allowed to get away with this censoring and silencing, and ultimately, we will win. Our country can't take this abuse anymore."[454] It should be added that until the ban on Trump, Facebook had justified non-interference with political advertising and/or political speech with this argument:

> Our approach is grounded in Facebook's fundamental belief in free expression, respect for the democratic process, and the belief that, in mature democracies with a free press, political speech is already arguably the most scrutinized speech there is. Thus, when a politician speaks or makes an ad, we do not send it to third party fact checkers.[455]

Subsequently, when President Muhammadu Buhari of Nigeria banned Twitter for deleting one of his posts for breaching its rules, Trump congratulated Buhari for banning Twitter. Trump wrote, "Congratulations to the country of Nigeria, who just banned Twitter because they banned their President." He urged more countries to "ban Twitter and Facebook for not allowing free and open speech". He questioned: "Who are they to dictate good and evil, if they themselves are evil?" Trump suggested he would have banned Facebook when he was President, had Mark Zuckerberg not "kept calling me and coming to the White House for dinner telling me how great I was".[456]

Deplatforming Trump had the effect, Wolff indicates, of taking away the final two weeks of a presidency that had defined itself largely through its television and social media presence, as there was practically no administration left capable of any action (Wolff 2021a: Chapter 11). Strictly in terms of his relationship with the media, and by extension with the wider public, banning or deplatforming Trump is comparable to Tutuola's "The Complete Gentleman" giving up all the body parts and material substances that he borrowed to prop himself up Humpty-Dumpty-like to dazzle and glitter with a spectacular larger-than-life sense of ephemeral achievement and visibility. It was as if Drezner's "Toddler-in-Chief" (Drezner 2020) had been deflated into realising, at long last, that there was nothing chiefly about him even in the wishful and fantasy spaces of television and social media.

In recalcitrant toddler fashion, it would appear that Trump remained Trump throughout his four years in office. As Wolff observes, the Trump that left office "was the same Trump who had come into office". There had been "no transformational moment". "He didn't learn, he didn't grow, he didn't change. He was a simple machine: he got punched, and he punched back. As long as he still stood, he was still punching." Trump never admitted, never apologised, never backed down, but attacked (Wolff 2021a: Chapter 11). If attacked in turn, he saw it as an attack against "his people", those he "fights for". Hence, "the more he is pursued the stronger he remains" (Wolff 2021a: Epilogue). His "stubborn refusal to listen to more considered and cautious counsel or to tolerate anyone whose talents might actually be clear and need to be credited" had reduced him to "a team of one", and ensured that even when apparently surrounded by others, "He walked into the storm alone and came out alone" (Wolff 2021a: Chapter 12). This makes the case to add to the shopping basket the idea of Trump as ultimately a lone ranger, even when in the company of others. Like Tutuola's "The Complete Gentleman", Trump rode into Washington DC unaccompanied, and left, more or less, unaccompanied.

I hope you have read this multidimensional book not as an attempt to fill in all the gaps in between the extremes and binary oppositions that ambitions of completeness have a tendency to impose and that are evident in how value is attributed or denied "populism". On the contrary, what I have attempted to do is to use "Trumpism" – as a political style – as a guiding thread and Tutuola's tale of "The Complete Gentleman" as an analytical filter in reflecting social sentiments beyond the noise of populist rhetoric. Instead of claiming completeness – as works explaining populism often seem to do when trying to answer a range of questions on the phenomenon – this book encourages its readers to embrace incompleteness. This it does through an exploration of a range of literature and concepts like mobility, elitism, belonging and citizenship, and inclusion and exclusion, but not in an effort to establish a causal narrative. The point has not been to assign blame, explain the roots of populist symptoms or establish a how-to-avoid-falling-victim-to-populism wisdom.

Amos Tutuola's story serves to rattle truth–fake binaries and frame social realities as being in permanent motion. I hope his story helps in understanding how any attempt to use a populist rationale to concretise belonging and define who does and does not fit established frameworks of "the people" demonstrates ignorance of our interconnections and interdependencies as humans, and the reality of one being and becoming a citizen only through relationships with others. Mobility here takes on meaning in terms of flexibility – rather than of distinguishing elites from the rest (part of populist language repertoires). Mobility as a quest for extending beyond the world in its pretence, because there is always a lot more or a lot less to things than meets the eye.

The pursuit of completeness at the core of populist claims is elusive and illusory and can only unleash sterile ambitions of conquest and zero-sum games of superiority. Incompleteness as a social organising principle, on the other hand, moves in a very different direction – one that invites exploration, contemplation and openness to infinite interconnections, fluidities and conviviality. If one, for lack of space in one's shopping basket, were to retain only one idea from this book, I would suggest the following: Mobility is a permanence because incompleteness is an enduring condition. It sums up perfectly the very sterility of many of the ambitions that motivate claiming the support of "the people". It also creates an eye-opening imagery, illustrating that there is no such thing as a "The

Complete Gentleman" that is not the product of compositions and extensions.

What Have We Learnt about Trump, Populism, Democracy and Citizenship?

We have learnt, among other things, that absolute regressive Republican white tribalism has been Trump's instinctive first port of call. Second, we have learnt that he has seemed patient with democracy only to the extent that he is victorious, even if this takes corrupting the rules of the game by putting in place his own referees to ensure the game is played in his favour (Leonnig and Rucker 2021; Wolff 2021a). "Trumpism corrupts, and absolute Trumpism corrupts absolutely," writes Wilson (2020: Part 1).

Inclusivity and cosmopolitanism are the fruit of a world on the move. Yet, they have not been part of Trump's rhetoric and campaign slogans of "America First" and "Make America Great Again". He has left few in doubt that *his* America is one increasingly without a sense of history and on a crusade of purity and purification. It is an America that has little sympathy for anyone who is not unapologetically and supremely white and autochthonous – even if, paradoxically, his idea of autochthony does not seem to extend beyond white settlers from Europe whose claim to nativity would be disqualified by Native American history (Wong 2010; Ioanide 2015; Fukuyama 2018; Mercieca 2018; Reid 2019; Trump, M. L. 2021; Geary et al. 2020).

This passage by Reid captures the challenge of zero-sum articulations of belonging in and as Americans, which Trump was expected to inspire Americans away from towards greater inclusivity and conviviality:

> Trump voters shared a sense that "being American" used to mean being like them, and now that was changing in a way that they found hard to accept. They were convinced that an amorphous "they" was pouring into America—not to "assimilate" and become American, like their forefathers did, but to exploit the good graces of Uncle Sam to steal federal benefits paid for with the hard-earned money of "real" Americans (Reid 2019: Chapter 1).

The word "stranger" and its aliases such as "Alien, intruder, interloper, foreigner, *novus homo*, newcomer, immigrant, guest, outsider, outlander", as Shack reminds us, "are convenient labels that social groups habitually apply to persons who, by reasons of custom, language, or social role, stand on the margin of society" (Shack 1979: 2). He argues that as an appellation, the word "stranger" is full of ambiguities, drawing on Georg Simmel's point that the stranger's position is fundamentally determined by the fact that unlike those who see themselves as insiders/hosts to a given group, the perceived stranger has not belonged to the group "from the beginning" and that she or he "imports qualities into it which do not, and cannot, stem from the group itself" (Shack 1979: 2). In this regard, the stranger is at best an outsider within (Harrison 2008), and often feels caught betwixt and between (Shack 1979). An obvious ambiguity is in how the group doing the differentiation, between insiders and strangers, tends to ignore the history of mobility and population or settlement of a given space or place. Such reasoning validates claims to bona fide insider status, which, by implication, would also mark the end of history. Powerful settlers willy-nilly, through political machinations, manipulation of history and the privileging of their own mobilities over the mobilities of those they encounter, turn themselves into natives and natives into settlers (Mamdani 1996; Nyamnjoh 2016), as well as make permanent minorities of less powerful settlers (Mamdani 1998, 2020), even when these minorities become majorities demographically, which is what the US is projected to become by 2045.[457] Such violence and disregard freeze the processes of nativisation and belonging outside of the histories and sociologies that produce and contest them. Being a native or a settler is more than just legal realities; these are historical and sociological realities as well (Laclau 2005; De Vries et al. 2019; Castells and Lategan 2021), and are determined by and determining of the sort of identity politics at play and its capacity to accommodate and actively promote experimentation, creativity and rejuvenation in the interest of inclusivity and justice (Lategan 2021).

Trump might claim to be unequivocally on the side of "the American people", especially his supporters and attendees at his rallies, whom he loves to call "true patriots", as he did those who stormed the Capitol (Bender 2021), but in reality, he is no friend to the common person whom "he holds in contempt" while making the millions of his voters amongst them believe that "he's somehow one of them" (Res 2020: Chapter 7). On this score, and touting his successes as a businessman, Trump often contrasts himself with liberal elites, or the Washington establishment, who have betrayed the patriotic values he professes to share with the American people. But in view of his often-undiluted subscription in rhetoric and pronouncements to a right-wing white-only America, he could be said to be no different from the elites who engage in hierarchies of meritocracy. In putting in place a hierarchy of Americanness informed by race, ethnicity, citizenship, belonging and patriotism *à la* Trump, Trump, in his populism, falls short of rising above the very contradictions of which he blames the liberal and conservative elites who disagree with him. Additionally, as Fuchs demonstrates, Trump's rise is much more "the story of how a billionaire came to political power" than of bringing about "a non-elitist people's politics" – which certainly did not happen. If anything, Trump ensured "the rise of the capitalist class as directly ruling and dominating politics" (Fuchs 2018: 86).

At the bottom rungs of ever-diminishing indicators of Americanness, Trump has consistently located Africans and Latinos, the ultimate revulsions (in his view) around which he built his build-a-wall anti-immigrant campaign for the office of President. All manner of crimes and afflictions are fabricated and projected onto these purportedly reckless sweat-footed "barbarians" or "animals" from "shithole countries" who keep knocking at the doors of civilisation that whiteness and its unfathomable genius have made possible in Europe and the United States of America. Racial Darwinism is a constant insinuation in Trump's speeches and tweets.

Some would see in Trump's insinuations on racial superiority a suggestion that he shares in the belief that it is possible and indeed desirable to invest in producing thoroughbred human beings as implied in racehorse theory eugenics. As Isenberg argues and substantiates in *White Trash*, eugenicists have the habit of comparing "good human stock to thoroughbreds, equating the wellborn with superior ability and inherited fitness" (Isenberg 2016: Chapter 8). Enchanted by the idea of "human thoroughbreds", it is not uncommon in a political rally in an overwhelmingly white state such as Minnesota for Trump to suggest racial superiority by telling his white audience: "You have good genes, you know that, right?" He touts his "Ivy league education", being a "smart guy" and "good genes" in which "I'm a believer". If and when he claims his German roots, it is to indicate how proud he is of his German blood, and the order and strength with which it imbues him.[458] Trump has said he would prefer "short guys that wear yarmulkes every day" to count his money than have "Black guys counting my money!" Even though his daughter and son-in-law are Jewish and American, Trump sometimes comes across as unable to imagine Jews being loyal to any other political community than Israel, refuses to criticise rabid anti-Semites and shares in anti-Semite conspiracy theories, including stereotypes about Jews as "money-grubbing chislers".[459]

With reference to African, Haitian and Latino immigrants, during an immigration agenda-setting meeting in 2018 at the White House, Trump reportedly slurred: "Why are we having all these people from shithole countries come here?" He singled out and summarily condemned Haitians as all infected with HIV/AIDS. "Why do we need more Haitians? Take them out", he instructed his immigration administrators, adding that if he had his way, more immigrants should be attracted from Europe, especially from the Scandinavian countries such as Norway.[460] Is this what is at the heart of his campaign slogan of "Make America Great Again"? The slogan is reportedly code for "Make America White Again". If there is little or no room for blacks, browns, LGBTQI+ people, Muslims and Jews in such a carefully distilled idea and ideal of being American and being great again, what does the future hold for the mobile "shitholes" of the world? If white lives matter to Trump as president, why should this cancel out the fact that black and brown lives matter as well? What democracy is possible with a president who seeks legitimacy only among an estimated one-third of the nationals and citizens of the country he leads? What are the merits of a leader without a sense of the history of mobility of persons, ideas and ideals that has gone into the making of the unity in diversity of being American, which he is called upon to protect, preserve and enrich with visionary creativity, imagination and unrelenting open-mindedness?

Those inclined to a more inclusive America during the Trump administration must have felt truly demotivated when the Supreme Court decided by a vote of 5 to 4 to uphold as constitutional the third version of Trump's Travel Ban. The Trump policy applied to travellers from five countries with overwhelmingly Muslim populations – Iran, Libya, Somalia, Syria and Yemen. It also affected two non-Muslim countries, North Korea and some Venezuelan government officials and their families. This decision came despite the acknowledgement by "Chief Justice Roberts […] that Mr. Trump had made many statements concerning his desire to impose a 'Muslim ban'". He recounted the president's call for a "total and complete shutdown of Muslims entering the United States", and he noted that the president had said that "Islam hates us" and had asserted that the United States was "having problems with Muslims coming into the country".[461] Justice Sonia Sotomayor, one of the four who dissented (the others being Justices Stephen Breyer, Ruth Bader Ginsburg and Elena Kagan), said: "History will not look kindly on the court's misguided decision today, nor should it", adding that "a reasonable observer would conclude that the Proclamation was motivated by anti-Muslim animus". According to Justice Sotomayor, the majority of judges had reached their judgement by "ignoring the facts, misconstruing our legal precedent and turning a blind eye to the pain and suffering the Proclamation inflicts upon countless families and individuals, many of whom are United States citizens".[462] A much more unifying presidency would have given the judges a much more accommodating, productive and enriching case for citizenship as belonging that is constantly renegotiated with inspiration from mobility and incompleteness as universals.

Trump poses as a non-elitist anti-establishment populist and is hailed as a champion by those Hillary Clinton regrettably referred to during the 2016 presidential campaign as "deplorables". Among those who hail him are millions of American nationals who genuinely fall through the cracks of the material fulfilment of citizenship and The American Dream, despite the drudgery and sacrifices of toiling to make a decent living (Bruder 2017; Wilkerson 2020). Some, Wilkerson maintains, are "willing to accept short-term discomfort, forgo health insurance, risk contamination of the water and air, and even die to protect their long-term interest" in the caste system and racialised hierarchy as they have known it (Wilkerson 2020: 327). Trump, however, is unashamedly dedicated to stripping everyone else of the dignity of citizenship and/or humanity (Reid 2019). His idea of populism, citizenship and belonging are thus driven by a zero-sum logic of absolute winners and absolute losers, one that defines and pursues a regressive nationalism of ever diminishing circles of inclusion. Ultimately, pursued to its logical conclusion, Trump ends us as the last man standing; his idea of citizenship starts and ends with him.

As we noted from the outset, populism is like a container that leaves its users the choice to fill it up as they see fit. How do you fill yours up? Is there room for others in your Noah's Ark of populism? How would you go about deciding whom to include and those to exclude? What criteria would you use for the choices you make? Are the choices permanent or could there be reason to revisit them? What reasons would push you to revisit them? What idea of society or community informs what we choose to fill our populism container with? The questions are endless, but they provide some food for thought on the work in progress, nature and contingency of citizenship and belonging together, and the risks we run when we treat others as less deserving to be included, or as debris.

In this regard, J. D. Vance reminds us that "for those [...] lucky enough to live the American Dream, the demons of the life [...] left behind continue to chase" them (Vance 2016: Introduction). What, for example, does it mean for one's solidarities, to emerge as a middle-class white from a community of working-class whites who share a common ethnicity? The left-behinds can make or mar. They invite or remind us not to be overly effusive in our celebration of personal success, especially when this has not been adequately extended to include others with whom we share affinities, be these by race, ethnicity or gender, to name a few. Success does not amount to much if it is not inclusive. That J. D. Vance is a rising star within Republican ranks, reportedly being seriously considered as a senatorial candidate for his state of Ohio, is indicative of the fact that elites are not always born or reproduced, and that elitism can be achieved.[463] The history of the USA is full of examples of people who rose from ordinary beginnings into elite circles, with some, like Barack Obama, making it all the way to the presidency. Vance has in common with Trump the fact of being a prestigiously educated elite speaking on behalf of his people, in addition to the fact of doing so through the Republican party (Lauret 2020), and drawing attention to fact that it is possible to claim a racial and an ethnic identity in the US concurrently. The fact of elitism being acquired should come as no surprise to anyone in Africa, where memories are still fresh of how colonialism and colonial education turned the tables on the traditional political, cultural and economic elites, bringing about a new meritocratic elite that has distinguished itself at whitening up and zombie-like mimicry of Europe and North-America, while paying lip service to the imperatives of contestation, decolonisation, Africanisation and sovereignty (Nyamnjoh 2012, 2016).

Many of the arguments against populism, even when sympathetic to the issues it raises, are skewed because they are mostly garnered by a belief in the superiority and/or universality of liberal democracy and the elite forms of governance it inspires (Müller 2016: 75–99). It seems to be taken for granted that populism is a negative development in the danger it poses to liberal democracy, which is presented as the most perfected form of government possible. Stated and unstated assumptions of completeness also underpin these arguments. Many seem to argue – implicitly or explicitly – for a return to cherished values, traditions and the idea of nation-states frozen out of history and bound together by common cultures, beliefs and practices that are equally bounded. Very few seem to problematise the notion that such coherent cultures and value systems ever existed as uncontested and the extent to which they can continue to be justified in an increasingly multicultural context. This begs the question of which or whose values should be embraced, and with what consequences for those who are excluded, delegitimated or relegated to the margins. For anyone who falls through the cracks of conventional or taken-for-granted parameters of identity and identification, anyone who blurs the boundary markers of neat and predictable dichotomies in citizenship, belonging and nationality, the apparent consensus in much of the arguments I have examined should make one uncomfortable, because it feels like minority rights and the rights of the majority poor (defined quantitatively or qualitatively, culturally, politically or economically), in the end, will have to be sacrificed for the good of a contrived elite consensus.

Hence my opening argument in this book in favour of locating our discussion and theorisation of populism, citizenship and belonging within the framework of incompleteness. It is a framework that invites us to disabuse ourselves of problematic dichotomies and zero-sum games of absolute winners and absolute losers. It fosters recognition and provision for interconnections and interdependencies, which in the case of populism points to the need for elites and those labelled as populists to embrace much more convivial forms of co-existence. Thus, as Kazin has argued, "while populism can be dangerous, it may also be necessary" in that it challenges "those who wield political or economic power [to] live up to the ideals of equal opportunity and self-government to which they routinely pay lip service" (Kazin 2017[1995]: xv). Kazin's argument echoes Müller's invitation for us to see populism as "a permanent shadow of modern representative democracy, and a constant peril" that should help us understand "the distinctive features" as well as "the shortcomings" of democracies beyond liberalism (Müller 2016: 11).

Rauch does well to remind us that, "In a war of all against all, charlatans, demagogues, and sociopaths thrive, roaming and pillaging like warlords in a stateless Hobbesian world" (Rauch 2021: 41). Rauch defines a sociopath as:

> [...] someone who does not feel that social norms apply to her and who feels free to pursue naked self-interest whenever she can get away with it. She may conform to laws and constraints imposed from without, but only because doing so is to her benefit. (Rauch 2021: 156).

Put differently, and with Trump in mind, a sociopath is a law to themselves. It is either their way or no way. With a sociopath, no compromise is possible. In a zero-sum context, if everyone were to be a sociopath, what type of society or community would be possible? What does it take for the centre to hold? How do we outwit our biases by creating social truths that are shared, cosmopolitan and not simply confined to our warring but socially distant echo chambers?

Once again, I would like to think the answer lies in incompleteness as a universal attribute of being, and in the humility of compromise and conviviality that comes with recognising and providing for incompleteness. I suppose it is in this sense that Wehler calls for moderation, compromise and civility at the service of hope as a healing balm for American politics post-Trump (Wehler 2019). A much more negotiated and inclusive consensus would entail a deliberate effort to transcend unproductive relativism and dramatising the politics of polarisation, partisanship and contempt. For, as Klein reminds us, polarisation begets polarisation, because:

[…] to appeal to a more polarized public, political institutions and political actors behave in more polarized ways. As political institutions and actors become more polarized, they further polarize the public. This sets off a feedback cycle: to appeal to a yet more polarized public, institutions must polarize further; when faced with yet more polarized institutions, the public polarizes further, and so on (Klein 2020: xix).

The American system, Klein believes, is one which, though defined by political parties, calls for a balance in which there is mistrust for ideologues and partisans, and veneration for centrists, moderates and independents (Klein 2020: 11). It is a system that appeals to recognition and provision for incompleteness and the potential for humility and conviviality it inspires as a way of rising above polarisation and divisiveness.

There is need to interrogate on a constant basis often taken-for-granted tendencies to standardise, routinise and simplify identities. Such tendencies encourage problematic, stereotypical and summary distinction, often on the basis of superficial indicators, between insiders and outsiders, the popular and the elite. This tends to be the case even if some concession is made to a measure of inclusivity and levelling of the cultural, social, economic and political playing fields. In this connection, the following observation by Fareed Zakaria is pertinent. He recognises the "the fissure between relatively better-educated urbanites and less-educated rural populations" as "the new dividing line in Western politics". Those who see themselves or who are perceived as outsiders in terms with such class, economic or cultural fissures, "feel ignored or looked down upon and feel deep resentment toward metropolitan elites", who are perceived to be at the origin of such cleavages.[464] Zakaria writes:

> […] we seem to need a handful of brainiacs who will, with computers and robots, chart the course for the future. So […] the ordinary person, who doesn't have a fancy degree, who doesn't attend TED Talks, who doesn't have capital or connections, will reasonably wonder: Where does that leave me?[465]

Zakaria's sentiment is echoed by Badones, who sees in populism "a strategy of desperation, pursued by people whose policy preferences have been excluded from the political debate", although, as he points out, "the populists usually lose" in such debates. If populism, "as a response to the rhetorical dominance of liberal intellectuals in polite political society" is not to be ignored, as Badones and many others have argued, one cannot expect to attend to populism and its legitimate demands satisfactorily within a framework of zero-sum games of absolute winners and absolute losers that sell the illusion that completeness is possible and achievable (Badones 2018: Chapter 5). What populism needs is salesmen and women who are firmly grounded in the nuanced complexities of the communities and situations they inhabit locally, nationally and globally, and not those who are more eager in salesmanship, willing and dealing than in the substance of a sale, a deal or a transaction. Populism could very well be "a last-gasp strategy for breaking through the expert consensus on the universe of sound policy options, a strategy for challenging the authority of experts to determine the boundaries of legitimate political discourse" (Badones 2018: Chapter 5). Known for far fewer clear-cut long-term victories than the short-term enthusiasm it generates, populism is a timely wake up call to take seriously the reality of incompleteness and the conviviality for which it calls.

If populism is a problem, it is not one the elites, liberal or otherwise, can wish away or hope to solve alone or in gestures of goodwill to the dispossessed and debris of their modernism – neoliberalism or otherwise – and globalisation endeavours (Judis 2018; Lind 2020). In this connection, Badones warns of the danger posed if "liberal intellectuals increasingly dismiss the moral right of less-educated people to have opinions that conflict with the consensus wisdom of the expert class". For, as he contends, it is only normal to expect of functioning democracies "that the most exalted experts engage seriously with the mundane views of ordinary citizens". In this regard, far from being something negative to be disparaged and demonised, populism ensures that the liberal intellectuals and expert class live up to this expectation. "It forces the political class to respect the dignity of the electorate" (Badones 2018: Chapter 5).

Could populism serve as "the Biblical flood that has the potential to wash away a dysfunctional party system and its sterile political covenants"? As Badones sees it, populists as wells as the elites that have given them cause for action would have to disabuse themselves of the illusive pursuit of completeness in the spirit of zero-sum games of absolute winners and absolute losers. This would require paying close attention to factors that produce and/or offer an enabling environment for the likes of Trump (and varying degrees thereof) to make opportunism of opportunities, and socialising the young to domestic and not celebrate narcissism. For "the survivors of that flood to rebuild a better political home for the people and their representatives", as Badones (2018: Chapter 5) rightly calls for, incompleteness and the conviviality it inspires should be embraced wholeheartedly in thought and in practice.

Institutions, communities, societies, nations and civilisations, like Tutuola's "The Complete Gentleman", do not spontaneously occur. Each and every one of them are the produce of human creativity and ingenuity through mobility, encounters and interactions anchored on the reality of debt and indebtedness that activate (charge, discharge, recharge) the incompleteness of being and becoming. Humans are not born cultivated, even as they are born into communities, cultures, and particular institutional contexts and social configurations. Neither "The people" nor "The Elites" are a spontaneous occurrence; they are actively produced and purposefully imbued with a programme of action and can thus be deactivated and reactivated with a new consciousness to fulfil much more inclusive pursuits. Cultural values, just as patriotism, are learnt and can be unlearnt and relearnt, with time, vision and practice.

It is possible for a human being to acquire cosmopolitan credentials through their capacity and appetite for encountering, navigating and negotiating multiple cultural margins that make of them a truly composite being with an Ubuntu disposition. As long as this does not intoxicate them with pretensions of superiority and completeness, they are all the better for it and can serve as an example to others about the sort of bridging of divides that is possible. Just like Tutuola's "The Skull", as humans, we produce, reproduce and/or contest our worlds and our realities through our relationships and interactions with one another, as well as with our physical, social, cultural, economic and political environments. As every human effort, the world and realities we embrace and are familiar with can be tinkered with, remade in part or in whole, or completely discarded with the passage of time, from one generation to another, or when the debt collectors come knocking with impatient insistence and rupture-seeking zero-sum rage.

Incompleteness and dynamism in human effort should spur us to explore more convivial ways of being and becoming in our creative diversity, with humility and openness. We do not have to unravel to a sterile completely deactivated essence of our incompleteness in the manner of Tutuola's "The Skull" to learn the important lesson that we are all incomplete. Life and living are the produce of activating mobility and contact and constantly acknowledging and being humbled about being who we are because of others (humans and non-humans). Put differently, everything does not have to be rooted in a disembodied I and the unified and singular self. Nor do we need to fear and stigmatise being dependent and interdependent once we take seriously the ubiquity of incompleteness. Everything does not have to be mine or yours, us and others in radically dichotomised terms and compartments, as if the very idea of community, mobility and interaction were dead and buried forever. Serious consideration should be given to a form of co-existence informed by inextricable entanglements – manglements even (in the sense of the seamless blending into a cosmopolitan whole of all the borrowings by "The Skull" in the process of self-activation towards metamorphosing into "The Complete Gentleman") – that imposes the need for an ethic of eating and being eaten to guarantee living and letting live (Nyamnjoh 2018a).

All we really need is not so much a radical break through debts completely repaid, for that would mark the very death of the idea of sociality and humanity. Rather, what we need is an arrangement in which we recognise and provide for debt and indebtedness as a permanent feature of being and becoming as the incomplete and otherwise dependent beings that we all are (Nyamnjoh 2015). With humility, and disabused of all ambitions of completeness, we can free ourselves and our world of various, and ultimately unproductive, forms of violence and violations, by imagining and actualising a truly convivial existence. This, I admit, is a tall challenge, with the current world fuelled by ambitions of dominance, and the erroneous belief that completeness is possible and attainable and that a shared truth is beyond attainment. As long as we limit ourselves to prevailing prisms of oppressive individuality devoid of recognition of attachment and connection through productive encounters and shared stories, we will always be confronted with the question: How do we make space for conviviality and the practice of humility when there is so much anger and disparity in the world? How is conviviality possible with such skewed power relations among races, ethnicities, cultures, geographies, classes, genders, sexes and generations?

What a conundrum. How would we feel if life were reduced to a perpetual cycle or eternal rerun of violence and violation, as victims turn the tables, however short-lived, on their oppressors without ever really tackling the fact of oppression? How comfortable would we be trading one dogma for another instead of systematically challenging the very idea of a world dictated by and framed around rigid dogmatic thinking? "Dogmatic people," Bergland claims, "may be less likely to resolve uncertainty by seeking new facts."[466] However painful our experiences of injustice, the world cannot become a better place if all we do is wait for our turn to be on top – to take our turn at intolerance, arrogance and zero-sum pretensions to power and achievement, and to inflict injustice in turn on those who inflicted it on us, or on a new set of victims. Or to become disrespectful and violent when we feel the rug of privilege moving beneath us.

There is much to be gained in an inclusivity that provides for both perceived victors and perceived losers. As Reno reminds us, "whatever is strong—strong loves and strong truths—leads to oppression, while liberty and prosperity require the reign of weak loves and weak truths". In addressing inclusion as one of "our leading imperatives", Reno suggests we yield for "a god who softens differences" to "open things up", not a strong god of absolutes and dictatorship, be this informed by a commitment to a single truth or to relativism without limits (Reno 2019: Introduction).

Similarly, Bretherton stresses the need to seek ways of rendering productive what he terms the "mutual antagonistic suspicion" that is an inevitable and justifiable feature of democracies, with the understanding that "What is popular can be idiotic and simplistic, and what is done by elites can be self-serving, corrupt, and oppressive even while it proclaims itself enlightened, progressive, and for the good of all." He sees "Democratic politics" as "that process through which these antagonisms are addressed peaceably rather than violently" (Bretherton 2019: 28).

Thus, even as one agrees with Reno that those who "deserve to rule" are those "who trumpet diversity, innovation, and transgression" – "Those who transgress, break down boundaries, and include the marginalized are seen as exemplary citizens" – and "not the 'clingers' who are susceptible to 'nostalgia' and vulnerable to 'fear,' if not outright racism" (Reno 2019: Chapter Four), it is important, even in such a model of leadership, to accommodate beyond tokenism the latter category of citizenry.

Hence the need to take seriously, Lind's idea of democratic pluralism of political checks and balances reinforced by social checks and balances, along with a healthy respect for "hard-won and lasting consensus among negotiating parties, classes and creeds" and not merely "on fluctuating numerical majorities" (Lind 2020: Chapter 9).

I hope this book has been plentiful in perspectives about what we choose to fill our populism container with, always conscious, as we should be, that we do not have a monopoly of the populism container or of its contents, just as we do not have a monopoly of incompleteness or of ambitions of self-activation. Non-exclusivity of being, I hope, is important towards making us better appreciate and cherish each interaction with people (familiar and strange), because it creates a less hierarchical scheme of relationships.

In a world of interconnecting and interdependent incompleteness, there is need to foster greater social and cultural integration with selflessness and commitment to our common humanity. This points to a future trapped neither in delusions of superiority nor in the celebration of victimhood. A future disabused of the raging inferno of sterile relativism in a post-truth world of algorithms gone wild is possible, a future in which echo chambers and their universes of splintered reality give way to the circulation of diverse narratives that reflect the true complexities, predicaments and interdependencies of people and cultures. However, the failure to enable greater integration beyond elite circles combines with ignorance and arrogance to guarantee the continued production of malcontents (Brabazon et al. 2019).

Permanent alertness must prevail – alertness to the divisiveness and frustrations that slow socioeconomic transformation and the reconfiguration of attitudes, beliefs and relationships favouring greater mutual recognition and accommodation (Welfens 2019). It is through recognition of the capacity of all and sundry, in the USA and everywhere else in an interconnected world, to act and interact, bearing in mind the realities of others in time and space, that an appropriate citizenship inspired by the universality of incompleteness, mobility, debt and indebtedness actualises beyond the pages of a Constitution and its Bill of Rights and an imaginary America Dream or other dream.

Fruitful democracy and citizenship are far from possible in contexts where the myth of self-cultivation, self-activation and self-management is uncritically internalised and reproduced in abstraction with effortless abundance and callous disregard for the debris it generates and multiplies. If belonging to bubbles and echo chambers comes naturally to us as humans, there is little in our nature as humans, to stop us from cultivating empathy by belonging to bubbles and echo chambers which cut across divides that are narrowly framed and articulated along racial, ethnic, cultural, class, geographical, gender, sexual, generational, religious or educational lines. What holds promise are democracy, citizenship and belonging inspired by the imperatives of the universality of incompleteness, not as a negative condition that must be transcended by perpetuating the illusion of "The Complete Gentleman" as a permanence but as a reality and a disposition with enormous potential for efficacy in action and interaction among a myriad of incomplete beings.

Afterword

You Have been Warned – Ideas Have Consequences

So – ideas *do* matter. The images, concepts and patterns of thought which we use as tools to understand ourselves and to make sense of the world around us, *do* shape who we are, how our identities are formed, what we experience as "reality" and how we consequently behave and act in this world. We cannot escape the deeply embedded hermeneutical nature of our existence. Like all living things, we prevail by virtue of a constant process of communication, interpretation, response and re-interpretation.

This is the lasting impression with which the reader is left after perusing Nyamnjoh's wide-ranging, rich and comprehensive analysis of populism – with Trump as its ultimate and erratic exponent. Hidden under the more visible manifestations of the phenomenon is a deep structure which steers and, in many instances, predetermines the outcome on the surface.

In the case of populism, Nyamnjoh shows how the whole conundrum is premised on a set of binary oppositions in the form of either/or choices, "them" and "us" divisions and inclusive or exclusive behaviours. The inability of populism to break out of this binary mould severely limits its options for response. At the root of these phenomena lies an inward-looking, restrictive and constantly shrinking concept of identity which is set in opposition to and experienced as being under threat from other identities – identities which are likewise conceived in exclusivist terms. Identity itself consequently becomes a site of resistance which translates into a permanent anti-attitude, incapable of any meaningful compromise, co-operation and solidarity. No wonder that violence in the end becomes the only remaining course of action (as the events on 6 January 2021 at the United States Capitol illustrate), resulting in a kind of identity politics which rips social cohesion apart. The mindset of exclusion also creates silos of isolation in other areas like the media and truth regimes – leading to the emergence of "fake news" and the fabrication of "alternative facts". Because there is no willingness or obligation to engage, these alternative realities are withdrawn from critical scrutiny and the usual processes of verification, enabling the emergence of alternative (but sequestered) realities. Longing for a more simplistic world, the rejection of complexity lies at the core of the appeal of populism.

The basic inward orientation and inherent propensity for exclusion consequently attract related and compatible concepts, attitudes and practices. Collectively, these form an intricate web which determines the mindset undergirding populism in its various guises. Because the latter is usually hidden from view, operating almost unconsciously, it cannot be countered with a single or simple remedy, but requires an equally comprehensive response – in other words, an alternative matrix of interrelated concepts, values and strategies.

The Achilles heel of populism in its present form – relying on binary oppositions, unbridgeable chasms and exclusive, mono-identities – is that it is strikingly unsuitable to meet the challenges of a complex, interconnected and increasingly globalised world. Binary thinking may have demonstrated its power in the development of our digital world in a spectacular way, but that is not the case in an interwoven, multi-faceted and pluralistic environment. In all fairness, it must be acknowledged that populism is in essence a protest against this engulfing world and it could therefore hardly be expected to be in harmony with its "enemy". But whatever the merits of the movement, in the end it has to contend with the fact that isolation is always relative and that it inescapably forms part of a larger whole which it cannot ignore. The inability to break out of its binary mould renders populism incapable of responding effectively to a complex world which it no longer can control nor contain. This mismatch leads to a constant stream of aberrant responses – responses which are ineffective at best and destructive at worst.

As an alternative to this state of affairs, Nyamnjoh takes his cue from *incompleteness* which becomes the "master symbol" of his proposal – the "prism" and the "framework" he utilises for his analysis.

It is important to observe more closely how this alternative approach comes into being. It starts with *conceptualising* a different idea, to whose emergence a number of factors can contribute – it is something which is imagined (visual), but also contemplated (cognitive) and finally implemented (performative). The birth of a new idea is a fascinating process in itself, but conceptualising an alternative is just the first step. Secondly, it needs to be *interpreted*. "Incompleteness" functions as a shibboleth – it is such a concentrated word with a range of (often widely differing) associations that it needs to be closer defined. For some, it has negative associations – a task which was not completed, and thus failed. For others it is a passive term, lacking dynamism and energy. Such generic concepts can lead to both positive and negative outcomes. Nyamnjoh is thus at pains to explicate what he has in mind. For him, the essence is the *openness,* and thus the potential *inclusivity*, which the term signifies. In a hundred-and-eighty-degree turnaround from the inward-looking focus of populism, the orientation is now in the opposite direction – fanning outwards in ever widening circles. This openness and willingness to include is complemented by the concept of the *mobility* of ideas and of people, signifying the readiness to engage, to cross borders, to consider alternatives and to change one's mind. Recognising the limits of one's own insights and abilities (thus not claiming to be the "perfect gentleman") engenders *humility* and the willingness to entertain what is different and strange, to co-operate, negotiate and to find common ground, even if only in transit on an ever-unfolding journey of inclusivity and its unfathomableness. The desire to dominate is replaced by the acknowledgement of one's indebtedness to others and the fostering of a spirit of *conviviality.* This prepares the ground to move from seeing the self as something static and unalterable to the concept of an enriched and multi-faceted identity in which the self is constantly renewed and expanded in interaction with the other – as a "permanent work in progress".

In this way, Nyamnjoh offers a different matrix of interrelated and mutually supporting ideas to serve as the basis for an alternative approach to the challenges of a complex world. However, in order to be effective, a third step is needed in addition to conceptualisation and interpretation, namely a strategy which will ensure the effective *implementation* of these concepts. Such an approach should reflect the same inclusiveness and complexity of the alternative matrix – simply rejecting and replacing the matrix of populism with a different approach, as if it were another zero-sum game, militates against the very spirit of inclusiveness and incompleteness and merely continues a binary mode of thinking. Not only *what* we think, but also *how* we think needs to be changed if an alternative matrix is to make a difference. In essence this would mean to understand the "local" and the "global" not as opposites, but to find a more balanced and differentiated way to conceptualise and explore the dynamic interrelatedness between these two poles.

We are therefore challenged to develop a more nuanced, inclusive and nimble-footed way of thinking and acting. This would require us to move beyond the mere rejection of or opposition to populism and to develop a fuller understanding of what makes this movement so attractive. A starting point could be to acknowledge the validity of populism's protest against the excesses of unbridled globalisation and the arrogance of elites who often regard "ordinary people" with disdain and subject them to an own brand of exclusivism. But the desire to participate in how you are governed must be balanced with the need for expertise, a strong sense of belonging while embracing global mobility and a firm set of values, including the tolerance of other views.

Ironically, populism can also be understood as a plea for inclusion by those who feel left behind. The same applies to the nationalist longing to "reassert the primacy of the nation over distant and unaccountable international organizations", as long as it is understood that this "nation" remains surrounded by and depends on the recognition of and interaction with other nations in a network of conviviality driven by the comparative advantage of incompleteness. Withdrawal into bunkered enclaves of isolation is not a sustainable strategy. Retreat and regrouping have value only as a temporary respite to prepare for a better *re*-entry into the world of multiple relations and complex interaction in which a compositeness of identity and identification is welcomed and encouraged. Separate states and nations form part of a larger reality from which they can never totally isolate themselves. Like in a living cell, borders are necessary to allow the cell to grow and prosper, but these are always porous and never permanent.

What applies to collective identity also holds for the self-consciousness of the individual. The trend towards mono-identities cannot be countered by suppressing or denying the power of identity itself. The well-being of the individual depends on a healthy self-consciousness and the positive acceptance of the self. This "rootedness" should rather be valued and used as a sound basis on which to build a more enriched and diverse identity and to harness its power to expand the horizons, perspectives and capabilities of the self.

In a situation where the mediating role of the media has become so pervasive, resulting in an intensified contestation of facts, veracity and "reality", the plurality of perspectives and the diversity of experience inevitably give rise to disparate and often conflicting renditions of the truth and the proffering of "alternative realities". In a time when the constructed nature of what we call "reality" is generally acknowledged, it comes as no surprise that populists forge their own version. It is when this configuration is presented as the absolute truth with uncontested validity and withdrawn from the normal processes of verification and the scrutiny of rigorous peer review and validation that the possibility of finding common ground evaporate.

To repeat – the *way* we think is as important as *what* we think. Not only the concept, but the *modus* in which an alternative matrix is nursed and nudged into being should reflect the same inclusiveness, humility, indebtedness, incompleteness and conviviality which gave rise to the idea in the first place.

For this, we need to become comfortable with complexity itself, not constantly seeking to contain or simplify it, but explore the myriad of possibilities which it opens. Likewise, mobility provides us with the room to manoeuvre, navigate and reconfigure the world. It also requires that we make peace with the mediated nature of our existence, with the fundamental hermeneutical processes which underlie our interactions with all we encounter and through which we arrive at insights, ideas and alternatives – and use this hermeneutical potential to venture into the unknown and to act in terms of newly discovered alternatives.

Ideas, after all, *should* have consequences.

Bernard C. Lategan
Professor, Founding Director,
Stellenbosch Institute for Advanced Study (STIAS)

Notes

[1] Karin Priester (cited in Benveniste et al. (2016: 3) refers to populism as a chameleon phenomenon.

[2] David Klemperer, Interview: Chantal Mouffe on democracy, populism, and why the Left needs to read Spinoza, 19 August 2021. https://tocqueville21.com/blog-info/interview-chantal-mouffe-on-democracy-populism-and-why-the-left-needs-to-read-spinoza/

[3] Centre for Development and Enterprise (CDE), Francis Fukuyama on Contemporary Populism. https://www.cde.org.za/wp-content/uploads/2019/08/Contemporary-Populism-final.pdf, August 2019

[4] Donald Trump inauguration speech full transcript, January 21, 2017. www.belfasttelegraph.co.uk/news/world-news/donald-trump-inauguration-speech-full-transcript-35386639.html

[5] David Smith and Philip Oltermann. Merkel and Trump can't hide fundamental differences in first visit. www.theguardian.com/us-news/2017/mar/17/trump-merkel-white-house-trade-refugees-wiretapping

[6] M. S. The Economist explains: What is populism? www.economist.com/the-economist-explains/2016/12/19/what-is-populism

[7] Maureen Dowd, Trump has been wearing a mask for years, 24 May 2020. https://www.irishtimes.com/news/world/us/maureen-dowd-trump-has-been-wearing-a-mask-for-years-1.4261242; Covid Dreams, Trump Nightmares, 23 May 2020, https://www.nytimes.com/2020/05/23/opinion/sunday/trump-mask-coronavirus.html

[8] Marcia Pally: 'Throw the bastards out': an American tradition from settlers to Trump (The Guardian, 8 Sep 2016). https://www.theguardian.com/us-news/2016/sep/08/donald-trump-us-history-religion-change

[9] Marcia Pally: 'Throw the bastards out': an American tradition from settlers to Trump (The Guardian, 8 Sep 2016). https://www.theguardian.com/us-news/2016/sep/08/donald-trump-us-history-religion-change

[10] Centre for Development and Enterprise (CDE), Francis Fukuyama on Contemporary Populism. https://www.cde.org.za/wp-content/uploads/2019/08/Contemporary-Populism-final.pdf, August 2019

[11] Michael Penn, Why is populism so unpopular in Japan? 10 June 2021. https://www.aljazeera.com/features/2021/6/10/why-is-populism-so-unpopular-in-japan

[12] Pankaj Mishra: The Divided States: Trump's inauguration and how democracy has failed (The Guardian, 13 Jan 2017).

https://www.theguardian.com/books/2017/jan/13/divided-states-trump-america-failed-democracy

[13] David Klemperer, Interview: Chantal Mouffe on democracy, populism, and why the Left needs to read Spinoza, 19 August 2021. https://tocqueville21.com/blog-info/interview-chantal-mouffe-on-democracy-populism-and-why-the-left-needs-to-read-spinoza/

[14] David Klemperer, Interview: Chantal Mouffe on democracy, populism, and why the Left needs to read Spinoza, 19 August 2021. https://tocqueville21.com/blog-info/interview-chantal-mouffe-on-democracy-populism-and-why-the-left-needs-to-read-spinoza/

[15] Robert Costa, Seung Min Kim and Josh Dawsey, Trump calls governors 'weak,' urges them to use force against unruly protests, 2 June 2020. https://www.washingtonpost.com/politics/trump-governors-george-floyd-protests/2020/06/01/430a6226-a421-11ea-b619-3f9133bbb482_story.html

[16] Clare Foran: American Secessionists Dream of Declaring Independence (The Atlantic, 2016). https://www.theatlantic.com/politics/archive/2016/07/secession-trump-brexit/489689/

[17] Ian Bremmer: The Era of American Global Leadership Is Over. Here's What Comes Next (TIME, 19 Dec 2016). https://time.com/4606071/american-global-leadership-is-over/

[18] Michael J. Mazarr: The Once and Future Order: What Comes After Hegemony? (Foreign Affairs, Jan/Feb 2017). https://www.foreignaffairs.com/articles/2016-12-12/once-and-future-order

[19] Yascha Mounk: Illiberal Democracy or Undemocratic Liberalism? (Project Syndicate 9 June 2016). https://www.project-syndicate.org/commentary/trump-european-populism-technocracy-by-yascha-mounk-1-2016-06

[20] Neil Vigdor, Rush Limbaugh, Awarded Presidential Medal of Freedom at State of the Union, 4 February 2020. https://www.nytimes.com/2020/02/04/us/politics/rush-limbaugh-medal-of-freedom.html

[21] Yascha Mounk: Illiberal Democracy or Undemocratic Liberalism? (Project Syndicate 9 June 2016). https://www.project-syndicate.org/commentary/trump-european-populism-technocracy-by-yascha-mounk-1-2016-06

[22] Anatole Kaletsky: Nationalism Will Go Bankrupt (Project Syndicate, 20 Jun 2018). https://www.project-syndicate.org/commentary/nationalism-fails-to-lift-living-standards-by-anatole-kaletsky-2018-06

[23] James Petras: Anglo-America: Regression and Reversion in the Modern World (Global Research, 31 May 2016). https://www.globalresearch.ca/anglo-america-regression-and-reversion-in-

the-modern-world/5528214

[24] Edward Luce: The Anglo-American democracy problem (Financial Times, 14 Jun 2017). https://www.ft.com/content/58bf0c00-5052-11e7-bfb8-997009366969

[25] Ivan Krastev: The Rise and Fall of European Meritocracy (The New York Times). https://www.nytimes.com/2017/01/17/opinion/the-rise-and-fall-of-european-meritocracy.html

[26] Daniel Gros: Is Globalization Really Fueling Populism? (Project Syndicate, 6 May 2016). https://www.project-syndicate.org/commentary/understand-factors-behind-rising-populism-by-daniel-gros-2016-05

[27] Federico Pieraccini: The Strategic Triangle That Is Changing The World (Strategic Culture Foundation, 11 March 2017). https://www.strategic-culture.org/news/2017/03/11/strategic-triangle-that-changing-world/

[28] John Lloyd: Political decency is going to hell (Jakarta Globe, 3 June 2016). https://jakartaglobe.id/news/political-decency-going-hell/

[29] John Lloyd: Political decency is going to hell (Jakarta Globe, 3 June 2016). https://jakartaglobe.id/news/political-decency-going-hell/

[30] Javier Corrales: Polarize and Conquer (The New York Times, 8 Oct 2017). https://www.nytimes.com/2017/10/08/opinion/political-polarization-trump.html

[31] Richard J. Evans: The Breakup (The Nation, 17 Dec 2019). https://www.thenation.com/article/archive/empire-democracy-simon-reid-henry-book-review

[32] John Gray, David Cameron and the great sell-out, 21 April 2021. https://www.newstatesman.com/politics/uk/2021/04/david-cameron-and-great-sell-out

[33] BBC, Archbishop Tutu in his own words, 22 July 2010, accessed 13 June 2021. https://www.bbc.com/news/world-africa-10734471

[34] Jill Lepore: A New Americanism: Why a Nation Needs a National Story (Foreign Affairs, March/April 2019 (5 Feb 2019)). https://www.foreignaffairs.com/articles/united-states/2019-02-05/new-americanism-nationalism-jill-lepore

[35] Whither nationalism? (The Economist, 19 Dec 2017). https://www.economist.com/christmas-specials/2017/12/19/whither-nationalism

[36] Whither nationalism? (The Economist, 19 Dec 2017). https://www.economist.com/christmas-specials/2017/12/19/whither-nationalism

[37] Whither nationalism? (The Economist, 19 Dec 2017). https://www.economist.com/christmas-specials/2017/12/19/whither-

nationalism

³⁸ The ideas of liberalism's greatest thinkers (The Economist, 2 Aug 2018). https://www.economist.com/leaders/2018/08/02/the-ideas-of-liberalisms-greatest-thinkers

³⁹ Gavin Jacobson: The complex roots of populism (New Statesman, 28 Nov 2018). https://www.newstatesman.com/culture/books/2018/11/populism-book-review-muller-eatwell-goodwin-mudde-kaltwasser-mouffe

⁴⁰ Robert Kagan: The strongmen strike back (The Washington Post, 14 Mar 2019). https://www.washingtonpost.com/news/opinions/wp/2019/03/14/feature/the-strongmen-strike-back

⁴¹ Andrew A. Michta: The Sources of the West's Decline (The American Interest, 22 Feb 2019). https://www.the-american-interest.com/2019/02/22/the-sources-of-the-wests-decline/

⁴² Matthijs Rooduijn: Why is populism suddenly all the rage? (The Guardian, 20 Nov 2018). https://www.theguardian.com/world/political-science/2018/nov/20/why-is-populism-suddenly-so-sexy-the-reasons-are-many

⁴³ Rogers Brubaker: Why "Civilization" Is Replacing the Nation (Foreign Affairs, 6 Dec 2017). https://www.foreignaffairs.com/articles/europe/2017-12-06/new-language-european-populism

⁴⁴ John Gray, David Cameron and the great sell-out, 21 April 2021. https://www.newstatesman.com/politics/uk/2021/04/david-cameron-and-great-sell-out

⁴⁵ Keeping Up Appearances S03E04 How To Go On Holiday Without Really Trying. https://www.dailymotion.com/video/x6tcs5s

⁴⁶ Yoni Applebaum, June 24, 2016, "Brexit Right: The U.K.'s vote to leave the European Union betrays a failure of empathy and imagination among its leaders. Will America's political establishment fare any better?".

⁴⁷ Chris Hedges: The New European Fascists (Truthdig, undated). https://www.truthdig.com/articles/the-new-european-fascists/

⁴⁸ *The Economist*, The disruptive rise of English nationalism. https://www.economist.com/britain/2021/03/20/the-disruptive-rise-of-english-nationalism, accessed 25 March 2021

⁴⁹ M. K. Bhadrakumar: Trump and the meltdown of the European project (*Asia Times*, 1 Jul 2018). https://asiatimes.com/2018/07/trump-and-the-meltdown-of-the-european-project/

⁵⁰ Satyajit Das: The world's economic crises are entering a political stage (*Independent*, 24 Jul 2016). https://www.independent.co.uk/voices/world-economic-crisis-brexit-eu-referendum-spain-italy-us-political-stage-results-dangerous-a7153256.html

⁵¹ Tom Batchelor: World on brink of 'post-Western age' as influence of

Europe and US declines, warns report (*Independent*, 14 Feb 2017).
https://www.independent.co.uk/news/world/politics/world-brink-post-western-age-donald-trump-brexit-europe-us-declines-munich-security-conference-a7580511.html

[52] Eric Kaufmann: Good Fences Make Good Politics (*Foreign Affairs*, Sep/Oct 2018). https://www.foreignaffairs.com/reviews/review-essay/2018-08-13/good-fences-make-good-politics

[53] Ivan Krastev and Stephen Holmes: How liberalism became 'the god that failed' in eastern Europe (The Guardian, 24 Oct 2019).
https://www.theguardian.com/world/2019/oct/24/western-liberalism-failed-post-communist-eastern-europe

[54] Eric Kaufmann: Good Fences Make Good Politics (Foreign Affairs Sep/Oct 2018). https://www.foreignaffairs.com/reviews/review-essay/2018-08-13/good-fences-make-good-politics

[55] Our Schumpeter columnist pens a dark farewell (The Economist, 20 Dec 2016). https://www.economist.com/business/2016/12/20/our-schumpeter-columnist-pens-a-dark-farewell

[56] Benjamin Mouffitt, The Trouble with Anti-Populism: Why the Champions of Civility Keep Losing, 14 February 2020.
https://www.theguardian.com/politics/2020/feb/14/anti-populism-politics-why-champions-of-civility-keep-losing

[57] Adam Kirsch and Liesl Schillinger: Which Force is More Harmful to the Arts: Elitism or Populism? (The New York Times, 13 Apr 2017).
https://www.nytimes.com/2017/04/13/books/review/which-force-is-more-harmful-to-the-arts-elitism-or-populism.html

[58] Adam Kirsch and Liesl Schillinger: Which Force is More Harmful to the Arts: Elitism or Populism? (The New York Times, 13 Apr 2017).
https://www.nytimes.com/2017/04/13/books/review/which-force-is-more-harmful-to-the-arts-elitism-or-populism.html

[59] https://en.wikipedia.org/wiki/Keeping_Up_Appearances

[60] Keeping Up Appearances S03E04 How To Go On Holiday Without Really Trying. https://www.dailymotion.com/video/x6tcs5s, accessed 31 May 2021

[61] David Brooks: Is Radicalism Possible Today? (The New York Times, 13 Jun 2017). https://www.nytimes.com/2017/06/13/opinion/is-radicalism-possible-today.html

[62] Andrew Sheng and Xiao Geng: Anger in America (Project Syndicate, 25 Jun 2018). https://www.project-syndicate.org/commentary/angry-americans-elite-failure-by-andrew-sheng-and-xiao-geng-2018-06

[63] Gary Younge: From Trump to Boris Johnson: how the wealthy tell us what 'real folk' want (The Guardian, 23 Nov 2018).
https://www.theguardian.com/commentisfree/2018/nov/23/trump-boris-johnson-rightwing-populists

[64] Larry Elliot: Crash course: what the Great Depression reveals about our future (The Guardian, 4 March 2017). https://www.theguardian.com/society/2017/mar/04/crash-1929-wall-street-what-the-great-depression-reveals-about-our-future

[65] Ian Buruma: The End of the Anglo-American Order (The New York Times Magazine, 29 Nov 2016). https://www.nytimes.com/2016/11/29/magazine/the-end-of-the-anglo-american-order.html

[66] Sophie McBain: The death of American optimism (New Statesman, 13 Feb 2019). https://www.newstatesman.com/2019/02/death-american-optimism

[67] Francis Fukuyama: The Dangers of Disruption (The New York Times, 6 Dec 2016). https://www.nytimes.com/2016/12/06/opinion/the-dangers-of-disruption.html

[68] Dirk Kurbjuweit: One-Hundred Years of Fear: America Has Abdicated Its Leadership of the West (14 Nov 2016). https://www.spiegel.de/international/world/trump-election-means-europe-must-now-lead-west-a-1120929.html

[69] Ken Moak: Democracy is not dying, it is dysfunctional (Asia Times, 14 May 2018). https://asiatimes.com/2018/05/democracy-is-not-dying-it-is-dysfunctional/

[70] Kemal Derviş: The Win-Win Fantasy of Liberal Democracy (Project Syndicate, 5 Dec 2016). https://www.project-syndicate.org/commentary/failure-to-predict-brexit-and-trump-by-kemal-dervis-2016-12

[71] Kemal Derviş: The Win-Win Fantasy of Liberal Democracy (Project Syndicate, 5 Dec 2016). https://www.project-syndicate.org/commentary/failure-to-predict-brexit-and-trump-by-kemal-dervis-2016-12

[72] Duncan Espenshade, Populism in American Elections: Bernie Sanders and Donald Trump, 10 June 2020. https://www.fpri.org/article/2020/06/populism-in-american-elections-bernie-sanders-and-donald-trump/

[73] Paul Mason: The Soviet Union collapsed overnight. Don't assume western democracy will last for ever (The Guardian, 5 Dec 2016). https://www.theguardian.com/commentisfree/2016/dec/05/soviet-union-collapsed-overnight-western-democracy-liberal-order-ussr-russia

[74] Ari Berman: How Endangered Is American Democracy? (The New York Times, 13 Apr 2018). https://www.nytimes.com/2018/04/13/books/review/steven-levitsky-daniel-ziblatt-how-democracies-die.html

[75] Oliver Burkeman: The age of rage: are we really living in angrier times? (The Guardian, 11 May 2019).

https://www.theguardian.com/lifeandstyle/2019/may/11/all-fired-up-are-we-really-living-angrier-times

[76] Christiane Hoffmann: How To Counter the Attack on Democracy (Der Spiegel, 25 Jul 2016).
https://www.spiegel.de/international/world/spiegel-editorial-how-to-counter-the-attack-on-democracy-a-1104567.html

[77] Wolfgang Münchau: The Revenge of globalisation's losers. Its failure in the west is down to democracies' inability to cope with the economic shocks (24 April 2016)
https://www.ft.com/content/a4bfb89a-0885-11e6-a623-b84d06a39ec2

[78] Ian Buruma: The End of the Left/Right Divide? (Project Syndicate, 8 May 2017). https://www.project-syndicate.org/commentary/macron-end-of-left-right-divide-by-ian-buruma-2017-05

[79] Fareed Zakaria: Populism on the March: Why the West Is in Trouble (Foreign Affairs, Nov/Dec 2016).
https://www.foreignaffairs.com/articles/united-states/2016-10-17/populism-march

[80] Martin Wolf: Trump's clash of civilisations v global community (Financial Times, 11 Jul 2017). https://www.ft.com/content/876bd8d8-658a-11e7-8526-7b38dcaef614

[81] Martin Wolf: The Economic Origins Of The Populist Surge (Financial Times, 27 Jun 2017). https://www.ft.com/content/5557f806-5a75-11e7-9bc8-8055f264aa8b

[82] Bret Stephens: The Dying Art of Disagreement (The New York Times, 24 Sep 2017). https://www.nytimes.com/2017/09/24/opinion/dying-art-of-disagreement.html

[83] David Brooks: The Future of American Politics (The New York Times, 30 Jan 2020). https://www.nytimes.com/2020/01/30/opinion/us-politics.html

[84] Timur Kuran: What Kills Inequality: Redistribution's Violent History (Foreign Affairs, Sep/Oct 2017).
https://www.foreignaffairs.com/reviews/review-essay/2017-08-15/what-kills-inequality

[85] Rob Picheta: The flat earth conspiracy is spreading around the globe. Does it hide a darker core? (CNN, 17 November 2019).
https://edition.cnn.com/2019/11/16/us/flat-earth-conference-conspiracy-theories-scli-intl/index.html (version updated 18 November 2019)

[86] Duncan Kelly: When Democracy Dies Not in Darkness but in Dysfunction (The New York Times, 3 Nov 2017).
https://www.nytimes.com/2017/11/03/books/review/ac-grayling-democracy-and-its-crisis.html

[87] Thomas B. Edsall: Democracy Can Plant the Seeds of Its Own Destruction (The New York Times, 19 Oct 2017).

https://www.nytimes.com/2017/10/19/opinion/democracy-populism-trump.html

[88] Ganesh Sitaraman: Our Constitution Wasn't Built for This (The New York Times, 16 Sep 2017). https://www.nytimes.com/2017/09/16/opinion/sunday/constitution-economy.html

[89] Bob Bauer, Trump Is the Founders' Worst Nightmare, 2 December 2019. https://www.nytimes.com/2019/12/02/opinion/trump-impeachment.html

[90] Gideon Rachman: The authoritarian wave reaches the West (Financial Times, 22 Feb 2017). https://www.ft.com/content/6b57d7ae-f74a-11e6-bd4e-68d53499ed71

[91] Noah Barkin: Davos elites struggle for answers as Trump era dawns (Eyewitness News, 15 Jan 2017). https://ewn.co.za/2017/01/15/davos-elites-struggle-for-answers-as-trump-era-dawns-1

[92] K. Mahbubani and L. H. Summers: The Fusion of Civilizations: The Case for Global Optimism (*Foreign Affairs* May/June 2016).

https://www.foreignaffairs.com/articles/2016-04-18/fusion-civilizations

[93] K. Mahbubani and L. H. Summers: The Fusion of Civilizations: The Case for Global Optimism (*Foreign Affairs* May/June 2016).

https://www.foreignaffairs.com/articles/2016-04-18/fusion-civilizations

[94] Emma Green: The Meaningless Politics of Liberal Democracies (*The Atlantic*, 8 June 2016).

https://www.theatlantic.com/international/archive/2016/06/the-meaningless-politics-of-liberal-democracies/486089/

[95] Matthew J. Goodwin: Old Labour, New Labour, No Labour (The New York Times, 11 Jan 2017). https://www.nytimes.com/2017/01/11/opinion/old-labour-new-labour-no-labour.html

[96] Jørgen Ørstrøm Møller: Left Behind: How Privatization Disenfranchises the Poor and Endangers Democracies (The National Interest, 22 Jan 2019). https://nationalinterest.org/feature/left-behind-how-privatization-disenfranchises-poor-and-endangers-democracies-42247

[97] Jonathan Freedland: Welcome to the age of Trump. (The Guardian, 19 May 2016). https://www.theguardian.com/us-news/2016/may/19/welcome-to-the-age-of-trump

[98] Dani Rodrik: The Politics of Anger (Project Syndicate, 9 March 2016). https://www.project-syndicate.org/commentary/the-politics-of-anger-by-

dani-rodrik-2016-03

[99] Laurence Peter: Will Trump-style revolt engulf Europe? (BBC News, 11 Nov 2016). https://www.bbc.com/news/election-us-2016-37935120

Peter asks whether Trump's victory in the US might turn into a "tsunami" that will change European politics. He discusses several specific country cases – Italy, Austria, the Netherlands, France and Germany – which are all countries were right-wing populists had gained ground recently (November 2016), and which were soon to hold referendums or elections. Peter does not really answer his own question, but leaves the reader to judge what might happen.

[100] Arthur C. Brooks: How to Get Americans Moving Again (The New York Times, 20 May 2016). https://www.nytimes.com/2016/05/21/opinion/how-to-get-americans-moving-again.html

[101] Joseph S. Nye: Donald Trump's Message (Project Syndicate, 4 March 2016). https://www.project-syndicate.org/commentary/donald-trump-parochial-appeal-by-joseph-s-nye-2016-03

[102] Dominique Moisi: Trump Versus the West (Project Syndicate, 28 Sep 2016). https://www.project-syndicate.org/commentary/trump-versus-the-west-by-dominique-moisi-2016-09; see also Ruth Ben-Ghiat: An American Authoritarian (The Atlantic, 10 Aug 2016). https://www.theatlantic.com/politics/archive/2016/08/american-authoritarianism-under-donald-trump/495263/

[103] Harold Meyerson: America's white working class is a dying breed (The Washington Post, 4 November 2015). https://www.washingtonpost.com/opinions/the-white-working-class-is-a-dying-breed/2015/11/04/f2220170-8323-11e5-a7ca-6ab6ec20f839_story.html

[104] Harold Meyerson: America's white working class is a dying breed (The Washington Post, 4 November 2015). https://www.washingtonpost.com/opinions/the-white-working-class-is-a-dying-breed/2015/11/04/f2220170-8323-11e5-a7ca-6ab6ec20f839_story.html

[105] Amanda Taub: Trump's Victory and the Rise of White Populism (The New York Times, 9 Nov 2016). https://www.nytimes.com/2016/11/10/world/americas/trump-white-populism-europe-united-states.html

[106] Jonathan Martin and Maggie Haberman, Fear and Loyalty: How Donald Trump Took Over the Republican Party, 21 December 2019. https://www.nytimes.com/2019/12/21/us/politics/trump-impeachment-republicans.html

[107] Philip Rucker, Trump says he misled on virus to instill calm. But he's governed with scare tactics. 9 September 2020.

https://www.washingtonpost.com/politics/trump-woodward-coronavirus-panic/2020/09/10/5376cd7c-f375-11ea-999c-67ff7bf6a9d2_story.html

[108] Ben Judah: Donald Trump's greatest weapon is white Americans' fear that they're quickly becoming a minority – because they are (Independent, 7 Nov 2016). https://www.independent.co.uk/voices/donald-trump-us-elections-hillary-clinton-race-hispanic-black-vote-white-americans-fear-minority-a7402296.html

[109] Will Hutton: Trade is the lifeblood of humanity. Closed doors lead to closed minds. (The Guardian, 13 Nov 2016). https://www.theguardian.com/commentisfree/2016/nov/13/america-trade-deals-donald-trump-nafta-isolationism

[110] Ivan Krastev: Sorry, NATO. Trump Doesn't Believe in Allies. (The New York Times, 11 Jul 2018). https://www.nytimes.com/2018/07/11/opinion/trump-nato-summit-allies.html

[111] Julia Ioffe, Trump Is Waging War on America's Diplomats, 3 December 2019. https://www.gq.com/story/trump-is-waging-war-on-american-diplomats

[112] Andrew Sullivan: A tyrant in the making? (The Sunday Times, 8 May 2016). https://www.thetimes.co.uk/article/a-tyrant-in-the-making-wnl7clrs5

[113] Barack Obama has described Sarah Palin's brand of populism as "folksy populism", quoting what Palin said of him as a presidential candidate during the campaign in which she was running mate to John McCain, "In small towns, we don't quite know what to make of a candidate who lavishes praise on working people when they're listening, and then talks about how bitterly they cling to their religion and guns when those people aren't listening." (Obama 2020: Chapter 8).

[114] Andrew Sullivan: A tyrant in the making? (The Sunday Times, 8 May 2016). https://www.thetimes.co.uk/article/a-tyrant-in-the-making-wnl7clrs5

[115] Louis René Beres: America Becomes what Its Founders Feared. We the people want comfort and easy wealth, but very little else (1 May 2016). https://nationalinterest.org/feature/america-becomes-what-its-founders-feared-16000

[116] Simon Johnson: Donald the Destroyer (Project Syndicate, 31 May 2016). https://www.project-syndicate.org/commentary/trump-threat-global-prosperity-security-by-simon-johnson-2016-05

[117] Trump's world – The new nationalism (The Economist, 19 Nov 2016). https://www.economist.com/leaders/2016/11/19/the-new-nationalism

[118] Simon Johnson: Donald the Destroyer (Project Syndicate, 31 May 2016). https://www.project-syndicate.org/commentary/trump-threat-global-prosperity-security-by-simon-johnson-2016-05

[119] Philip Freeman: Ancient Rome's Donald Trump (Project Syndicate, 5

April 2016). https://www.project-syndicate.org/commentary/donald-trump-of-ancient-rome-by-philip-freeman-2016-04

120 Pepe Escobar: Trumpquake (Sputnik News, 9 Nov 2016). https://sputniknews.com/columnists/201611091047255659-trump-elected-president-geopolitical-nine-eleven/

121 Ivan Krastev: Donald Trump and the Bieber Doctrine (The New York Times, 20 Nov 2016). https://www.nytimes.com/2016/11/21/opinion/donald-trump-and-the-bieber-doctrine.html

122 Decca Aitkenhead: So long, 2016: the year of the political earthquake (The Guardian, 24 Dec 2016). https://www.theguardian.com/news/2016/dec/24/2016-in-review-world-news-syria-terrorism-brexit-trump-decca-aitkenhead

123 D. Quah and K. Mahbubani: The Geopolitics of Populism (Project Syndicate, 9 Dec 2016). https://www.project-syndicate.org/commentary/populism-driven-by-geopolitical-change-by-danny-quah-and-kishore-mahbubani-2016-12

124 Ed Kilgore, The insurrection was a complex, yearslong plot, not a one-day event. And it isn't over, 5 September 2021. https://nymag.com/intelligencer/article/trump-campaign-steal-presidency-timeline.html

125 CISA, Joint Statement From Elections Infrastructure Government Coordinating Council & The Election Infrastructure Sector Coordinating Executive Committees, 12 November, 2020. https://www.cisa.gov/news/2020/11/12/joint-statement-elections-infrastructure-government-coordinating-council-election

126 Michael Balsamo, Disputing Trump, Barr says no widespread election fraud, 1 December 2020. https://apnews.com/article/barr-no-widespread-election-fraud-b1f1488796c9a98c4b1a9061a6c7f49d

127 Alayna Treene, McConnell congratulates Joe Biden on becoming president-elect, 15 December 2020. https://www.axios.com/mcconnell-biden-electoral-college-1f38ad08-3138-497a-8dc8-e5da0f7318a8.html

128 Peter Baker, Maggie Haberman and Annie Karni, Pence Reached His Limit with Trump. It Wasn't, 12 January, 2021, Pretty. https://www.nytimes.com/2021/01/12/us/politics/mike-pence-trump.html

129 Peter Baker, Maggie Haberman and Annie Karni, Pence Reached His Limit with Trump. It Wasn't, 12 January, 2021, Pretty. https://www.nytimes.com/2021/01/12/us/politics/mike-pence-trump.html

130 Stephanie Grisham resigned after Melania Trump turned down her suggestion to send out a tweet condemning the lawlessness and violence of the mob. She recounts: "At 1:25 p.m., I texted her, 'Do you want to tweet that peaceful protests are the right of every American, but there is no place for lawlessness and violence?'". In response, "Melania Trump sent me back a

one-word response: 'No.'" (Grisham 2021: Introduction).

131 Barbara Ortutay, Twitter, Facebook remove Trump video amid Capitol violence, 6 January 2021. https://www.fox13now.com/news/national-news/twitter-facebook-remove-trump-video-amid-capitol-violence

132 Barbara Ortutay, Twitter, Facebook remove Trump video amid Capitol violence, 6 January 2021. https://www.fox13now.com/news/national-news/twitter-facebook-remove-trump-video-amid-capitol-violence

133 Mary Kay Linge, Violence erupts at Trump rally as thousands protest election in DC 12 December, 2020. https://nypost.com/2020/12/12/violence-erupts-at-trump-rally-as-thousands-protest-election/

134 Greg Miller, Greg Jaffe and Razzan Nkahlawi, A mob insurrection stoked by false claims of election fraud and promises of violent restoration, 10 January 2021. https://www.washingtonpost.com/national-security/trump-capitol-mob-attack-origins/2021/01/09/0cb2cf5e-51d4-11eb-83e3-322644d82356_story.html

135 Craig Timberg and Drew Harwell, Pro-Trump forums erupt with violent threats ahead of Wednesday's rally against the 2020 election, 5 January 2021. https://www.washingtonpost.com/technology/2021/01/05/parler-telegram-violence-dc-protests/

136 Washington Post, Homeland Security Bulletin Warms Americans about Violence by Grievance-fueled Domestic Extremists, 27 January 2021. https://www.washingtonpost.com/national/homeland-security-bulletin-warns-americans-about-violence-by-grievance-fueled-domestic-extremists/2021/01/27/4182f864-60c3-11eb-ac8f-4ae05557196e_story.html

137 Yascha Mounk, After Trump, Is American Democracy Doomed by Populism?, 14 January, 2021. https://www.cfr.org/in-brief/after-trump-american-democracy-doomed-populism

138 Blake Ellis and Melanie Hicken, They stormed the Capitol to overturn the results of an election they didn't vote in, 1 February 2021. https://edition.cnn.com/2021/02/01/us/capitol-rioters-non-voters-invs/index.html

139 David Frum, There's a Word for What Trumpism Is Becoming, 13 July 2021. https://www.theatlantic.com/ideas/archive/2021/07/theres-word-what-trumpism-becoming/619418/

140 Guardian staff and agencies, FBI chief calls Capitol attack domestic terrorism and rejects Trump's fraud claims, 11 June 2021. https://www.theguardian.com/us-news/2021/jun/10/capitol-attack-fbi-christopher-wray-congress

141 James Hohmann, The Daily 202: Trump's refusal to comply with the House subpoenas depends on an absolutist view of executive power, 9 October 2019. https://www.washingtonpost.com/news/powerpost/paloma/daily-

202/2019/10/09/daily-202-trump-s-refusal-to-comply-with-house-subpoenas-depends-on-an-absolutist-view-of-executive-power/5d9d69d088e0fa747e6d51e8/

[142] Sasha Polakow-Suransky: White Nationalism Is Destroying the West (The New York Times, 12 Oct 2017). https://www.nytimes.com/2017/10/12/opinion/sunday/white-nationalism-threat-islam-america.html

[143] Chris Patten: In defense of democracy during challenging times (Asia Times, 3 Feb 2018). https://asiatimes.com/2018/02/weekend-defense-democracy/

[144] David Brooks: The Chaos After Trump (The New York Times, 5 March 2018). https://www.nytimes.com/2018/03/05/opinion/the-chaos-after-trump.html

[145] Thomas B. Edsall: Trump Is Waiting and He Is Ready (The New York Times, 12 Feb 2020). https://www.nytimes.com/2020/02/12/opinion/trump-campaign-2020.html

[146] Matthew Continetti: Who Really Rules The United States? (The Washington Free Beacon, 17 Feb 2017). https://freebeacon.com/columns/rules-united-states/

[147] Matthew Continetti: Who Really Rules The United States? (The Washington Free Beacon, 17 Feb 2017). https://freebeacon.com/columns/rules-united-states/

[148] Katie Benner and Adam Goldman, Justice Dept. Is Said to Open Criminal Inquiry Into Its Own Russia Investigation, 24 October 2019. https://www.nytimes.com/2019/10/24/us/politics/john-durham-criminal-investigation.html; Matt Zapotosky and Spencer S. Hsu, Justice Department authorised prosecutors to charge Andre McCabe, 12 September 2019. https://www.washingtonpost.com/national-security/justice-dept-authorized-prosecutors-to-charge-andrew-mccabe/2019/09/12/5b0d48ea-d418-11e9-9343-40db57cf6abd_story.html; Adam Goldman and Katie Benner, Justice Dept. Rejects Andrew McCabe's Bid to Avoid Charges, 12 September 2019. https://www.nytimes.com/2019/09/12/us/politics/andrew-mccabe-fbi.html

[149] David Brooks: Our Elites Still Don't Get It (The New York Times, 16 Nov 2017). https://www.nytimes.com/2017/11/16/opinion/elites-taxes-republicans-congress.html

[150] David Brooks: Our Elites Still Don't Get It (The New York Times, 16 Nov 2017). https://www.nytimes.com/2017/11/16/opinion/elites-taxes-republicans-congress.html

[151] Sophie McBain: The death of American optimism (New Statesman, 13 Feb 2019). https://www.newstatesman.com/2019/02/death-american-optimism

[152] David Brooks: An Era Defined by Fear (The New York Times, 29 Apr 2019). https://www.nytimes.com/2019/04/29/opinion/politics-fear.html

153 A. MacGillis and ProPublica: The Original Underclass (The Atlantic, September 2016). https://www.theatlantic.com/magazine/archive/2016/09/the-original-underclass/492731/

154 Dominic Tierney: Does American Need an Enemy? (The National Interest, 19 Oct 2016). https://nationalinterest.org/feature/does-america-need-enemy-18106

155 Ronald Brownstein: Why Trump Looks Eerily Familiar to Germans. (The Atlantic, 12 May 2016). https://www.theatlantic.com/international/archive/2016/05/atlantic-crossings/482448/

156 Francis Fukuyama: American Political Decay or Renewal?: The Meaning of the 2016 Election (Foreign Affairs, July/August 2016).

157 Alix Kroeger, JD Vance: Trump whisperer turned Senate hopeful, 18 April 2021. https://www.bbc.com/news/world-us-canada-56748047, accessed 18 April 2021

158 Natalie Y. Moore, Why did 53% of white women vote for Trump? The story of Phyllis Schlafly tells why, 21 May 2020, https://chicago.suntimes.com/columnists/2020/5/21/21266599/phyllis-schlafly-feminism-equal-rights-amendment-mrs-america-era-culture-wars

159 According to Newman, it was when Obama mocked at Trump at "the 2011 White House Correspondents' dinner at the Washington, DC, Hilton", that Trump decided to run for president in 2016, with the aim of taking "his revenge on Obama's humiliating him in front of all those influential people" (Newman 2018: Chapter 4).

160 Thomas J. Sugrue: A Look at America's Long and Troubled History of White Poverty (The New York Times, 24 June 2016). https://www.nytimes.com/2016/06/26/books/review/white-trash-by-nancy-isenberg.html

161 Arthur C. Brooks: The Dignity Deficit (Foreign Affairs, March/April 2017). https://www.foreignaffairs.com/articles/united-states/2017-02-13/dignity-deficit

162 Anatole Kaletsky: Pensioners and Populism (Project Syndicate, 28 Oct 2016). https://www.project-syndicate.org/commentary/voting-data-show-little-economic-link-with-brexit-by-anatole-kaletsky-2016-10

163 Ian Buruma: The West's Race Problem (Project Syndicate, 13 Sep 2018). https://www.project-syndicate.org/commentary/west-race-problem-chemnitz-by-ian-buruma-2018-09

164 https://www.msnbc.com/transcripts/11th-hour-with-brian-williams/2020-05-22-msna1361986

165 Carlos Lozada: How Does Donald Trump Stack up Against American Literature's fictional dictators? Pretty well actually (9 June 2016). https://www.washingtonpost.com/news/book-party/wp/2016/06/09/how-

does-donald-trump-stack-up-against-american-literatures-fictional-dictators-pretty-well-actually/

166 Nail Ferguson: Ageing white America is sick, like the rabid rantings of its hero Trump. https://www.thetimes.co.uk/article/ageing-white-america-is-sick-like-the-rabid-rantings-of-its-hero-trump-k7h2p9lbpt5

167 Rod Dreher: Trump: Will The West Survive? (The American Conservative, 6 Jul 2017). https://www.theamericanconservative.com/dreher/trump-will-the-west-survive-poland/

168 Allan Smith, HARRY REID: 'Donald Trump is the Republican Party's Frankenstein', 2 March 2016. https://in.news.yahoo.com/weather/harry-reid-donald-trump-republican-172936301.html

169 Harold James: The Death of Anglo-American Conservatism (Project Syndicate, 27 Sep 2019). https://www.project-syndicate.org/commentary/the-death-of-conservatism-by-harold-james-2019-09

170 Paul Krugman: Populism, Real and Phony (The New York Times, 23 Dec 2016). https://www.nytimes.com/2016/12/23/opinion/populism-real-and-phony.html

171 Henry Scott Wallace: American Fascism, in 1944 and Today (The New York Times, 12 May 2017). https://www.nytimes.com/2017/05/12/opinion/american-fascism-trump.html

172 Paul R. Pillar: A President Without Purpose (The National Interest, 1 Sep 2017). https://nationalinterest.org/blog/paul-pillar/president-without-purpose-22160

173 Maureen Dowd, Covid Dreams, Trump Nightmares, 23 May 2020. https://www.nytimes.com/2020/05/23/opinion/sunday/trump-mask-coronavirus.html

174 Jennifer Szalai, In 'Surviving Autocracy,' Masha Gessen Tells Us to Face the Facts. 3 June 2020. https://www.nytimes.com/2020/06/03/books/review-surviving- autocracy-masha-gessen.html

175 Masha Gessen, Donald Trump's Fascist Performance, 3 June 2020. https://www.newyorker.com/news/our-columnists/donald-trumps-fascist-performance

176 Francis Fukuyama: American Political Decay or Renewal?: The Meaning of the 2016 Election (Foreign Affairs, July/August 2016).

177 David Brooks: Let's Not Do This Again (The New York Times, 8 Nov 2016). https://www.nytimes.com/2016/11/08/opinion/lets-not-do-this-again.html

178 Natalie Y. Moore, Why did 53% of white women vote for Trump?

The story of Phyllis Schlafly tells why, 21 May 2020.
https://chicago.suntimes.com/columnists/2020/5/21/21266599/phyllis-
schlafly-feminism-equal-rights-amendment-mrs-america-era-culture-wars

[179] Javier Solana and Strobe Talbott: The Decline of the West, and How
to Stop It (The New York Times, 19 Oct 2016).
https://www.nytimes.com/2016/10/20/opinion/the-decline-of-the-west-
and-how-to-stop-it.html

[180] Philip Stephens: The perils of a populist paean to ignorance (23 June
2016). https://www.ft.com/content/bfb5f3d4-379d-11e6-a780-
b48ed7b6126f

[181] Gary Younge: Trump and the Brexiters must own the mess they lied
us into (The Guardian, 10 Jan 2019).
https://www.theguardian.com/commentisfree/2019/jan/10/donald-trump-
brexitiers-tailspin-left-must-act

[182] William Davies: Boris Johnson, Donald Trump and the Rise of
Radical Incompetence (The New York Times, 13 Jul 2018).
https://www.nytimes.com/2018/07/13/opinion/brexit-conservatives-boris-
trump.html

[183] Ian Buruma: Hoping for the Best Against Trump (Project Syndicate,
10 Jan 2017). https://www.project-syndicate.org/commentary/hoping-
against-trump-by-ian-buruma-2017-01

[184] The right way to help declining places (The Economist, 2017).
https://www.economist.com/leaders/2017/10/21/the-right-way-to-help-
declining-places

[185] Paul Krugman: The Age of Fake Policy (The New York Times, 6 Jan
2017). https://www.nytimes.com/2017/01/06/opinion/the-age-of-fake-
policy.html

[186] Paul Krugman: The Age of Fake Policy (The New York Times, 6 Jan
2017). https://www.nytimes.com/2017/01/06/opinion/the-age-of-fake-
policy.html

[187] Emilee Larkin, Biden Slams Trump Efforts to Dismantle Obamacare,
25 June 2020. https://www.courthousenews.com/biden-slams-trump-efforts-
to-dismantle-obamacare/

[188] Andrea Kendall-Taylor and Erica Frantz: How Democracies Fall
Apart: Why Populism Is a Pathway to Autocracy (Foreign Affairs, 5 Dec
2016). https://www.foreignaffairs.com/articles/2016-12-05/how-
democracies-fall-apart

[189] Gideon Rachman: Donald Trump, Vladimir Putin and the lure of the
strongman (Financial Times, 16 May 2016).
https://www.ft.com/content/1c6ff2ce-1939-11e6-b197-a4af20d5575e

[190] David J Lynch and Josh Dawsey, Trump adviser gives conflicting
accounts on whether Chinese offered information on Hunter Biden, 10
October 2019.

https://www.washingtonpost.com/business/economy/trump-advisor-gives-conflicting-accounts-on-whether-chinese-offered-information-about-hunter-biden/2019/10/10/35f32a14-eb80-11e9-9306-47cb0324fd44_story.html

191 Andrew Duehren and Gordon Lubold, White House Shifted Authority Over Ukraine Aid Amid Legal Concerns, 10 October, 2019. https://www.wsj.com/articles/white-house-shifted-authority-over-ukraine-aid-amid-legal-concerns-11570717571

192 Conor Finnegan, 'I think Putin thinks he can play (Trump) like a fiddle': Former national security adviser John Bolton in exclusive interview, 18 June 2020. https://abcnews.go.com/Politics/putin-thinks-play-trump-fiddle-national-security-adviser/story?id=71307801

193 Lisa Mascaro And Mary Clare Jalonick, 'All roads lead to Putin': Impeachment ties Ukraine, Russia, 7 December, 2019. https://apnews.com/article/donald-trump-nancy-pelosi-ap-top-news-politics-russia-57518f0072af442af2a43f359f32d541

194 Adam Entous, House majority leader to colleagues in 2016: 'I think Putin pays' Trump, 17 May 2017. https://www.washingtonpost.com/world/national-security/house-majority-leader-to-colleagues-in-2016-i-think-putin-pays-trump/2017/05/17/515f6f8a-3aff-11e7-8854-21f359183e8c_story.html

195 Greg Miller and Greg Jaffe, Trump revealed highly classified information to Russian foreign minister and ambassador, 15 May, 2017. https://www.washingtonpost.com/world/national-security/trump-revealed-highly-classified-information-to-russian-foreign-minister-and-ambassador/2017/05/15/530c172a-3960-11e7-9e48-c4f199710b69_story.html

196 Greg Miller, Trump has concealed details of his face-to-face encounters with Putin from senior officials in administration, 13 January 2019. https://www.washingtonpost.com/world/national-security/trump-has-concealed-details-of-his-face-to-face-encounters-with-putin-from-senior-officials-in-administration/2019/01/12/65f6686c-1434-11e9-b6ad-9cfd62dbb0a8_story.html

197 Julian E. Barnes and Matthew Rosenberg, Charges of Ukrainian Meddling? A Russian Operation, U.S. Intelligence Says, 22 November, 2019. https://www.nytimes.com/2019/11/22/us/politics/ukraine-russia-interference.html

198 AP, Putin says US 'political dramas' diverting focus from Russia, 20 November 2019. https://apnews.com/article/trump-impeachment-inquiry-donald-trump-joe-biden-russia-impeachments-ed2b2f90c74a420a8beb076c1c25df32; see also, Philip Rucker and Shane Harris, Tumult at home, ailing alliances abroad: Why Trump's America has been a 'gift' to Putin, 24 October, 2020. ttps://www.washingtonpost.com/politics/trump-russia-

putin/2020/10/24/4edb462e-13bb-11eb-ba42-ec6a580836ed_story.html

[199] David Brooks: Vladimir Putin, the Most Influential Man in the World (The New York Times, 2 Apr 2018). https://www.nytimes.com/2018/04/02/opinion/vladimir-putin-most-influential.html

[200] Suzanne Moore: Nervous States: How Feeling Took Over the World by William Davies – review (The Guardian, 28 Oct 2018). https://www.theguardian.com/books/2018/oct/28/nervous-states-how-feeling-took-over-the-world-william-davies-review

[201] Gregory Feifer: Where Trump and Putin Diverge (Foreign Affairs, 15 Feb 2017). https://www.foreignaffairs.com/articles/russian-federation/2017-02-15/where-trump-and-putin-diverge

[202] According to Rick Wilson (2018: Chapter 13), "If you're looking for weaponized, white-hot, immigrant-hating trailer-trash postconservative nationalist populism, look no further than Donald Trump's loudest screaming section, Breitbart 'News.'"

[203] Michael S. Schmidt and Maggie Haberman, Macabre Video of Fake Trump Shooting Media and Critics, 13 October 2019. https://www.nytimes.com/2019/10/13/us/politics/trump-video.html; see also Paul LeBlanc, New York Times: Fake video of Trump shooting media and critics played at his resort, 14 October 2019. https://edition.cnn.com/2019/10/13/politics/trump-fake-video-shooting-media-critics-doral/index.html

[204] William H. McRaven, Opinion: Revoke my security clearance, too, Mr. President, 16 August 2018. https://www.washingtonpost.com/opinions/revoke-my-security-clearance-too-mr-president/2018/08/16/8b149b02-a178-11e8-93e3-24d1703d2a7a_story.html

[205] Walden Bello: People Are Likening the Next Philippine President to Donald Trump. Here's Why. (Foreign Policy in Focus, 19 May 2016). https://fpif.org/people-likening-next-philippine-president-donald-trump-heres/

[206] Cleve Kevin Robert Arguelles: The rise and rise of Rodrigo Duterte (Asia Times, 25 Dec 2016). https://asiatimes.com/2016/12/rise-rise-rodrigo-duterte/

[207] Mustafa Akyol: Turkey's Populists See an Unlikely Ally (The New York Times, 16 Nov 2016). https://www.nytimes.com/2016/11/17/opinion/turkeys-populists-see-an-unlikely-ally.html

[208] Patrick Cockburn: Think the American political system will stop Donald Trump exercising ultimate power? The same was said about Turkey's President Erdogan (Independent, 13 Jan 2017). https://www.independent.co.uk/voices/donald-trump-president-elect-turkey-

president-erdogan-absolute-power-terrifying-parallels-patrick-a7526176.html

209 Nick Wadhams, Jennifer Jacobs and Saleha Mohsin, Trump-Erdogan Call Led to Lengthy Quest to Avoid Halkbank Trial, 16 October 2019. https://www.bloomberg.com/news/articles/2019-10-16/trump-erdogan-call-led-to-lengthy-push-to-avoid-halkbank-trial

210 Samara Lynn, 'Don't be a tough guy': President Trump sent threatening letter to Turkish President Erdogan on day of invasion, 17 October 2019. https://abcnews.go.com/International/dont-tough-guy-president-trump-threatening-letter-turkish/story?id=66333927

211 Roger Cohen: Trump, Johnson and the Hole in the Doughnut (The New York Times, 5 Jul 2019). https://www.nytimes.com/2019/07/05/opinion/boris-johnson-donald-trump.html

212 Roger Cohen: Trump, Johnson and the Hole in the Doughnut (The New York Times, 5 Jul 2019). https://www.nytimes.com/2019/07/05/opinion/boris-johnson-donald-trump.html

213 Donald Trump - America's African President: The Daily Show. https://www.youtube.com/watch?v=2FPrJxTvgdQ, accessed 26 March 2021

214 Roger Southall, Zuma and Trump half a world apart yet similarly paranoid and dangerous. https://theconversation.com/zuma-and-trump-half-a-world-apart-yet-similarly-paranoid-and-dangerous-120599, accessed 25 March 2021

215 Reuters, Jacob Zuma reps condemn 'emotional, angry' South African court for his jail sentence, 1 July 2021. https://www.reuters.com/world/africa/jacob-zuma-reps-condemn-emotional-angry-south-african-court-his-jail-sentence-2021-06-30/

216 Marianne Thamm, Nine lost days: SA government was uniquely placed to stop the July insurrection – but it didn't, 29 July 2021. https://www.dailymaverick.co.za/article/2021-07-29-nine-lost-days-sa-government-was-uniquely-placed-to-stop-the-july-insurrection-but-it-didnt/

217 Mark Niquette and Naomi Nix, Trump sues Facebook, Twitter and Google over social media bans, 7 July 2021. https://www.aljazeera.com/economy/2021/7/7/trump-sues-facebook-twitter-and-google-over-social-media-bans

218 Salvador Rodriguez, Facebook changes company name to Meta, 28 October 2021. https://www.cnbc.com/2021/10/28/facebook-changes-company-name-to-meta.html

219 BBC, Trump to Kim: My nuclear button is 'bigger and more powerful', 3 January 2018. https://www.bbc.com/news/world-asia-42549687

220 Megan Keneally, From 'fire and fury' to 'rocket man,' the various barbs traded between Trump and Kim Jong Un, 12 June 2018. https://abcnews.go.com/International/fire-fury-rocket-man-barbs-traded-

trump-kim/story?id=53634996; Lauren Gambino, Donald Trump boasts that his nuclear button is bigger than Kim Jong-un's, 3 January 2018.
https://www.theguardian.com/us-news/2018/jan/03/donald-trump-boasts-nuclear-button-bigger-kim-jong-un; Simon Denyer, North Korea responds to Trump's 'Rocket Man' comment with 'senile dotard' jibe, 5 December 2019.
https://www.washingtonpost.com/world/north-korea-responds-to-trumps-rocket-man-comment-with-senile-dotard-jibe/2019/12/05/1dba85f6-176c-11ea-80d6-d0ca7007273f_story.html

221 Doug Bandow: What Trump Has in Common with the Last German Emperor (The National Interest, 31 Jan 2017).
https://www.cato.org/publications/commentary/what-trump-has-common-last-german-emperor

222 William J. Burns, The Demolition of U.S. Diplomacy, 14 October, 2019. https://www.foreignaffairs.com/articles/2019-10-14/demolition-us-diplomacy

223 Kevin Freking and Zeke Miller, Book: Trump said of virus, 'I wanted to always play it down', 9 September 2020.
https://www.washingtonpost.com/politics/book-trump-said-of-virus-i-wanted-to-always-play-it-down/2020/09/09/68d4f7cc-f2bf-11ea-8025-5d3489768ac8_story.html

224 See also, William Cummings, 'This is not a reality TV show': Trump criticized for tweets on TV ratings as coronavirus death toll rises, 29 March 2020. https://www.usatoday.com/story/news/politics/2020/03/29/trump-tweets-touting-tv-ratings-coronavirus-briefings/2936761001/

225 Ashley Parker, For a numbers-obsessed Trump, there's one he has tried to ignore: 100,000 dead, 28 May 2020.
https://www.washingtonpost.com/politics/for-a-numbers-obsessed-trump-theres-one-he-has-tried-to-ignore-100000-dead/2020/05/27/0a9c58ee-9f63-11ea-9590-1858a893bd59_story.html

226 "Opinion: The hustle — white saviors and hashtag activism", by Angela Bruce-Raeburn, 12 June 2020.
https://www.devex.com/news/opinion-the-hustle-white-saviors-and-hashtag-activism-97463

227 "Coronavirus: Obama criticises Trump administration's virus response", 17 May 2020. www.bbc.com/news/world-us-canada-52694872

228 "Trump concedes pandemic to 'get worse before it gets better'", by Anthony Zurcher, 22 July 2020. https://www.bbc.com/news/world-us-canada-53494766

229 "Bolsonaro's politics of death, Covid-19 and racial inequality in Brazil", by Carolina Parreiras and Viviane Mattar, 8 July 2020.
https://www.coronatimes.net/bolsonaro-politics-death-covid-19-race-brazil/

230 "The time of masks: everyone to themselves and Covid-19 for us all", by Divine Fuh, 8 May 2020.

http://publicanthropologist.cmi.no/2020/05/08/the-time-of-masks-everyone-to-themselves-and-covid-19-for-us-all/

231 "Coronavirus: Donald Trump vows not to order Americans to wear masks", 18 July 2020. https://www.bbc.com/news/world-us-canada-53453468

232 Watch "Trump again says Covid-19 will 'disappear' in first virus briefing in months, The 11th Hour, MSNBC", by Brian Williams, 21 July 2020. https://www.youtube.com/watch?v=3JV5LuqCm90&feature=youtu.be

233 "Trump concedes pandemic to 'get worse before it gets better'", 22 July 2020. https://www.bbc.com/news/world-us-canada-53494766

234 "Tracking Covid-19 cases in the US", by Sergio Hernandez, Sean O'Key, Amanda Watts, Byron Manley and Henrik Pettersson, 23 September 2020. https://edition.cnn.com/interactive/2020/health/coronavirus-us-maps-and-cases/#!

235 "Trump mocks Biden for wearing mask: 'Did you ever see a man that likes a mask as much as him?'", by Paul LeBlanc, 3 September 2020. https://amp.cnn.com/cnn/2020/09/03/politics/trump-biden-coronavirus-mask/index.html

236 "Lancet Editor Spills the Beans and Britain's PM Surrenders to the Gates Vaccine Cartel," by Alliance for Human Research Protection (AHRP), 5 June 2020. https://ahrp.org/lancet-editor-spills-the-beans-and-britains-pm-surrenders-to-the-gates-vaccine-cartel/; see also, "Surgisphere: mass audit of papers linked to firm behind hydroxychloroquine Lancet study scandal," by Melissa Davey and Stephanie Kirchgaessner, 10 June 2020. https://www.theguardian.com/world/2020/jun/10/surgisphere-sapan-desai-lancet-study-hydroxychloroquine-mass-audit-scientific-papers

237 "The Lancet changes editorial policy after hydroxychloroquine Covid study retraction," by Melissa Davey, 22 September 2020. https://www.theguardian.com/world/2020/sep/22/the-lancet-reforms-editorial-policy-after-hydroxychloroquine-covid-study-retraction

238 "Trump retweeted a video with false covid-19 claims. One doctor in it has said demons cause illnesses", by Travis M. Andrews and Danielle Paquette, 29 July 2020. https://www.washingtonpost.com/technology/2020/07/28/stella-immanuel-hydroxychloroquine-video-trump-americas-frontline-doctors/

239 "Stella Immanuel - the doctor behind unproven coronavirus cure claim", by Dickens Olewe, 29 July 2020. https://www.bbc.com/news/world-africa-53579773

240 "Coronavirus: Hydroxychloroquine ineffective says Fauci", by BBC, 29 July 2020. https://www.bbc.com/news/world-us-canada-53575964

241 "Coronavirus: Why are Americans so angry about masks?", by Tara McKelvey 21 July 2020. https://www.bbc.com/news/world-us-canada-53477121

242 "Fighting alone: I'm a GOP governor. Why didn't Trump help my state with coronavirus testing?", by Larry Hogan, 16 July 2020. https://www.washingtonpost.com/outlook/2020/07/16/larry-hogan-trump-coronavirus/

243 "My statement on Donald Trump's continued failure to control Covid-19", by Joe Biden, 19 July 2020. https://medium.com/@JoeBiden/my-statement-on-donald-trumps-continued-failure-to-control-covid-19-1d0bddb9504f

244 "After 200,000 coronavirus deaths, the US faces another rude awakening," by Ed Pilkington, 22 September 2020. https://www.theguardian.com/world/2020/sep/22/us-coronavirus-deaths-trump-autumn

245 "UN chief criticizes lack of global cooperation on Covid-19", by Edith M. Lederer, 24 June 2020. https://abcnews.go.com/US/wireStory/chief-criticizes-lack-global-cooperation-covid-19-71417094

246 "SA exports 800 000 masks to Italy, as the WHO warns of a global mask shortage due to Covid-19," by Jay Caboz, 5 March 2020. https://www.businessinsider.co.za/the-world-faces-a-mask-shortage-due-to-covid-19-the-who-warns-as-sa-exports-800-000-to-italy-2020-3

247 "Taking back responsibility: A joint effort to increase the production of medical masks in Europe", by Sanne van der Lugt, 2 April 2020. https://www.clingendael.org/publication/joint-effort-increase-production-medical-masks-europe

248 "Trump Covid: President criticised over drive-past," by BBC, 5 October 2020. https://www.bbc.com/news/election-us-2020-54415532

249 "Trump Tests Positive for the Coronavirus," by Peter Baker and Maggie Haberman, 2 October 2020. https://www.nytimes.com/2020/10/02/us/politics/trump-covid.html

250 "Trump says he is doing well, but next couple of days the 'real test'," by the BBC, 4 October 2020. https://www.bbc.com/news/election-us-2020-54405734

251 "Trump health monitored after weekend of confusion," by BBC, 5 October 2020. https://www.bbc.com/news/election-us-2020-54413536

252 "Trump to leave hospital on Monday after weekend Covid treatment," by BBC, 5 October 2020. https://www.bbc.com/news/election-us-2020-54427390

253 BBC, Trump tells Republican supporters to get vaccinated. 16 March 2021. https://www.bbc.com/news/world-us-canada-56424614, accessed 17 March 2021

254 Michael T. Taussig, Trump Studies, January 18, 2017. https://culanth.org/fieldsights/trump-studies

255 Matthew Sharpe, Understanding the appeal of Donald Trump,

accessed 24 May 2021. https://this.deakin.edu.au/society/understanding-the-appeal-of-donald-trump

256 Adam Goldman and Mark Mazzetti, Activists and Ex-Spy Said to Have Plotted to Discredit Trump 'Enemies' in Government, 13 May 2021. https://www.nytimes.com/2021/05/13/us/politics/mcmaster-fbi-trump-project-veritas.html

257 Dion Forster, Trump is out, but US evangelicalism remains alive and well in Africa, January 17, 2021. https://theconversation.com/trump-is-out-but-us-evangelicalism-remains-alive-and-well-in-africa-151117

258 Jim Quinn: Trump a New Jacksonian Era? (Burning Platform, 13? Feb 2017). https://www.marketoracle.co.uk/Article58140.html

259 Timothy Egan: A Tyrant's Ghost Guides Trump (The New York Times, 3 Feb 2017). https://www.nytimes.com/2017/02/03/opinion/a-tyrants-ghost-guides-trump.html

260 Michael Crowley: The Man Who Wants to Unmake the West (Politico Magazine, March/April 2017). https://www.politico.com/magazine/story/2017/03/trump-steve-bannon-destroy-eu-european-union-214889

261 Fareed Zakaria: The threat to democracy – from the left (The Washington Post, 13 Sep 2018). https://www.washingtonpost.com/opinions/a-new-threat-to-democracy--from-the-left/2018/09/13/7e3fbb72-b790-11e8-94eb-3bd52dfe917b_story.html

262 Timothy Egan: A Tyrant's Ghost Guides Trump (The New York Times, 3 Feb 2017). https://www.nytimes.com/2017/02/03/opinion/a-tyrants-ghost-guides-trump.html

263 Walter Russell Mead: The Jacksonian Revolt (Foreign Affairs, March/April 2017). https://www.foreignaffairs.com/articles/united-states/2017-01-20/jacksonian-revolt

264 Daniel W. Drezner: America the unexceptional (The Washington Post, 1 Feb 2017). https://www.washingtonpost.com/posteverything/wp/2017/02/01/america-the-unexceptional/

265 Stephen M. Walt: The End of Hubris (Foreign Affairs, 16 Apr 2019). https://www.foreignaffairs.com/articles/2019-04-16/end-hubris

266 Larry Diamond: It Could Happen Here (The Atlantic, 19 Oct 2016). https://www.theatlantic.com/international/archive/2016/10/trump-democracy-election-2016/504617/

267 Frank Rich, What Will Happen to The Trump Toadies?, 7 January 2020. https://nymag.com/intelligencer/2020/01/what-will-happen-to-trumps-republican-collaborators.html

268 Dan Balz, The Senate trial will shape the president's legacy and also that of his Republican Party, 17 January 2020.

https://www.washingtonpost.com/politics/the-senate-trial-will-shape-both-the-presidents-legacy-but-also-that-of-his-republican-party/2020/01/16/60b5d18c-388f-11ea-9541-9107303481a4_story.html

269 Carlos Lozada: American democracy is on a break. Welcome to 'Trumpocracy.' (The Washington Post, 18 Jan 2018). https://www.washingtonpost.com/news/book-party/wp/2018/01/18/american-democracy-is-on-a-break-welcome-to-trumpocracy/

270 Dominic Tierney: The Global Spread of Trumpism (The Atlantic, 19 Jul 2016). https://www.theatlantic.com/international/archive/2016/07/trump-brexit-far-right/491786/

271 Zhang Tengjun: 'Trumpism' unavoidable new norm, research concept for world (Global Times, 2 Jan 2018). http://www.globaltimes.cn/content/1083000.shtml

272 Stephanie Ruhle and Carol E. Lee, In private speech, Bolton suggests some of Trump's foreign policy decisions are guided by personal interest, 12 November, 2019. https://www.nbcnews.com/politics/donald-trump/private-speech-bolton-suggests-some-trump-s-foreign-policy-decisions-n1080651

273 Ian Buruma: Trump and the Cosmopolitans (Project Syndicate, 8 Aug 2017). https://www.project-syndicate.org/commentary/stephen-miller-cosmopolitan-ignorance-by-ian-buruma-2017-08

274 David S. Glosser, Stephen Miller Is an Immigration Hypocrite. I know Because I am His Uncle, 13 August 2018. https://www.politico.com/magazine/story/2018/08/13/stephen-miller-is-an-immigration-hypocrite-i-know-because-im-his-uncle-219351/

275 Eric Kaufmann: White majorities feel threatened in an age of mass migration – and calling them racist won't help (New Statesman, 17 Oct 2018). https://www.newstatesman.com/politics/uk/2018/10/white-majorities-feel-threatened-age-mass-migration-and-calling-them-racist-won

276 Chris Patten: The Return of Violent Identity Politics (30 Apr 2019). https://www.project-syndicate.org/commentary/sri-lanka-christchurch-attacks-identity-politics-by-chris-patten-2019-04

277 Eric Kaufmann: White majorities feel threatened in an age of mass migration – and calling them racist won't help (New Statesman, 17 Oct 2018). https://www.newstatesman.com/politics/uk/2018/10/white-majorities-feel-threatened-age-mass-migration-and-calling-them-racist-won

278 CDA Taylor, Op-Ed in Novoye Vremya by CDA Taylor: Ukraine's Committed Partner, 10 November, 2019. https://ua.usembassy.gov/op-ed-in-novoye-vremya-by-cda-taylor-ukraines-committed-partner/

279 Robert D. Kaplan: Trump's Budget Is American Caesarism (Foreign Policy, 26 May 2017). https://foreignpolicy.com/2017/05/26/trumps-budget-is-american-caesarism/

[280] The Associate Press, Chairman of Joint Chiefs says no role for military in presidential election, 29 August, 2020. https://www.nbcnews.com/politics/2020-election/chairman-joint-chiefs-says-no-role-military-presidential-election-n1238772; Jonathan Swan, Scoop: Generals privately brief news anchors, promise no military role in election, 3 November 2020. https://www.axios.com/milley-tv-anchors-call-military-no-election-role-1570714a-3532-4102-8f24-69fbd2d375e2.html

[281] Opinion by Ashton Carter, Dick Cheney, William Cohen, Mark Esper, Robert Gates, Chuck Hagel, James Mattis, Leon Panetta, William Perry and Donald Rumsfeld, All 10 living former defense secretaries: Involving the military in election disputes would cross into dangerous territory, 4 January 2021. https://www.washingtonpost.com/opinions/10-former-defense-secretaries-military-peaceful-transfer-of-power/2021/01/03/2a23d52e-4c4d-11eb-a9f4-0e668b9772ba_story.html, accessed 04 January 2021

[282] Jeffrey Goldberg, James Mattis Denounces President Trump, Describes Him as a Threat to the Constitution, 4 June 2020. https://www.theatlantic.com/politics/archive/2020/06/james-mattis-denounces-trump-protests-militarization/612640/

[283] Thom Geier, Jim Carrey Taunts Bubble-Boy Trump's Former Chief of Staff John Kelly in New Cartoon, 17 October 2020. https://www.thewrap.com/jim-carrey-john-kelly-cartoon-general-braveheart/

[284] Max Stier, A time to heal and embark on a peaceful, effective transfer of presidential power, 8 January 2021. https://ourpublicservice.org/blog/a-time-to-heal-and-embark-on-a-peaceful-effective-transfer-of-presidential-power/

[285] The Editorial Board, Donald Trump's Final Days: The best outcome would be for him to resign to spare the U.S. another impeachment fight, 7 January 2021. https://www.wsj.com/articles/donald-trumps-final-days-11610062773?

[286] Robert D. Kaplan: Trump's Budget Is American Caesarism (Foreign Policy, 26 May 2017). https://foreignpolicy.com/2017/05/26/trumps-budget-is-american-caesarism/

[287] Eliot A. Cohen: Trump's Lucky Year (Foreign Affairs, 20 Jan 2018). https://www.foreignaffairs.com/articles/2018-01-20/trumps-lucky-year

[288] Amanda Taub: How Stable Are Democracies? 'Warning Signs Are Flashing Red' (The New York Times, 29 Nov 2016). https://www.nytimes.com/2016/11/29/world/americas/western-liberal-democracy.html

[289] Anatole Kaletsky: Ten Consequences of Trump (Project Syndicate, 28 Nov 2016). https://www.project-syndicate.org/commentary/ten-consequences-of-trump-by-anatole-kaletsky-2016-11

[290] Sam Kim: 'Korea's Trump' Rises in Polls as Voter Anger Fuels Populism (Bloomberg, 25 Nov 2016).

https://www.bloomberg.com/news/articles/2016-11-24/harnessing-trump-and-sanders-korean-populist-rises-in-polls

291 Julie Carr Smyth, What's in an adjective? 'Democrat Party' label on the rise, 27 February 2021. https://apnews.com/article/donald-trump-us-news-ohio-elections-f39b9370f14fd698a76285b83a2ef4c6

292 Neil Clark: 1917 and its lessons for 2017: Learning from Lenin (RT, 4 Jan 2017). https://www.rt.com/op-ed/372668-lenin-revolution-ussr-soviet/

293 Joseph S. Nye, Jr.: Will the Liberal Order Survive? (Foreign Affairs, Jan/Feb 2017). https://www.foreignaffairs.com/articles/2016-12-12/will-liberal-order-survive

294 Aditya Chakrabortty: Panic is on the agenda at Davos – but it's too little too late (The Guardian, 23 Jan 2019). https://www.theguardian.com/commentisfree/2019/jan/23/panic-davos-inequality-global-elite

295 Andy Beckett: The new left economics: how a network of thinkers is transforming capitalism (The Guardian, 25 Jun 2019). https://www.theguardian.com/news/2019/jun/25/the-new-left-economics-how-a-network-of-thinkers-is-transforming-capitalism

296 Jonathan Rutherford: Goodbye to the liberal era (New Statesman, 6 Feb 2017). https://www.newstatesman.com/politics/2017/02/goodbye-liberal-era

297 Pål Steigan: It Hurts When Empires Fall (Information Clearing House, 8 Oct 2017). http://www.informationclearinghouse.info/47972.htm

298 Ian Buruma: Hoping for the Best Against Trump (Project Syndicate, 10 Jan 2017). https://www.project-syndicate.org/commentary/hoping-against-trump-by-ian-buruma-2017-01

299 Carlo Invernizzi-Accetti and Daniel Steinmetz-Jenkins: Can Christian democracy save America from Trump? (The Guardian, 7 Apr 2018). https://www.theguardian.com/commentisfree/2018/apr/07/christian-democracy-authoritarianism-trump

300 David Smith: The decade that shook America (The Guardian, 21 Dec 2019). https://www.theguardian.com/us-news/2019/dec/21/decade-that-shook-america-donald-trump-barack-obama-us-politics-race-division

301 Bret Stephens: This Decade of Disillusion (The New York Times, 20 Dec 2019). https://www.nytimes.com/2019/12/20/opinion/decade-millennials.html

302 Lee Edwards, Taking Back 'We The People' From The Left, 23 April 2019. https://www.theamericanconservative.com/articles/taking-back-we-the-people-from-the-left/

303 J. Bradford DeLong: Which Thinkers Will Define Our Future? (Project Syndicate, 28 June 2016). https://www.project-syndicate.org/commentary/thinkers-who-define-future-by-j--bradford-delong-2016-06

[304] David van Reybrouck: Why elections are bad for democracy (The Guardian, 29 June 2016). https://www.theguardian.com/politics/2016/jun/29/why-elections-are-bad-for-democracy

[305] Dani Rodrick: The Politics of Anger (9 March 2016). https://www.project-syndicate.org/commentary/the-politics-of-anger-by-dani-rodrik-2016-03

[306] Max Fisher and Amanda Taub: Overrun,' 'Outbred,' 'Replaced': Why Ethnic Majorities Lash Out Over False Fears (The New York Times, 30 Apr 2019). https://www.nytimes.com/2019/04/30/world/asia/sri-lanka-populism-ethnic-tensions.html

[307] Nikos Konstandaras: The Timeless Temptation of Despots (The New York Times, 3 June 2016). https://www.nytimes.com/2016/06/04/opinion/the-timeless-temptation-of-despots.html

[308] Steven B. Smith: Beware the Tyranny Trap (The National Interest, 14 Aug 2016). https://nationalinterest.org/feature/beware-the-tyranny-trap-17342

[309] Kevin Baker: The America We Lost When Trump Won (The New York Times, 21 Jan 2017). https://www.nytimes.com/2017/01/21/opinion/sunday/the-america-we-lost-when-trump-won.html

[310] Kevin Breuninger, Trump lashes out at enemies during National Prayer Breakfast speech following acquittal in impeachment trial, 6 February 2020. https://www.cnbc.com/2020/02/06/trump-lashes-out-during-national-prayer-breakfast-speech-after-acquittal.html

[311] Josh Dawsey, Robert Costa and Greg Miller, Trump lambastes his critics as he moves to target perceived enemies over impeachment, 7 February 2020. https://www.washingtonpost.com/politics/trump-lambastes-his-critics-as-he-considers-how-else-to-target-his-perceived-enemies-over-impeachment/2020/02/06/571003a0-4924-11ea-9475-535736e48788_story.html

[312] Peter Baker, Instead of Reconciliation, a Promise of Payback, 7 February 2020. https://www.nytimes.com/2020/02/07/opinion/letters/trump-impeachment-acquittal.html

[313] David Nakamura and Greg Miller, 'Not just chilling but frightening': Inside Vindman's ouster amid fears of further retaliation by Trump, 9 February 2020. https://www.washingtonpost.com/politics/not-just-chilling-but-frightening-inside-vindmans-ouster-amid-fears-of-further-retaliation-by-trump/2020/02/08/7d5ae666-4a90-11ea-bdbf-1dfb23249293_story.html

[314] Toluse Olorunnipa, Tom Hamburger, Josh Dawsey and Greg Miller, Trump ousts Vindman and Sondland, punishing key impeachment witnesses

in post-acquittal campaign of retribution, 8 February 2020.
https://www.washingtonpost.com/politics/trump-ousts-vindman-and-sondland-punishing-key-impeachment-witnesses-in-post-acquittal-campaign-of-retribution/2020/02/07/dafbdb90-49be-11ea-bdbf-1dfb23249293_story.html

315 Sonam Sheth and John Haltiwanger, Impeachment witness Alexander Vindman and his twin brother were abruptly fired and escorted from the White House as part of Trump's payback, 7 February 2020.
https://www.businessinsider.com/impeachment-witness-alexander-vindman-escorted-out-of-the-white-house-2020-2?IR=T

316 Donald Ayer, Bill Barr Must Resign, 17 February 2020.
https://www.theatlantic.com/ideas/archive/2020/02/donald-ayer-bill-barr-must-resign/606670/; David Rohde, 13 January 2020.
https://www.newyorker.com/magazine/2020/01/20/william-barr-trumps-sword-and-shield; David Rohde, Why Is William Barr Really Criticizing Donald Trump?, 14 February 2020.
https://www.newyorker.com/news/daily-comment/who-is-william-barr

317 Michael D. Shear and Maggie Haberman, Trump Places Loyalists in Key Jobs Inside the White House While Raging Against Enemies Outside, 13 February 2020. https://www.nytimes.com/2020/02/13/us/politics/trump-roger-stone.html

318 Masha Gessen, autocracy rules for survival, accessed 25 May 2021.
https://www.newyorker.com/news/our-columnists/one-year-after-trumps-election-revisiting-autocracy-rules-for-survival

319 Joseph E. Stiglitz: Trump's Rogue America (Project Syndicate, 2 Jun 2017). https://www.project-syndicate.org/commentary/trump-rogue-america-by-joseph-e--stiglitz-2017-06

320 Larry Elliott: Joseph Stiglitz: 'Trump has fascist tendencies' (The Guardian, 16 Nov 2017).
https://www.theguardian.com/business/2017/nov/16/joseph-stiglitz-trump-fascist-globalisation-bernie-sanders

321 Jason Stanley: Our Increasingly Fascist Public Discourse (Project Syndicate, 25 Jan 2019). https://www.project-syndicate.org/onpoint/our-increasingly-fascist-public-discourse-by-jason-stanley-2019-01

322 Patrick Cockburn: Is Donald Trump a fascist? (The Independent, 7 Jun 2019). https://www.independent.co.uk/voices/trump-fascism-populism-authoritarianism-hitler-mussolini-a8949496.html

323 James Jay Carafano: Maybe "Civilizations" Aren't the Problem (The National Interest, 7 Jul 2018). https://www.heritage.org/civil-society/commentary/maybe-civilizations-arent-the-problem

324 Paul Craig Roberts: The Assault on Trump (Paul Craig Roberts Institute for Political Economy, 18 May 2017).
https://www.paulcraigroberts.org/2017/05/18/the-assault-on-trump/

[325] Paul Craig Roberts: The Assault on Trump (Paul Craig Roberts Institute for Political Economy, 18 May 2017). https://www.paulcraigroberts.org/2017/05/18/the-assault-on-trump/

[326] Costica Bradatan: Democracy Is for the Gods (The New York Times, 5 Jul 2019). https://www.nytimes.com/2019/07/05/opinion/why-democracies-fail.html

[327] Sławomir Sierakowski: What Trump's Win Means for Eastern Europe (Project Syndicate, 18 Nov 2016). https://www.project-syndicate.org/commentary/trump-poland-russia-eastern-europe-by-slawomir-sierakowski-2016-11

[328] Philip Stephens: Donald Trump would tear up the Pax Americana (Financial Times, 5 May 2016). https://www.ft.com/content/f195226c-11ff-11e6-839f-2922947098f0

[329] Philip Auerswald and Joon Yun: As Population Growth Slows, Populism Surges (The New York Times, 22 May 2018). https://www.nytimes.com/2018/05/22/opinion/populist-populism-fertility-rates.html

[330] Sarah Churchwell: End of the American dream? The dark history of 'America first' (The Guardian, 21 Apr 2018). https://www.theguardian.com/books/2018/apr/21/end-of-the-american-dream-the-dark-history-of-america-first

[331] See also Jason Silverstein, Trump tells Democratic congresswomen of color to "go back" to their countries, 15 July 2019. https://www.cbsnews.com/news/donald-trump-racist-tweets-progressive-democratic-congresswomen-go-back-to-countries-nancy-pelosi-slam-president/

[332] Jason Silverstein, Trump tells Democratic congresswomen of color to "go back" to their countries, 15 July 2019. https://www.cbsnews.com/news/donald-trump-racist-tweets-progressive-democratic-congresswomen-go-back-to-countries-nancy-pelosi-slam-president/

[333] George Conway, Trump Is A Racist President, 15 July, 2019. https://www.washingtonpost.com/opinions/george-conway-trump-is-a-racist-president/2019/07/15/b13c0bd4-a740-11e9-9214-246e594de5d5_story.html

[334] Anonymous, I Am Part of the resistance Inside the Trump Administration, 5 September 2018. https://www.nytimes.com/2018/09/05/opinion/trump-white-house-anonymous-resistance.html

[335] Caroline Cournoyer, A Warning by "Anonymous" will be released next week. Here are the highlights.16 November 2019. https://www.cbsnews.com/news/a-warning-by-anonymous-released-next-week-here-are-the-highlights-2019-11-16/; see also Lloyd Green, A Warning

review: Anonymous Trump book fails to make a name for itself, 18 November 2019. https://www.theguardian.com/us-news/2019/nov/18/a-warning-review-anonymous-trump-book

[336] See also, Julian Borger, Mark Milley, US general who stood up to Trump, founders over Kabul strike, 18 September 2021. https://www.theguardian.com/us-news/2021/sep/18/mark-milley-us-general-who-stood-up-to-trump-founders-over-kabul-strike

[337] Paul R. Pillar: Brexit and the Transnational Triumph of Ignorance (*The National Interest,* 25 June 2016). https://nationalinterest.org/blog/paul-pillar/brexit-the-transnational-triumph-ignorance-16733

[338] David Brooks: The Danger of a Dominant Identity (The New York Times, 18 Nov 2016). https://www.nytimes.com/2016/11/18/opinion/the-danger-of-a-dominant-identity.html

[339] Benjamin Mouffitt, The Trouble with Anti-Populism: Why the Champions of Civility Keep Losing, 14 February 2020. https://www.theguardian.com/politics/2020/feb/14/anti-populism-politics-why-champions-of-civility-keep-losing

[340] Benjamin Mouffitt, The Trouble with Anti-Populism: Why the Champions of Civility Keep Losing, 14 February 2020. https://www.theguardian.com/politics/2020/feb/14/anti-populism-politics-why-champions-of-civility-keep-losing

[341] Benjamin Mouffitt, The Trouble with Anti-Populism: Why the Champions of Civility Keep Losing, 14 February 2020. https://www.theguardian.com/politics/2020/feb/14/anti-populism-politics-why-champions-of-civility-keep-losing

[342] Benjamin Mouffitt, The Trouble with Anti-Populism: Why the Champions of Civility Keep Losing, 14 February 2020. https://www.theguardian.com/politics/2020/feb/14/anti-populism-politics-why-champions-of-civility-keep-losing

[343] Maaza Mengiste, "The Moment of Encounter: History, Disruptions, and Transformations", 19 May 2021, accessed 31 May 2021. https://www.pluralism.ca/event/maaza-mengiste-8th-annual-pluralism-lecture/; https://www.youtube.com/watch?v=I5ztss4ojTY

[344] Benn Steil: The Marshall Plan and "America First" (4 Aug 2017). https://www.project-syndicate.org/onpoint/the-marshall-plan-and-america-first-by-benn-steil-2017-08

[345] Nikolas K. Gvosdev: Trump Takes a Gamble on Davos (The National Interest, 25 Jan 2018). https://nationalinterest.org/feature/trump-takes-gamble-davos-24218

[346] Fareed Zakaria: Say hello to a post-America world (The Washington Post, 27 Jul 2017). https://www.washingtonpost.com/opinions/say-hello-to-a-post-america-world/2017/07/27/aad19d68-7308-11e7-8f39-

eeb7d3a2d304_story.html

347 Fareed Zakaria: The Self-Destruction of American Power (Foreign Affairs, 11 Jun 2019). https://www.foreignaffairs.com/articles/2019-06-11/self-destruction-american-power

348 Michael Hudson: Trump's Brilliant Strategy to Dismember U.S. Dollar Hegemony (Counterpunch, 1 Feb 2019). https://www.counterpunch.org/2019/02/01/trumps-brilliant-strategy-to-dismember-u-s-dollar-hegemony/

349 Patrick Cockburn: Unlike the US with Trump, Britain doesn't have the political clout to suffer a fool like Boris Johnson (The Independent, 3 Aug 2018). https://www.independent.co.uk/voices/boris-johnson-donald-trump-brexit-us-populism-nationalism-a8476476.html

350 John Rentoul: Do we have Obama and Blair to thank for Trump and Brexit? (The Independent, 24 Sep 2018). https://www.independent.co.uk/news/long_reads/barack-obama-donald-trump-bernie-sanders-tony-blair-brexit-jeremy-corbyn-populism-a8532871.html

351 Bret Stephens: The Rudderless West (The New York Times, 17 Jan 2019). https://www.nytimes.com/2019/01/17/opinion/brexit-western-powers.html

352 David Brooks: Choosing Leaders: Clueless or Crazy (The New York Times, 5 July 2016). https://www.nytimes.com/2016/07/05/opinion/choosing-leaders-clueless-or-crazy.html

353 Stephen M. Walt: The End of Hubris (Foreign Affairs, 16 Apr 2019). https://www.foreignaffairs.com/articles/2019-04-16/end-hubris

354 Simon Wren-Lewis: Why are we governed by incompetents? (New Statesman, 7 May 2019). https://www.newstatesman.com/politics/staggers/2019/05/why-are-we-governed-incompetents

355 David Brooks: When the World Is Led by a Child (The New York Times, 15 May 2017). nytimes.com/2017/05/15/opinion/trump-classified-data.html

356 Masha Gessen: Trump's Incompetence Won't Save Our Democracy (The New York Times, 2 Jun 2017). https://www.nytimes.com/2017/06/02/opinion/sunday/trumps-incompetence-wont-save-our-democracy.html

357 Masha Gessen, autocracy rules for survival, accessed 25 May 2021. https://www.newyorker.com/news/our-columnists/one-year-after-trumps-election-revisiting-autocracy-rules-for-survival

358 Tyler Durden: Beppe Grillo: "The Amateurs Are Conquering The World Because The 'Experts' Destroyed It" (ZeroHedge, 21 Nov 2016). https://www.zerohedge.com/news/2016-11-20/beppe-grillo-amateurs-are-

conquering-world-because-experts-destroyed-it;
https://www.euronews.com/2016/11/14/political-amateurs-are-conquering-the-world-beppe-grillo-tells-euronews

359 Fareed Zakaria: These foreign admirers are cheering Trump. What do they have in common? (The Washington Post, 17 Nov 2016). https://www.washingtonpost.com/opinions/these-foreign-admirers-are-cheering-trump-what-do-they-have-in-common/2016/11/17/bdd48978-ad0d-11e6-8b45-f8e493f06fcd_story.html

360 Michel Wieviorka: France, Without a Struggle, Is at a Loss (The New York Times, 10 Feb 2017). https://www.nytimes.com/2017/02/10/opinion/france-without-a-struggle-is-at-a-loss.html

361 David Brooks: The Coming War on Business (The New York Times, 22 Sep 2017). https://www.nytimes.com/2017/09/22/opinion/business-war-trump.html

362 Ken Moak: Why Trump could win another term (Asia Times, 3 Mar 2020). https://asiatimes.com/2020/03/why-trump-could-win-another-term/

363 Chris Patten: From Tolstoy to Trump (Project Syndicate, 18 March 2016). https://www.project-syndicate.org/commentary/trump-populism-in-europe-and-america-by-chris-patten-2016-03

364 Chris Patten: Tough times for the tough guys (Project Syndicate, 23 Aug 2018). https://www.project-syndicate.org/commentary/authoritarian-leaders-scandals-crises-by-chris-patten-2018-08

365 Andrew Solomon: Against the Wall: from Mexico to Calais, why the idea of division is taking hold (Andrew Solomon, 16 Sep 2016). http://andrewsolomon.com/articles/against-the-wall/

366 The new political divide (The Economist, 30 Jul 2016).

https://www.economist.com/leaders/2016/07/30/the-new-political-divide

367 John Oliver, Last Week Tonight, 12 November 2018. https://www.youtube.com/watch?v=5HS2TstPfW4

368 Stephen M. Walt: America's Corruption Is a National Security Threat (Foreign Policy, 19 Mar 2019). https://foreignpolicy.com/2019/03/19/americas-corruption-problem-is-a-national-security-threat/

369 Justin E. H. Smith: No, He's Not Hitler. And Yet … (New York Times, 2016). https://www.nytimes.com/2016/06/05/opinion/sunday/no-hes-not-hitler-and-yet.html

370 Jonathan Rauch: How American Politics Went Insane (The Atlantic, July/August 2016).

https://www.theatlantic.com/magazine/archive/2016/07/how-american-politics-went-insane/485570/

371 PS editors: A Comeuppance for Populism? (Project Syndicate, 16 Jun 2017). https://www.project-syndicate.org/onpoint/a-comeuppance-for-populism-2017-06

372 Basillioh Rukanga, Evelyne Musambi and Natasha Booty, Cameroon president wears mask after foreign trip, BBC, 17 August 2021. https://www.bbc.com/news/live/world-africa-47639452?

373 Peter Nicholas, Donald Trump Is All Alone, 7 November 2019. https://www.theatlantic.com/politics/archive/2019/11/donald-trump-all-alone-white-house/601537/

374 Maggie Haberman, Glen Thrush, and Peter Baker, Inside Trump's Hour-by-Hour Battle for Self-Preservation, 9 December 2017. https://www.nytimes.com/2017/12/09/us/politics/donald-trump-president.html

375 David Smith, Interview: The right man for the job: how Bob Woodward pinned Trump to the page, 20 September 2020. https://www.theguardian.com/media/2020/sep/19/bob-woodward-donald-trump-rage-interview

376 Greg Sargent, Want Trump removed? New data shows Fox News is a huge obstacle, 21 October 2019. https://www.washingtonpost.com/opinions/2019/10/21/want-trump-removed-new-data-shows-that-fox-news-is-huge-obstacle/

377 Reuter Staff, Fact check: Trump did not call Republicans "the dumbest group of voters", 28 May 2020. https://www.reuters.com/article/uk-factcheck-trump-republicans-meme-idUSKBN2342S5

378 David Klemperer, Interview: Chantal Mouffe on democracy, populism, and why the Left needs to read Spinoza, 19 August 2021. https://tocqueville21.com/blog-info/interview-chantal-mouffe-on-democracy-populism-and-why-the-left-needs-to-read-spinoza/

379 BBC, Donald Trump balloon: Baby blimp acquired by Museum of London, 18 January 2021. https://www.bbc.com/news/uk-england-london-55694910,

380 Robert Costa, Sarah Ellison and Josh Dawsey, Hannity's rising role in Trump's world: 'He basically has a desk in the place' 18 April 2018. https://www.washingtonpost.com/politics/hannitys-rising-role-in-trumps-world-he-basically-has-a-desk-in-the-place/2018/04/17/e2483018-4260-11e8-8569-26fda6b404c7_story.html

381 Bess Levin, Report: Tucker Carlson Is Dictating Trump's Policy On Iran, 9 January 2020. https://www.vanityfair.com/news/2020/01/tucker-carlson-donald-trump-iran

382 Robert Costa, Sarah Ellison and Josh Dawsey, Hannity's rising role in

Trump's world: 'He basically has a desk in the place' 18 April 2018.
https://www.washingtonpost.com/politics/hannitys-rising-role-in-trumps-world-he-basically-has-a-desk-in-the-place/2018/04/17/e2483018-4260-11e8-8569-26fda6b404c7_story.html

383 Gabriel Sherman, "It's Management Bedlam": Madness At Fox News As Trump Faces Impeachment, 26 September 2019, https://www.vanityfair.com/news/2019/09/madness-at-fox-news-as-trump-faces-impeachment-lachlan-murdoch

384 Tommy Christopher, Elizabeth Warren Critics Miss the Point: Starving Racism is More Important Than Winning Fox News Viewers, 15 May 2019. https://www.mediaite.com/opinion/elizabeth-warren-critics-miss-the-point-starving-racism-is-more-important-than-winning-fox-news-viewers/

385 See also, Maggie Haberman and Michael S. Schmidt, Trump Has Considered Firing Intelligence Community Inspector General, 12 November 2019. https://www.nytimes.com/2019/11/12/us/politics/trump-michael-atkinson-inspector-general.html

386 Mary L. Trump, (2020), *Too Much and Never Enough: How My Family Created the World's Most Dangerous Man*, New York: Simon & Schuster.

387 "The World's Most Dangerous Man": Mary Trump on Her Uncle, President Trump, & Why He Must Be Ousted, 7 August 2020. https://www.democracynow.org/2020/8/7/mary_trump_how_dysfunctional_family_shaped

388 Michael Moore. https://www.facebook.com/mmflint/posts/so-now-trump-has-earned-your-trust-a-note-of-covid-caution-from-michael-moorethe/10157263999686857/

389 If Trump's former personal attorney and confident, Michael Cohen is to be believed in his claim that Trump has no friends (Cohen 2020), then Piers Morgan's allusion to 15 years of friendship with Trump was more his feeling about the relationship and not necessarily a reflection of how Trump categorised it.

390 Piers Morgan: An open letter to President Trump from his (now unfollowed) friend PIERS MORGAN: Cut the covid crap, stop whining, get serious and show some damn empathy - or it will cost you the White House (27 April 2020). https://www.dailymail.co.uk/news/article-8261275/PIERS-MORGAN-open-letter-President-Trump-unfollowed-friend-cut-covid-crap.html

391 Philip Rucker and Carol Leonnig, "It's Like A Foreign Language": Donald Trump's Encounter With The Constitution Did Not Go Well, 20 January 2020. https://www.vanityfair.com/news/2020/01/donald-trump-disastrous-encounter-with-the-constitution-very-stable-genius

392 Elisabeth Dwoskin, Twitter labels Trump's tweets with a fact check for the first time, 27 May 2020. https://www.washingtonpost.com/technology/2020/05/26/trump-twitter-

label-fact-check/

[393] Kate Conger and Mike Isaac, Twitter Permanently Bans Trump, Capping Online Revolt. 8 January 2021. https://www.nytimes.com/2021/01/08/technology/twitter-trump-suspended.html

[394] Michael D. Shear, Maggie Haberman, Nicholas Confessore, Karin Yourish, Larry Buchanan and Keith Collins, How Trump Reshaped the Presidency in Over 11,000 Tweets, 2 November 2019. https://www.nytimes.com/interactive/2019/11/02/us/politics/trump-twitter-presidency.html

[395] Jordan Hollinger, Trump, social media and the first Twitter-based Presidency, 7 May 2018. https://www.diggitmagazine.com/articles/Trump-Twitter-Based-Presidency, accessed 08 January 2020

[396] Michael Humphrey, I analyzed all of Trump's tweets to find out what he was really saying, 8 February 2021. https://theconversation.com/i-analyzed-all-of-trumps-tweets-to-find-out-what-he-was-really-saying-154532

[397] Statement from the Office of the Former President, 25 January 2021. https://www.45office.com/news/statement-from-the-office-of-the-former-president

[398] See BBC, Donald Trump plans social media comeback, says adviser, accessed 22 March 2021. https://www.bbc.com/news/world-us-canada-56479316; see also Jazmin Goodwin, Trump is returning to social media in a few months with his own platform, spokesman says. https://edition.cnn.com/2021/03/21/media/donald-trump-social-media-network/index.html, accessed 22 March 2021

[399] Drew Hartley and Josh Dawsey, Trump is sliding towards online irrelevance. His new blog isn't helping, 22 May 2021, accessed 25 May 2021. https://www.iol.co.za/news/world/trump-is-sliding-towards-online-irrelevance-his-new-blog-isnt-helping-359ab8c1-4e1c-5511-87a0-4e84778bf584

[400] Richard Luscombe, Trump closes his 'beacon of freedom' website a month after launching it, 2 June 2021. https://www.theguardian.com/us-news/2021/jun/02/trump-closes-website-beacon-of-freedom

[401] Mark Niquette and Naomi Nix, Trump sues Facebook, Twitter and Google over social media bans, 7 July 2021. https://www.aljazeera.com/economy/2021/7/7/trump-sues-facebook-twitter-and-google-over-social-media-bans

[402] The Observer view on Donald Trump's Truth Social: Observer editorialhttps://www.theguardian.com/commentisfree/2021/oct/24/the-observer-view-on-donald-trump-truth-social, 24 October 2021, accessed 07 November 2021.

[403] Itzu Díaz The Century We Put the Idiots on Pedestals (March 2021).

https://www.nationalreview.com/2021/03/the-century-we-put-the-idiots-on-pedestals/

[404] Scott Barry Kaufman, What Collective Narcissism Does to Society, 6 November 2021. https://www.theatlantic.com/family/archive/2021/11/group-narcissism/620632/

[405] Itzu Díaz The Century We Put the Idiots on Pedestals (March 2021). https://www.nationalreview.com/2021/03/the-century-we-put-the-idiots-on-pedestals/

[406] Michael Lind, How right-wingers use semantic tricks to kill government, 18 May 2013, accessed 31 May 2021. https://www.salon.com/2013/05/18/how_right_wingers_use_semantic_tricks_to_kill_government/

[407] David Smith, Trump has a new favourite news network – and it's more rightwing than Fox, 15 June 2019. https://www.theguardian.com/tv-and-radio/2019/jun/15/oan-oann-fox-news-donald-trump; see also Kevin Poulsen, Trump's New Favorite Channel Employs Kremlin-Paid Journalist, 22 July 2019. https://www.thedailybeast.com/oan-trumps-new-favorite-channel-employs-kremlin-paid-journalist

[408] Michael de Groot: Why do many British people not like Donald Trump? (20 April 2020). https://medium.com/typewriting/why-do-many-british-people-not-like-donald-trump-9810d1485509

[409] De Trollenkoning (The Troll King) , accessed 31 May 2021. https://aegtte.weebly.com/de-trollenkoning-the-troll-king.html

[410] Francis Fukuyama: American Political Decay or Renewal?: The Meaning of the 2016 Election (Foreign Affairs, July/August 2016).

[411] Mary Trump: "He feels no shame. He has no humility", MSNBC, 28 August 2020. https://www.facebook.com/msnbc/videos/777334146424835

[412] Tony Schwartz on Donald Trump, 5 May 2017. https://www.youtube.com/watch?v=-2JmC_yDL2k

[413] The Late Show with Stephen Colbert, Trump's Disregard For Human Life Has Resulted In 200K Deaths And CDC Guidance That Can't Be Trusted, 23 September 2020. https://www.youtube.com/watch?v=8DG_4ZY48iQ; see also, Stephen Colbert Refuses to Watch Night 3 of the R.N.C. https://www.nytimes.com/2020/08/27/arts/television/stephen-colbert-republican-convention.html

[414] Tony Schwartz, Why Trump can't change, no matter what the consequences are, 18 October, 2019. https://www.washingtonpost.com/outlook/why-trump-cant-change-no-matter-what-the-consequences-are/2019/10/18/cf502cf6-f117-11e9-89eb-ec56cd414732_story.html

[415] Inae Oh, Watch Toni Morrison Explain the "Profound Neurosis" of

Racism, 6 August 2019.
https://www.motherjones.com/politics/2019/08/watch-toni-morrison-explain-the-profound-neurosis-of-racism/

[416] Carlos Lozada: Review of White Trash (The Washington Post, 23 Jun 2016). https://www.washingtonpost.com/

[417] Timothy Shenk: The secret history of Trumpism (The Guardian, 16 Aug 2016). https://www.theguardian.com/news/2016/aug/16/secret-history-trumpism-donald-trump

[418] Ian Buruma: Reading the Signs of the Times (Project Syndicate, 9 Jul 2018). https://www.project-syndicate.org/commentary/how-to-tell-democracy-is-in-peril-by-ian-buruma-2018-07

[419] Ian Buruma: Reading the Signs of the Times (Project Syndicate, 9 Jul 2018). https://www.project-syndicate.org/commentary/how-to-tell-democracy-is-in-peril-by-ian-buruma-2018-07

[420] Robert Kagan: This is How Fascism comes to America. Trump captures the nation's attention on the campaign trail (18 May 2016). https://www.washingtonpost.com/opinions/this-is-how-fascism-comes-to-america/2016/05/17/c4e32c58-1c47-11e6-8c7b-6931e66333e7_story.html

[421] Max Boot: How the 'Stupid Party' Created Donald Trump (The New York Times, 31 July 2016). https://www.nytimes.com/2016/08/01/opinion/how-the-stupid-party-created-donald-trump.html

[422] Jay Nordlinger, How Populists Talk, 18 February 2021, accessed 23 April 2021. https://www.nationalreview.com/magazine/2021/03/08/how-populists-talk/#slide-1

[423] Jay Nordlinger, How Populists Talk, 18 February 2021, accessed 23 April 2021. https://www.nationalreview.com/magazine/2021/03/08/how-populists-talk/#slide-1

[424] Peter, Suderman, Josh Hawley's Toxic Populism: Is the senator's authoritarian grandstanding the dark future of the GOP?, 6 April 2021. https://reason.com/2021/03/06/josh-hawleys-toxic-populism/

[425] Peter, Suderman, Josh Hawley's Toxic Populism: Is the senator's authoritarian grandstanding the dark future of the GOP?, 6 April 2021. https://reason.com/2021/03/06/josh-hawleys-toxic-populism/

[426] Max Boot: How the 'Stupid Party' Created Donald Trump (The New York Times, 31 July 2016). https://www.nytimes.com/2016/08/01/opinion/how-the-stupid-party-created-donald-trump.html

[427] Robert Kagan: This is how fascism comes to America. (Washington Post, 18 May 2016). https://www.washingtonpost.com/opinions/this-is-how-fascism-comes-to-america/2016/05/17/c4e32c58-1c47-11e6-8c7b-6931e66333e7_story.html

[428] Andrew A. Michta: Losing the Nation-State (The American Interest, 1

Jul 2017). https://www.the-american-interest.com/2017/07/01/losing-nation-state/

429 Dani Rodrik: Why nation-states are good (Aeon, 2 Oct 2017). https://aeon.co/essays/capitalists-need-the-nation-state-more-than-it-needs-them

430 Jørgen Ørstrøm Møller: Democracies Are Fighting for Their Lives (The National Interest, 11 Dec 2018). https://nationalinterest.org/feature/democracies-are-fighting-their-lives-38467?page=0%2C1

431 Tom Nichols: How America Lost Faith in Expertise (Foreign Affairs, March/April 2017). https://www.foreignaffairs.com/articles/united-states/2017-02-13/how-america-lost-faith-expertise

432 Michiko Kakutani: The Death of Expertise (The New York Times, 21 March 2017). https://www.nytimes.com/2017/03/21/books/the-death-of-expertise-explores-how-ignorance-became-a-virtue.html

433 See also, Tom Nichols: How America Lost Faith in Expertise (Foreign Affairs, March/April 2017). https://www.foreignaffairs.com/articles/united-states/2017-02-13/how-america-lost-faith-expertise

434 William Davies: The Age of Post-Truth Politics (The New York Times, 24 Aug 2016). https://www.nytimes.com/2016/08/24/opinion/campaign-stops/the-age-of-post-truth-politics.html

435 See Editorial, Lobbying for and against climate solutions, Nature Climate Change volume 9, page 427 (2019). https://www.nature.com/articles/s41558-019-0499-4

436 David Masci, Darwin in America: The Evolution Debate in the United States, 6 February 2019. https://www.pewforum.org/essay/darwin-in-america/

437 Jason Husser, Why Trump is reliant on evangelicals. 6 April 2020. https://www.brookings.edu/blog/fixgov/2020/04/06/why-trump-is-reliant-on-white-evangelicals/

438 Mark Galli, Christianity Today editorial, Trump Should Be Removed from Office, 19 December 2019. https://www.christianitytoday.com/ct/2019/december-web-only/trump-should-be-removed-from-office.html

439 Mark Galli, Christianity Today editorial, Trump Should Be Removed from Office, 19 December 2019. https://www.christianitytoday.com/ct/2019/december-web-only/trump-should-be-removed-from-office.html

440 Melissa Barnhart, Nearly 200 evangelical leaders slam Christianity Today for questioning their Christian witness, 22 December 2019. https://www.christianpost.com/news/nearly-200-evangelical-leaders-slam-christianity-today-for-questioning-their-christian-witness.html

[441] Episcopal Church Office of Public Affairs, Presiding Bishop Michael Curry's statement on President Donald Trump's use of St. John's, Holy Bible, 1 June 2020. https://www.episcopalnewsservice.org/pressreleases/presiding-bishop-michael-currys-statement-on-president-donald-trumps-use-of-st-johns-holy-bible/

[442] Michael Horton, The Cult of Christian Trumpism, 16 December 2020. https://www.thegospelcoalition.org/article/cult-christian-trumpism/

[443] Peter Wehner, Evangelicals Made a Bad Bargain With Trump, 18 October 2020. https://www.theatlantic.com/ideas/archive/2020/10/the-evangelical-movements-bad-bargain/616760/

[444] William Davies: The age of pain (15 November 2016). https://www.newstatesman.com/politics/uk/2016/11/age-pain

[445] Jean Seaton, Tim Crook and DJ Taylor: Welcome to dystopia – George Orwell experts on Donald Trump (The Guardian, 25 Jan 2017). https://www.theguardian.com/commentisfree/2017/jan/25/george-orwell-donald-trump-kellyanne-conway-1984

[446] Casey Williams: Has Trump Stolen Philosophy's Critical Tools? (The New York Times, 17 Apr 2017). https://www.nytimes.com/2017/04/17/opinion/has-trump-stolen-philosophys-critical-tools.html

[447] BBC, Kellyanne Conway: Key moments from her White House career. 24 August 2020. https://www.bbc.com/news/world-us-canada-53889605

[448] Noah Feldman, The Myth of America's Anglo-Saxon Political Traditions, 20 April 2021. https://www.bloomberg.com/opinion/articles/2021-04-20/the-myth-of-america-s-anglo-saxon-political-traditions

[449] Casey Williams: Has Trump Stolen Philosophy's Critical Tools? (The New York Times, 17 Apr 2017). https://www.nytimes.com/2017/04/17/opinion/has-trump-stolen-philosophys-critical-tools.html

[450] John Gray: Europe's states of disorder (New Statesman, 12 Dec 2016). https://www.newstatesman.com/politics/2016/12/europes-states-disorder

[451] Satyajit Das: Brexit and Donald Trump promised easy solutions to hard problems – but what happens when they don't deliver? (The Independent Online, 26 March 2017). https://www.independent.co.uk/voices/brexit-europe-president-donald-trump-make-america-great-again-easy-solutions-a7650621.html

[452] David Brooks, How to Destroy Truth, 1 July 2021. https://www.nytimes.com/2021/07/01/opinion/patriotism-misinformation.html

[453] Olivier Douliery, Facebook bans former US president Trump for 2 years, 4 June 2021, accessed 5 June 2021.

https://www.enca.com/news/facebook-bans-former-us-president-trump-2-years; see also, BBC, Facebook suspends Trump accounts for two years, accessed 5 June 2021. https://www.bbc.com/news/world-us-canada-57365628

454 Olivier Douliery, Facebook bans former US president Trump for 2 years, 4 June 2021. https://www.enca.com/news/facebook-bans-former-us-president-trump-2-years; see also, BBC, Facebook suspends Trump accounts for two years. https://www.bbc.com/news/world-us-canada-57365628

455 Sue Halpern, The problem of political advertising on Social Media, 24 October 2019. https://www.newyorker.com/tech/annals-of-technology/the-problem-of-political-advertising-on-social-media

456 BBC, Nigeria's Twitter ban: Donald Trump hails Buhari, accessed 10 June 2021. https://www.bbc.com/news/world-africa-57408179

457 William H. Frey, The US will become 'minority white' in 2045, Census projects, 14 March 2018. https://www.brookings.edu/blog/the-avenue/2018/03/14/the-us-will-become-minority-white-in-2045-census-projects/

458 Seema Mehta, Trump's touting of 'racehorse theory' tied to eugenics and Nazis alarms Jewish leaders, 5 October 2020. https://www.latimes.com/politics/story/2020-10-05/trump-debate-white-supremacy-racehorse-theory.

459 Ryan Cooper, What Donald Trump has said about Jews, 18 April 2019. https://theweek.com/articles/835714/what-donald-trump-said-about-jews

460 See "President Trump Called El Salvador, Haiti 'Shithole Countries': Report", accessed 29 May 2018. http://time.com/5100058/donald-trump-shithole-countries/?xid=homepage

461 See Adam Liptak and Michael D. Shear, "Trump's Travel Ban Is Upheld by Supreme", accessed 27 June 2018. https://www.nytimes.com/2018/06/26/us/politics/supreme-court-trump-travel-ban.html

462 See Mark Sherman, "Supreme Court upholds Trump ban on travel from several mostly Muslim countries", accessed 27 June 2018. http://www.chicagotribune.com/news/nationworld/ct-supreme-court-trump-travel-ban-20180626-story.html; see also "The Rachel Maddow Show 6/26/2018| MSNBC NEWS June 26, 2018", accessed 27 June 2018. https://youtu.be/9BNJyv27-6k

463 Alix Kroeger, JD Vance: Trump whisperer turned Senate hopeful, 18 April 2021, accessed 18 April 2021. https://www.bbc.com/news/world-us-canada-56748047

464 Fareed Zakaria: The new dividing line in Western politics (Washington Post 13 Dec 2018). I found the article reproduced in full on Zakaria's website. https://fareedzakaria.com/columns/2018/12/13/the-new-dividing-line-in-

western-politics

[465] Fareed Zakaria: The new dividing line in Western politics (Washington Post 13 Dec 2018). I found the article reproduced in full on Zakaria's website. https://fareedzakaria.com/columns/2018/12/13/the-new-dividing-line-in-western-politics

[466] Christopher Bergland, One Way Dogma Can Perpetuate Rigid Opinions, 22 November 2020. https://www.psychologytoday.com/za/blog/the-athletes-way/202011/one-way-dogma-can-perpetuate-rigid-opinions

References

Abrams, S. (2020) *Our Time Is Now: Power, Purpose, and the Fight for a Fair America*, New York: Henry Holt and Co.

Abutaleb, Y. and Paletta, D. (2021) *Nightmare Scenario: Inside the Trump Administration's Response to the Pandemic that Changed History*, New York: Harper.

Achter, P. J. (2018) "Great Television: Trump and the Shadow Archetype", in: Ryan Skinnell (ed.), *Faking the News: What Rhetoric Can Teach Us about Donald J. Trump*, Exeter: Imprint Academic.

Albertazzi, D. and Vampa, D. (eds) (2021) *Populism and New Patterns of Political Competition in Western Europe*, London: Routledge.

Albright, M. (2018) *Fascism: A Warning*, New York: Harper.

Angelo, N. (2019) *One America? Presidential Appeals to Racial Resentment from LBJ to Trump*, New York: Suny Press.

Anonymous (A Senior Trump Administration Official) (2019) *A Warning*, New York: Twelve.

Applebaum, A. (2020) *Twilight of Democracy: The Seductive Lure of Authoritarianism*, New York: Doubleday.

Attwell, D. (2020) "Populism vs. the Popular in South African Literature", *English Studies in Africa*, 63(1): 119–29.

Ayyangar, S. (2017) "The Promise and Perils of Populism: Global Perspectives", *Commonwealth & Comparative Politics*, DOI: 10.1080/14662043.2017.1290748.

Babones, S. (2018) *The New Authoritarianism: Trump, Populism, and the Tyranny of Experts*, Cambridge: Polity.

Bahi, A. (2013) *L'Ivoirité Mouvementée: Jeunes, Médias et Politique en Côte D'Ivoire*, Bamenda: Langaa RPCIG.

Banywesize, E. M. (2013) "The Facets and Offshoots of Populism in Sub-Saharan Africa", in: Sergiu Gherghina, Sergiu Mişcoiu and Sorina Soare (eds), *Contemporary Populism: A Controversial Concept and Its Diverse Forms*, Newcastle: Cambridge Scholars Publishing, pp. 203–233.

Barber, W. J. (2020) *We Are Called to Be a Movement*, New York: Workman Publishing.

Barrett, W. (2016[1992]) *Trump: The Greatest Show on Earth: The Deals, The Downfall, The Reinvention*, New York: Regan Arts.

Bartlett, R. C. (2020) *Against Demagogues: What Aristophanes Can Teach Us About the Perils of Populism and the Fate of Democracy*, Oakland: University of California Press.

Bender, M. C. (2021) *"Frankly We Did Win This Election": The Inside Story of How Trump Lost*, New York: Twelve.

Benen, S. (2020) *The Impostors: How Republicans Quit Governing and Seized American Politics*, New York: William Morrow.

Ben-Ghiat, R. (2020) *Strongmen: Mussolini to the Present*, New York: W.W. Norton & Company.

Bennett, M. (2019) *Dividing America: How Russia Hacked Social Media and Democracy*, Denver.

Benveniste, A., Campani, G., & Lazaridis, G. (2016) "Introduction. Populism: The Concept and Its Definitions", in: G. Lazaridis, G. Campani & A. Benveniste (eds), *The Rise of the Far Right in Europe Populist Shifts and 'Othering'*, London: Palgrave Macmillan, pp.1–24.

Bernstein, C. and Woodward, B. (1974) *All the President's Men*, New York: Simon & Schuster.

Boczkowski, P. J. and Papacharissi, Z. (2018) "Introduction", in: P. J. Boczkowski and Z. Papacharissi (eds), *Trump and the Media*, Cambridge, Massachusetts: The MIT Press, pp. 1–7.

Bolton, T. (2020) *The Room Where It Happened: A Memoir*, New York: Simon & Schuster.

Brabazon, T. Redhead, S. and Chivaura, R. S. (2019) *Trump Studies: An Intellectual Guide to Why Citizens Vote Against Their Interests*, Bingley: Emerald Publishing.

Braun, C. N. (2021) "The Morality of Resisting Trump", *Academia Letters*, Article 183, DOI: 10.20935/AL183.

Bretherton, L. (2019) "Good and Bad Forms of Populism: Who Speaks for the People"., *Christian Century*, 19 June 2019, p. 28.

Brooke, C. G. (2018) "How #Trump Broke/red the Internet", in: Ryan Skinnell (ed), *Faking the News: What Rhetoric Can Teach Us about Donald J. Trump*, Exeter: Imprint Academic.

Bruder, J. (2017) *Nomadland: Surviving America in the Twenty-First Century*, New York: W. W. Norton & Company.

Burke, C. B. (2018) *America's Information Wars: The Untold Story of Information Systems in America's Conflicts and Politics from World War II to the Internet Age*, Lanham: Rowman & Littlefield.

Burns, W. J. (2019) *The Back Channel: A Memoir of American Diplomacy and the Case for Its Renewal*, New York: Random House.

Carbone, G. (2005) *'Populism' Visits Africa: The Case of Yoweri Museveni and No-Party Democracy in Uganda*, Crisis States Programme, Working Paper series No. 73, Crisis States Research Centre, DESTIN, LSE, Houghton Street, London.

Carpini, M. X. D. (2018) "Alternative Facts: Donald Trump and the Emergence of a New U.S. Media Regime", in: P. J. Boczkowski and Z. Papacharissi (eds), *Trump and the Media*, Cambridge, Massachusetts: The MIT Press, pp. 17–23.

Castells, M. and Lategan, B. (eds) (2021) *National Identity and State Formation in Africa*, Cambridge: Polity.

Chandler, A. (2020) "Populism and Social Policy: A Challenge to Neoliberalism, or a Complement to It?", *World Affairs*, Vol. 183(2): 125–154.

Cheeseman, N. and Larmer, M. (2015) "Ethnopopulism in Africa: Opposition Mobilization in Diverse and Unequal Societies", *Democratization*, Vol. 22(1): 22–50.

Chini, C. and Moroni, S. (2018) "Introduction", in: Chiara Chini and Sheyla Moroni (eds), *Populism: A Historical Category*, Cambridge: Cambridge Scholars Publishing, pp. 1–6.

Coates, T.-N. (2017) *We Were Eight Years in Power: An American Tragedy*, New York: One World.

Cohen, M. (2020) *Disloyalty: A Memoir*, New York: Skyhorse Publishing.

Coles, T. J. (2017) *President Trump, Inc. How Big Business and Neoliberalism Empower Populism and the Far-Right*, Sussex: Clairview Books Ltd.

Comey, J. (2018) *A Higher Loyalty: Truth, Lies and Leadership*, London: Macmillan.

Cooper, F. (1987) "Who Is the Populist?", *African Studies Review*, Vol. 30, No. 3 (Sep., 1987), pp. 99–103.

Coppins, M. (2015) *The Wilderness: Deep Inside the Republican Party's Combative, Contentious, Chaotic Quest to Take Back the White House*, New York: Little Brown and Company.

Cowls, J. and Schroeder, R. (2018) "Tweeting All the Way to the White House", in: P. J. Boczkowski and Z. Papacharissi (eds), *Trump and the Media*, Cambridge, Massachusetts: The MIT Press, pp. 151–157.

Cox, M. (2017) "The Rise of Populism and the Crisis of Globalisation: Brexit, Trump and Beyond", *Irish Studies in International Affairs*, Vol. 28, pp. 9–17.

De la Cadena, M. and Starn, O. (eds) (2007) *Indigenous Experience Today*, Oxford: Berg.

De la Torre, Carlos (2015a) "Introduction: Power to the People. Populism, Insurrections, Democratization", in: Carlos de la Torre, (ed.), *The Promise and Perils: Global Perspectives*, Lexington: The University Press of Kentucky, pp 1–28.

De la Torre, Carlos (ed.) (2015b) *The Promise and Perils: Global Perspectives*, Lexington: The University Press of Kentucky.

De Vries, L., Englebert, P. Schomerus, M. (eds) (2019*) Secessionism in African Politics: Aspiration, Grievance, Performance and Disenchantment*, New York: Palgrave Macmillan.

Dean, J. W. and Altemeyer, R. A. (2020) *Authoritarian Nightmare: Trump and His Followers*, Brooklyn: Melville House Publishing.

Deneen, P. J. (2018) *Why Liberalism Failed*, New Haven: Yale University Press.

Dietze, G. and Roth, J. (2020) "Right-Wing Populism and Gender: A Preliminary Cartography of an Emergent Field of Research", in: Gabriele Dietze and Julia Roth (eds), *Right-Wing Populism and Gender: European Perspectives and Beyond*, Bielefeld: transcript Verlag, pp. 7–21.

Dionne, E. J. (2020) *Code Red: How Progressives and Moderates Can Unite to Save Our Country*, New York: St. Martin's Press.

Dreher, R. (2020) *Live Not By Lies: A Manual for Christian Dissidents*, New York: Sentinel.

Drezner, D. W. (2020) *The Toddler in Chief: What Donald Trump Teaches Us About the Modern Presidency*, Chicago: Chicago University Press.

Du Mez, K. K. (2020) *Jesus and John Wayne: How White Evangelicals Corrupted a Faith and Fractured a Nation*, New York: Liveright Publishing Corporation.

Dunlap, R. E. and Jacques, P. J. (2013) "Climate Change Denial Books and Conservative Think Tanks: Exploring the Connection", *American Behavioral Scientist*, Vol. 57(6): 699–731.

Eatwell, R. and Goodwin, M. (2018) *National Populism: The Revolt against Liberal Democracy*, London: Pelican.

Elias, N. (1994) *The Civilising Process*, Oxford: Blackwell Publishing.

Espejo, P. O. (2017) "Populism and the Idea of the People", in: C. R. Kaltwasser, P. A. Taggart, P. O. Espejo and P. Ostiguy (eds), *The Oxford Handbook of Populism*, Oxford: Oxford University Press.

Finchelstein, F. (2017) *From Fascism to Populism in History*, Oakland: University of California Press.

Fowler, I. (2020) "The Trump Brand and the Mocking of Christian Values", in: R. J. Sider (ed.), *The Spiritual Danger of Donald Trump: 30 Evangelical Christians on Justice, Truth, and Moral Integrity*, Eugene: Cascade Books.

Frum, D. (2018) *Trumpocracy: The Corruption of the American Republic*, New York: HarperCollins.

_____ (2020) *Trumpocalypse: Restoring American Democracy*, New York: Harper.

Fuchs, C. (2018) *Digital Demagogue Authoritarian Capitalism in the Age of Trump and Twitter*, London: Pluto Press.

Fukuyama, F. (1992) *The End of History and the Last Man*, New York: The Free Press.

_____ (2018) *Identity: The Demand for Dignity and the Politics of Resentment*, New York: Farrar, Straus and Giroux.

Gagnon, J.-P., Beausoleil, E., Son, K.-M., Arguelles, C., Chalaye, P. and Johnston, C. N. (2018) "Editorial: What is Populism? Who is the Populist?", *Democratic Theory*, Vol. 5(2): v-xxvi, doi: 10.3167/dt.2018.050201.

Geary, D., Schofield, C. and Sutton, J. (eds) (2020) *White Nationalism: From Apartheid to Trump*, Manchester: Manchester University Press.

Geschiere, P. (2009) *The Perils of Belonging: Autochthony, Citizenship, and Exclusion in Africa and Europe*, Chicago, IL: University of Chicago Press.

Gessen, M. (2020) *Surviving Autocracy*, New York: Riverhead Books.

Gherghina, S. and Soare, S. (2013) "Introduction: Populism – A Sophisticated Concept and Diverse Political Realities", in: Sergiu Gherghina, Sergiu Mișcoiu and Sorina Soare (eds), *Contemporary Populism: A Controversial Concept and Its Diverse Forms*, Newcastle: Cambridge Scholars Publishing, pp. 1–14.

Goodhart, D. (2017) *The Road to Somewhere: The Populist Revolt and the Future of Politics*, London: Hurst & Company.

Grewal, I. (2020) "Authoritarian Patriarchy and Its Populism", *English Studies in Africa*, Vol. 63(1): 179–198.

Grisham, S. (2021) *I'll Take Your Questions Now: What I Saw at the Trump White House*, New York: Harper.

Guerrero, J. (2020) *Hate Monger: Stephen Miller, Donald Trump and the White Nationalist Agenda*, New York: William Morrow.

Gunn, J. (2018) "Donald Trump's Perverse Political Rhetoric", in: Ryan Skinnell (ed), *Faking the News: What Rhetoric Can Teach Us about Donald J. Trump*, Exeter: Imprint Academic.

Guth, J. L. (2019) "Are White Evangelicals Populists? The View from the 2016 American National Election Study", *The Review of Faith & International Affairs*, Vol. 17:3, 20–35.

Hampton, K. N. (2018) "Social Media or Social Inequality: Trump's "'Unexpected'" Election", in: P. J. Boczkowski and Z. Papacharissi (eds), *Trump and the Media*, Cambridge, Massachusetts: The MIT Press, pp. 159–166.

Harrison, F. V. (2008) *Outsider Within: Reworking Anthropology in the Global Age*, Illinois: University of Illinois Press.

Hart, G. (2014) *Rethinking the South African Crisis: Nationalism, Populism, Hegemony*, Athens: University of Georgia Press.

Hassan, S. (2019) *The Cult of Trump: A Leading Cult Expert Explains How the President Uses Mind Control*, New York: Free Press.

Hauser, M. (2018) "Metapopulism in-between Democracy and Populism: Transformations of Laclau's Concept of Populism with Trump and Putin", *Distinktion: Journal of Social Theory*, Doi: 10.1080/1600910X.2018.1455599.

Hawkins, K., Dudley, R. and Tan, W. J. (2016) "Made in US: Populism Beyond Europe", in: Alberto Martinelli (ed.), *Beyond Trump: Populism on the Rise*, Milano: Milano: Edizioni Epoké – ISPI, pp. 93–111.

Hawkins, E. T. and Hawkins, K. (2018) "National-Populism in Trump's First Year of Presidency", in: Alberto Martinelli (ed.), *When Populism Meets Nationalism: Reflections on Parties in Power*, Milano: Ledizioni Ledi Publishing, pp. 47–69.

Hazony, Y. (2018) *The Virtue of Nationalism*, New York: Basic Books.

Heinisch, R., Holtz-Bacha, C. and Mazzoleni, O. (2017) "Preface", in: Reinhard Heinisch, Christina Holtz-Bacha and Oscar Mazzoleni (eds), *Political Populism: A Handbook*, Baden-Baden: Nomos Verlagsgesellschaft, pp. 5–8.

Hochschild, A. R. (2016) *Strangers in their Own Land: Anger and Mourning on the American Right*, New York: The New Press.

Hofstadter, R. (1963) *Anti-intellectualism in American Life*, New York: Alfred A. Knopf.

_____ (2008[1965]) *The Paranoid Style in African Politics and Other Essays*, New York: Vintage Books.

Holden, C. J., Messitte, Z. and Podair, J. (2019) *Republican Populist: Spiro Agnew and the Origins of Donald Trump's America*, Charlottesville: University of Virginia Press.

Honig, E. (2021) *Hatchet Man: How Bill Barr Broke the Prosecutor's Code and Corrupted the Justice Department*, New York: Harper.

Hoover, S. (2020) "Myth 'Today': Reading Religion Into Research on Mediated Cultural Politics", *International Journal of Communication*, Vol. 14(2020), Feature 1–25.

Hountondji, P. (ed.) (1997) *Endogenous knowledge: Research Trails*, Dakar: CODESRIA.

Hunter, J. D. and Owen IV, J. M. (2018) "Foreword", in: Patrick J. Deneen (author), *Why Liberalism Failed*, New Haven: Yale University Press, pp. ix–xi.

Ignatieff, M. (1995) *Blood and Belonging: Journeys into the New Nationalism*, New York: Farrar, Straus and Giroux.

Ingram, J. D. (2017) "Populism and Cosmopolitanism", in: C. R. Kaltwasser, P. A Taggart, P. O. Espejo and P. Ostiguy (eds), *The Oxford Handbook of Populism*, Oxford: Oxford University Press.

Ioanide, P. (2015) *The Emotional Politics of Racism: How Feelings Trump Facts in an Era of Color Blindness*, Stanford: Stanford University Press.

Ionescu, G. and Gellner, E. (1969) "Introduction", in: G. Ionescu and E. Gellner (eds), *Populism: Its Meanings and National Characteristics*, Letchworth, Hertfordshire: The Garden City Press, pp. 1–5.

Isenberg, N. (2016) *White Trash: The 400-Year Untold History of Class in America*, New York: Viking.

Journal of Global Faultlines (2017) "Editorial: The Rise of 'Authoritarian Populism' in the 21st Century: From Erdoğan's Turkey to Trump's America", *Journal of Global Faultlines*, Vol. 4(1): 3–6.

Judis, J. B. (2016) *The Populist Explosion: How the Great Recession Transformed American and European Politics*, New York: Columbia Global Reports.

_____ (2018) *The Nationalist Revival: Trade, Immigration, and Revolt against Globalization*, New York: Columbia Global Reports.

Kakutani, M. (2018) *The Death of Truth*, London: William Collins.

Kalb, M. (2018) *Enemy of the People: Trump's War on the Press, the New McCarthyism, and the Threat to American Democracy*, Washington D.C.: Brookings Institution Press.

Kaltwasser, C. R., Taggart, P., Espejo, P. O. and Ostiguy, P. (2017) "Populism: An Overview of the Concept and State of the Art", in: C. R. Kaltwasser, P. Taggart, P. O. Espejo and P. Ostiguy (eds), *The Oxford Handbook of Populism*, Oxford: Oxford University Press.

Kapanga, K. M. (2020) "UDPS Opposition Populism in the DRC and Its Reflection in Two Congolese Novels", *English Studies in Africa*, Vol. 63(1): 167–178.

Karl, J. (2020) *Front Row at the Trump Show*, New York: Dutton.

Kazin, M. (2016) "Trump and American Populism: Old Whine, New Bottles", *Foreign Affairs*, (November/December 2016) Vol. 95(6): 17–24.

_____ (2017[1995]) *The Populist Persuasion: An American History*, Ithaca: Cornell University Press.

Kellner, D. (2016) *American Nightmare: Donald Trump, Media Spectacle, and Authoritarian Populism*, Boston: Sense Publishers.

Kenny, P. D. (2017) *Populism and Patronage: Why Populists Win Elections in India, Asia, and Beyond*, Oxford: Oxford University Press.

Kessler, G., Rizzo, S. and Kelly, M. (2020) *Donald Trump and His Assault on Truth: The President's Falsehoods, Misleading Claims and Flat-Out Lies*, New York: Scribner.

Kivisto, P. (2017) *The Trump Phenomenon: How the Politics of Populism Won in 2016*, Bingley: Emerald Publishing.

Klein, E. (2020) *Why We're Polarized*, New York: Avid Reader Press.

Knopff, R. (1998) "Populism and the Politics of Rights: The Dual Attack on Representative Democracy", *Canadian Journal of Political Science/Revue canadienne de science politique*, Vol. 31(4): 683–705.

Krämer, B. (2017) "Populist and Non-Populist Media: Their Paradoxical Role in the Development and Diffusion of a Right-Wing Ideology", in: Reinhard Heinisch, Christina Holtz-Bacha and Oscar Mazzoleni (eds), *Political Populism: A Handbook*, Baden-Baden: Nomos Verlagsgesellschaft, pp. 405–420.

Kreiss, D. (2018) "The Media Are about Identity, Not Information", in: P. J. Boczkowski and Z. Papacharissi (eds), *Trump and the Media*, Cambridge, Massachusetts: The MIT Press, pp. 83–99.

Krieger, M. (2008) *Cameroon's Social Democratic Front: Its History and Prospects as an Opposition Political Party (1990-2011)*, Bamenda: Langaa RPCIG.

Laclau, E. (2005) *On Populist Reason*, London: Verso.

Lanier, J. (2013) *Who Owns the Future?* New York: Simon & Schuster.

_____ (2018) *Ten Arguments for Deleting Your Social Media Accounts Right Now*, New York: Henry Holt and Company.

Lasch, C. (1991[1979]) *The Culture of Narcissism: African Life in an Age of Diminishing Expectations*, New York: W. W. Norton.

_____ (1995) *The Revolts of the Elites and the Betrayal of Democracy*, New York: W.W. Norton.

Lategan, B. (2021) "Identiteitspolitiek: Sukses, Paradoks en Onvoorsiene Gevolge", *LitNet Akademies*, Jaargang 18, Nommer 2, 2021:.434–457.

Laterza, V. (2021) "Could Cambridge Analytica Have Delivered Donald Trump's 2016 Presidential Victory? An Anthropologist's Look at Big Data and Political Campaigning", *Public Anthropologist* 3, pp.119–147, doi:10.1163/25891715-03010007.

Lauret, M. (2020) "Populism and Dog Whistle Writing: The Memoirs of J. D. Vance and Ta-Nehisi Coates", *English Studies in Africa*, Vol. 63(1): 130–147.

Lazaridis, G., Campani, G. and Benveniste, A. (eds) (2016) *The Rise of the Far Right in Europe Populist Shifts and 'Othering'*, London: Palgrave Macmillan.

Leonnig, C. (2021) *Zero Fail: The Rise and Fall of the Secret Service*, New York: Random House.

Leonnig, C. and Rucker, P. (2021) *I Alone Can Fix It: Donald J. Trump's Catastrophic Final Year*, New York: Penguin Press.

Levitsky, S. and Ziblatt, D. (2018) *How Democracies Die*, New York: Crown.

Lind, M. (2020) *The New Class War: Saving Democracy from the Managerial Elite*, New York: Portfolio/Penguin.

Magcamit, M. (2017) "Explaining the Three-Way Linkage between Populism, Securitization, and Realist Foreign Policies: President Donald Trump and the Pursuit of 'America First' Doctrine", *World Affairs*, doi/full/10.1177/0043820017746263.

Maghimbi, S. (2012) *Populist Theory in Russia and Tanzania: A Collage of Ideas*, Professorial Inaugural Lecture Serial No. 51, 2012, Dar es Salaam: University of Dar es Salaam.

Magri, P. (2016) "Introduction", in: Alberto Martinelli (ed.), *Beyond Trump: Populism on the Rise*, Milano: Milano: Edizioni Epoké – ISPI, pp. 7–12.

Makulilo, A. B. (2013) "Populism and Democracy in Africa", in: Sergiu Gherghina, Sergiu Mișcoiu and Sorina Soare (eds), *Contemporary Populism: A Controversial Concept and Its Diverse Forms*, Newcastle: Cambridge Scholars Publishing, pp. 167–202.

Mamdani, M. (1996) *Citizen and Subject: Contemporary Africa and the Legacy of Late Colonialism*, Cape Town: David Philip.

_____ (1998) *When does a settler become a Native? Reflections of the colonial roots of citizenship in Equatorial and South Africa*, 208 (n.s.), Cape Town: University of Cape Town.

_____ (2020) *Neither Settler nor Native: The Making and Unmaking of Permanent Minorities*, Cambridge, Massachusetts: The Belknap Press of Harvard University Press.

Manucci, L. (2017) "Populism and the Media", in: Cristóbal Rovira Kaltwasser, P. Taggart, P. O. Espejo and P. Ostiguy (eds) *The Oxford Handbook of Populism*, Oxford: Oxford University Press.

Marcotte, A. (2018) *Troll Nation: How The Right Became Trump-Worshipping Monsters Set On Rat-F*cking Liberals, America, and Truth Itself*, New York: Skyhorse Publishing.

Martinelli, A. (2016) "Populism and the Crisis of Representative Democracy", in: Alberto Martinelli (ed.), *Beyond Trump: Populism on the Rise*, Milano: Edizioni Epoké – ISPI, pp. 13–31.

_____ (2018) "Populism & Nationalism: The (Peculiar) Case of Italy", in: Alberto Martinelli (ed.), *When Populism Meets Nationalism: Reflections on Parties in Power*, Milano: Ledizioni LediPublishing, pp. 13–45.

Maskovsky, J. and Bjork-James, S. (2020a) "Introduction", in: Jeff Maskovsky and Sophie Bjork-James (eds), *Beyond Populism: Angry Politics and the Twilight of Neoliberalism*, Morgantown: West Virginia University Press, pp. 1–19.

Maskovsky, J. and Bjork-James, S. (eds) (2020b), *Beyond Populism: Angry Politics and the Twilight of Neoliberalism*, Morgantown: West Virginia University Press.

Mazrui, A. A. and Engholm, G. F. (1968) "Rousseau and Intellectualized Populism in Africa", *The Review of Politics*, Vol. 30(1): 19–32.

Mazzarella, W. (2019) "The Anthropology of Populism: Beyond the Liberal Settlement", *Annual Review of Anthropology*, Vol. 48: 45–60.

McCabe, A. G. (2019) *The Threat: How the FBI Protects America in the Age of Terror and Trump*, New York: St. Martin's Griffin.

McCallion, K. F. (2019) *Treason & Betrayal: The Rise and Fall of Individual #1*, New York: Bryant Park Press.

Melber, H. (2018) "Populism in Southern Africa under liberation movements as governments", *Review of African Political Economy*, Vol. 45:158: 678–686.

Mercieca, J. R. (2018) "Afterword: Trump as Anarchist and Sun King", in: Ryan Skinnell (ed), *Faking the News: What Rhetoric Can Teach Us about Donald J. Trump*, Exeter: Imprint Academic.

Miller, G. (2018) *The Apprentice: Trump, Russia and the Subversion of American Democracy*, New York: Custom House.

Mills, D. Q. and Rosefielde, S. (2017) *The Trump Phenomenon and The Future of US Foreign Policy*, Singapore: World Scientific Publishing.

Mounk, Y. (2018) *The People Vs. Democracy: Why Our Freedom Is in Danger and How to Save It*, Cambridge, Massachusetts: Harvard University Press.

Mudde, C. (2019) *The Far Right Today*, Cambridge: Polity Press.

Mudde, C. and Kaltwasser, C. R. (2017) *Populism: A Very Short Introduction*, Oxford: Oxford University Press.

Muirhead, R. and Rosenblum, N. L. (2019) *A Lot of People Are Saying: The New Conspiracism and the Assault on Democracy*, Princeton: Princeton University Press.

Müller, J.-W. (2016) *What is Populism*, Philadelphia: University of Pennsylvania Press.

Nance, M. (2019) *The Plot to Betray America: How Trump Team Embraced Our Enemies, Compromised Our Security, and How We Can Fix It*, New York: Hachette Books.

Newman, O. M. (2018) *Unhinged: An Insider's Account of the Trump White House*, London: Simon & Schuster.

Nichols, T. (2017) *The Death of Expertise: The Campaign Against Established Knowledge and Why It Matters*, Oxford: Oxford University Press.

_____ (2021) *Our Own Worst Enemy: The Assault from within on Modern Democracy*, Oxford: Oxford University Press.

Norris, P. and Inglehart, R. (2019) *Cultural Backlash: Trump, Brexit, and Authoritarian Populism*, Cambridge: Cambridge University Press.

Nyamnjoh, F. B. (1999) "Cameroon: A Country United by Ethnic Ambition and Difference", *African Affairs*, Vol. 98(390): 101–118.

_____ (2005) *Africa's Media: Democracy and the Politics of Belonging*, London: CODESRIA–Zed Books.

_____ (2006) *Insiders and Outsiders: Citizenship and Xenophobia in Contemporary Southern Africa*, London: CODESRIA–Zed Books.

_____ (2012) "Potted Plants in Greenhouses: A Critical Reflection on the Resilience of Colonial Education in Africa", *Journal of Asian and African Studies*, Vol. 47(2): 129–154.

_____ (2015) *"C'est l'homme qui fait l'homme": Cul-de-Sac Ubuntu-ism in Côte d'Ivoire*, Bamenda: Langaa RPCIG.

374

_____ (2016) *#RhodesMustFall: Nibbling at Resilient Colonialism in South Africa*, Bamenda: Langaa RPCIG.

_____ (2017) *Drinking from the Cosmic Gourd: How Amos Tutuola Can Change Our Minds*, Bamenda: Langaa RPCIG.

_____ (2018b) *The Rational Consumer: Bad for Business and Politics: Democracy at the Crossroads of Nature and Culture*, Bamenda: Langaa RPCIG.

_____ (2019) "ICTs as Juju: African Inspiration for Understanding the Compositeness of Being Human Through Digital Technologies", *Journal of African Media Studies*, Vol. 11(3): 279–291

Nyamnjoh, F. B. (ed.) (2018a), *Eating and Being Eaten: Cannibalism as Food for Thought*, Bamenda: Langaa RPCIG.

Obama, B. (2020) *A Promised Land*, New York: Crown.

Oborne, P. and Roberts, T. (2017) *How Trump Thinks: His Tweets and the Birth of a New Political Language*, London: Head of Zeus Ltd.

O'Brien, T. L. (2015[2005]) *TrumpNation: The Art of Being the Donald*, New York: Open Road.

Opoku, K. A. (2012) "Skinny but imperishable truth: African religious heritage and the regeneration of Africa", *Studia Historiae Ecclesiasticae*, Vol. 38, Supplement, pp 141–151.

Parmar, I. (2017) "The Legitimacy Crisis of the U.S. Elite and the Rise of Donald Trump", *Insight Turkey*, Trump's America Changes, Challenges Expectations and Uncertainties, Vol. 19(3): 9–22.

Pearce, K. E. (2018) "Creeping Toward Authoritarianism?", in: P. J. Boczkowski and Z. Papacharissi (eds), *Trump and the Media*, Cambridge, Massachusetts: The MIT Press, pp. 119–124.

Pfeiffer, D. (2020) *Un-Trumping America: A Plan to Make America a Democracy Again*, New York: Twelve.

Phiri, A. (2020) "Trumping the House that Race Built: Deracinating 21st-Century American Politics", *English Studies in Africa*, Vol. 63(1): 45–58.

Pickard, V. (2018) "When Commercialism Trumps Democracy: Media Pathologies and the Rise of the Misinformation Society", in: P. J. Boczkowski and Z. Papacharissi (eds), *Trump and the Media*, Cambridge, Massachusetts: The MIT Press, pp. 195–201.

Pieper, C. and Henderson, M. (2020) "10 Reasons Christians Should Reconsider Their Support of Trump", in: R. J. Sider (ed.), *The Spiritual Danger of Donald Trump: 30 Evangelical Christians on Justice, Truth, and Moral Integrity*, Eugene: Cascade Books.

Posner, S. (2020) *Unholy: Why White Evangelicals Worship at the Altar of Donald Trump*, New York: Random House.

Rauch, J. (2013[1993]) *Kindly Inquisitors: The New Attacks on Free Thought*, Chicago: Chicago University Press.

_____ (2021) *The Constitution of Knowledge: A Defense of Truth*, Washington D.C.: The Brookings Institution Press.

Reid, J.-A. (2019) *The Man Who Sold America: Trump and the Unravelling of the American Story*, New York: William Morrow.

Reno, R. R. (2019) *Return of the Strong Gods: Nationalism, Populism, and the Future of the West*, New Jersey: Regnery Gateway.

Res, B. A. (2020) *Tower of Lies: What My 18 Years of Working with Donald Trump Reveals about Him*, Los Angeles: Graymalkin Media, LLC.

Resnick, D. (2014) *Urban Poverty and Party Populism in African Democracies*, New York: Cambridge University Press.

_____ (2015) "Varieties of African Populism in Comparative Perspective", in: Carlos de la Torre, (ed.), *The Promise and Perils: Global Perspectives*, Lexington: The University Press of Kentucky, pp 317–348.

Resnick, D. E. (2017) "Populism in Africa", in: Cristóbal Rovira Kaltwasser, P. Taggart, P. O. Espejo and P. Ostiguy (eds), *The Oxford Handbook of Populism*, Oxford: Oxford University Press.

Roberts-Miller, P. (2018) "Charisma Isn't Leadership, and Other Lessons We Can Learn from Trump the Businessman", in: Ryan Skinnell (ed.), *Faking the News: What Rhetoric Can Teach Us about Donald J. Trump*, Exeter: Imprint Academic.

Robinson, S. (2018) "Trump, Journalists, and Social Networks of Trust", in: P. J. Boczkowski and Z. Papacharissi (eds), *Trump and the Media*, Cambridge, Massachusetts: The MIT Press, pp. 187–193.

Rohde, D. (2020) *In Deep: The FBI, The CIA, The Truth About America's "Deep State"*, New York: W.W. Norton & Company.

Roncarolo, F. (2017) "Media Politics and Populism as a Mobilisation Resource", in: Reinhard Heinisch, Christina Holtz-Bacha and

Oscar Mazzoleni (eds), *Political Populism: A Handbook*, Baden-Baden: Nomos Verlagsgesellschaft, pp. 391–403.

Rucker, P. and Leonnig, C. (2020) *A Very Stable Genius: Donald J. Trump's Testing of America*, New York: Penguin Press.

Russell, A. (2018) "Making Journalism Great Again: Trump and the New Rise of News Activism", in: P. J. Boczkowski and Z. Papacharissi (eds), *Trump and the Media*, Cambridge, Massachusetts: The MIT Press, pp. 203–12.

Samuels, R. (2016) *Psychoanalyzing the Left and Right after Donald Trump: Conservatism, Liberalism and Neoliberal Populisms*, New York: Palgrave Macmillan.

Sanders, B. (2011) *The Speech: A Historic Filibuster on Corporate Greed and the Decline of Our Middle Class*, New York: Nation Books.

_____ (2016) *Our Revolution: A Future to Believe In*, New York: Thomas Dunne Books.

_____ (2018) *Where We Go from Here: Two Years in the Resistance*, New York: Thomas Dunne Books.

Saul, J. (1969) "Africa", in: G. Ionescu and E. Gellner (eds), *Populism: Its Meanings and National Characteristics*, Letchworth, Hertfordshire: The Garden City Press, pp. 122–150.

Schlesinger, P. (1978) *Putting 'Reality' Together: BBC News*, London: Constable.

Serwer, A. (2021) *The Cruelty Is the Point: The Past, Present, and the Future of Trump's America*, New York: One World.

Shack, W. A. (1979) "Introduction", in: William A. Shack and Elliot P. Skinner (eds), *Strangers in African Societies*, Berkeley: University of California Press.

Sider, R. J. (ed.) (2020a) *The Spiritual Danger of Donald Trump: 30 Evangelical Christians on Justice, Truth, and Moral Integrity*, Eugene: Cascade Books.

_____ (2020b) "Afterword", in: R. J. Sider (ed.), *The Spiritual Danger of Donald Trump: 30 Evangelical Christians on Justice, Truth, and Moral Integrity*, Eugene: Cascade Books.

Simpson, G. and Fritsch, P. (2019) *Crime in Progress: Inside the Steele Dossier and the Fusion GPS Investigation of Donald Trump*, New York: Random House.

Sims, C. (2019) *Team of Vipers: My 500 Extraordinary Days in the Trump White House*, New York: Thomas Dunne Books.

Singh, R. (2017) "'I, the people': A Deflationary Interpretation of Populism, Trump and the United States Constitution", *Economy and Society*, https://doi.org/10.1080/03085147.2017.1302060.

Sinn, S. and Harasta, E. (eds) (2019) *Resisting Exclusion. Global Theological Responses to Populism*, Leipzig: Evangelische Verlangsanstalt GmbH (on behalf of The Lutheran World Federation).

Skinnell, R. (ed.) (2018a) *Faking the News: What Rhetoric Can Teach Us about Donald J. Trump*, Exeter: Imprint Academic.

_____ (2018b) "What Passes for Truth in the Trump Era: Telling It Like It Isn't", in: Ryan Skinnell (ed.), *Faking the News: What Rhetoric Can Teach Us about Donald J. Trump*, Exeter: Imprint Academic.

Slavitt, A. (2021) *Preventable: The Inside Story of How Leadership Failures, Politics and Selfishness Doomed the U.S. Coronavirus Response*, New York: St. Martin's Press.

Snyder, T. (2017) *On Tyranny: Twenty Lessons from the Twentieth Century*, New York: Crown.

Sonnevend, J. (2018) "Facts (Almost) Never Win Over Myths", in: P. J. Boczkowski and Z. Papacharissi (eds), *Trump and the Media*, Cambridge, Massachusetts: The MIT Press, pp. 87–92.

Stelter, B. (2020) *Hoax: Donald Trump, Fox News, and the Dangerous Distortion of the Truth*, New York: One Signal Publishers/ATRIA Books.

Stengel, R. (2019) *Information Wars: How We Lost the Global Battle Against Disinformation & What We Can Do About It*, New York: Atlantic Monthly Press.

Stenner, K. (2005) *The Authoritarian Dynamic*, Cambridge: Cambridge University Press.

Steudeman, M. J. (2018) "Demagoguery and the Donald's Duplicitous Victimhood", in: Ryan Skinnell (ed.), *Faking the News: What Rhetoric Can Teach Us about Donald J. Trump*, Exeter: Imprint Academic.

Stevens, S. (2020) *It Was All a Lie: How the Republican Party Became Donald Trump*, New York: Alfred A. Knopf.

Strzok, P. (2020) *Compromised: Counterintelligence and the Thread of Donald. J. Trump*, Boston: Houghton Mifflin Harcourt.

Sullivan, A. (2021) *Out on a Limb: Selected Writing 1989-2021*, New York: Avid Reader Press.

Tasini, J. (2015) *The Essential Bernie Sanders and his Vision for America*, Vermont: Chelsea Green Publishing.

Taveira, R. and Nyerges, A. (2016) "Introduction: Populism and Propaganda in the US Culture Industries", *Australasian Journal of American Studies*, Vol. 35, No. 1, *The State and US Culture Industries* (July 2016), pp. 3–10.

Titlestad, M. (2020) "Introduction: Cultures of Populism", *English Studies in Africa*, Vol. 63(1): 1–4.

The Washington Post (2019) *The Mueller Report*, New York: Scribner.

Thurman, C. (2020) "God hates a lying tongue", in: R. J. Sider (ed.), *The Spiritual Danger of Donald Trump: 30 Evangelical Christians on Justice, Truth, and Moral Integrity*, Eugene: Cascade Books.

Toobin, J. (2020) *True Crimes and Misdemeanors: The Investigation of Donald Trump*, New York: Doubleday.

Traverso, E. (2019) *The New Faces of Fascism: Populism and the Far Right*, London: Verso.

Trump, D. J. with Schwartz, T. (1987) *The Art of the Deal*, New York: Ballantine Books.

Trump, I. (2009) *The Trump Card: Playing to Win in Work and Life*, New York: Simon & Schuster.

Trump, M. L. (2020) *Too Much and Never Enough: How My Family Created the World's Most Dangerous Man*, New York: Simon & Schuster.

_____ (2021) *The Reckoning: Our Nation's Trauma and Finding a Way to Heal*, New York: St. Martin's Press.

Turner, F. (2018) "Trump on Twitter: How a Medium Designed for Democracy Became an Authoritarian's Mouthpiece", in: P. J. Boczkowski and Z. Papacharissi (eds), *Trump and the Media*, Cambridge, Massachusetts: The MIT Press, pp. 143–149.

Tutuola, A. (1952) *The Palm-Wine Drinkard*, London: Faber and Faber.

_____ (1954) *My Life in the Bush of Ghosts*, London: Faber and Faber.

Twenge, J. M. and Campbell, W. K. (2009) *The Narcissism Epidemic: Living in the Age of Entitlement*, New York: Free Press.

Urbinati, N. (2019) "Political Theory of Populism", *Annual Review of Political Science*, Vol. 22: 111–127, doi.org/10.1146/annurev-polisci-050317-070753.

Van Slyck, A. (2020) "Responding to Xenophobia: Politics, Populisms and Our Teaching", *English Studies in Africa*, Vol. 63(1): 104–118.

Vance, J. D. (2016) *Hillbilly Elegy: A Memoir of a Family and Culture in Crisis*, New York: HarperCollins.

Vindman, A. S. (2021) *Here, Right Matters: An American Story*, New York: Harper.

Wahl-Jorgensen, K. (2018) "Public Displays of Disaffection: The Emotional Politics of Donald Trump", in: P. J. Boczkowski and Z. Papacharissi(eds), *Trump and the Media*, Cambridge, Massachusetts: The MIT Press, pp. 79–86.

Waisbord, S., Tucker, T. and Lichtenheld, Z. (2018) "Trump and the Great Disruption in Public Communication", in: P. J. Boczkowski and Z. Papacharissi (eds), *Trump and the Media*, Cambridge, Massachusetts: The MIT Press, pp. 25–32.

Watts, C. (2018) *Messing with the Enemy: Surviving in a Social Media World of Hackers, Terrorists, Russians, and Fake News*, New York: Harper.

Wehner, P. (2019) *The Death of Politics: How to Heal Our Frayed Republic After Trump*, New York: Harper One.

Wehner, P. (2020) "The Deepening Crisis in Evangelical Christianity", in: R. J. Sider (ed.), *The Spiritual Danger of Donald Trump: 30 Evangelical Christians on Justice, Truth, and Moral Integrity*, Eugene: Cascade Books.

Welfens, P. J. J., (2019) *The Global Trump Structural US Populism and Economic Conflicts with Europe and Asia*, Cham: Palgrave Macmillan.

West, C. (2017) "The Trump Era: Hope in a Time of Escalating Despair", *Transition*, No. 122, White A$$holes, pp. 22–41.

Weyland, K. and Madrid, R. L. (eds) (2019) *When Democracy Trumps Populism: European and Latin American Lessons for the United States*, Cambridge: Cambridge University Press.

Wilkerson, I. (2020) *Caste: The Origins of Our Discontents*, New York: Random House.

Will, G. F. (2013) "Foreword", in: Jonathan Rauch, *Kindly Inquisitors: The New Attacks on Free Thought*, Chicago: Chicago University Press, pp. xiii–xvii.

Wilson, R. (2018) *Everything Trump Touches Dies: A Republican Strategist Gets Real About the Worst President Ever*, New York: Free Press.

_____ (2020) *Running Against the Devil: A Plot to Save America from Trump – and Democrats from Themselves*, New York: Crown Forum.

Wingard, J. (2018) "Trump's Not Just One Bad Apple: He's the Product of a Spoiled Bunch", in: Ryan Skinnell (ed.), *Faking the News: What Rhetoric Can Teach Us about Donald J. Trump*, Exeter: Imprint Academic.

Wolff, M. (2008) *The Man Who Owns the News: Inside the Secret World of Rupert Murdoch*, New York: Broadway Books.

_____ (2018) *Fire and Fury: Inside the Trump White House*. London: Little Brown.

_____ (2019) *Siege: Trump Under Fire*, New York: Henry Holt and Company.

_____ (2021a) *Landslide: The Final Days of the Trump Presidency*, New York: Henry Holt and Company.

_____ (2021b) *Too Famous: The Rich, the Powerful, the Wishful, the Notorious, the Damned*, New York: Henry Holt and Company.

Wong, C. J. (2010) *Boundaries of Obligation in American Politics: Geographic, National, and Racial Communities*, Cambridge: Cambridge University Press.

Woodward, B. (2018) *Fear: Trump in the White House* New York: Simon & Schuster.

_____ (2020) *Rage*, New York: Simon & Schuster.

Woodward, B. and Costa, R. (2021) *Peril*, New York: Simon & Schuster.

Wu, T. (2016) *The Attention Merchants: The Epic Scramble to Get Inside Our Heads*, New York: Alfred A. Knopf.

Wylie, C. (2019) *Mindf*ck: Cambridge Analytica and the Plot to Break America*, New York: Random House.

Young, A. M. (2018) "Rhetorics of Fear and Loathing: Donald Trump's Populist Style", in: Ryan Skinnell (ed.), *Faking the News: What Rhetoric Can Teach Us about Donald J. Trump*, Exeter: Imprint Academic.

Zada, J. (2021) *Veils of Distortion: How the News Media Warps Our Minds*, Canada: Terra Incognita.

Zito, S. and Todd, B. (2018) *The Great Revolt: Inside the Populist Coalition Reshaping African Politics*, New York: Crown Forum.

Index

392